CHICANO!

The History of the Mexican American Civil Rights Movement

F. Arturo Rosales

ARTE
PÚBLICO
PRESS

1997

This volume is made possible through grants from the Charles Stewart Mott Foundation, the Ewing Marion Kauffman Foundation, and The Rockefeller Foundation.

Recovering the past, creating the future

Arte Público Press
University of Houston
452 Cullen Performance Hall
Houston, Texas 77204-2004

Rosales, F. Arturo (Francisco Arturo)
    Chicano! The history of the Mexican American civil rights movement / by Francisco A. Rosales.
        p.   cm.
    Based on the four-part television series of the same name.
    Includes bibliographical references (pp. 269-77) and index.
    ISBN 978-1-55885-201-3 (alk. paper)
    1. Mexican Americans—Civil rights—History. 2. Civl rights movements—United States—History—20th century. I. Chicano! (Television program) II. Title.
    E184.M5R634   1996   96-5979
    973'.046872—dc20   CIP

♾ The paper used in this publication meets the requirements of the American National Standard for Information Sciences—Permanence of Paper for Printed Library Materials, ANSI Z39.48-1984.

CHICANO!

The History of the Mexican
American Civil Rights Movement

Para Mamá Cuca y Mamá Mechi,
who raised me and whose memories served as
the prism to my Mexican-American past.

CHICANO!

The History of the Mexican
American Civil Rights Movement

ACKNOWLEDGMENTS

Researching and writing history are usually solitary efforts. In this case, however, the production of this book was truly a collaborative effort. I would like especially to acknowledge the tremendous level of support provided by Nicolás Kanellos from Arte Público Press and Jesús Treviño of the National Latino Communications Center (NLCC). On the surface, it would seem that writing this work was the business as usual of the historian. I was sequestered away at home before my personal computer for five months, pressing away in order to finish the task and meet the deadline established by Arte Público Press. And when I was not at home, usually visiting my parents in Tucson, my laptop accompanied me. I could not afford to break my rhythm of writing; otherwise the manuscript would not be completed.

But this work was not completed by following the usual methods of the historian. I certainly did the writing, but Nicolás Kanellos and Jesús Treviño provided an ongoing and dedicated assistance, without which this work would never have seen the light of day. Immediately after I agreed to write this work, the NLCC staff from Los Angeles and Galán Productions in Austin sent me five boxes of the interview transcripts which they used to create the television series *Chicano!* Then Nicolás Kanellos provided me with moral and financial support to start the project and so I could be released from teaching duties to concentrate full-time on writing the manuscript.

But the critical help came with the research and writing. Unlike previous experiences, I did not have the luxury of sending off a manuscript to a friend and then waiting a month or two for a response. Nick returned my chapter drafts within two to three days with numerous copyediting changes which I quickly incorporated into another draft and quickly sent off again. Jesús Treviño made numerous editorial suggestions as well as providing factual information and interpretations of the interviews. He more than anyone else at the NLCC was intimate with the content of the interviews. His input was essential to my finishing. Needless to say, I was on the phone constantly with both Jesús and Nick throughout the five months it took me to complete the final version.

Moreover, the staff at Arte Público Press, the NLCC and Galán Productions were extremely helpful. I would especially like to thank Rose Hansen and Tim Aikens for their effort in helping provide photographs to accompany the text. Rita Mills and her staff at Arte Público deserve special kudos for the extraordinary production efforts they made to publish this in time for the airing of *Chicano!*

Unfortunately, time constraints did not allow me to collaborate with other colleagues as much as I would have liked. Nonetheless, I owe a great deal to the published works of many scholars—more than the citations suggest. But I was also very fortunate to have close at hand Edward Escobar and Christine Marín, who both have published some fine works on the Chicano Movement. Not only did I constantly call them at all hours of the day, but both generously shared their collections of Chicano Movement materials.

In addition, I appreciate the ideas of my fellow Chicano Movement associates, Alfredo Gutiérrez and Miguel Montiel, who refreshed my memory on happenings in Arizona. Ignacio García, John Aguilar, Miguel Tinker Salas, Eleazar Risco and Armando Valdez also provided me with significant insights on interpretation. To my wife, Graciela, who endured my being in the house constantly for five months and who patiently listened to my ruminating on ideas as I wrote, I am also very grateful.

I would like to acknowledge the cooperation of Retha Warnicke, my department chair, in providing me with leave time, and my graduate students, Jaime Aguila and Patrick Lukens, for teaching my classes while I wrote. My graduate assistant, Nick Tapia, who was always around for doing various and sundry tasks, also deserves a special thanks.

Special thanks go to Gladys Ramírez and Doris Clark for designing and setting the type for this beautiful book.

CHICANO!

The writing of this book would not have been possible without the enormous amount of development, research and production that went into the film series on which it is based and which has provided so many of the interviews and other research materials incorporated into the book.

The development of *Chicano! The History of the Mexican American Civil Rights Movement* began with an initial idea by José Luis Ruiz. As director of the National Latino Communications Center, José Luis Ruiz dedicated more than six years of his life, working tirelessly with funders and PBS to bring about the funding that made the series possible. It was the sustained institutional support of the National Latino Communications Center that allowed the project to stay alive even when funding options looked dim.

Sharing key credit for bringing the project to life are Luis R. Torres and Jesús Salvador Treviño. Torres was essential in conceiving the project in its earliest stages, and it was he who almost single-handedly developed the concept for more than three years. He was instrumental in obtaining the initial seed monies that carried the project forward. Jesús Salvador Treviño was also involved early on. He worked diligently to shape the intellectual and historical content of the four programs, supervised pre-production research, wrote funding treatments and oversaw the editorial vision of the series to completion.

The series would not have been possible without the initial encouragement of Dr. Tomás Ybarra-Frausto, who secured a seed grant (and later, a production grant) from the Rockefeller Foundation. The series is indebted to Andrea Taylor and Christina Cuevas for facilitating a generous grant from the Ford Foundation, to Patricia Botero and Woodward Wickham for their help in securing an equally generous grant from the John D. and Catherine T. MacArthur Foundation, and to Donald Marbury and Jennifer Lawson for their help in securing funding from the Corporation for Public Broadcasting/Public Broadcasting Service Challenge Fund. Thanks also to Douglas Patiño, William White and David Harris for their help in securing a grant from the Charles Stewart Mott Foundation to make educational outreach materials available to secondary schools, colleges and universities.

Once the series was underway, through the leadership of José Luis Ruiz, the National Latino Communications Center was able to sustain the series by convening regular meetings of scholars and undertaking a series of field interviews. Thanks go to those interview researchers who conducted the first set of more than 100 interviews with Chicano Movement activists. These researchers included Enrique Berumen, Claire Jones, Myléne Moreno, Susan Racho, and Luis R. Torres.

The film series is indebted to the many scholars who gave of their time and resources to help the project along in key moments. Not only were these scholars available for meetings at which the themes and issues of the series were discussed, but often gave of their time through telephone conference calls, by providing photocopies of pertinent data or by reviewing treatment and script drafts. Among the many scholars who were part of the advisory committee are: Dr. Blandina Cárdenas, Dr. Clayborne Carson, Dr. Mario García, Dr. Juan Gómez-Quiñones, Dr. Alicia González, Dr. José Limón, Dr. Teresa McKenna, Dr. Amalia Mesa Baines, Dr. Douglas Monroy, Dr. Carlos Muñoz Jr., Dr. Louise Año Nuevo Kerr, Dr. Ricardo Romo, Dr. Vicki Ruiz, Dr. Adaljiza Sosa Riddell, Dr. Carlos Vélez-Ibáñez, Dr. Julie Leininger Pycior and Dr. Mary Logan Rothschild. Particularly outstanding in their assistance beyond the call of duty were Dr. Juan Gómez-Quiñones, Dr. Mario García and Dr. Vicki Ruiz.

To familiarize the producers of the series with the themes and issues of the times, an intensive two-week "school" was convened at which movement activists and scholars spoke and shared their insights. The many participants at the school included Alurista, Tomás Atencio, Dr. Rodolfo Acuña, Santa Barraza, Jerry Cohen, Bert Corona, Dr. Rudolfo de la Garza, Moctezuma Esparza, Hermán Gallegos, Dr. Ignacio García, Nita González, Dr. Juan Gómez-Quiñones, José Angel Gutiérrez, Dr. Vincent Harding, Ester Hernández, Severita Lara, Lydia López, Theo Majka, Rev. Vahac Mardirosian, César Martínez, Elizabeth Martínez, Vilma Martínez, Esq., José Montoya, Antonio Morales, Judge

Alberto Peña, Dr. Beatrice Pesquera, Eleazar Risco, Dr. Rodolfo Rosales, Alfonso Sánchez, Dr. Christina Sierra, Juan Sepúlveda, Ernesto Vigil and Dr. Thomás Ybarra-Frausto.

Also helpful to the producers were the numerous people who gave of their time, insight and resource materials during the production of the series. These included Sherry Adams, Emilia Alvarado, Richard Baiz, Gregg Barrios, Frances Crisóstomo, Robert Cyclona, Richard B. Davies, Mark R. Day, Antonio Delgado, Bob Dickson, Gerald Dodd, Charles Dodge, Jesse De La Cruz, Alicia Escalante, Rodolfo Espinosa, Ventura González, Sonia Green, Terri Kennedy and the staff at Blackside, Inc., Father John Luce, Jesse C. Maldonado, Richard Maldonado, Mario Obledo, Antonio Orendáin, Martín Quiroz, Eleazar Risco, Fred Ross, Paul Shrade, Mary M. Torres, Pete Velasco, Devra Weber, Sam Yorty and Raúl Yzaquirre.

In addition, to establish news media and professional photo archives, the series would not have been possible were it not for the many film, video and photo collections provided by Chicano filmmakers, photographers and movement activists. Film and photo collections for the series included ABC Video Source Joe Aguerrebere Collection; *Albuquerque Journal*; AP Worldwide Photos; Lillian Apodaca Collection; Archive Films; George Ballis Collection; Benson Latin American Collection of the University of Texas at Austin; Ed Brostoff Collection; California History Center Foundation; California State University; Ray Carey Collection; Sal Castro Collection; Oscar Castillo Collection; CBS News Archives; Chris Cebada Collection; Leroy Chatfield Collection; Copeland Productions; Corpus Christi State University; Crusade for Justice Collection; Crystal City High Yearbook; Denver Historical Society; Denver Public Library; Western History Department; *The Denver Post*; Moctezuma Esparza Collection; Sissy Farenthold Collection; Film Audio Services; Fred Glass Collection; Sherman Grinberg; Dr. Shifra Goldman Collection; José Angel Gutiérrez Collection; Alfred Hernández Collection; Ester Hernández Collection; *The Houston Chronicle*, Image Bank; Institute of Texan Cultures; KBDI-TV, Denver; KCBS-TV, Los Angeles; KCET-TV, Los Angeles; KMGH-TV, Denver; KMIR-TV, Denver; KPBS-TV, San Diego; KRON-TV, San Francisco; KSDK-TV, St. Louis; KQED-TV, San Francisco; LBJ Library; Lisa Johnson Collection; *The Los Angeles Times*, Carlos Montes Collection; Sylvia Morales Collection; Museum of New Mexico; George Meany Memorial Archive; Eliseo Medina Collection; NBC News Archives; Library of Congress; New Mexico State Records Center; Gil Padilla Collection; Diana Palacios Collection; Jack Pandol Collection; Hart Perry Collection; Harvey Richards Collection; George Rodríguez Collection; Rudy Rodríguez Collection; Edward Roybal Collection; Phoenix Film Archives; Raúl Ruiz Collection; St. Mary's University Yearbook; Stanford University; Lionel Sternberg Collection; Harry Sweet Collection; Texas State Library Archive; Teatro Campesino Collection; Jesús Salvador Treviño Collection; María Varela Collection; George Velásquez Collection; UCLA Film and Television Archives; University of Texas, Arlington; University of New Mexico, Albuquerque; United Farmworkers Unions; AFL-CIO; UPI/Bettman; Bobby Verdugo Collection; Ernesto Vigil Collection; Wayne State University and the *Westminster Herald*.

Particularly helpful was Dr. Félix Gutiérrez, who secured from the University of Southern California an extensive collection of news footage from Spanish-language station KMEX (1963-1980) and donated it to the National Latino Communications Archives, making possible the use of this rare footage in the series.

Lastly, though most importantly, was the team of creative men and women who sacrificed long hours and hard work to make the series a reality. Special recognition goes to Héctor Galán, who supervised the overall production of the documentary series through his company, Galán Productions of Austin, Texas.

Other credits include the following:

For Episode One (Quest for a Homeland): producers Héctor Galán and Myléne Moreno; associate producer Karen Kocher, editor Brian Beasley, assistant editor Leah Marino.

For Episode Two (The Struggle in the Fields): producer Sylvia Morales, associate producer Susanne Mason, editor Joan Zapata; assistant editor Sandra Guardado.

For Episode Three (Taking Back the Schools): producer Susan Racho, associate producer Claire Jone, editor Crager Couger, assistant editor Leah Marino.

For Episode Four (Fighting for Political Power): producer Robert Cozens, associate producer Ray Santiesteba, editor Brian Beasley, assistant editor Leah Marino.

Series producer Héctor Galán, series consultant Steve Fayer, series associate producer Rose Hansen, series production executive Susan Racho, series unit manager Mónica Flores, series production coordinator Steve Akers; original music for series Joseph Julián González; series editors: Brian Beasley, Crager Couger and Joan Zapata; series assistant editors Leah Marino and Sandra Guardado; camera Dieter Kaupp and Tom Taylor; field sound Mack Melson and Gerardo Rueda; series post production supervisors Crager Couger and Leah Marino; series production assistants Jessica A. Bega, Bryan Horch and Alejandro Hinojosa; series researchers, Enrique Berumen, Claire Jones, Velia La Garda and Myléne Moreno; post production editor Glenn Dill; sound mix Chris Erlon; the staff at the National Latino Communications Center, including Luis R. Torres, Elena Minor, Marisa Leal, Katherine Burgueño and Angel Zapata; educational outreach coordinators Toby Levine and Cecilia García of Toby Levine Communications, Inc.

And thanks to Steve Kulczycki, Jackie Kain and especially co-executive producer Joyce Campbell of KCET-TV, Los Angeles, who helped get the series accepted for broadcast at PBS. Executive producers for the series were José Luis Ruiz and Jesús Salvador Treviño.

FOREWORD

Like many college students of the 1960s, I was inexorably drawn to the atmosphere of protest that was so typical of campuses during this era. But the seeds of my politicization went back further. My case, not in its particulars but in historical context, is typical of how other participants in the Chicano Movement became involved. In recalling my days as an enlisted aircraft mechanic stationed at a U.S. Air Force base in Great Britain during early 1960s, I now realize how that experience taught me a great deal about racial perceptions that were current in that era. The lesson politicized me and has helped shape my present thoughts on this complex process.

At that time, the civil rights movement was in full force "back in the states." I had dropped out of high school to enlist in the Air Force and was not particularly politicized. But I read in British newspapers and in the *Stars and Stripes* that, back home Black children were killed when a church was bombed, that civil rights workers were slain and that Bull Conners turned dogs loose on peaceful demonstrators. To my dismay and discomfort, some white sergeants openly delighted in this terrorism. This was a shocking lesson on the degree to which racism permeated our country.

Although my memory is fuzzy, while I was in the Air Force, I did not want to admit or I was not aware that, as a Mexican, I too could be an object of such abject hatred. The prospect was too ugly and threatening. To be sure, there were other manifestations of prejudice aimed at me in these politically incorrect surroundings, but similar barbs were also aimed at the Italian Americans and Polish Americans in my flight group. Because these Air Force career men waited until Black airmen were out of earshot before venting murderous hatreds, but spoke freely in front of me, perhaps I unconsciously assumed that white

America's racial malice for Mexicans did not sink as low. Moreover, some of these same white airmen, who literally anguished over Black GIs going out with white English girls, did not seem to extend their anxiety to Mexican Americans doing the same. In fact, a couple of my fellow Chicano airmen married to English women befriended southern whites who celebrated racist violence against Blacks. At times, I saw Mexican American GIs join in racial bashing.

No, it did not seem to me that we Mexicans were in the same boat, figuratively speaking, when it came to racism from whites. Thus when some liberal-minded whites, usually young enlisted boys like myself and one or two sergeants, argued against anti-Black violence and for integration, I chimed in. More than anything, I had been moved by the horror of white airmen airing their crude, hateful racism right before my very eyes; I did not read about it in the abstract conduit of newspaper stories or history textbooks. My revulsion was provoked by sympathy for Blacks and their predicament, not because of how the situation affected Chicanos. I suppose I fancied myself more like the white freedom bus riders, whom I read about and came to admire, making a decision to help Blacks because I was more privileged.

Many times, treatment from fellow whites, however, compromised my ability to speak from that position. One sergeant would constantly call me *pachuco* and tell me how he helped clean up "Mexican town" in Los Angeles during World War II. I might have shrugged that off as not being particularly racial because American GIs were always talking about doing something similar to English "Teddy Boys" in the town of Newmarket, which was located next to the base.

But more was revealed to me. In my outfit there was a white sergeant in his forties—the quality control specialist—who often spoke softly and lovingly about our mutual home state of Arizona as he inspected my work. He came from the central part of the state – the Wickenburg-Prescott mining-ranching area known for turbulent Mexican-Anglo relations. I had grown up in southern Arizona, where I assumed, with an eighteen-year-old brashness, that we were equal to Anglos. But in these flight-line discussions on race, the normally genial and likable World War II veteran metamorphosed and reminded me angrily that, back in Arizona when he was growing up, they hanged uppity Mexicans like me.

That was more shocking to me than knowing some GIs cleaned up "Mexican town." My great desire by then was to go to college upon my return to the States, repair what I considered a misspent youth and become a contender in something. I was tired of the military caste system that so rigidly separated us "fly-boy grunts" from officer pilots with their polished college exterior. The Arizona sergeant's posturing, exaggerated as it might have been, provided one of my first real

indications that Mexicans shared with Blacks a debilitating burden of oppression. Such a revelation discouraged my aspirations to acquire social mobility. I therefore put his admonition out of my mind, perhaps by not believing him. Nonetheless, while this career Air Force man who had grown up in the Arizona of my parents and immigrant grandparents may have exaggerated, he was not lying. Fortunately, when I found out that it was true, that *Mexicans were lynched in Arizona* because of racism, I was not defeated by a victimization mentality but was well into pursuing my educational aspirations.

The dynamics of Anglo-American racism towards Mexicans reflects this interplay. Indeed, I was not aware of the degree to which antipathy existed towards Mexicans, precisely because the process has a distinct historical construction from the one affecting Blacks.

F. Arturo Rosales
Tempe, Arizona
November 20, 1995

INTRODUCTION

Today many of my students, Mexican Americans included, know little about or have never heard of the Chicano Movement (*el movimiento,* as it became known to its thousands of participants). The passing of time has much to do with this—because the height of this political movement occurred at the end of the 1960s and the beginning of the 1970s. For an even greater number of young students, the names of movement stalwarts such as Reies López Tijerina, Rodolfo "Corky" Gonzales and José Angel Gutiérrez meant nothing before they enrolled in my history class. More of them recognize farm-worker union leader César Chávez because the United Farm Workers continues to organize workers into the present day and because his untimely death raised the farm-worker leader's stature. In addition, the message and goals of the farm-worker movement transcended those of the other Chicano leaders, whose appeal was widespread mainly within the historical context of that period.

But the Chicano Movement indeed ushered in a new era. It was a time when young people from ethnic and mainstream groups in various parts of the country sought to express their hopes for the country. In the history of the U.S., no other era embodies the rise of youthful self-conscious idealism. The period produced a generation that questioned the premises and values sacred to their parents. In fact, a guiding axiom, whose etymology is unclear, was "don't trust anyone over thirty."

Young white Americans, usually middle-class and living in large urban concentrations, participated in a counterculture which they expressed in art and in politics. The most visible representatives of the counterculture were known as "hippies." But the counterculture contained more than love-peace proclaiming "flower children" whose mecca was the Haight Ashbury district of San Francisco. For the first time, young Americans felt confident in themselves and liberated from the ideological constraints which had hamstrung free discourse since the end of World War II, a period dominated by the Cold War. In their liberation, many turned to a unique brand of American radical politics.

The seeds of this phenomenon were partially sown by the "beatniks" of the 1950s, such as Jack Kerouac, Neal Cassidy and Allen Ginsberg. These intellectual rebels defined a uniquely American anti-establishment critique. They had indicted a "silent generation" of Americans whose race for the "good life" resulted in banality and unquestioning conformity. They believed that Cold War politics silenced free expression and stifled lifestyles which did not conform to all-American models.

This 1950s phenomenon mushroomed into a huge movement in the subsequent decade. One of the first indications of this movement emerged at the University of California-Berkeley in a tempest called the "Free Speech Movement." Led by Mario Savio, an undergraduate student at the time, this activity questioned the premises of the conventional curriculum in mainstream institutions of higher education. Savio and his associates attracted hundreds of Berkeley students to teach-ins designed to raise consciousness and stimulate free thinking.

Indeed, the Cold War mentality of the 1950s had stifled academic learning. Few professors, many of whom were products of the post-war world, dared or wanted to question the American system. Nonetheless, some academics, such as

Marxist scholar Herbert Marcuse at the University of California-San Diego, welcomed the burgeoning intellectual ferment and served as its mentor. The restless young, however, did not study or apply a strict Marxist prescription to the ills they protested against. Rather, they chose an eclectic and vague but strident vision of reform.

The Black civil rights movement also challenged the system. It served as a catalyst to the unrest of young people who wondered how the ideals of democracy and equality, for which the nation supposedly stood, could exist alongside the repression of racial minorities. In the university environment, the civil rights movement encountered a more comfortable environment in which to conduct its work.

Such a heady mix was bound to inspire Mexican American youth, who in high-school and college mall or neighborhood rap sessions excitedly discussed the condition of their people, whom they knew had been repressed. They reflected the new consciousness in the common language of the time: the enemy became the Establishment and its supposed minions were the older Mexican American political leaders. But for many future activists, the path to politicization did not directly result from the identification of their own people as an oppressed minority to the degree that was current among African-American activists. Three reasons accounted for this. One, the media and white liberals were not as interested in Mexican American issues as they were in the abhorrent treatment of Blacks, especially in the South. Two, in the Mexican American era of civil rights struggle, the extent of racism and oppression was either denied or masked over by an overly optimistic appraisal of access to the U.S. opportunity structure. Three, a common notion was that Mexican Americans did not suffer from the same racism to which Black Americans were subjected.

Thus, for many future Chicano activists, the Black civil rights struggle was crucial in persuading them to pursue the path that eventually led them to the *movimiento.* Many made the decision to help Blacks as if Mexican Americans did not need to engage in a similar struggle. In the early 1960s, hallmark years for the African American civil rights movement, María Varela, who became an active Chicano Movement participant in New Mexico during the late 1960s, joined the National Student Association, which worked hand in hand with the Student Non-violent Coordinating Committee (SNCC). It was not until she met Reies López Tijerina in 1966 that she started to turn her energies to Chicano activism. Carlos Muñoz, now a professor at Berkeley and a founder of the 1960s United Mexican American Students (UMAS) at California State College Los Angeles, remembers, "When I was at Cal State LA and working with SNCC and other civil rights organizations, all of a sudden in my mind I said, Wait, what am I doing?. . . We've got our own revolution. . . We don't have civil rights. . . . That's when we started organizing."[1]

The Black civil rights movement served also to teach strategies to Mexican Americans activists. Farm-worker leader César Chávez, for example, the Chicano Movement leader who came the closest to projecting a Martin Luther King image, acknowledges the influence of that monumental American figure. In an interview taken just before he passed away, he was asked how much influence King had on him.

> A lot. . . Although he wasn't known around the *mexicanos* and strikers. They didn't see him as a teacher. I learned a lot from him. And I was totally in awe with what he did.... I was an organizer, so I know what he was going through...so I got to know him and we became friends. And I began to see—I got involved with some of the things he was doing and then also looked to him for...advice, guidance. Not so much asking, but just seeing what he was doing.[2]

As Mexican Americans recognizing the

---

[1] Interview with Carlos Muñoz by Susan Racho, National Latino Communications Center - Galán Productions. All subsequent references to these video-taped and/or transcribed interviews will be abbreviated as NLCC-GP.

[2] Interview with César Chávez by Luis Torres, April 20, 1992, NLCC-GP.

oppression of Black Americans looked at their own condition, they first attended to those who appeared the most repressed—the poverty-stricken farm workers who had been completely bypassed by the good life of the 1950s and 1960s. Lionel Steinberg, a farmer in the Coachella Valley in California, acknowledged this in a recent interview:

> In the 1950s and 1960s, farm workers unfortunately were considered just another item in producing. . . . like fertilizers. . . . most growers didn't treat their workers with any degree of respect or dignity. . . so there was a natural scenario for bitterness. . . . [there] were legitimate grievances by workers.[3]

Moreover, youthful discontent rose with the escalation of American involvement in the Vietnam conflict. As the U.S. committed resources and human lives to the war, which had been unpopular from the beginning, American youth became disenchanted. World War II, and to a lesser degree the Korean conflict, had brought out a general patriotic fervor among Americans; Vietnam did not. Many Chicano youths shared the increasing antiwar sentiment that permeated the country. As it became evident that war casualties came from the working class, Chicanos began to view this bias from a nationalistic-racial perspective: Chicanos and minorities carried the burden of the war. The antiwar effort became a crucial issue that gave the *movimiento* impetus.

Cultural renewal and the search for identity became pivotal parts of the overall 1960s ambience. The flower children, young people who committed themselves to communal living and sharing everything from food to sex, were the most ardent representatives of this cultural transformation. While a minority, these "hippies" had an impact on the rest of society. Chicano culture likewise was becoming transformed, and mainstream Mexican American society was affected—consciously and unconsciously.

In essence, challenges to racial conformity

thrived. African-American civil right leaders and their white liberal allies softened much of the American public to a tolerant position, encouraging a more aggressive stance on the part of those who wanted to protest everything from racism to the war. But the youth movement also influenced the cultural direction Americans were taking. Full-time professionals, college students and even working-class adults who continued to lead conformist lives sported longer hair, mustaches, beards and an exuberant flower-laden "mod" dress.

This does not mean there was no resistance to change. As happened in the American South when Blacks escalated their demands for desegregation and voting rights, government officials resorted to repression when antiestablishment activities seemed to threaten the status quo. In the initial years of protest, police, the national guard, the FBI and other enforcers were employed to suppress manifestations of discontent. They often acted violently. Chicano activists, especially in Los Angeles, where the heart of the classical manifestations of the *movimiento* resided, were treated likewise.

The white counterculture was suppressed as well—albeit not as violently. It was undoubtedly more difficult to use violence on middle-class white youngsters than on brown and black protesters. Still, as was seen at Berkeley and at Kent State, whites met with fierce repression at times. Throughout the sixties and in the early seventies, denouncement of youthful radicals was constant, and even President Nixon overreacted to the perceived threat. In 1968 Congressman Joe Pool, a member of the House Committee on Un-American Activities, spoke for many Americans who disapproved of the underground newspapers that had mushroomed among dissident youth:

> These smut sheets are today's Molotov cocktails thrown at respectability and decency in our nation. . . . They encourage depravity and irresponsibility, and they nurture a

---

[3] Interview with Lionel Steinberg by Sylvia Morales, December 7, 1994, NLCC-GP.

breakdown in the continued capacity of the government to conduct an orderly and constitutional society.[4]

How white and African-American protest fits into this era of social unrest is well-known to most Americans because it has been documented time and time again in both the print and electronic media. However, the story of the Mexican American civil rights struggle in the 1960s and the 1970s is practically untold. That the Chicano Movement did not leave the same legacy as the Black civil rights movement and its Promethean Martin Luther King is not because of its relative lack of importance. Perhaps the Chicano Movement was not as central to American consciousness because the plight of Mexican Americans was not as recognized as the sin of slavery. Perhaps it was too fragmented and did not coalesce around the figure of a dynamic religious leader. Perhaps it was not as well covered by the media because so much of its ideas and grassroots organizing was expressed in the Spanish language. Or perhaps it was because Mexican Americans were still viewed as foreigners.

In the throes of *movimiento* activity, while participants agreed on the need for militancy (the main unifying variable), they were in constant disagreement on ideology, long-term strategy and choice of representative movement symbols. In many ways this internal intellectual struggle is what made the movement attractive and exciting.

Just as *el movimiento* did not follow a strategic plan, a coherent ideology, it did not have designated leaders. In fact, César Chávez, who led the United Farm Workers (UFW); Reies López Tijerina, founder of the movement to reclaim land grants, the Alianza Federal de las Mercedes; and Rodolfo "Corky" Gonzales, leader of the Crusade for Justice, did not have the slightest premonition they would become leading symbols of the Chicano Movement.

The issues addressed by the *movimiento* were not as broadly defined as the integration struggle for Blacks. For example, even though activists used walkouts to bring attention to educational inequities, the underlying nature of these problems differed from region to region as did the solutions that were sought. In the inner city schools of East Los Angeles, where *de facto* segregation created an almost exclusive Mexican American student body, grievances arose when activists compared the poorly funded barrio schools with educational institutions in affluent areas of the city and its suburban communities. The walkouts in Crystal City, Texas, where all students regardless of race, attended the same high school, stemmed from blatant unequal treatment of Anglos and Mexicans within the school itself. There, Mexican American participation in extracurricular symbols of success, such as cheerleading, was limited through quotas. In Phoenix, students walked out of Phoenix Union High School to protest *de facto* segregation and inadequate funding. But here the constant racial tension between Mexican Americans and Black students had provided the impetus for action.

Besides a lamentable educational system, the Chicano Movement was stimulated by many other issues such as racism, economic deprivation and police brutality. A crucial part of mobilization revolved around the issue of identity and racial pride. These had been important in Mexico, where European racial asthetics had predominated among a population where the majority was of Indian ancestry. After the Mexican Revolution of 1910, official policy tended to mollify racial denial. Class affiliation and cultural homogeneity, regardless of race, somewhat softened racism although it is still a significant problem in that country.

Mexicans in the U.S., however, have had to deal with a more acute sense of what is racially acceptable than in Mexico because of more intense and qualitatively different Anglo-American racism. Additionally, extreme ethnic differences separating Mexicans from Anglo-Americans exacerbated prejudice. The Chicano Movement confronted racism and racial self-hate head on, using

[4] *The Chicano Student*, June 12, 1968.

the slogan "brown is beautiful" and promoting an allegiance and affection to Indian-mestizo physical features. A virulent cultural nationalism[5] came to be an integral part of the *movimiento* although its expression differed depending on region.

Spurring the Chicano Movement was a perception that Mexicans living in the United States encountered repressive conditions that needed rectification. Indeed, the *raison d'etre* of the movement was the conviction that mainstream society was prejudiced against Mexicans because of cultural antipathy and because they were racially different. This notion paralleled the posture of the contemporary Black civil rights movement, which in large part movement activists emulated. While the analysis was correct that Mexicans suffered from racist oppression, the causes and manifestations of this unfortunate condition differed from those of Blacks in many respects. The legal and moral justification for demanding an end to unequal treatment resided in the founding principles of the United States. In essence, while both Blacks and Chicanos charged these guarantees were violated or hypocritically never meant to include them, the specifics of the violations were disparate.

THE FOUNDATION FOR EQUAL RIGHTS

In 1776 Thomas Jefferson wrote one of the most quoted passages ever set on paper when he authored the document which declared independence for the thirteen colonies from Great Britain.

> We hold these truths to be self-evident, that all men are created equal, that they are all endowed by their Creator with certain unalienable Rights, that among these are Life, Liberty and the pursuit of Happiness.

These words became the foundation of a revolution which resulted in removing the yoke of colonization by a European power from an emerging European enclave in the Americas. In the 1788 Constitution, the document which chartered the new course of government that is still in existence today, the spirit of equality was institutionalized. The Bill of Rights, ten amendments added after the Constitution's ratification, further provided basic freedoms such as the right to a jury trial, protection from illegal search and seizure and the right to form militias and bear arms. As inspiring as these initial guarantees were, the equality they established was for a select group: white males of property. Women, for example, were still not allowed to vote or own property while married. The situation was worse for African Americans, who at the time these documents were created, were enslaved as private property and had no rights under the Constitution whatsoever. These constitutional rights were also denied to Native Americans, whose tribes were treated as separate nations while living within the borders of the emerging United States. Mexicans who lived in what became part of the United States were still subjects of Spain in the early years of independence. The questions of what rights they would merit under equality guarantees would have to wait until the U.S. takeover of the Southwest or what was Mexico's extreme north.

But even if the Founding Fathers had not wanted to include nonwhite males in this supposed democratic Eden, the very structure of the Constitution and its Bill of Rights provided the mechanisms to include other groups. After the conclusion of the Civil War, the thirteenth (1865) and fourteenth (1868) amendments were added to the Bill of Rights. These constitutional changes made slavery illegal and provided citizenship to hundreds of thousands of former slaves. Similarly, women were given broader freedoms in 1920 with the nineteenth amendment, which forbade the preventing of voting based on sex. In 1964 Congress added the Equal Rights Amendment to the Constitution. This was the latest far-reaching attempt to protect the rights of citizens. This amendment, in essence, provided all citizens with the right to vote, disallowing obstacles such as the poll taxes designed to discourage minorities and the poor from voting.

---

[5] Constructing group or national identity based on a set of shared cultural and, in this case, racial traits.

While the Bill of Rights provided former slaves freedom and the rights of citizens, many white Americans balked at the idea of these mandates being fulfilled. In an experiment known as Reconstruction, the federal government established the Freedman's Bureau to assure that former slaves would be accorded the freedoms designed by the amended Constitution after 1868. However, within a few short years, Congress and the president lost their desire to continue overseeing the complex transition which liberated slaves had to make in a free society. By 1877, the Freedman's Bureau was dismantled and Reconstruction came to an end. Fierce opposition from Southern politicians combined with poor administration of Reconstruction brought an end to the program.

After this, former slaves were at the mercy of white-dominated state and local governments which lost no time in dismantling the gains African Americans had made during Reconstruction. A series of Jim Crow laws were established to assure severe segregation of Blacks in public facilities, transportation and schools. These same laws also prevented African Americans from voting. Poll taxes, intimidation and grandfather clauses—to vote, a person had to have had a grandfather who voted—kept former slaves from the polls. To assure social compliance, a reign of terror was unleashed on Blacks, in which violence became a favorite tactic. The infamous Klu Klux Klan spread throughout the South as the main enforcer. Thousands of Blacks were maimed or lynched for violating the social contract expected by whites.

Black leaders were aware that the constitutional guarantees were being abrogated, so they resisted as best they could. African Americans knew that the nation's courts could decide if the guarantees in the U.S. Constitution were being honored; so in 1896 a man named Plessy challenged through the court the segregation of African-Americans in the New Orleans train system. He won the case in a lower court but appealed the decision to the highest court. The Supreme Court in a critical decision decided segregation was legal—as long as "separate but equal" facilities were provided for Blacks. This provided the foundation for a system of apartheid, and while facilities provided Blacks were separate, they were far from being equal.

African Americans adapted to this system of apartheid, protesting periodically. In the twentieth century, however, as modernization and urbanization provoked a massive migration of Blacks from the rural South to the North, the African-American aspirations rose, provoking an intense civil rights movement that challenged and eventually ended "Jim Crow" legal codes. In 1954 African-Americans won a landmark decision when lawyers working for the National Association for the Advancement of Colored People (NAACP) won a favorable decision from the Supreme Court in a case where a Topeka, Kansas, student named Linda Brown sued the Board of Education of that city's school system to desegregate the schools.

This milestone decision reversed the *Plessy vs Furgeson* case that had served for more than half a century to ensure legal segregation and discrimination. The court, under Chief Justice Earl Warren, ruled that "in the field of public education the doctrine of 'separate but equal' has no place. Separate educational facilities are inherently unequal." Individual states were then called upon by the court to integrate the schools "with deliberate speed."[6]

This achievement provoked an intense movement by Black to demand an end to the now unconstitutional segregation and previously sanctioned denial of equal rights. This movement produced great historical figures, such as Martin Luther King Jr., who because of their sacrifices have properly earned heroic status.

Mexican Americans and other minorities in this country—"new immigrants" (eastern and southern Europeans), Native Americans, Puerto Ricans and women — have also had to struggle to obtain the lofty ideals of equality that were so

---

[6] Quoted in Edwin C. Rozwenc and Thomas Bender, *The Making of American Society* (New York: Alfred A. Knopf, 1978), p. 512.

eloquently put forth by the Constitution's framers. As will be seen in the beginning chapters of this text, Mexican Americans have struggled for civil rights in the United States since the mid-nineteenth century. In recent years, Mexican Americans have joined in the struggle to achieve the promises evident in the documents discussed above: the Declaration of Independence, the founding Constitution and the ensuing Bill of Rights. But as indicated, the particulars of denying Mexican Americans these rights differed from those of the Black experience. As shall be seen in the following pages, the conditions that led to the inequality of Mexican Americans are steeped first in a legacy of conquest and then in labor exploitation with little regard to their welfare.

RACE AND MEXICANS

Historians have pointed to numerous examples in which Mexicans were cast as undesirable because of their Indian features. It is also true that eastern and southern Europeans and even the Irish were treated with a similar hostility when they first arrived in the U.S. The image of extreme poverty, exacerbated by cultural differences, was what Anglo-Americans found most objectionable in the case of the white "new immigrants."

The construction of Mexicans as a race apart by white Americans, however, was very much different from the prejudices held against the European ethnic groups. While many new immigrants and their descendants were looked upon with racist disdain, as John Higham pointed out in his classic book on immigration, *Strangers in the Land*, that designation changed considerably in the post-World War II period. The descendants of the "new immigrants" have largely assimilated and acquired economic parity while Mexicans —along with Black and Native Americans and most other Latin Americans of color—have not.

According to such scholars as Arnoldo De León, David Weber, Raymund Paredes and Cecil Robinson, to name but a few, beginning with the initial contacts with Mexicans on the frontier in the nineteenth century, Anglo-Americans exhibited contempt for the mixed-race Mexicans.[7] During the process of annexation and conquest of what became the U.S. Southwest, this initial contempt turned to full-blown racism. David Weber indicates that, when the U.S. acquired Lousiana (1803) and Florida (1821), the Hispanics whom Anglos met there were mainly white. Few Hispanics owned vast tracts of land, and competition and violence were thus minimal in that area. As a consequence, the Anglos did not vilify the Hispanics of the Southeast. But the Anglos did

An editorial in the *New York Sun* during 1847, indicated that "the [Mexican] race is perfectly accustomed to being conquered, and the only new lesson we shall teach is that our victories will give liberty, safety, and prosperity to the vanquished, if they know enough to profit by the appearances of our stars." To "liberate and ennoble," the *Sun* reporter editorialized, "not to enslave and debase is our mission."

Most historians believe the reason all of Mexico was not annexed had to do with the race question. For example, the Richmond *Whig* editorialized during this period, "We have far more to dread from the acquisition of a debased population who have been so summarily manufactured into American citizens than to hope from the extension of our territorial limits."[8]

---

[7] David J. Weber, "The Spanish Legacy in North America and the Historical Imagination," *Western Historical Quarterly*, 23/1 (February 1992) p. 11.

[8] All quotes from David G. Gutiérrez, *Walls and Mirrors: Mexican Americans, Mexican Immigrants and the Politics of Ethnicity* (Berkeley: University of California Press, 1995), pp. 15-16.

despise the racial mixture of northern Mexicans, deeming it a mongrelization of the lowest order. And by subordinating northern Mexicans as inferior, they built up a case for appropriating their lands, even through violence. Since then, Anglos have perceived Hispanic society in the Southwest in very negative terms.

As the nineteenth century progressed, however, Anglos and Mexicans learned to live with each other and, in fact, relations improved, but with the rise of large-scale immigration at the turn of the century and the rise of border violence during the Mexican Revolution, acrimony towards Mexicans was revived with a vengeance.

The racial animosity that begins early in the nineteenth century, while showing some signs of abatement as the century came to an end, was resurrected as more and more Anglos settled along the long, contiguous border with Mexico. In this century, proximity to Mexico, massive immigration of undocumented poor people from Mexico, their continued use as cheap labor, drug smuggling across the border and constant reminders of corruption in Mexican politics racialized Mexicans even further.

Historian Carl Degler, in *Neither Black Nor White*, compares the experience of Blacks in Brazil with those in the U.S. He concludes that lighter-skinned Brazilian Negroes, known as *mulatos*, experienced less racism than their darker brothers. To protect this advantage, *mulatos* distanced themselves from the blacker African-Brazilians with the effect of muting a potential nationwide civil rights movement. In contrast, light-skinned African-Americans in the U.S. did not achieve such preferential treatment. This fact unifies African-Americans to such a degree that they have launched one of the most massive ongoing civil rights struggles in the history of the world.

In contrast, prior to the ascendancy of the *movimiento,* the Mexican American civil rights movement had not succeeded in dramatizing or publicizing the plight of Mexican Americans as racial injustice to the degree that Black activists had throughout this century. The very weight of oppression kept Black civil rights efforts in the news. It is no coincidence that, even for future

movimiento activists, atrocities against the Negro provided the first pangs of outrage which served to raise a consciousness that was necessary before Chicanos took the first steps into activism.

One reason that Mexican Americans did not dramatize their plight as effectively as Blacks was that they enjoyed an escape hatch like the one Degler described for Blacks in Brazil. Those Mexicans who were not directly impacted by extreme doses of racial prejudice—because of where they lived, their class or the color of their skin—were able to ignore the plight of their more subordinated brothers. But as members from the more subordinated Mexican classes in the U.S. became educated, the quest for civil rights became a grassroots effort known as the Chicano Movement.

This book is designed to accompany a television documentary series also called *Chicano! The History of the Mexican American Civil Rights Movement,* which strives to remind not only students but the nation that, during the turbulent 1960s, Chicanos also struggled for justice and equality. A mission of this book, like the documentary, is to reconstruct the classical era of the Chicano Movement—the period from about 1965 to 1975. But this cannot be done without providing a historical context. The *movimiento* did not appear in a vacuum. It was intricately anchored in a history linked to a past of civil rights struggles waged by Mexican people in the U.S. since the mid-nineteenth century. This is little known to most Americans. In the early *movimiento* days, young Chicanos made the mistake of assuming that the effort to end discrimination, prejudice and subordination began with the Chicano Movement. What the *movimiento* did was to accelerate concerns previously articulated by Mexicans in the U.S., and it intensified a style of confrontational protest that premovement activists were already employing or had employed in the past. Just as important, it reinvigorated the Mexican American quest to identify and assert a positive place in American society.

To capture such a history, the book designates four episodes of the Mexican civil rights struggle in the United States. Chapter One features efforts of the "lost-land" generation (Southwest Mexican natives) to stem property losses, maintain their culture and assert civil rights given them by the Treaty of Guadalupe Hidalgo after the U.S. takeover of the Southwest in the mid-nineteenth century. The second portion, Chapters Two to Five, studies attempts by Mexican immigrants in the early part of this century to protect themselves from a hostile American public. In the effort to safeguard their civil rights, an elaborate *México Lindo* (Pretty Mexico) nationalism emerged that immigrants used to rally around issues of repression. This process was aided and abetted by the Mexican government.

Chapters Six and Seven look at the optimistic Mexican American generation made up primarily of the first generation of children who did not have ties to Mexico. Not only did this generation demand the civil rights to which they were entitled, but they also strove to acculturate to Anglo-American culture without turning their backs on their Mexican heritage. In addition, Mexican Americans in this era made the greatest attempts to empower themselves as workers.

The final and most lengthy section of the book looks at the most important outgrowth of the Mexican American generation: the Chicano Movement. While this generation remained committed to the ideals of the Mexican American era, it realized that the promises which propelled optimism in the previous generation had evaporated. The *movimiento* is assessed within the context of the previous manifestations because, in the formation of ideology and identity, it borrowed, sometimes unconsciously, from past ideals while at the same time reflecting the general discontent that permeated contemporary America. It is specifically these chapters, Eight to Fourteen, which relate most directly to the documentary film series, *Chicano!*

In 1992 Peter Torres Jr., a San Antonio-based Mexican American legislator and political organizer who opposed La Raza Unida Party, was interviewed by the executive coproducer of the *Chicano!* documentary series, filmmaker Jesús Treviño. In the first question Treviño, obviously interested in gaining information on the movement era, asked Torres for his insights on the activism of the late sixties and to expound on such figures as César Chávez and Reies López Tijerina. Torres immediately shot back, "Yeah. There was certainly a lot of activism that had been going around prior to that," and then cited the Viva Kennedy campaigns, the formation of Political Association of Spanish-Speaking Organizations (PASO) and the Crystal City Hall takeover prior to the rise of La Raza Unida Party in 1963.

CHAPTER ONE

Americans by Conquest

1. Rounding up cattle at the San Gabriel Mission in early California.

Chicano activists believe that the U.S. violently invaded Mexico, wrested from it what became the American Southwest and then subjugated its inhabitants; this event has been portrayed as the first of a series of actions casting Mexicans as victims of U.S. imperialism. It follows, then, that a second *raison d'etre* of the Chicano Movement is the notion that the U.S. violated basic tenets of the Treaty of Guadalupe Hidalgo, which ended the war with Mexico in 1848 and established conditions under which conquered Mexicans were to live. But immigration from Mexico, a full-blown process initiated even before the end of the nineteenth century, challenged the Chicanos' claims of an unbroken heritage in the Southwest as a sizable proportion of Mexican Americans today are descended from late nineteenth- and twentieth-century immigrants.

THE MEXICAN NORTH—TODAY'S SOUTHWEST

As Mexicans witnessed the gradual immersion of their culture and economy into a powerful Anglo-American political and industrial monolith, native Mexicans in the Southwest perceived their "lost land" in an ideological perspective. The loss was felt more in northern New Mexico, south Texas and coastal California, where the Mexicans who remained outside Mexico's shrunken borders were concentrated. In spite of resistance to Anglo domination and a marked reluctance on the part of Anglo-Americans to incorporate Mexicans, in the initial contact years an uneasy symbiosis evolved in which the two groups cooperated at different social and economic levels.

By 1853 about 80,000 Spanish-speaking settlers lived in the territories lost by Mexico as a consequence of the Texas Rebellion (1836), the Mexican War (1848) and the Gadsden Purchase (1853). Dispersed in sparsely settled areas throughout the lost territories, they were descendants of the actual Mexican settlers who migrated from the interior of Mexico by conquering or pushing aside the indigenous groups who occupied the land before them. Officially, these Hispanics were not considered immigrants because the Treaty of Guadalupe Hidalgo conferred on them U.S. citizenship. But in reality, incoming Anglo-Americans, who claimed a "Manifest Destiny" to live in the conquered territories, saw them as foreigners.

Some nineteenth-century Mexicans accepted the alteration of their national status and welcomed U.S. citizenship. However, many Americans did not really accept them, often manifesting this attitude through political and social rejection. Moreover, Mexico's proximity compelled Americans to live close to a culture viewed as incompatible along one of the longest borders between any two nations. This closeness has bred some affinity, but mainly offensive and defensive forms of con-

"It seems to me that there never was a more peaceful or happy people on the face of the earth than the Spanish, Mexican, and Indian population of Alta California before the American conquest. We were the pioneers of the Pacific coast, building towns and missions while General Washington was carrying on the war of the Revolution, and we often talk together of the days when a few hundred large Spanish ranches and mission tracts occupied the whole country from the Pacific to the San Joaquin. No class of American citizens is more loyal than the Spanish Californians, but we shall always be especially proud of the traditions and memories of the long pastoral age before 1840."[1]

---

[1] Guadalupe Vallejo, "Ranch and Mission Days in Alta California," *The Century Magazine* 41/ 2 (1881): p. 183.

tempt have characterized relations between the two peoples.

The present states of Texas, New Mexico, Arizona, California and parts of Nevada, Utah, Colorado, Oklahoma and Kansas were at one time Mexican territory. Mexico inherited this vast territory when it acquired its independence from Spain in 1821. Within a short period—thirty-three years—this vast Mexican hinterland passed into the hands of the U.S. The first severance of Mexican territory came in 1836 with the Texas Rebellion. Since 1821, when Stephen F. Austin had signed an agreement to bring four hundred non-Hispanic Catholic families into Texas to settle this vast underpopulated Mexican region, immigrant Anglos continued to flock into the area. In 1824 the Mexican congress passed a law allowing even more non-Mexicans into the northern reaches and provided free and cheap land to the settlers. Most of these newcomers settled in what was the state of Texas-Coahuila.

By 1830 the area had twenty thousand Anglos living under Mexican rule, most in the northern part of the province. Soon, however, these outsiders tired of living under Mexican rule. The Texans, for example, complained that the Mexican government did not protect them from Comanche raids. Also they could not adapt to the Mexican legal code, especially to Spanish-language legal procedures. They disliked that the state legislature was located in the Coahuila part of the state—in Saltillo—hundreds of miles from Anglo population centers near present-day Austin, San Antonio and Houston. In 1836 Anglo and Mexican Texans declared their independence from Mexico. This was primarily because the central Mexican government, under the strongman Antonio López de Santa Anna, was attempting to bring the dissident Texans under control. The Texas Rebellion was successful after Anglo Texans defeated General Santa Anna himself, who brought troops from central Mexico to squelch the uprising. When Santa Anna's troops defeated the Texans at the Alamo mission in San Antonio and at Goliad, he gave an order to take no prisoners (a *degüello* order). Despite his surrender to Sam Houston in April, 1836, the *degüello* command resulted in massacres that became part of a

2. General Antonio López de Santa Anna.

litany of resentment which Texans held against Mexicans for a long time thereafter.

Mexico never accepted or recognized the independence of Texas as the Lone Star Republic and threatened war with the U.S. if it ever tried to annex the state. Mexican officials, with good reason, suspected U.S. connivance in the Texas rebellion and remained antagonistic to further American inroads. In 1845 Mexico's worst fears were confirmed when the U.S. Congress ratified a treaty to annex Texas. In July of 1845 President James K. Polk sent General Zachary Taylor across the Nueces River to enforce U.S. claims to Texas extending all the way to the Rio Grande River. The Mexicans asserted the new border to be the Nueces River, some one hundred miles to the north.

Anglo-Americans wanted to fulfill a "Manifest Destiny" of expanding their country all the

3. The Battle of Churubusco during the Mexican War.

way to the Pacific coast. Indeed many Americans believed that God had provided signs that these lands could be taken from Mexico with impunity. After the annexation, in November of 1845 President Polk sent John Slidell to Mexico with an offer of twenty-five million dollars for New Mexico and California, but Mexican officials refused even to see him. Polk then sent General Zachary Taylor across the Nueces River to blockade the mouth of the Rio Grande River at Port Isabel. On April 25, 1846, Mexicans retaliated by crossing the river and attacking U.S. troops, inflicting casualties. Now able to justify war immediately, Polk went to Congress and obtained a declaration of war against Mexico.

The U.S. invasion took place from four different directions. Taylor's troops crossed north across the Rio Grande while General Stephen Watts Kearny took an army overland to New Mexico and then to California. There he encountered considerable resistance from the *californios*[2] at the Battle of San Pascual before reaching Los Angeles. Commodore John C. Fremont assaulted California by sea through Monterey.

General Winfield Scott engineered the most decisive drive, leading to Mexico's defeat. In 1847 his troops bombarded Veracruz and then proceeded west with the most sizable American force to Mexico City, where Mexicans offered the greatest amount of resistance at Churubusco. By September Scott's troops occupied Mexico City. Selected as Mexican president in December of 1846, General Santa Anna attempted hopelessly to fend off the invasion, and

4. General Winfield Scott.

---

[2] *Californios* is a term Hispanic colonists who lived in California before the U.S. conquest used to identify themselves.

5. Pío Pico, the last Mexican governor of California.

in November he resigned in disgrace. The Mexicans, nonetheless, refused to come to the bargaining table until they were thoroughly routed. Finally in February of 1848, they signed the Treaty of Guadalupe Hidalgo, which brought the war officially to an end. That the war lasted as long as it did is quite remarkable. From the time the U.S. annexed Texas until the war ended in 1847, six different Mexican presidents attempted to make foreign policy—often at odds with each other. Some Mexicans, called *polkos* (after President Polk), even had military drills to prepare and fight on the American side.

For fifteen million dollars, the U.S. acquired the vast territories of New Mexico, Arizona, California and parts of Nevada, Utah and Colorado.

Provisions in the treaty gave Southwest Mexicans who remained in U.S. territory the constitutional rights of citizens and ostensibly protected their property, culture and religion—that is, if they did not retreat behind Mexico's shrunken border. These conditions, which the Mexican negotiators at the town of Guadalupe Hidalgo had insisted on, seemed protective of the former Mexican citizens, but these stipulations were only as good as the ability and desire to uphold the promises. As we shall see later, one of the most important issues in the Chicano Movement was the charge that the U.S. did not live up to those promises.

MEXICANS UNDER UNITED STATES RULE

An early source of Anglo-American antipathy towards Hispanics is found in the "Black Legend." This interpretation has sixteenth-century English propagandists discrediting the reputation of the Spaniards in the New World in order to further their own imperialistic plans. As a consequence, Anglo-Americans held negative views even before confronting Mexicans on New Spain's frontiers, where the encounter itself deepened prejudices and provided at least one important rationale for "Manifest Destiny." The violence of the Texas Rebellion and the Mexican War further fueled the antipathy.

But an underlying cause of the antipathy Anglo-Americans held for Mexicans was a pre-existing ideology of racism. According to Arnoldo De León, "Most whites who first met Tejanos in the 1820s had never had prior experiences with Mexicans nor encountered them anywhere else. Yet their reaction was contemptuous, many thinking the Mexicans abhorrent." The reason for this racist orientation, De Léon argues, was because

> cultural heirs to Elizabethans and Puritans, those [Anglos] moving into the hinterlands sensed an "errand into the wilderness" and felt a compelling need to control all that was beastly—sexuality, vice, nature, and other peoples [read other races]. . . . Coming into constant encounter with peoples of color in wilderness settings, these

Tiburcio Vásquez, the famous California "bandit" or social rebel, gave these reasons for striking out at the Anglo population: "My career grew out of the circumstances by which I was surrounded as I grew into manhood. I was in the habit of attending balls and parties given by the native Californians, into which the Americans, then beginning to become numerous, would force themselves and shove the native-born men aside, monopolizing the dances and the women. This was about 1852.

"A spirit of hatred and revenge took possession of me. I had numerous fights in defense of what I believed to be my rights and those of my countrymen. The officers were continuously in pursuit of me. I believe that we were unjustly and wrongfully deprived of the social rights which belonged to us. So perpetually was I involved in these difficulties that I at length determined to leave the thickly-settled portion of the country, and did so."[4]

sensitive whites struggled against noncivilization.[3]

The Treaty of Guadalupe Hidalgo did not apply to Texas because of an 1855 Supreme Court decision, but Mexicans in Texas were supposedly protected under the 1836 Texas constitution and the state constitution of 1845. The territorial acquisition delineated in the Treaty of Guadalupe Hidalgo did not include southern Arizona and southwestern New Mexico, a region extending from the present-day Yuma along the Gila River (twenty-five miles south of Phoenix) all the way to the Mesilla Valley, where Las Cruces, New Mexico, is situated. Under pressure from the Americans, General Santa Anna sold this region to the U.S. during his return to power in 1853. (He was exiled after losing to the invading Americans in 1847.) Gadsden Treaty perimeters gave Mexicans in the purchased territory the same rights provided by the Treaty of Guadalupe Hidalgo. In the process of these territorial severances, many Southwest Mexicans felt insecure that provisions protecting Mexicans would be honored; others were embittered because they felt Mexico had betrayed them. As a consequence, out of the tens of thousands of Mexicans living in the Southwest, about three thousand took advantage of official Mexican attempts to repatriate marooned Mexicans in the newly acquired American territories.

The experience of oppression of Mexicans who remained behind in the U.S. was cited regularly by Chicano Movement activists as a basis for charges of historical mistreatment. In essence, it is true that, because of an Anglo-American unwillingness to accept Mexicans as equals, they often ignored treaty agreements that gave Mexicans all the rights of citizens. In New Mexico because there were so many Hispanics—perhaps sixty-thousand were living in the territory in 1848—they forged some political self-determination. But even there the new Hispanic U.S. citizens encountered systematic discrimination. In the newly acquired areas outside of New Mexico, conditions were worse. In Texas, where the population increased from an ethnically mixed population of thirty thousand in 1836 to one hundred forty thousand in 1846, the influx of Anglos overwhelmed Mexicans by a ratio of six to one.

The 1836 constitution provided citizenship rights in the new republic to all Mexican and white residents living in Texas at the time of the rebellion. But that same document stipulated that the government could suspend the privileges of anyone who had been disloyal during the rebellion. Embittered Anglos who wanted the land of the outnumbered Mexicans or who resented their presence forced them off their property, claiming they had been disloyal. To avoid persecution, many Mexicans abandoned their land and simply crossed the border to Mexico. In 1857 in order to eliminate Mexican teamster competition because they dominated South Texas transportation, Anglo merchants hired cowboy hooli-

[3] Arnoldo De León, *They Called Them Greasers: Anglo Attitudes Toward Mexicans in Texas, 1821-1900* (Austin: University of Texas Press, 1983), p. 1.

[4] Tiburcio Vásquez interview by the *Los Angeles Star*, May 16, 1874.

6. Joaquín Murieta.

The anonymous ballad, "Corrido de Joaquín Murieta," includes this boast by the most famous of all "bandits," who reeked havoc among the mid-nineteenth-century Anglo residents of California in revenge for his gold mine claim being stolen and his wife and brother being killed by the claim jumpers:

Ahora salgo a los caminos	Now I go out onto roads
A matar a americanos	To kill Americans
Tú fuistes el promotor	You were the cause
De la muerte de mi hermano	Of my brother's death
Lo agarrastes indefenso	You took him defenseless
Desgraciado americano.	You disgraceful American.
A los ricos y avarientos	From the rich and avaricious
Yo les quité su dinero	I took their money
A los humildes y pobres	To the humble and poor
Yo me quitaba el sombrero	I tipped my hat
Ay, qué leyes tan injustas	Oh, what unjust laws
Voy a darme a bandolero.	I'm going to become a bandit.

Novelist Amparo Ruiz de Burton described the complicity of government, railroads and individuals in expropriating lands from the Californios: "I think but few Americans know or believe to what extent we have been wronged by Congressional action. And truly, I believe that Congress itself did not anticipate the effect of its laws upon us, and how we could be despoiled, we the conquered people.

"I am afraid there is no help for us native Californians. We must sadly fade and pass away. The weak and the helpless are always trampled in the throng. We must sink, go under, never to rise.

"The Anglo-Saxon is, as we so often hear, very land-hungry. Many of the newcomers were accustomed to the almost boundless freedom of the Western squatters; the right to squat on vacant land had come to seem to them traditional and inalienable; [Consequently,] that all the rights of the Californians should ultimately be respected was, indeed, in view of our rapacious Anglo-Saxon land-hunger, and of our national bigotry in dealing with Spanish-Americans, impossible."[5]

gans to force the Mexican carters off wagon routes. Although not completely successful, these attempts, combined with other violations, demonstrate not only an antipathy towards Mexicans but also show that Anglo-Americans felt Mexicans did not have the constitutional rights which they themselves prized.

California also experienced ethnic violence, especially in the intense competition of the Gold Rush. Anglo miners simply pushed Mexicans off their claims through force or by murder. A rash of lynchings, murders and expulsions of Hispanics provoked a reaction that

[5] From *The Squatter and the Don*, Arte Público Press reprint of the 1885 original edition, pp. 67 and 177.

In 1856 *El Clamor Público* published Pablo de la Guerra's impassioned speech to the California legislature, which reveals much about the sentiments of native Californios during the loss of their lands and rights:

"[The Californios] are the conquered who lay prostate before the conqueror and ask for his protection in the enjoyment of the little which their fortune has left them. They are the ones who had been sold like sheep—those who were abandoned and sold by Mexico. They do not understand the language which is now spoken in their own country. They have no voice in this Senate, except such as I am now weakly speaking on their behalf. . . . I have seen old men of sixty and seventy years of age weeping like children because they have been cast out of their ancestral home. They have been humiliated and insulted. They have been refused the privilege of taking water from their own wells. They have been refused the privilege of cutting their own firewood. And yet those individuals who have committed these abuses have come here looking for protection, and, surprisingly, the Senate sympathizes with them. You Senators do not lis-

gave rise to the Joaquín Murieta legend and produced more flesh-and-blood bandits symbolizing resistance such as Juan Flores and Tiburcio Vásquez. In addition, Anglo newcomers, many from the southern United States, brought grim traditions of prejudice against racial minorities.

Generally, the loss of property provides the greatest historical evidence of victimization. Indeed, the 1960s Alianza Federal de las Mercedes (Federal Land Grant Alliance), started by the militant Reies López Tijerina, known as "El Tigre" (The Tiger), was predicated on righting wrongs caused by property loss. Provisions regarding the safeguarding of Hispanic holdings were vague in the Treaty of Guadalupe Hidalgo, but the document made a definite commitment in this area. Southwest land values rose as the Anglo population increased and as the area became more economically developed. Inevitably, intense land competition followed, and Mexican property was coveted by developers and Anglo farmers who often justified their yearning by evoking the idea that lazy Mexicans were not industrious and used the land inefficiently. Divesting Mexicans of their property was facilitated by the fact that landholding systems in Mexico differed considerably from property record keeping in the U.S. Subsequently, in territories acquired by the U.S. from Mexico, Mexicans were immediately burdened with the difficulty of proving land ownership in the American system while using old Spanish and Mexican records.

In one of the first U.S. government attempts to address this issue, Congress passed the 1851 California Land Act. Ostensibly the legislators framed this enactment so that *californios* could legalize land they claimed prior to the U.S. takeover, but far from doing this, procedures specified by the act sometimes forced the California Mexicans to litigate for years. Because they could not afford the fees demanded by prolonged proceedings, *rancheros* paid their lawyers with huge tracts of land. Then Congress passed the 1862 Homestead Act, which allowed squatters to settle and claim vacant lands in frontier areas. *Californios* soon found thousands of Anglo settlers squatting on their lands, creating a morass of legal disputes that courts more often settled in favor of the squatters. In many cases, land speculators used homesteaders as front men to obtain the "free" lands owned by Mexicans, which they later sold at huge profits.

In 1854 the Surveyor of General Claims Office was established in the New Mexico territory to resolve land disputes between Hispanics and newcomers. This system was even slower than the one in California. At times it took fifty years to settle just a few claims, and in the meantime Hispanic New Mexicans were defrauded in land grabs similar to those in California. When the Santa Fe, Atchison and Topeka railroad was built from Kansas through the northern part of the territory in the 1890s, land speculators organized into the "Santa Fe Ring" and engineered schemes in which hundreds of Hispanic landowners lost their farms and ranches. In response, the Mexicans organized into bands of hooded night riders known as Las Gorras Blancas (The White Caps) and set out in forays to tear down fences and derail trains, hoping

7. The Lugo family of Californios at Bell Gardens, California, ca. 1888.

ten to the complaints of the Spanish citizens. You do not sufficiently appreciate their land titles and the just right to their possessions."

to frighten Anglo land developers and railroad companies into abandoning New Mexico. Then the establishment of state parks during the early twentieth century contributed to even further erosion of the land holdings in New Mexico (see Chapter Nine for discussion of this process as part of the Chicano Movement).

Because of a previous history of mistreatment and violence by the law enforcers, Chicano Movement activists also pointed to a historical pattern of oppression at the hands of the law and made it one of the main issues on the *movimiento* agenda. Because so many defendants could not speak English, some Texas communities during the 1880s still allowed court proceedings to be conducted in Spanish and installed monolingual Spanish-speaking jurors. Such privileges were limited, however, to border areas where Mexicans managed a modicum of political control. In the rest of Texas, an 1856 law prohibiting Spanish in the courts was vigorously enforced. Nineteenth-century Texas, which by 1900 had the largest Mexican population and the longest border

Juan Nepomuceno Cortina led a rebel band against the Anglos who had moved into Texas and abused the native population and disrupted life and culture. He issued a proclamation in 1859 in which he spoke eloquently for the self-preservation, dignity, freedom and the retention of land guaranteed by the Constitution:

"Our object, as you have seen, has been to chastise the villainy of our enemies, which heretofore has gone unpunished. These have connived with each other, and form, so to speak, a perfidious inquisitorial lodge to prosecute and rob us, without any cause, and for no other crime on our part than that of being of Mexican origin, considering us, doubtless, destitute of those gifts which they themselves do not possess."

Juan Nepomuceno Cortina issued a second proclamation on a broadside on November 23, 1859, in which he eloquently expressed the complaints of Texas Mexicans against discrimination, oppression and expropriation of lands and rights:

"Mexicans! When the state of Texas began to receive the new organization which its sovereignty required as an integral part of the Union, flocks of vampires, in the guise of men, came and scattered themselves in the settlements, without any capital except the corrupt heart and the most perverse intentions. Some, brimful of laws, pledged to us their protection against the attacks of the rest;. . . while others, to the abusing of our unlimited confidence, when we entrusted them with our titles, which secured the future of our families, refused to return them under false and frivolous pretexts.... Many of you have been robbed of your property, incarcerated, chased, murdered, and hunted like wild beasts, because your labor was fruitful, and because your industry excited the vile avarice which led them. . . .

"¡Mexicans! My part is taken; the voice of rev-

8. Juan Nepomuceno Cortina.

elation whispers to me that to me is entrusted the work of breaking the chains of your slavery."

with Mexico, experienced the greatest clashes with the legal system. From the time of Texas's independence in 1836, the region between the Nueces and the Rio Grande Rivers was plagued by warfare. During Texas's Lone Star Republic era, "cowboys" crossed the Nueces River, forcibly "rounding up thousands of head of livestock" as retribution for property destroyed by the Mexican army during the Texas Rebellion. Mexican *vaqueros* retaliated across the Nueces by driving back "equally large herds."[6]

Significantly, Mexican banditry angered Anglos more than anything else. Brigands easily crossed the Rio Grande to Mexico if conditions became "too hot" because of retaliatory Anglo rampages. The most famous and cited example of this activity is that of Juan Nepomuceno Cortina, a landowner in the Brownsville area. He precipitated years of warfare and brigandage between Mexicans and Anglos in 1859 when he killed a Brownsville deputy sheriff for mistreating a Mexican vagrant. It became a tradition for Texas Rangers zealously to suppress local bandits and Mexicans who struck from across the Rio Grande. In the process they harassed local Mexican Americans, maliciously breaking up *fandangos* and raiding homes of citizens not involved in bandit activity. Anglos had long memories and continued to harbor ill will because of atrocities committed against their people during the Texas Rebellion. The attitude of "Big Foot" Wallace is a good example. He came to Texas and joined the Rangers to kill "greasers" and avenge the execution of his brother and cousin at the 1836 Goliad Massacre.

[6] Robert J. Rosenbaum, *Mexicano Resistance in the Southwest: "The Sacred Right of Self-Preservation"* (Austin: University of Texas Press, 1981), p. 40.

9. Texas Rangers pose with a Mexican prisoner in 1894.

Sometimes Mexican Americans presented a threat for quite improbable reasons. In April 1898, as U.S. forces engaged Spain in Cuba and the Philippines, rumors circulated that Spaniards living in Mexico organized and paid Mexican marauders to conduct raids across the border, maneuvers Anglos suspected the Mexican government supported. Even Texas Mexicans were suspected of aiding and linking with brigrands.

Indeed, violence against Anglos was very real. In 1886 Mexicans raided a local saloon in Alpine, Texas, killing numerous Anglos. When news of the massacre spread, Anglos armed themselves and in retribution went on a murderous rampage. Typically, border-residing Anglos in towns such as Rio Grande City and Brownsville feared border Mexicans more than those further

inland in Texas. Along the border Mexicans, who vastly outnumbered whites, were considered "arrogant and aggressive." Moreover, Anglos knew that in any altercation Mexicans south of the Rio Grande could join their brothers on the American side.[7]

In Texas, Anglos commonly lynched Mexicans. The number of lynchings increased during and immediately after the Civil War, primarily in South and West Texas, but the phenomenon did not abate until the end of the century. It was not just minorities who suffered the illegal reprisals, but as historian Arnoldo De León puts it, "Lynchings of Blacks and Mexicans were accompanied by ritualistic tortures and sadism not displayed in other lynchings—such treatment being justified by reference to the supposed sexual threat posed by

[7] De León, *They Called Them Greasers*, p. 68.

10. Texas Rangers bring in fugitives dead: "Mexican bandits."

Cowboy Andrew García (1853-1943) wrote in his memoirs of life on the frontier about the type of justice that was meted out and how frontier elections were conducted: "They always see to it that their own kind of people are elected to enforce the law, and when they are not, they always seem to be able to elect them who will play on both sides of the fence. Where they had all the say in the election, you can imagine what chance for an honest deal the people got, it is no wonder that the justice you sometimes got was crooked and rotten as hell."[9]

the Blacks and the cruelty and depravity of Mexicans. In one case a Mexican who killed a white boy in Eagle Pass was tortured and mutilated before he was thrown, still alive, into a fire.[8]

In California, where law officers were rare, vigilantes dispensed justice probably more than anywhere else in the West. Between 1850 and 1895, mobs hanged 184 white persons, 131 Mexicans, 24 Chinese, 23 Indians and 1 Black. This was a grossly disproportionate number of Mexicans executed illegally. Mexicans were never more than fifteen percent of the California population in the nineteenth century. California also merits the dubious distinction of having the first lynching of a Mexican woman in the U.S. In 1851 Anglo miners lynched "Juanita" in Downieville after she stabbed an Anglo-American to death. This infamous story has many versions, but all conclude that she was definitely lynched.

In Arizona early Anglo-Mexican encounters provoked this brand of justice as well. Few Mexicans in nineteenth-century Arizona, for instance, served on juries, but they were disproportionately sentenced to jail and given longer sentences. A particularly vicious lynching occurred in 1859 when Santa Cruz Valley rancher John Ware was murdered and the constabulary arrested one of his "peons." Local cowboy

[8] Ibid., pp. 90-91.

[9] From *Tough Trip through Paradise* (Boston: Houghton Mifflin, 1967).

Sam Rogers and his friends, all known for cruel treatment of Mexicans and who had brutally killed at least one, kidnapped the manacled Mexican and hanged him from a tree.

Legal mistreatment affected Mexicans more in central Arizona, where they settled at the same time as Anglos in the 1860s after the U.S. had acquired the Southwest. The population of the Salt River Valley (the Phoenix area) increased five-fold during the 1870s, and many Anglo newcomers did not share the more benign view of Mexicans held by white settlers in the previous decade. A depression stalling the Arizona economy coincided with this influx, making for acute competition. The slightest hint of Mexican wrongdoing was met with severe reproach. One newspaper writer in 1872 declared, "The Indian is now a nuisance and the Sonoran a decided annoyance, but both of these are sure to disappear before civilization as sure as the noonday sun."[10]

Vigilante committees sprang up to deal with Mexican banditry, and a number of Mexicans were lynched. At a mass meeting in Phoenix on April 19, 1872, citizens organized for protection against "Sonorians" and elected county sheriff T. C. Warden as captain of the Safety Committee. All suspicious Mexicans deemed not to have legitimate business in the Valley were to be run out of town. Land and trade competition precipitated other struggles which account for the disproportionate lynchings of minorities in both Arizona and California during the 1870s depression.

While the Treaty of Guadalupe Hidalgo did not precisely define the rights of Mexicans, it did guarantee them the same rights as U.S. citizens. It is clear this guarantee was not upheld. As a result, the economic and political fortunes of Southwest Mexicans declined considerably during their experience with Anglo domination. But by the 1890s, considerable immigration from Mexico resulted in the swelling of Mexican communities throughout the Southwest, inexorably changing the character of Mexican life in the U.S.

CASUAL PRE-INDUSTRIAL IMMIGRATION

To base an identity on being "conquered," even for some immigrants, is historically well grounded without resorting to the Chicano Movement rationale. In the mid-nineteenth century, U.S. territorial aggrandizement separated many Hispanics who remained in the conquered territories from their political and cultural roots by an invisible and, for a time, unpatrolled boundary line. But some were actually born just south of what became a border in small villages and towns close to the new demarcation line. In migrating across the border, they were moving north within what they considered their home areas, in some cases traveling only a few miles. For example, property interests and family kinship attracted settlers from northern Sonora to what became southern Arizona after the Gadsden Purchase. Similarly, northeastern Mexicans who crossed the Rio Grande into South Texas found affinity with the people and the geography. Even migrants originating in Sonora and Chihuahua found cultural and family links in northern New Mexico or California during this era.

In essence, Mexicans living along the U.S.-Mexico border had been accustomed to traveling back and forth prior to the Mexican War. After the war, they continued this pattern of travel and re-settlement with little regard to the treaty signed by the U.S. and Mexico. Nonetheless, this early influx, while considerably more casual than later immigration, was still induced by increased economic opportunity such as the discovery of gold in California. After 1836 thousands of peons fled the large haciendas of northeast Mexico, seeking their freedom in South Texas; the border was much closer now.

Still, economic inducements in the U.S. for Mexican immigrants before the 1870s were minimal. Anglos who arrived in the Southwest during this early period invested in an economy that supplied the growing population with pre-industrial foodstuffs and artisan goods which depended in no small degree on Mexicans for their cultivation

---

[10] *Weekly Arizona*, November 30, 1872.

11. Mexican workers hauling hay in the San Gabriel Valley, California, 1890s.

and manufacture. An expanding market also appeared, especially in Arizona and New Mexico, as U.S. military efforts to subdue and destroy the nomadic Indian tribes intensified. Private merchant houses in Santa Fe, Albuquerque and Tucson, sometimes owned and operated by Mexicans or in which they definitely participated as employees, flourished as U.S. Army forts and Indian reservations needed provisions.

Mexicans continued traveling in and out of the Southwest after 1848 because the economies of both countries increasingly intertwined. Before railroads, goods were transported through the isthmus of Central America bound for California and the New Mexico and Arizona Territories; they were unloaded in Guaymas, Sonora, and then taken north. Tampico, on the Gulf of Mexico, served southern planters as a conduit to ship out cotton to British mills during the American Civil War when southern ports were blocked off by the Union. Thus, in the early years of immigration, the first immigrants shared a strong "lost homeland" sense of identity with longer-termed residents as the U.S. institutions increased

their hegemony.

Furthermore, these Southwest Mexicans never acquired a strong link to Mexico. Their community identification did not "grow up," as it were, with the evolution of modern "Mexicaness" during the reign of Porfirio Díaz (1876-1911) and the years of the Mexican Revolution of 1910. Mexicans in some of these regions, in New Mexico primarily, maintained a strong link with their past and a heritage that they traced to the Southwest and to colonial New Spain. This was less true in California and Texas, where massive immigration from Mexico at the turn of the century blurred this background.

Mainstream society promoted a separate identification of Mexicans, even as they were being incorporated into the Union. In 1847 as U.S. troops were registering victory after victory in the Mexican War, the *Illinois State Register* opposed annexation because the U.S. would have to absorb a mixed race "little removed from the Negro." Senator John C. Calhoun from North Carolina felt that racially impure Mexicans were "not [even] as good as the Cherokees or

Choctaws."[11] A continuation of such rejection served to keep Mexicans marginalized and from assimilating even when they wanted to. Members of the elite, many who were white or appeared to be without Indian or African physical features, hawked a racial identity which separated themselves from the markedly *mestizo* Mexican lower classes. Carey McWilliams called this the "Fantasy Heritage." This myth asserts that old Southwest families are of pure Spanish descent unlike the mixed-blood immigrants who came later from Mexico. The "Fantasy Heritage" was also perpetuated by influential Anglos.

POLITICAL AND ECONOMIC INTEGRATION

As stated earlier, Mexicans in Texas were supposedly fully protected under the 1836 Texas constitution and then under the U.S. Constitution after 1845. When Texas joined the Union in 1845, only one Texas Mexican was elected as a delegate to the convention which created the new state constitution. An attempt by convention delegates to disenfranchise Mexicans of the vote, however, was not successful. Nonetheless, Texas Mexicans were kept from voting through intimidation, with the result that few politicians were Mexicans. Between 1836 and 1845, the era of the Texas Republic, only a few rich San Antonio Mexicans were empowered politically. Juan Seguín was elected the first mayor of San Antonio but was forced out after the Anglo population increased. A bitter Seguín went to Mexico and fought the invading Americans during the Mexican War.

After Texas was annexed into the U.S., even fewer Mexicans participated in politics. Of sixty-four members in the state legislature during 1850, none was Texas- or Mexican-born. Often when Mexicans did vote, their choices were limited because local political bosses exerted influence over whom they voted for. In addition, white-only primaries and grandfather clauses

barred Mexicans from participating and, since the Democratic Party dominated in Texas, the elections were really decided in the primaries. Poll taxes, the custom of charging for voting, also deterred poor citizens from voting, a barrier that included most Mexicans.

But Southwest Mexicans also managed to obtain key positions in local governments, which especially benefited their people in court cases. In New Mexico many of the Hispanic elite who made the transition into the new economic and political structure after 1848 were in the best position to help their *paisanos*. But this was also true in South Texas. Historian Arnoldo De León points out that in South Texas "Mexican American leaders had consistent success in getting themselves elected or appointed to a variety of county and city offices in the last half of the Nineteenth century."[12]

Except during the early years of the U.S. takeover, before the *californio* population was diluted by the large numbers of outsider gold seekers, Mexicans participated little in the California political system. Even then, their integration was minimal. Only eight Mexican-Californians out of the forty-eight delegates participated in the 1849 state constitutional convention. This was the last major political event where Mexicans had any influence because, as in Texas, they soon were outnumbered. Because of the Gold Rush, an even greater imbalance existed in the ratio of Mexicans to Anglos than existed in Texas.

In 1850 fifteen percent of the population was Mexican; twenty years later, that figure dropped to only four percent. Mexicans saw their political and economic influence decline first in the north, where the gold mining areas attracted the majority of Anglos. As *californio* political influence declined, legislation contrary to their interests was enacted. In 1851, for example, property taxes in the six southern counties where most Mexicans resided were five times the rate of

[11] Gutiérrez, *Walls and Mirrors*, p. 16.

[12] De León, *Not Room Enough: Mexicans, Anglos and Socioeconomic Change in Texas, 1850-1900* (Albuquerque: University of New Mexico Press, 1993), p. 44.

northern entities where the majority of Anglos lived. The so-called "greaser laws," clearly aimed at suppressing *californio* customs, were enacted in 1855 to prohibit bull fights, bear fights and cock fights. Vagrancy codes in local governments were also mainly directed at Mexicans and were applied selectively when a community wanted to force Mexicans out. The 1850 Foreign Miners Tax, which levied a charge to stake out claims to anyone who was not a U.S. citizen, was one of the most onerous laws affecting Hispanics. French, Australian and Irish immigrants were drawn by the lure of gold, but Mexicans or South Americans, who possessed superior mining skills, comprised the bulk of the "foreigners." This tax was undoubtedly designed to eliminate the Hispanic competition in the gold diggings.

Economic and political participation was more extensive in New Mexico for Mexicans than in any other region because there Hispanic New Mexicans maintained their numerical majority until the turn of the century. The southeastern part of the state was quickly dominated by Anglos, but Hispanics politically controlled the north: the Santa Fe and Albuquerque areas. Essentially, Hispanics dominated most key political slots statewide and controlled the territorial legislature until the 1890s. In fact, the U.S. Congress delayed New Mexico's statehood because many members objected to a new state dominated by Mexicans.

Mexicans conserved political and economic power in Arizona, which was part of the New Mexican territory until 1863 and in the area purchased with the Gadsden Treaty in 1853. This was especially true in the southern part of the state around Tucson. That town was the territo-

The case of Henry Garfias provides a good example of how Mexican officials helped their people. Garfias was the highest elected Mexican American official in any town in the Salt River Valley during the nineteenth century. He had come to Phoenix from California in 1875 and established a freighting business; then in 1881 he was elected town marshal of Phoenix. After serving his full term as marshal, he went on to a number of other city offices: constable, town assessor, tax collector and street superintendent. In these positions he was able to provide patronage and protection for his constituents. He also published *El Progreso*, a Spanish-language newspaper, which helped him garner the Mexican vote.

The anonymous ballad, "El corrido de los americanos" (Ballad about the Americanos), protested in the late nineteenth century the coming of the *gringos* and the threat they represented to land and culture:

Voy a hablar del extranjero y lo que digo es verdad, quieren tenernos de esclavos, pero eso no les valdrá.	I'm going to talk about the foreigner and what I say is true, they want to have us as slaves, but it won't do them any good.
Señores, pongan cuidado a la raza americana, vienen a poseer las tierras, las que les vendió Santa Anna	People, be careful of the American race, they're coming to take the lands that Santa Anna sold them.
Vienen dándole al cristiano y haciéndole al mundo guerra, vienen a echarnos del país y a hacerse de nuestra tierra.	They come preaching Christianity and making war on the world, they're coming to throw us out and take over our land.

rial capital after Arizona separated from New Mexico. Anglos and Mexicans cooperated more in this area because economic activity depended greatly on trade through the state of Sonora.

In 1876 in Maricopa County, where Phoenix is located, more than twenty percent of the registered voters were Mexican, and the importance of their role was evident even earlier. In the controversial election of 1871, held to decide where to locate the county seat, all sides vied for the votes of Mexicans who, according to some historians, were mere pawns in the hands of political bosses. According to one story, Jack Swilling, who was married to a Mexican, wanted the seat located next to his properties, but he heard that his opponents had bribed and intimidated Mexicans and used Papago Indians to pose as Mexicans, so he immediately established a similar network.

Mexican voters, however, had more to gain in these early elections than a bribe or the insurance that they would not be bullied by Anglos. Considering the heavy investment that Mexican farmers, merchants and workers had in the canal systems, local government and justice issues, they voted to protect and promote their interests as property owners and citizens.

In the 1880s, however, the building of railroads drastically reduced the need for Southwest pre-industrial crafts and beast-powered merchant transportation, activities in which Mexicans participated on a large scale. A different type of Anglo immigrant arrived who started seeing Mexicans as irrelevant for anything but brute labor. The relationship between both groups became more strained as a new influx of Anglos who did not need to cooperate with Mexicans overwhelmed the older Anglo population. This demographic shift reduced the little political power that Mexicans were able to amass. Prescott in northern Arizona became the new territorial seat, away from Mexicans, and as Phoenix became more important, the city became the capital. Southern Arizona Mexicans retained some political power. Practically all the few Arizona Hispanic legislators, until the 1950s, came from that part of the state.

The desire to be a force at the ballot box was evident even in the early immigrant era but mainly in communities where Mexicans had long-standing residence such as in San Antonio and Tucson.

HABLAR EN CRISTIANO: MAINTAINING SPANISH IN THE SOUTHWEST

The most crucial measure for resisting cultural domination for Southwest Mexicans was the maintenance of Spanish. In the Chicano Movement it was central. A great many of the activists did not speak the language, a situation they explained as "cultural annihilation" by the Anglo establishment. "Corky" Gonzales, the founder of Denver's Crusade for Justice and who had attended four grade schools, three junior high schools and two high schools, once remarked that what the educational system accomplished was "how to forget Spanish, to forget my

The following poem, "Sinfonía de Combate" (Combat Symphony) by Santiago de la Hoz, is high-sounding and neo-classic and inspires combat in the abstract, but probably was an exhortation to Mexicans to resist their oppressive situation in the United States. The poem was published in Los Angeles in *El cuaderno libertario* (Libertarian Notebook) in 1904.

"¡Pueblo despierta ya!
Tus hijos crecen
Y una herencia de oprobio no merecen,
Vuelve ya en ti de esa locura insana:
Si siguen criando siervos tantas madres,
Tus hijos, los esclavos de mañana,
Renegarán del nombre de sus padres!"

(People, wake up at once! Your children grow older
And do not deserve a heritage of oppression,
Come out of that unhealthy insanity:
If so many mothers raise servile children,
Your children, the slaves of tomorrow,
Will deny their parents' names!)

An editorial in the Las Cruces newspaper, *El Labrador* (December 30, 1904), expressed the need to protect the Spanish language in New Mexico under Anglo-American rule: "It has become fashionable here in New Mexico to treat with a kind of reproach and contempt not only those who speak Spanish, but the language itself. It is as if they were guilty of some crime in speaking the language which came down from their forefathers, and as if it is not one of the most respected and best perfected of modern languages that is spoken in Europe and America. They try to demand that all the native people of New Mexico know the national language, which is English, though knowing this has been impossible because we have not had the means or the facilities to learn it. Even knowing this, there has been no lack of those who want Spanish to be a prohibited language, and those who speak it to be despoiled of their franchises and rights of citizenship."

heritage, to forget who I was."[13]

Many activists who had used English first names for most of their young lives changed them to Spanish. Making the frustration even greater was the systematic subordination of the language by the educational establishment, which at times came perilously close to suppressing it.

The very force of occupation brought the first notions of Mexican American nationalism and resistance in the nineteenth century—predating the Chicano Movement by about one hundred years. Francisco P. Ramírez, through his Los Angeles Spanish-language weekly, *El Clamor Público,* proposed the term "la raza" to denote Mexican Californians. Other self-identifiers were *la población, la población California* and *nuestra raza española.* Richard Griswold del Castillo,

12. Francisco Ramírez, editor of *El Clamor Público.*

however, noted that, in the Mexican culture in California, "the increasing use of 'La Raza' as a generic term in the Spanish-language press was evidence of a new kind of ethnic consciousness."[14]

The hallmark of resistance still was the maintenance of Spanish. That Mexicans kept their language in the U.S. territory longer than most other ethnic groups is partially due to continuous Mexican immigration but also to the resistance to Anglo domination offered in previous generations. Explorers from Spain and central New Spain (today's Mexico) introduced Castillian into the northern reaches of Spanish territories, today's Southwest, before the first English colonies were founded in North America. Until the Anglo takeover in the mid-nineteenth century, educated officials and clergy from Spain and Mexico brought to the frontier the whole written tradition. Among civilians, members of the upper classes educated their children and themselves in the written word. The lower classes maintained Spanish mainly at the oral, folk level. Virtually all the established Spanish and Mexican institutions in what became the Southwest effected and documented their work in written, formal Spanish. After the Anglo conquest, Southwest Mexicans continued to speak their language, regardless of political and cultural

---

[13] Quoted in Christine Marín, *A Spokesman of the Mexican American Movement: Rodolfo "Corky" Gonzales and the Fight for Chicano Liberation, 1966-1972* (San Francisco: R and E Research Associates, 1977), p. 12.

[14] Quoted in David G. Gutiérrez, *Walls and Mirrors,* p. 36.

domination. And they published hundreds of Spanish-language newspapers not only to print news and advertising but to support their ideas about language and culture.

The Mexican leadership conserved Spanish for other reasons. For example, during the 1880s, Tejano politicians delivered speeches in both English and Spanish because they ran at the local level, and "it was there that ordinary people came in close contact with politics and therefore the occasion called for politicians who spoke and understood Tejano ways."[15]

Spanish was also preserved in Texas because Jim Crow laws compelled many Texas Mexican entrepreneurs to conduct business only among their own people and, even though they were somewhat upwardly mobile within Anglo society, these businessmen maintained a closeness to their culture and Spanish because, in addition to their ethnic pride, their clientele demanded it

13. Jean Baptiste Lamy.

Churches and church schools were also crucial vehicles in preserving Spanish. In the nineteenth century, when Bishop Jean Baptiste Lamy took control of the Catholic Church in New Mexico, he attempted to wrest control away from local Hispanic leaders; nonetheless, he had to allow the use of Spanish in Catholic schools. Also in nineteenth-century New Mexico, schools newly established by Baptist churches taught Spanish along with English so that future ministers could be effective in proselytizing New Mexicans. In California, mission churches ministered in Spanish, offering a continuity lasting from the colonial period until the end of the nineteenth century.

But as Anglo domination increased, Spanish was pushed out of areas dominated by Anglos; at times it was vilified and almost always subordinated by them. Immediately after the war with Mexico, for example, most official and economic activity was conducted in English. In the political arena, Mexican Americans promoted bilingualism in the legislatures of New Mexico and California, yet proceedings almost always took place in English. As Spanish-speaking politicians improved their English or lost their power, Spanish was eradicated. In Texas, before the 1845 annexation to the U.S., the joint legislature of the Republic adopted a resolution which would eliminate the printing of laws in Spanish.

In South Texas, for example, Tejanos (native Texans of Mexican origin) still owned numerous but small farmsteads and ranches, and there, as historian Arnoldo De León points out, "Lo mexicano' prevailed over 'lo americano,' manifested in the population predominance of Mexicans, in the use of the Spanish language and Mexican work patterns, in the persistence of Mexican social traditions."[16]

[15] Arnoldo De León, *The Tejano Community, 1836-1900* (Albuquerque: University of New Mexico Press, 1982), p. 48.

[16] Ibid., pp. 31, 48; quote from p. 78.

According to noted folklorist Arthur Campa, repression of Spanish was a shock for a region that for several centuries had lived under the Spanish-Mexican system and to whom communication in Spanish meant *hablar en Cristiano (speak in the Christian tongue)*. It was a cultural shock from which many never recovered, and echoes of that shock persist to the present day.[17]

John R. Chávez, in *The Lost Land*, accuses Southwest Mexicans of depriving immigrants of the Southwest heritage because of a desire to distinguish themselves from new arrivals. Their "Fantasy Heritage" held that Mexican southwesterners had a more direct tie to Spain than Mexican immigrants. In this assessment, the myth is inexorably linked to Anglo subordination. By promoting the image to distinguish themselves from "Indian peon" immigrants in the twentieth century, they became more acceptable to Anglos. Chávez also asserts that, because the "Fantasy Heritage" was inclusive to "Spanish" southwesterners, it denied immigrant Mexicans an identification with the

The relationship between native Southwest Mexicans and Anglo institutions and customs evolved within a milieu of conflict where two ethnic groups competed for trade, mining, land and livestock. Punishing or sanctioning Mexicans who deviated from Anglo law and mores was a corresponding process that became a legacy for the immigrants who came later. But native southwestern Hispanics had more time to adapt in the fifty years in which they made the transition from being the dominant group in the Southwest regions they controlled to becoming subordinated by Anglos. Moreover, because the process occurred in their homeland, they resisted or accommodated from an anchored position. Eventually, Anglos accepted, even if grudgingly, that Mexicans living in the newly acquired territories had a right to live in the U.S. In addition, an upper class came with Southwest Mexicans, which Anglos found acceptable for socializing and even for marriage. A good example is the case of Representative J. T. Canales, a prominent South Texas Mexican who identified ethnically with Tejanos. In 1910 he married Annie Wheeler, a white Houston socialite. Immigration, however, changed this understanding between both groups.

MODERNIZATION AND IMMIGRATION

Large-scale immigration at the end of the nineteenth century weakened the link to the Southwest heritage claimed by Chicanos. As railroads induced Mexicans to migrate from regions further from the border, the strong ties that *norteño* (from the Mexican north) immigrants had forged with the Southwest and its native peoples diminished. The arrival of railroad transportation to the Southwest and northern Mexico in the 1880s dramatically changed the economies of both areas, greatly stimulating Mexican immigration. By 1900 127,000 Mexican-born persons augmented a population of perhaps 200,000 Mexicans native to the Southwest. The bulk of their entry took place in the 1890s. The impetus for massive immigration was a radical transformation of both the Southwest and Mexican economies. By 1900 Texas, New Mexico, Arizona and California were integrated with northern Mexico and parts of central Mexico.

During the Porfiriato in Mexico (the four decades of rule by Porfirio Díaz), foreign interests, mainly American, financed the construction of railways in both areas, linking crucial markets of the industrial basin in the Midwest and the Northeast to raw materials produced in northern Mexico and the Southwest. The result was a transformation along adjacent areas on both sides of the border which generated commercial agriculture and mining activity that depended completely on the same railroad work. With railroads, more Anglos and Europeans arrived as laborers, farmers, clerks, small merchants, wealthy entrepreneurs and land developers. As these entrepreneurs and Eastern capital generated a

---

[17] Arthur Campa, *Hispanic Culture in the Southwest* (Norman: University of Oklahoma Press, 1979), p. 183.

14. Mexican workers building the Pacific Electric Railroad, which by 1900 was the largest suburban transportation system.

huge Southwest agribusiness and mining development, it became evident that the resident Mexican population was not sufficient to meet growing labor needs. In Texas poor whites and Blacks competed with Mexicans, but the low wages offered in agriculture discouraged many from remaining in the same labor force. Eventually, Mexicans became the main labor source.

California, endowed with vast fertile valleys, temperate weather and plenty of runoff water from the great Sierra Nevada range, developed intensive commercial agriculture year-round. The building of the transcontinental railroads in the 1860s and 1870s allowed for marketing regional products. The main labor source was at first Chinese, but restrictive immigration laws curtailed their entry. Farmers had used other Asians extensively—Japanese and East Indians—but their entry was also restricted. Western employers also resorted to European laborers, but Eastern industry absorbed Europeans and only a small number filtered to the Southwest. Along the border states, a dependence on Mexican labor was the first and only option.

After the 1880s the building of an American-financed railroad network spurred industrial mining and commercial agriculture, also dependent on Mexican workers. Northern Mexico sources no longer sufficed, but as railway construction in Mexico dipped further south, the denser, more populated, landlocked areas of central Mexico were

Southwest. As Chávez puts it, the myth was "an attitude that made the new arrivals feel alien in the Southwest, despite the familiar geography and Mexican culture of the region."[18]

Critics of nineteenth-century Southwest Hispanics have overstated adherence to the fantasy heritage, confusing class prejudice with the desire to ingratiate themselves with Anglos. Many of the elites who allegedly kowtowed to Anglo whims were responsible for resisting Anglo cultural domination and continuing Mexican cultural, if not Mexico's political, heritage in the Southwest. A case in point is General Mariano Vallejo, who built up tremendous properties during the Mexican period only to lose them after the Anglo conquest. According to literary analyist Genaro Padilla, much of what Vallejo had to say about his life demonstrates great contradictions that mirror the turmoil which characterized his life. Vallejo on the one hand welcomed the Anglos but also lamented the cultural decline caused after the United States takeover. For example, he became highly resentful that French- and German-language instruction was offered in the

[18] John R. Chávez, *The Lost Land: The Chicano Image of the Southwest* (Albuquerque: University of New Mexico Press, 1984), p. 86.

schools of San Francisco while Spanish was disdained. This he saw as part of the decline. Writing became a way of surviving, and in Vallejo's case it assured that Anglo historians, such as Hubert Bancroft, would not tell the history of California without the consultation of *californios*. Felipe Fierro, a contemporary of Vallejo and editor of *La Voz del Nuevo Mundo*, felt that it was incumbent on *californios* to tell their story over generations; otherwise they would disappear. In essence, Padilla's explicit interpetation is that *californios* resisted through their writing.

now tapped for workers. Thousands of men and women, known as *los del interior* (from the interior) —mostly from Jalisco, Guanajuato, Michoacán, Aguascalientes, San Luis Potosí and Zacatecas, i.e., Mexican regions experiencing a labor surplus—migrated as seasonal laborers to work in nearby railway construction and maintenance. After that, they made their way to the Mexican north, where many crossed the border to the U.S., where wages were much higher.

Although *los del interior* identified somewhat with the Southwest, which at the turn of the century still maintained Hispanic traits, they were still immigrants in every sense of the word. Subject to a new political jurisdiction and immigrant regulations, most did not understand or speak English and were confronted with racism and discrimination. Native Mexican Americans faced a similar rejection, but because of their longer exposure to the "gringo," they acquired survival abilities and participated more within the U.S. system.

The kind of jobs Mexicans obtained varied; some were more difficult and less remunerative. While most immigrants were poor, some brought enough capital to start businesses to tide them over until they obtained jobs. Still others, who came from homes just across the border, could more easily bring their families than those whose origins were deep in Mexico. Nonetheless, before the 1910 revolution, practically all immigrants came from the lower classes; thus poverty was an endemic problem. For these immigrants, labor was the only commodity they could trade.

While west central Mexicans lived and worked alongside *norteños*, they were more mobile because they had not brought their families; once across the border, sometimes a thousand miles separated west central Mexicans from home. They responded more readily than Mexican Americans, as railroads recruited section gangs further north. This pattern resulted as early as 1910 in becoming the foundation for midwestern *colonias* (colonies) in such cities as Chicago and Kansas City. In contrast, northern Mexicans and Mexican Americans with Southwest kinship ties preferred to work closer to their home areas in Mexico and/or the Southwest, sometimes in commercial agricultural and mining sectors similar to those in northern Mexico. Immigrants from the Northeast followed wagon trails to West Texas and the Oklahoma cotton fields before 1910, then returned home to South Texas or south of the Rio Grande. This pattern continued into the automobile age except that, instead of returning to Mexico, many migrants made South Texas a permanent home.

Thus, when the U.S. required more labor during and after World War I, extensive migrant networks linked northern and central Mexican regions to the voracious labor markets wherever they emerged. To keep labor cheap, employers did all they could to encourage the flow. The Mexican Revolution, accelerated modernization in the U.S. during World War I and the "roaring twenties" combined to create the most intensive flow of Mexicans across the border. While Anglo-Americans reluctantly learned to live with native southwestern Mexicans and nineteenth-century immigrants, they were not prepared for the onslaught which occurred in the twentieth century.

The break that immigration brought to the mainspring ideal of the Chicano Movement, a claim to the Southwest heritage, presented *movimiento* ideologies with a challenge that was not simply ignored. Chicano activists, whose ancestors in the main had immigrated after the Southwest was acquired by the U.S., chose not to separate themselves from those who were actually conquered. They argued that Mexicans who came to the U.S. in large numbers were merely reclaiming Aztlán, the mythical homeland of the Aztecs, said to have been situated geographically in the area of the five southwestern states obtained by conquest from Mexico. Other activists, perhaps finding the Aztlán concept too fanciful, also claimed the heritage by posing more material-based arguments. U.S. economic domination, they said, kept Mexico impoverished, forcing this migration into what was once Mexican land. Both of these *movimiento* interpretations, simplified so that they could serve as usable political history, do have a basis in fact.

CHAPTER TWO

Legacy of the Mexican Revolution

15. Revolutionary generals Francisco Villa and Emiliano Zapata meet at Mexico City.

The Mexican Revolution remains a vivid memory and legacy for all Mexicans whether they remained at home or immigrated to the United States. Out of the struggles emerged a number of figures who were elevated into enduring symbols of the underdog for generations to come: Emiliano Zapata, Pancho Villa, La Adelita, and others. For Chicano Movement activists, the struggle not only confirmed the idea that Mexicans came from a revolutionary tradition, but the pantheon of heroes who took up arms inspired and justified modern-day Chicano militancy. The axiom apocryphally attributed to Emiliano Zapata, "It is better to die on your feet than to live on your knees," became one of the recurrent themes of the movement. At the same time, the Revolution heightened Mexican nationalism, basing it to a great degree on anti-Americanism. This process found its way to the United States and endured more than half a century to serve as a pillar of the Chicano Movement.

For more general Mexican American history, the Revolution was important because it made refugees out of Mexicans from all walks of life, creating early in the century a rich and heterogeneous immigrant society in the United States. Other byproducts of the struggle were border violence, smuggling and vice. These disturbed Anglo Americans to such a degree that a backlash, which historian Ricardo Romo dubbed the "Brown Scare," exacerbated an already existing antipathy towards Mexicans. Just as the persistence of apartheid after the abolition of slavery fueled civil rights for Blacks, for Mexican Americans the antipathy generated during this era provides an important part of the foundation for a civil rights movement.

From the time Francisco I. Madero's El Plan de San Luis Potosí (The San Luis Potosí Plan) called for an uprising for November 20, 1910, Mexicans endured twenty years of interminable bloodshed. Every political stage of the struggle unleashed new waves of violence. Regimes fell in and out of power, creating exiles of individuals who had held power or who found themselves on the losing side. Those who had no stake in the struggles did their best not to join; sometimes fleeing as refugees was the only solution. The majority of those who fled just wanted to escape the constant violence, pillage and rape which belligerents on both sides inflicted on the Mexican people.

Before the Revolution, emigration was a full-blown process, but a delicate set of conditions—usually economic—dictated when migrants left. Now, large numbers of middle- and upper-class Mexicans who lived comfortably before the conflagration joined the emigrant streams. For others who would eventually have emigrated anyway, the decision to leave was forced on them much earlier. Practically everyone departed under such duress that few refugees made the preparations that even the poorest of migrants make under more peaceful conditions. As a consequence, thousands of destitute émigrés with few or no resources for survival crossed the border, not knowing what awaited them on the other side. Few other immigrants to the United States had weathered such traumatic experiences as they exited their home country. It compares to the ordeal of

16. Francisco Madero.

refugees fleeing potato famine-ravaged Ireland in the 1840s or Eastern European Jews escaping state-inspired pogroms at the turn of the century. This made the social and economic adaptation of Mexican immigrants in the United States extremely challenging.

The Mexican Revolution had distinct regional origins: primarily in the northern states and the areas in the Valley of Mexico. Eventually, none of Mexico was left untouched by the struggle and as it spread, every citizen and foreigner in the republic was affected. The displacement of people from their homes followed the revolutionary tide southward. Most refugees were from the lower and middle classes, but families like the Creels and the Terrazas of Chihuahua and other wealthy *norteños* left their homes, accompanied by liquid assets deposited in American banks along the border. They were able to live comfortably in the United States.

The incessant battling that plagued Mexico between 1911 and 1914 took place north of Zacatecas and Guadalajara. For the most part, it was the inhabitants of these regions who suffered the most because of the struggle. In Alvaro Obregón's drive to defeat Victoriano Huerta's army in the west, he captured Guadalajara and then proceeded through the populous Bajío in order to reach Mexico City. Up to now, the revolutionary activity was mainly evident in this important agricultural center through numerous but isolated manifestations of rural and agrarian unrest. Rebel bands, including some followers of Zapata, had raided haciendas and small villages since 1913. The worst was still to come.

In July of 1913 during the initial phases of the Constitutionalist movement, rebels in Durango reportedly ravished some fifty young girls from the upper classes, causing them to commit suicide rather than continue living in such a "dishonored" condition. As knowledge of this kind of activity spread, fathers in the areas of the struggle sent their daughters, wives and young sons to the United States. In general, Mexicans from the more privileged classes left because they were threatened by *los de abajo* (the underdogs), who were emboldened as they enlisted in the ranks of revolutionaries. Many times they took out their resentment on the middle and upper classes, who then fled as emigrants in the wake of lower-class rebellion.

The ability of the economy to maintain and feed the people of Mexico, although barely at a subsistence level, had improved by the early 1920s and people were at least surviving. Conditions were not as severe as in 1915, 1916 and 1917, but in 1923 the Adolfo de la Huerta rebellion changed all of that. The conflict was precipitated by the former interim president because Alvaro Obregón did not select him as his successor. During that period, central and southern Mexico was devastated by another bloody upheaval.

In the Bajío region, Ocotlán, Jalisco, La Piedad, Michoacán and other towns were focal points of the many attacks which Obregón's armies initiated in order to dislodge de la Huerta's forces. Finally, in 1924, de la Huerta was defeated. This rebellion was quashed, but the all-too-familiar side effects lingered. Bajío agricultural production, which during the 1911-1915 struggle was able to produce on a relatively normal scale, in the course of this latest revolution was much more seriously curtailed. Spring planting was interrupted by the impressment of thousands of young men into military service, by the large movements of

José Cruz Cervantes, a native of a rural rancho in San Luis Potosí who was interviewed in Houston, Texas, recalled his boyhood experiences during the Revolution: "For the *pacífico* (nonparticipant) those were trying times. My father was a teacher on an hacienda and a part-time rancher. During the war, all the cattle disappeared and there was nothing to eat except maguey heart and *nopales*. They are nutritious; you could fry them and eat them with salt, if there was salt. It became our constant diet. Life on our rancho became impossible. In 1916, I went to Tampico when I became old enough to fend for myself."[1]

[1] Interview with José Cruz Cervantes by author, Houston, Texas, March 21, 1976.

troops across the countryside and by the bloody contests waged to gain control of cities around Lake Chapala. Thousands of peasants and farmers fled to the north and eventually to the United States.

BORDER VIOLENCE AND CREATION OF THE "BROWN SCARE"

A major diplomatic issue between the governments of Benito Juárez, Porfirio Díaz and various U.S. administrations concerned border banditry and contraband. The strained process was intimately related to American efforts to define the border through the establishment of customs stations and military installations as the economic importance of the Southwest increased. As part of this effort, the U.S. started to enforce smuggling and immigration laws more stringently and to crack down on lawbreakers regardless of the seriousness of their offenses. Mexican immigrants, accustomed to casual migration, trade and behavior modes, were rapidly transformed into criminals and undesirables. In essence, U.S. officials plugged up a porous border so that Mexico's people and culture could not as easily flow into the Southwest.

The United States efforts to establish a clear demarcation seemed to proceed successfully until the Mexican Revolution demonstrated that the idea of a border was more fragile than previously imagined. As a result, in one decade more antipathy was created towards Mexicans than that which had built up over the past fifty years. Warfare and border violence received prominent coverage in newspapers, popular magazines and the emerging cinema, provoking the "Brown Scare." American indignation also played into the hands of private interests who urged U.S. intervention to protect or enhance their investments in Mexico. In the long run, these events affected relationships between Anglos and U.S. Mexicans not involved in political

17. Ricardo and Enrique Flores Magón.

The fear of "dishonor" is captured in the words of Ana Navarro de Garza, an immigrant who went to East Chicago with her businessman husband, also a Mexican immigrant: "My father sent all of us from Chihuahua in 1913. He stayed behind taking care of his business, but my mother, my sisters and myself, we all went to El Paso to live. My father had heard of what the Villistas were doing to young girls and was afraid for us. My father finally joined us in El Paso, where he set up another real estate business."[2]

---

[2] Interview with Ana Navarro de Garza by author, Schererville, Indiana, 1975.

intrigue or in revolutionary activity.

Even before the start of hostilities, precursor plots by Mexican *revoltosos* (insurgents) on United States territory rankled Americans. U.S. authorities reserved the most zeal for pursuing the Flores Magón brothers and other members of the Partido Liberal Mexicano (Mexican Liberal Party—PLM), whom President Díaz had exiled immediately before the revolution. The press followed their activities closely and eventually officials jailed PLM members for violating United States neutrality laws. Anglo-American readers of any southwestern newspaper were subjected to a barrage of stories dealing with the activities of *revoltosos*.

Reports of harm to Americans in Mexico provoked a flurry of complaints, despite the exaggerated nature of the stories reaching the United States. Civilians wrote home either to relatives, to their government or to American newspapers and reported these infractions. Of central concern to expatriate Americans was Mexican government interference in their economic affairs. The popular notion of Porfirian Mexico pampering foreigners, especially Americans, is not altogether true. All foreign investors, including Americans, were often played off against each other and even betrayed by the Mexican government. At times, local power groups conspired with government officials to defraud Americans. Mexican judicial treatment of Americans also provoked disgruntlement. What Americans feared most were the extreme privations, the inefficiency and lack of common-law principles in legal proceedings. In addition, a sense of Anglo superiority incensed American families and American friends of accused criminals because they felt loved ones should be above Mexican law.

Even before hostilities began, border-dwelling Americans were aware that Mexican exiles operated on the U.S. side, and they associated the revolutionaries with border banditry. Rioting in Mexico in response to a Texas lynching intensified Anglo fear along the border. On November 2, 1910, enraged townspeople in Rock Springs, Texas, burned Antonio Rodríguez at the stake for killing a white woman named Mrs. Clem Anderson. Widely publicized in the Mexican press, the outrage provoked violent anti-American demonstrations in Mexico City and in Guadalajara. In the melee, rioters roughed up Americans and damaged their property. The events, misreported in the American press or exaggerated by Ambassador Henry Lane Wilson, provoked a heated backlash against Mexicans in the U.S., especially those living in Texas.

Backlash to the riots only marks the beginning of negative sentiment built up in response to revolution-linked border provocations. As called for in the Plan de San Luis Potosí, Madero entered Mexico on November 20, 1910, but returned to Texas when the uprising miscarried. Madero enjoyed support from influential Texas Anglos disenchanted with

Jovita Yáñez, interviewed in Houston during the 1970s, tells of her experiences as a fifteen-year-old girl on vacation in Aguascalientes: "In 1914, towards the end, we went on the train, and when we disembarked, there were a large number of soldiers on the platform. We were told they were Villistas. One of them who appeared to be an officer was staring at me. I was very beautiful in those days, I was told. My hair is white now, but I had long blond hair and blue eyes. The officer beckoned to his aide and said something to him, and immediately his aide came to us and spoke to me. 'My colonel wants you to accompany me.' He took me away. The officer, a tall man, said that I was to be his girl and travel with him. You can imagine my distress. I started pleading, and if it had not been for a group of heroic students who pulled me underneath one of the cars while the others distracted the soldiers, I don't know what would have happened to me. We returned promptly to Mexico City. My father eventually sent us all to Laredo and then we came here to Houston."[3]

---

[3] Interview with Jovita Yáñez by author, Houston, Texas, March 29, 1976.

Not surprisingly, Americans could not count on Mexican immigrant loyalty during this period. In 1927 Andrés Avila, a Tucson resident, remembered how Mexicans in the city prepared for war against the United States during the invasion. "Yes, if the Americans had advanced a little more, the *raza* here would have risen up in arms. All the plans had been made. We even had generals, and everything was ready." He claimed the plans included taking Nogales and Yuma. One of the conspirators was a Tucson deputy sheriff, Avila said, and concluded that President Wilson did not order further penetration of Mexico because he feared "thousands of Mexicans" in the United States would rebel (translations of all quotes by author).[4]

Díaz, but average Americans who read the newspapers resented Mexicans hatching plots on U.S. soil. In February 1913, Huerta ousted Madero and had him murdered. Woodrow Wilson, inaugurated as U.S. president the same month, recalled Ambassador Wilson, who had also been involved in the ouster. Then, because Woodrow Wilson refused to recognize his government, Huerta orchestrated a wave of anti-American agitation, which the press in both countries played up. Because of the resurgence of border insurrection in 1913, Mexican immigrants continued to be objects of Anglo-American antagonism and fear.

Tension in 1914 was already exacerbated by an agricultural recession which put thousands of Mexicans out of work in the Southwest. That month, purportedly to end political chaos, President Wilson directed U.S. troops to occupy Veracruz. American law officials were alerted that angry Mexicans and Mexican Americans might launch reprisals. In Los Angeles, with the largest Mexican population in the U.S., the *Times* and other newspapers engaged in sensationalist reporting that fueled suspicion of Mexicans. In fact, a police investigation landed a number of suspected Mexican subversives in jail. The imbroglio put El Paso Anglos in such an ugly mood that city officials warned Mexicans not to create a disturbance. In Austin on April 25, intimidated Mexicans assured Governor Colquitt they would not cause any commotion.

Throughout this strife-plagued period, refugees called *pacíficos* (neutral Mexicans) poured across the border, taxing U.S. resources. The agricultural depression in Texas during most of 1914 and part of 1915 reduced the desirability of immigration and added to resentment of the Mexican presence. By October 1915, 23,000 refugees were concentrated in El Paso. Many were starving and suffering from debilitating diseases such as diphtheria, which reportedly killed as many as 335 Mexicans each week. Hipólito Villa, Pancho's brother, slaughtered his own cattle to feed starving refugees.

Anglo retaliation to the Texas-based Plan de San Diego in 1915 is unparalleled in its degree of anti-Mexican violence by Anglos. The plan, whose origins remain unclear, was reportedly concocted by Texas Mexicans and called all racial minorities—Blacks, Native Americans, Asians and Mexicans—to rise up in arms and drive Anglos out of the Southwest. The declaration, which called for the execution of all Anglo males over sixteen years of age, was scheduled for February 20. Moreover, it was irreverently designed to coincide with George Washington's birthday. Most accounts indicate that major Anglo retaliation started only after Texas Mexicans Luis de la Rosa and Aniceto Pizaña actually led a small group of raiders on a short-lived reign of terror beginning in July of 1915. But violence was evident earlier. Texas officials released news of the proposed insurrection as soon as Basilio

---

[4] Interview with Andrés Avila, April 23, 1927, Manuel Gamio Papers, Bancroft Library, Box 1, File No. 3.

Ramos, Antonio González and Manuel Flores were caught smuggling the document across the border in January of 1915.

After the raids began, Texas Rangers and volunteers summarily executed hundreds of Mexicans in the Rio Grande Valley and forced thousands across the border. The Plan de San Diego also caused urban unrest. In July wary federal officers arrested twenty Mexicans who were recruiting adherents for revolutionary activity in San Antonio. During August, twenty-eight San Antonio men, identified as supporters of the plan, were arrested after rioting against police. Alarmed Los Angeles residents associated the plan with an alleged revolution of *magonistas* in Southern California. Although the origins of the plan were never ascertained, it is certain that at least a small number of Tejanos responded to its call to arms, and probably the sentiment the document expressed was shared by many South Texas Mexicans. Here we can find historical precedence for the ideals of separating the Southwest from the U.S., which many Chicano Movement activists flirted with in the 1960s.

VILLISTA PROBLEMS

Early in 1915, when revolutionary leader Francisco "Pancho" Villa's forces were in Ciudad Juárez, the populist leader was courting favor with Americans, hoping that with U.S. help he would prevail in the struggle against rival leader, Venustiano Carranza. Villa, who at the time still enjoyed a positive image in the U.S., hereafter became the greatest villain associated with anti-American activity. After President Wilson extended de facto recognition of Carranza as president of Mexico in October, Villa turned against the United States. In November his remaining army was almost destroyed in an attack on Agua Prieta, Sonora, a town of strategic importance if *villistas* were to remain major contenders. The U.S. played a major role because permission to use American railroads was granted Carranza to transport soldiers from Chihuahua to fortify Agua Prieta. With the defeat, Villa's bitterness increased.

Determined to continue sabotaging Carranza's relations with the United States and to wreak vengeance, during January 1916 37 Villa's men dragged from a train at Santa Ysabel, Chihuahua, seventeen American engineers slated to start operations for La Cusi Mining Company and killed them. The bodies were brought back from Chihuahua through El Paso in coffins draped with American flags. This image whipped Anglos into a frenzy of revenge, and they went on a rampage attacking every Mexican man they could lay their hands on.

Villa also staged a number of border incursions into Texas. But the most infamous of the *villista* raids was the March 9, pre-dawn invasion of Columbus, New Mexico. Eighteen American soldiers and civilians

Even after Huerta's ouster in July of 1914, border tension and suspicions remained high. In August the *Arizona Republic* revealed a plot brewing in the Salt River Valley. Nine conspirators were jailed after police tracked them for two months. According to this incredible story, Maricopa County officers uncovered a conspiracy, "which had for its object the capture of the city of Phoenix by hordes of banditti, the rifling of the stores and banks and the gradual spread of conditions of anarchy into other portions of the state, together with an armed attempt by a combined force of Indians and Mexicans against the government of the United States starting in this section."[5]

The foray was to yield munitions, money and supplies in order to conduct revolution in Mexico and in the United States. Five of the alleged plotters received two-year sentences in a trial held shortly after their arrest. The Phoenix newspaper claimed that the conspiracy was *magonista*-inspired and that it extended to numerous mining town barrios in southeastern Arizona.

[5] *Arizona Republican*, August 8, 1914.

were killed and many others were wounded while Villa's forces suffered more than two hundred casualties. The reaction was swift. U.S. troops led by General John Pershing pursued Villa into Chihuahua in the foray known as the "Punitive Expedition." The expedition was a failure, however. It succeeded mainly in demoralizing the expedition's soldiers and frustrating supporters back home while elevating "Pancho" Villa as a national hero, the defender of Mexican sovereignty in the face of the American invasion.

18. Venustiano Carranza.

In the meantime, Mexican consuls reported that outraged Mexicans of diverse loyalties considered returning to defend their country. Concurrently, Mexicans suspected of subversion suffered indignities at the hands of hostile Americans. In a two-day period in El Paso, for example, on March 10 and 11, officials rounded up two hundred Mexicans for being *villistas*, deported them and continued to arrest anyone showing anti-American feelings. Emilio Valenzuela of the newspaper *La Constitución,* and five of his employees were jailed when they criticized Pershing's expedition. In Los Angeles fear of Mexicans intensified after the Columbus raid as well. A rash of burglaries in Long Beach were blamed on *villistas* while local authorities enforced a ban on selling guns and liquor to Mexicans. In addition, the scare prompted Police Chief A. Snively to form a squad to spy on Mexicans.

During May a number of violent raids by *villistas* in the Texas Big Bend shook American sensibilities. That month, U.S. officials warned that the Plan de San Diego leader, Luis de la Rosa, planned to invade Texas sometime between May 10 and 15. On May 11 authorities arrested a number of Mexicans in Corpus Christi thought to be involved in this conspiracy. According to the *Houston Chronicle*, the uprising was to extend into New Mexico and Arizona.

As shown in the Los Angeles repression after the Villa raid, oppro-

In May, Plan de San Diego leader General León Caballo showed reporters a packet of letters from Mexicans in Texas who wanted to return to Mexico because of repression in Texas. Said Caballo, "These. . . are from my people who cannot live any longer in the state of Texas, as they are denied protection and many have been killed by irresponsible armed posses without reason. They are afraid to live there, and are leaving small farms which they have purchased with the savings of a lifetime. Leaving everything behind, they are coming back."[6]

[6] *The New York Times*, May 22, 1915.

19. *Carrancistas* in Charcas, Mexico, with leader of the Cruz Blanca nursing corps, Leonor Villegas de Magnón (center), 1914.

brium extended beyond the border. In May Santos Dávalos in Union City, Oklahoma, complained to the Mexican consul in Kansas City that Americans riled by the raids gave Mexicans twenty-four hours to leave town; otherwise they would be blasted out with guns. Diplomatic pressure persuaded the Oklahoma governor to intervene, and the threat was not carried out.

As Villa had expected, the border incursions corroded U.S.-Carranza relationships. In fact, *carrancistas* considered invading Texas to force Pershing's troops out of Mexico, a strategy canceled at the last moment. Nonetheless, Carranza still maintained pressure on the U.S. through small-scale raids, a strategy that persuaded the U.S. to make peace at a time when the war in Europe was the foremost foreign-policy concern.

In the end, diplomacy won out and on February 5, 1917, Pershing's army vacated Mexico, but Americans did not easily forget the bitterness they felt against Mexico.

In 1917 *villista*-inspired raids continued. Villa took advantage of Pershing's withdrawal to regain strategic positions in Chihuahua, and by October his men controlled areas around Ojinaga, which became a headquarters. United States soldiers stationed across the river at Presidio pursued bandits after every raid with unprecedented zeal. In December a frustrated Governor Hobby turned to Francisco Chapa, publisher of *El Imparcial de Texas* in San Antonio, to mediate in a meeting with Nuevo León Governor Nicéforo Zamorano. The Mexican official offered to cooperate with

20. *El Imparcial de Texas.*

The following quote from *The Los Angeles Times* reflects how the widespread xenophobia sweeping the nation during World War I was tied to the Mexican Revolution: "If the people of Los Angeles knew what was happening on our border, they would not sleep at night. Sedition, conspiracy and plots are in the very air. Telegraph wires are tapped, spies come and go at will. German nationals hob-nob with Mexican bandits, Japanese agents, and renegades from this country. Code messages are relayed from place to place along the border, frequently passing six or eight people from sender to receiver. Los Angeles is the headquarters for this vicious system, and it is there that the deals with German and Mexican representatives are made."[7]

Texas Rangers while Hobby promised protection to Texas Mexicans, but raids continued and so did the enmity of Americans against Mexicans.

World War I-induced xenophobia increased fear already felt towards Mexicans and created more doubt about the loyalty of those living in the U.S. Moreover, Mexican leaders Huerta and Carranza were suspected of having pro-German sympathies. The 1914 Yripanga incident, in which the U.S. Navy confiscated German arms bound for Huerta, convinced many Americans of his German leanings. After being ousted during 1914, Huerta languished in Spanish exile until 1915, planning a return to power. As an accomplice, he chose former enemy Pascual Orozco, and both colluded with Germans to restore them to leadership. The fear of Mexico becoming an ally of Axis powers heightened after the U.S. entered the war in April. Only the sending of troops to Europe precluded further intervention in Mexican affairs.

Fear of Mexicans heightened when U.S. officials in El Paso investigated reports that German agents in Mexico and American draft-evaders inspired border bandit raids. During June of 1918 in Nogales, Sonora, Mexicans kidnapped an American identified as Gus and held him for ransom. The bandits were paid ten thousand dollars by Gus's friends, but he was still not released. One of the ransomers in Los Angeles wrote a letter to Nogales in which he cast doubts that the Mexican government would help obtain the release of the kidnapped victim because "they do not like us, and are pro-German to the core,

---

[7] Quoted in W. Dirk Raat, *Revoltosos: Mexico's Rebels in the United States* (College Station: Texas A&M University Press, 1981), pp. 276-277.

21. *Soladaderas* in Carranza's army; the one at right was a spy.

and that is behind it all, if I know anything about it."[8]

Border violence created further tensions which by 1919 again brought the two nations close to war. After Americans were no longer burdened with the European war, they clamored for an invasion of Mexico. Rumors were so rife that, in mid-July, José Luis Velasco and Luis R. Alvarez were arrested in El Paso for publishing a story claiming the United States planned an invasion of Mexico. They even divulged U.S. military war plans which had probably been leaked to them by *carrancista* spies. Americans, doubting Carranzas's loyalty during World War I and tired of his resisting efforts to influence Mexico's economy, supported his political challenger, Alvaro Obregón.

In July of 1919, the Association for Rights of Americans in Mexico, an organization controlled in part by Senator Bacon Fall, listed 317 Americans killed in Mexico between 1910 and 1919. The organization, made up of American expatriates in Mexico, obtained the information from the Department of State and provided a "murder map" showing where Americans had been killed.

The images coming out of Mexico during the period of revolution portrayed Mexicans as violent, dangerous and treacherous. Few Anglos

Texas Congressman John C. Box argued against waiving immigration laws to allow entry of Mexican workers in 1920: "Americans found they could not live with them on genial terms in Texas 80 years ago. In a contest which arose then the Mexican showed both his inferiority and savage nature. The same traits which prevailed with them in the days of the Alamo and Goliad show themselves in the dealings with each other and with the Americans now. I could go on indefinitely for the story has no end. Villa, Huerta, Orozco, Carranza and their bands and the conditions of Mexico now are exhibits of Mexican character."[9]

---

[8] Quoted in Anita Harlan, "The Battles of 'Ambos Nogales,'" unpublished manuscript, MS 332, Arizona Historical Society Archives, p. 17.

[9] Quoted in Mark Reisler, *By the Sweat of Their Brow: Mexican Immigrant Labor in the United States: 1900-1940* (Westport, Connecticut: Greenwood Press, 1976), p. 159.

discerned that special circumstances in the Revolution created an atmosphere conducive to atrocities in Mexico. Instead, Americans believed this to be intrinsic to Mexican character, a conviction that justified mistreatment. As one historian has put it, "The additional hysteria of wartime America only amplified and aggravated the already existing prejudice and discrimination. It was a pretty sorry time when there was no justice for innocent, apolitical Mexican Americans."[10]

In Mexico resentment towards the United States also increased during the turmoil. It stemmed mostly from the treatment of Mexicans in the United States, but Mexicans were also sensitive to constant Mexico-bashing by U.S. politicians and the media. The pounding resumed in 1926 when President Plutarco Elías Calles repressed the Catholic Church and threatened to enforce Mexican subsoil rights. United States government criticism, while welcomed by militant Catholics, generally rankled Mexican nationalists. Then beginning in 1926, a violent Catholic reaction known as the *Cristero* Rebellion unleashed a lawlessness not seen since the 1910s. Again, some Americans were abused, creating demands for intervention.

In November of 1926, an editorial in *Excelsior* accused Americans of besmirching Mexico's reputation in order to continue exploiting Mexican resources with impunity. In addition, the piece charged that bashing also created a favorable atmosphere for U.S. citizens with cases before the Joint Claims Commission for property damage and deaths during the Revolution. The campaign made it appear that Mexicans were peculiarly prone to atrocities, said *El Universal*, and it ignored the heinous behavior of Europeans and Americans during World War I. In March of 1927, a San Antonio lawyer wrote to the Department of State, warning that Mexican immigrants were creating sentiment to align with an enemy country and start a revolution to regain lost lands.

BLAMING THE PURVEYOR: VICE ALONG THE BORDER

Through the reign of Porfirio Díaz, smuggling along the border had been both a constant source of diplomatic tension and intense anti-Mexican feelings among the Anglo population. This established way of border life acquired even more vibrancy during the Mexican Revolution when gun-running attracted thousands of new adherents. In addition, vice—gambling, prostitution, drugs and bootlegging—became part of border culture. It mattered little to judgmental Americans that this vice existed primarily for their countrymen's consumption.

Human contraband became more common with the rise of immigration in the first decade of the twentieth century when the U.S. began tightening its borders. After the 1917 Immigration Act, which demanded literacy from immigrants and an eight-dollar head tax, ferrying them across the Rio Grande illegally became a lucrative trade. Because of reverse migration during the 1921 depression, the alien smuggling trade shrank, but with economic recovery, the smuggling of people to the U.S. resumed, and soon an abundance of clients clamored to be ferried across. The 1924 National Origins Quota Act barred nonwhite immigrants from Asia and restricted southern and eastern Europeans. This created even more opportunities for runners because many Asians and Europeans tried to enter through the Mexican border clandestinely.

Despite the act's exclusion of the Western Hemisphere, Mexicans still paid a head tax and visa fee totaling eighteen dollars and needed to comply with requirements of the 1917 Literacy Act. In essence, the market remained lucrative for smugglers. After passage of the 1924 act restricting immigration, Mexicans also became unwanted. By the end of 1925 smuggling of liquor and aliens reached an all-time high, and Border Patrol agents now aimed more of the vigilance at

---

[10] Raat, *Revoltosos*, p. 265.

Mexicans. As harassment in 1926 heightened, the Mexican Chamber of Deputies passed a law requiring the government to extend protection to emigrants.

The Border Patrol, organized in 1924 to augment a thinly staffed customs agency, was given primary responsibility for curbing illegal entries, but lack of personnel limited its effectiveness. In 1925, for example, only nine men, responsible for some ninety miles of border, operated in the El Paso area. Previous to the restrictive laws of 1917 and 1924, the Immigration and Naturalization Service had maintained special inspectors on the border to halt Chinese entries, which were barred completely. To upgrade supervision of contravention, Secretary of Labor James J. Davis created three principal immigration districts with headquarters in San Francisco.

The War Prohibited Act in 1918, which set up dry zones along the length of the border to force abstention on U.S. soldiers, provoked the smuggling of a cheap but potent moonshine called *tesol*. After the more far-reaching 1919 Volstead Act ushered in full prohibition, by the mid-1920s extensive contraband rings emerged. A U.S. market for illegal drugs such as cocaine, morphine and opium further propelled the illegal trade. Cocaine, which just a few years prior went for thirteen dollars an ounce, commanded seventy-five in 1925. It was openly sold by druggists in Ciudad Juárez. Once smuggled across the Rio Grande, most drugs made their way to the eastern United States. As early as 1919 many El Paso Mexicans were organized into dope rings.

Contraband ring leaders came from a variety of ethnic groups. Anglo-Americans, Middle Easterners, Chinese and Mexican merchants ran the large operations, but ground troops were from the working class *barrios* of border towns. Independent operators known as "mules" smuggled most of the liquor across in small quantities. Juárez official Andrés Morán estimated that seventy-five percent of the city's population, mostly natives of the border area, engaged in some kind of smuggling activity.

In addition, every border town contained vice industries—prostitution, gambling, pornographic floor shows—that attracted Americans by the thousands. Eventually an outcry of public indignation, which blamed Mexico for border evils, demanded an end to smuggling and pressured politicians to act. The Klu Klux Klan (KKK) even entered into the picture as border moralists and vigilantes. During 1925 the Calexico KKK was among many lobbyist groups militating for restricting border interaction. Apparently in El Paso the KKK was more assertive. In 1921 an El Paso judge declared that KKK members who took the law into their own hands would be prosecuted.

Because of the border evils, Americans cast a critical eye towards

Sweeping generalizations about Mexicans and border vice are seen in a 1929 report on Texas criminality written by U.S. customs agent Frank Buckley, who said: "San Antonio, El Paso, Del Rio, Brownsville, and Laredo—All-American cities, but Mexican in population, atmosphere and morals. Law-enforcement conditions in most such places reflect the moral laxity of Latins; liquor, narcotics, gambling, and prostitution all flourish—openly in some places, under cover in others—but flourishing nevertheless. It is a fact, also, and an unfortunate one so far as moral texture of Texas border communities is concerned, that the annual immigration tide from the southern Republic leaves upon our doorsteps a horde of low-caste Mexicans—ignorant, immoral and unassimilable."[11]

[11] "Report of Frank Buckley of the Bureau of Prohibition, Treasury Department, Submitting Detailed Information Relative to a Survey of Prohibition Enforcement in the State of Texas," in *United States, 71st Congress, 3d Session, Enforcement of the Prohibition Laws; Official Records of the National Commission on Law Observance and Enforcement* Vol 4. (Washington, DC: United States Government Printing Office, 1931), p. 924.

Mexicans, assuming that border towns reflected their values. On the morning of May 21, 1929, two Mexican money couriers from the Aguacaliente Casino in Tijuana were taking the previous night's receipts to a San Diego bank. As their car turned a corner on the winding highway separating Tijuana from San Diego, a band of white "eastern types," hijackers, cut them down with machine-gun fire. The two casino employees, José Borrego and Nemesio Monroy, died instantly. San Diego police apprehended two of the six gang members soon after the robbery. They were tried and convicted of premeditated murder. Because of the brutality of the crime, the Mexican government pressed for a death sentence and general public opinion seemed to concur. Judge J.N. Andrews, however, sentenced the robbers, M.B. Colson and Robert Lee Cochran, to life imprisonment, a decision which sent shock waves through Mexican communities on both sides of the border. At the time of sentencing, Judge Andrews justified the lighter penalty by holding Mexico partially responsible for the misdeeds of the two holdup men.

CHAPTER THREE

Mexican Immigrants

22. Mexican miners in Arizona in the early 1900s.

No other concept is at more variance with the Chicano ideal of Aztlán than the term "illegal alien," which in the minds of most Americans means undocumented Mexican worker. In the initial stages of the Chicano Movement, however, immigration was not a major issue, and the Chicano's symbolic claim to the Southwest went unchallenged. It was not until the federal government stepped up efforts to apprehend undocumented Mexicans in the 1970s that this topic became controversial within *movimiento* circles. Before this, immigrants received the benefit of its activism only in a de facto manner— i.e., when their problems fell within the orbit of Chicano issues as when they protested police brutality. In fact, César Chávez's farm-worker union treated immigrants with great hostility. As a consequence, the Chicano Movement did not address many of the issues relevant to Mexican nationals such as raids by the Immigration and Naturalization Service, denigration of immigrants by both Anglos and Mexican Americans and the precariousness of "illegal alien" status.

A number of reasons account for this seeming lack of concern. The undocumented worker was not as visible to Chicanos themselves when the *movimiento* emerged in the 1960s as he became later on. In addition, Americans have always reacted most negatively to immigration during economic downturns. When the Chicano Movement appeared, the U.S. economy was booming. Because the *movimiento* reacted mainly to immediate issues such as police abuse and poor education and the "illegal alien" syndrome was not on the surface, it was ignored.

A final consideration is that the movement's *rasion d'etre* was predicated on being a conquered people, not an immigrant population. This notion endures to this day among many Chicano intellectuals. The denial of an immigrant heritage prevented Chicano Movement activists from embracing Mexican nationals as part of their world. The Americanizing Mexican American generation was unequivocal in its opposition to Mexican immigration. But as shall be seen below, the continued influx from Mexico has been a central factor in Mexican American life.

THE REVOLUTION, WORLD WAR I AND MASSIVE IMMIGRATION

Severe economic depression racked Mexico in the first decade of this century, creating extreme poverty. Francisco I. Madero initiated the revolt that led to the Mexican Revolution in November of 1910, and refugees immediately started to pour across the border. Revolutionary destruction worsened the already dire situation in which Mexicans lived, eventually rendering Mexicans among the most vulnerable immigrants ever to come to the U.S. In 1910, two hundred nineteen thou-

To the chagrin of immigrant elites, many Anglo Americans did not discern that immigrants were also middle class— and white. A November 1926 editorial in *The New York Times* warned about dangers stemming from unregulated inflow. It stated that there were two kinds of Mexicans in the United States: the old stock with more Spanish blood, thus desirable by American standards, and newer immigrants, more visibly Indian. Fortunately, said the *Times* editorial, "For the most part they return to their old homes as soon as laced by a few hundred dollars." It should be noted that the piece appeared during a recession when labor markets were saturated.[1]

[1] *The New York Times*, November 10, 1926.

sand Mexican nationals already lived in the U.S., but by 1930 that number had increased to close to one million. Their entry also coincided with the years of border violence which had provoked intense feelings of hostility towards Mexicans. Americans easily marginalized newly arrived Mexicans, who found a hostile and difficult-to-navigate environment in the U.S.

Normal migration resumed after 1917 only after a relative peace ensued and the government needed labor to repair railroads. During the lull, a food crisis prompted Mexicans to respond to the needs of a now-accelerating economy in the U.S. during World War I. Coinciding with difficulty in traveling to the border before 1916 was a sluggish Southwest economy, which had not quite recovered from the 1907-1908 recession. In 1914 farm prices dropped drastically and thousands of Mexicans wanted to return home but were without funds. Texas, with three entry ports and railroad connections to the Mexican interior, had absorbed the lion's share of indigent and destitute immigrants. During April the Mexican Labor Ministry inquired among henequen producers in the Yucatan if they could accommodate unemployed Mexican repatriates from Texas.

Recovery came quickly, however, spurred partially by irrigation projects financed through the Newlands Reclamation Act. Farmers planted lettuce on irrigated acreage in the Salt River Valley of Arizona and in California's Imperial Valley in 1915, and along with cotton, lettuce was responsible for the most important economic activity in both areas. In California, Asian labor continued to comprise a large bulk of the work force, but for Arizona, Mexico remained the only source.

By now the U.S. economy was achieving unparalleled growth, owing primarily to its position as a supplier to warring factions in Europe. Labor requirements had never been so great, yet wartime disruption in trans-Atlantic transportation and utilization of potential European emigrants in opposing armies hindered the influx of European workers. Then when the U.S. became directly involved in the struggle, thousands of U.S. workers were conscripted into military service, thus creating a vacuum in agriculture, mining, basic industry and transportation. These sectors looked

south of the border in order to meet labor requirements—at the same time when Mexico was experiencing one of its worst economic crises.

Access to Mexican labor during this period proved to be more difficult than would have been the case in previous years, however. In February of 1917 Congress responded to a restrictionist mood bolstered by wartime xenophobia; it enacted an immigration act that imposed a literacy requirement and an eight-dollar head tax on all immigrants. Passed before the U.S. entered the war, the act did not address the potential manpower shortages of a wartime economy. The bill was designed to curb an "undesirable" influx from southern and eastern Europe, where illiteracy rates were as high as seventy-five percent. Nevertheless, the act ultimately inhibited immigration from Mexico.

Prior to 1917 Mexicans complied with certain provisions of an immigration law passed in 1907 that prohibited entry to the diseased, criminal and insane and required a four-dollar head tax. Officials imposed the restriction more on European immigrants than on those from the Western Hemisphere. In the western part of the U.S., stopping oriental emigration preoccupied immigration officials the most. As a consequence, there was a greater need for Mexicans. Officials, in fact, exempted Mexicans, Canadians and Cubans from paying the head tax as long as they displayed sound mind and body—provisions rarely monitored along the Mexican border. The 1917 act, however, presented more difficulty for Mexicans because of the literacy requirement. Illiteracy rates in Michoacán, a major source of immigration, were eighty-five percent, and for most migrants arriving destitute at the border, the head tax was prohibitive.

Legal immigration from Mexico suffered a temporary setback in 1917. Surreptitious entry continued, but employers wanted legal, free and easy access to this valuable labor reserve to the south. As the summer harvests approached, agriculturists and related interest groups became desperate and pressured Congress to defer the law for Mexicans. In June Congress complied, but the waiver given to agricultural workers was good only after farmers complied with a tangle of bureaucratic requirements. Ultimately both employers and workers preferred illegal entry.

In May passage of the Selective Service Act emerged as another threat to the easy flow of Mexicans into the U.S. Only naturalized immigrants or those taking out first papers were eligible for the draft, but local draft boards required all immigrants, regardless of status, to register. Most Mexican immigrants were loathe to comply with this provision for fear of being drafted—with good reason. Local boards sometimes called up citizens of Mexico suspected of being Mexican Americans. The confusion provoked a mass exodus to Mexico. American employers who needed labor during wartime economic expansion became anxious about this voluntary repatriation. The Mexican government discouraged the return as well because the outflow had provided a safety valve for the unemployment besetting Mexico.

Both governments joined in a widespread campaign to assure fearful Mexicans they would not be drafted. President Woodrow Wilson even proclaimed publicly that Mexican citizens would not be drafted because of their importance as farm workers. The Mexican consuls and Spanish language newspapers also cooperated. *El Cosmopolita* in Kansas City, for example, ran a series of articles assuring Mexicans that the draft would not apply as long they proved Mexican citizenship. Similarly the two major San Antonio Spanish-language dailies, *El Imparcial de Texas* and *La Prensa,* throughout 1917 and most of 1918 reminded Mexicans to register, assuring them that their Mexican citizenship prevented conscription. Eventually, the conscription problem was resolved, and Mexican immigration resumed a normal flow.

During World War I, California became the main destination of Mexico's immigrants; Texas, however, continued to be the state with the greatest number of Mexicans until the 1940s. In California farmers had relied heavily on Asian immigrants in the past, but because its agricultural sector had been expanding so rapidly since 1915, the Asian pool no longer sufficed. In the meantime, in June 1917 Secretary of Labor William Wilson suggested extending the waiver to allow illiterate Mexicans to work in nonagricultural sectors such as transportation.

During 1918 Mexican American labor contractors (*enganchistas*) hired by American companies entered Mexico and recruited in areas where railroads offered easy transportation to the border. Since this was the first emigration for most workers, *enganchistas* many times exploited their vulnerability by not paying full wages or by overcharging for food and lodging. The recruits arrived at Laredo or El Paso in crowded cattle cars, and once there, contractors often abandoned boys under sixteen or those workers stricken with diseases such as tuberculosis because they did not meet entry requirements.

Indeed, Americans appeared to Mexican officials to hunger after their workers. In a move designed to improve strained relations between the two countries during World War I, the State Department invited a group of Mexican newspaper editors and publishers to New York during June 1918 to discuss a cultural exchange program. Once there, a representative of Secretary of Labor Wilson implored them to persuade their government to be more cooperative in allowing Mexican laborers to enter the U.S. On June 16, the same day that Wilson's aide approached the Mexican journalists, the waivers of the previous summer became applicable to all industries that needed Mexican labor, and automatic renewals continued as they were needed for the duration of the war.

When the warring factions in Europe declared armistice in December of 1918, Department of Labor officials, anticipating a surge of returning veterans, voided the waiver. Officials felt the presence of Mexican workers would create strife. Mexicans who had come in legally before dispensation ended could remain until the following summer season, but "illegal aliens" were enthusiastically rounded up and dumped across the border—south of Eagle Pass and Brownsville rather than at the more heavily used ports of entry of El Paso and Laredo. The move was calculated to disorient the deported Mexicans, thus hindering their return. Once there, they became destitute with no ability to earn a living, creating serious problems for Mexican border officials. This process of inviting Mexican laborers in during times of manpower shortage and repatriating them when they proved a threat to domestic laborers would continue in years to come.

The geographical distribution of Mexicans in the U.S. changed dramatically during the war years. Before 1915 Mexicans labored primarily in border-area agriculture, railroads and mining. When the war ended, automobile factories in Detroit and the Chicago stockyards employed large numbers of Mexicans. According to one estimate, as many as thirty-five thousand Mexican laborers resided outside the southwestern states, mostly in the Midwest. Mexicans, however, could now be found as far east as Florida, traditionally a Negro labor sector, and as far north as Buffalo, New York, and Bethlehem, Pennsylvania. The New York correspondent of the Mexico City daily, *El Demócrata,* reported that during the war Mexicans moved into textile factories, restaurants, hotels and transportation in the New York area, while, in Tennessee, bauxite mines employed them.

Even in the Southwest, where Mexican labor was an established tradition, wartime conditions hastened their entry into labor sectors that were previously the exclusive domain of U.S. citizens. This was the case, for example, in the oil fields of West Texas and the chemical industry in Freeport, a town near Houston, Texas. In the latter case, one spokesman indicated to a congressional committee that his company hired about two hundred Mexicans during the war to replace American workers who migrated out of the area; he attested to their being "very good working with sulphate gas."

In his message to the opening session of the Mexican Congress on September 1, 1919, Venustiano Carranza devoted a large portion of his speech, a vociferous attack on U.S. policy towards Mexico, to alleged injustices committed against Mexican workers in the U.S. These included such incidents as lynchings, indiscriminate murders in which law officials participated or did not investigate, the drafting of Mexican nationals into the U.S. Army and overt discrimination, especially in Texas. Carranza was not exaggerating. Mexicans felt so completely marginalized that many thought that owning property required citizenship.

On March 24, 1920, the Mexican consul in El Paso alleged in a report to the Foreign Ministry that police and border guards had indiscriminately killed hundreds of Mexicans since 1910 in various parts of the U.S. Two months later the governor of Chihuahua ordered migration officials at Ciudad Juárez completely to halt entry into El Paso after more than three hundred persons obtained documents to enter Texas during the course of one day. In that month, more than six thousand Mexicans entered legally. But then as now, more Mexicans crossed clandestinely than legally.

The inconsistent pattern of responses to Mexican immigration in the U.S. thoroughly frustrated Mexican government officials. By 1920 under

The Mexico City newspaper, *Gráfico,* warned that the heavy immigration of Mexican laborers was increasing vigilance by the Border Patrol, forcing many Mexicans to enter clandestinely. "Some have been shot because the border patrol has orders to shoot. Lozano, a well known resident of El Paso, was shot. A smuggler and many others have been shot. A strict examination is now required: eyes, chest, height. One has to be an Adonis to be able to cross, and as a result many are left across the border in Laredo."[2]

Smugglers demanded fifty dollars to cross the Mexicans clandestinely, the newspaper lamented, which sometimes were their last *centavos.*

[2] *The New York Times,* April 3, 1920.

the leadership of newly elected president Álvaro Obregón, Mexican leaders remained ideologically opposed to emigration, but economic conditions forced a continuation of an opportunistic and vacillating policy. In the meantime, *The New York Times* printed an editorial praising the salutary effects that Mexican labor had in southwestern agriculture, and John B. Carrington, the head of the San Antonio Chamber of Commerce, declared that "Mexican labor had put Texas on the map."

In 1920 more than four hundred thousand Mexican nationals were living in the U.S. No longer a temporary expedient, they became an integral part of the economy. In the Midwest, use of Mexican labor related more directly to the wartime labor shortages. Railroads, sugar beet farms, meat packing plants and heavy industries such as steel and coal mining sought out Mexicans to assure a plentiful supply of workers. Since midwestern industries did not receive Mexican workers through the special waivers to the 1917 law, a large number of undocumented immigrants resided there, becoming more vulnerable to the perils of being illegal. As the most recently arrived ethnic group, they stood out within a hierarchy of ethnic workers. More labor-union minded, midwestern workers' attitudes toward Mexicans by 1920 were poisoned by the use of Mexicans as scabs in strikes held during the previous decade.

Then early in 1921 definite signs of a post-war depression appeared, accompanied by a decrease in the desirability of Mexican immigrant labor. Severe unemployment marooned those already in the U.S., leaving them destitute and unable to return home. This situation drained the energy and resources of the Mexican government as it made a concerted effort to ease immigrant distress. This latest downturn surpassed those of 1908 and 1914, leaving Mexican immigrants more vulnerable to the usual privations. The destitution which affected Mexicans disproportionately during economic plunges magnified their presence to Americans, who perceived their situation as an unwanted "Mexican problem."

Five to six million workers in general were thrown out of work during 1921 in the U.S., and Mexicans were again deported en masse. During the war years, Mexicans had entered labor sectors where they supplied first-time competition with white workers. This fueled racism and encouraged nativist deportation sentiment. Mexicans were repatriated, however, because local governments did not want to take responsibility for the welfare of unemployed "undesirables" who, from their viewpoint, did not have a right to charity anyway.

The recession eased by 1923, and once again employers sought Mexican labor. Concurrently restrictive immigration legislation curtailed European labor; the vacuum was filled by Mexicans in many industrialized sectors. In 1924 the Department of Labor announced that more Mexicans had entered the U.S. during the fiscal year ending in June than in any other year in history. Contemporary observers were acutely aware of the reason for the increase. The *Houston Chronicle*, for example, in January of 1924 indicated that "Mexican immigration is due to increased demands for common labor among big eastern manufacturers and substitutes for similar European labor which had been curbed by the immigration act of 1917." The passage of even more restrictive legislation in 1921 and 1924 further stemmed European immigration, sustaining the demand for Mexican labor throughout the country.

Labor-hungry industries recruited massively, offering wages to entice west-central Mexicans, who at home earned but a few *centavos* a day. The recruitment efforts quickly created labor surpluses as the markets filled up in spite of the seemingly unlimited need for workers—a desirable situation for employers, but tragic for latecomer workers who did not nab limited jobs and tragic for the labor unions.

In 1926 push factors in the ailing Mexican economy combined with zealous overrecruitment to create an even greater incentive for emigration. Mexico declared the outflow as a threat to the nation's interests as well; newspapers, government officials and union leaders alike lamented that the country was losing too many inhabitants. But by summer even U.S. employers looked askance at the saturated labor markets, prompting what the *Hispano América* newspaper called "massive deportations." That fall, because the cotton yield in Texas and Arizona fell severely below normal expectations, the need for Mexicans was reduced even further. As winter approached, destitute Mexicans from throughout the country clamored for repatriation.

The Baptist Home Missions perceived the tide of Mexican immigration as a problem of such proportions that it sponsored a conference in El Paso to plan strategy on how to deal with educational and religious needs of the newcomers. The group estimated the 1926 population of Mexicans in the U.S. at one and one-half million, of which close to three hundred thousand had entered after the economy had recovered from the 1921 recession.

In 1926 a drop in the demand for Mexican labor prompted immigration officials to rethink their policy. The Department of Labor added new requirements to existing immigration regulations, which already barred applicants with a history of vice violations. They now included in this definition persons living in common-law liaisons. Single women not accompanied by husbands were required to have two character reference letters.

Prior to the restrictive laws of 1917 and 1924, the Immigration and Naturalization Service maintained special inspectors on the border to halt the entry of Chinese, the only aliens barred completely from entering the U.S. Mexicans were still allowed to cross more freely. The Naturalization Service and the Border Patrol, which was also responsible for stopping illegal entry, could no longer ignore illegal entries as they did during periods of labor shortage; efforts were stepped up to curb illegal entries of Mexicans—sometimes violently. In April of 1926 Border Patrol agents shot a record number of Mexicans attempting to cross into Texas.

Obviously, the welcome mat for Mexicans had worn thin as the 1920s booming economy slowed, but oblivious to changing attitudes, thousands of Mexicans entered illegally and showed little inclination to naturalize, even if their status was legal. Many Americans saw in this the rationale for marginalizing and deporting Mexicans. Just as important, Americans viewed Mexicans as racially unacceptable, and many could not understand that, if Asians were barred outright from entering and if southern and eastern European immigration was reduced by quotas, why were Mexicans neither barred nor put on quotas?

In turn, Mexicans felt Americans discouraged them from becoming citizens. Many believed that the naturalization ritual included spitting or stepping on the Mexican flag. This notion was undoubtedly apocryphal, but according to contemporary sociologist Helen Walker, American officials did discourage Mexicans from becoming citizens. Besides, Mexicans found themselves worse off as citizens than as aliens, she thought, because as aliens at least they were protected by the Mexican government.

In the 1920s nativists such as Texas Representative John C. Box had militated for curbing Mexican immigration through congressional legislation. But employer interests won out and legal immigration for Mexicans remained relatively unencumbered. His witnesses in congressional hearings conjured up images of inferior "half breeds" unable to assimilate properly into the American scene.

Others did not want to close the door completely. Texas Congressman James Blanton proposed before the Johnson immigration committee in January of 1928 that the entry of *braceros* be suspended for seven years, except during harvest time. He asked for a one million-dollar increase in the Department of Labor budget exclusively for deporting Mexicans. Congressman Lawrence Phipps of Colorado strongly opposed such a bill, however, primarily because of the need to keep Mexicans permanently in his state.

After 1926 diplomatic relations between Mexico and the U.S. had deteriorated after President Calles had decided to prosecute Catholics (*cristeros*) and enforce subsoil rights on foreign-owned properties. Also mistreatment of Americans in Mexico during this time of strained relations resulted in negative publicity against Mexico and Mexicans in general. As usual, events in Mexico reflected on Mexicans in the U.S. At the end of the decade, public opinion supported the ending of immigration from Mexico, an attitude that heartened restrictionists like John C. Box, who had fought an uphill battle with entrenched employer interests.

During the winter of 1927-1928, Los Angeles unemployment reached one hundred thousand, creating an army of homeless men who converged on city parks to loiter. Whites used Pershing Park while Mexicans lounged at *la placita*, a square surrounded by employment agencies. Every so often police raided these commons, picking up anyone not having a means of support. In January of 1928 the Mexican community came together in protest. Organizer Agustín García claimed that, once jailed, many prisoners were forced to work on public projects and, instead of wages, they earned a bus ticket to the nearest town. "These people are not vagrants," said García. "They are just unemployed" (translated by author).[3]

Similar tactics were employed in Long Beach during September 1928. City police put jobless Mexican farm workers on a train, sternly warning them never to return to town. According to *La Opinión*, a city council spokesman proclaimed, "We don't want vagrants here; we want people who will work" (translated by author).[4]

REPATRIATION DURING THE GREAT DEPRESSION

When it became obvious that the economy was failing and did not have a chance of recovery, Congress passed the 1929 immigration act. It served as a partial victory for John C. Box and other nativists who had pressed for a specific Mexican immigration ban throughout the 1920s. Although it was not aimed specifically at Mexico, it became the most restrictive legislation affecting Mexicans up to this point. Its provisions called for imprisonment of one year for those caught without documents a second time and a one thousand dollar fine. When William Doak was named secretary of labor in 1930 by President Herbert Hoover, he decided to use this new law against Mexicans. Throughout the country, Department of Labor agents zealously pursued Mexican undocumented immigrants, working hand in hand with local law enforcement officials.

The Great Depression of the 1930s, which dislocated the lives of all Americans, presented the greatest challenge to Mexican immigrants as the collapsed economy left millions of Americans homeless or without jobs. During the worse of the crisis, industrial cities like Detroit were plagued with seventy-five percent unemployment. By 1932 transient camps ringed every city in the country. In order to eat, the inhabitants depended on soup kitchens, if they were lucky, or on foraging among garbage dumps. This terrible ordeal obviously changed the evolution of the Mexican *colonias* (Mexican immigrant communities) as well. Mexicans, so desirable as workers in the previous decade, were now dis-

23. A migrant family of Mexicans with tire trouble, 1936. Photo by Dorothea Lange.

[3] *La Opinión*, February 14, 1928.

[4] *La Opinión*, September 23, 1928.

24. A truckload of Mexican migrants returning to their homes in the Rio Grande Valley, 1939.

charged from their jobs by the thousands and then pressured to leave by community authorities. Between 1929 and 1936 at least six hundred thousand Mexican nationals and their children, many of whom were born in the U.S., returned to Mexico—this represented about one third of the U.S. Mexican population. Economic downturns had been a constant factor in their lives, but nothing compared to the suffering created by this crisis.

Out of work and unable to acquire adequate shelter and food, most Mexican immigrants wanted to return home. But they resented the attitude shown by Americans that they had no right to be in the U.S. In the past, opposition to Mexicans living in the U.S.—from nativists and white workers—had not transformed into successful campaigns to expel them. This was mainly due to powerful employers who were anxious to protect the Mexican influx. But now nativists could do their worst.

The movement to repatriate Mexicans was the most intense in large industrial cities ravaged by unemployment such as Los Angeles, Chicago and Detroit. Similar conditions existed in Texas and Arizona mining communities, where the collapsed market for raw materials forced a drastic curtailment of production. In the industrial Calumet region of Indiana southeast of Chicago, the steel mills in tandem with local governments systematically coerced unemployed Mexican workers and their families to take free train rides back to the border. Relief to the needy in the cities of East Chicago and Gary, both located in Lake County, Indiana, came from various sources, but much of it was controlled by the local government.

The most zealous repatriation campaigns took place in Los Angeles.

In October 1929 Mexican Ambassador Manuel Téllez charged that, in Edinburg, Texas, a jail built for one hundred persons contained more than three hundred fifty Mexicans who were detained mainly for illegal entry. Once, the facility had housed more than four hundred Mexicans, creating such a crisis that the Hidalgo County Grand Jury, made up partially of Mexican Americans, demanded improvement. The jailing and deportations soon brought other defenders from the immigrant and Mexican American communities. When a Department of Labor agent had to pressure Hidalgo County officials to release three hundred Mexicans jailed for vagrancy, *La Prensa* chided that these unfortunates were considered criminals because hopes of finding work in the U.S. were unfulfilled. *El Defensor*, an Hidalgo County newspaper with ties to the League of United Latin American Citizens (LULAC), published a number of exposés on jail conditions, which pressured the Texas Prison Commission to demand renovations. As a result of this scrutiny, overcrowding conditions improved by the beginning of the 1930s.

In Albuquerque during the summer of 1929 Consul Guillermo L. Robinson read in the *State Tribune* that the New Mexico jail population had increased dramatically. Thirty-three persons were in the Santa Fe, Valencia and Los Lunas County jails and twelve were jailed in Bernalillo County, where Albuquerque is located. Suspecting the majority to be Mexican, Robinson toured the jails and, sure enough, thirty of the total were undocumented aliens. They had been treated well, Robinson indicated, but the four-year-old child of a married couple in the Albuquerque lockup was put in an orphanage since the jail did not provide for children—an extremely painful arrangement for both parents, he said. After talking to Mexican American warden Felipe Rubbel, the consul arranged for the child to stay with the mother in jail until the sentence was completed. Robinson himself provided milk and food for the child.

José Anguiano, a steel worker with a growing family who resisted returning, remembered in a 1974 interview how Mexicans were induced to return. He indicated, "A Mexican would go to the North Township

25. *Houston Chronicle* photo of repatriating Mexicans.

As seen above, even before the passage of the 1929 act, Los Angeles law officials conducted vagrancy sweeps to clear Los Angeles streets of unemployed workers, of which Mexicans figured disproportionately. The 1929 restrictions provided Los Angeles officials with another weapon to get rid of Mexicans. Charles P. Visel, Los Angeles County coordinator for unemployment relief, worked hand in hand with federal agents sent to Los Angeles by Secretary of Labor Doak and local Los Angeles police to arrest as many undocumented Mexicans as possible.

Officials knew that, even with beefed-up police manpower, it would be impossible to corral all of the undocumented Mexicans. A strategy was devised to intimidate aliens into leaving on their own by publicizing raids where hundreds of Mexicans were rounded up, regardless of whether or not they carried documents. On February 26, 1931, Los Angeles County deputies and Department of Labor agents took a number of newspapermen on a raid which netted four hundred Mexicans at *la placita*. The next day photographs of manacled Mexican men being led into paddy wagons appeared on the front pages of Los Angeles dailies. It turned out that only a small percentage of the Mexicans harassed in this manner were undocumented.

In 1931 President Hoover implemented the President's Emergency Committee for Employment (PECE), his solution to unemployment. It was no more than a public relations ploy to make people feel good about providing a marginal number of jobs through the private sector. But the PECE in Los Angeles, of which Charles Visel was a member, worked closely with county officials to coordinate the voluntary repatriation of Southern California Mexicans—i.e., those who were not deportable under the 1929 act. In 1931, Visel traveled to Mexico hoping to arrange a program to settle the thousands of Mexicans whom county officials and Visel wanted to repatriate.

The Mexican government did cooperate with various groups in the U.S., including Visel's program in Los Angeles County, that raised funds to send Mexicans to the border by promising to take responsibility for the repatriates once they crossed the border. Unfortunately, the engine of repatriation on the American side was more efficient than that south of the border and resulted in bottlenecks which left thousands of the discarded Mexicans marooned in border towns with little to eat and nowhere to sleep.

CONCLUSION

Historically a relatively generous U.S. immigration policy never met with the approval of Anglo-American nativists. The nativist ideology has not only been at odds with official procedures, but its adherents have often succeeded in influencing Congress to pass restrictive legislation, mainly against the "new immigrants" and Asians. When negative feelings on immigration focused on Mexicans, nativists in the West did not have the same power to restrict their entry. While, for the average American, Mexicans were seen as undesirables, the U.S. government pressed for their entry to fill labor needs. It was not until the collapse of the economy at the end of the 1920s that U.S. officials fell in step with general opinion and passed the 1929 immigration law, which made undocumented immigration a felony violation.

This law intensified the "illegal alien" notion, and the image became attached to Mexicans.

The Mexican government and Mexican Americans also became crucial players in the politics of immigration. Mexico did not want emigration during most of this period, but the economic climate was always so poor that at times it even encouraged the outflow. Significantly, restrictive legislation against Mexicans was not as severe or as effective as that against Asians and eastern and southern Europeans. Nonetheless, the lack of jobs resulted in the largest mass exodus in history of any one group from this country.

The zest and quickness with which Americans sent undocumented or destitute Mexicans packing back to their home country demonstrates that they were seen as a commodity that could be thrown out into a human junk heap once it was no longer of use. No matter that most Mexicans might have initially welcomed repatriation, many left because of the pressure brought to bear by those who wanted to rid their communities of Mexicans. In the process, the rights of many U.S.-born Mexican Americans—usually the children of Mexican nationals being returned—were not taken into consideration. Many Mexicans who were

Relief Center to get his weekly commodities and they would tell him, 'This is the last time we will help you, Sr. So and So, but we can give you a train ticket for you and your family or buy tires and give you gasoline for your truck so that you can go back to the border.'"[5]

The Indiana Harbor Welfare Committee, a private group that provided relief for unemployed workers and their families, cosponsored the American Legion effort. According to the *Calumet News* (March 21, 1930), its chairman, Maurice E. Crites, a Superior Court judge, opposed efforts by the Immigrant Protective League and local Spanish-language newspapers to help Mexicans file for naturalization. He told East Chicago high school students in 1930 that he doubted the ability of foreigners, especially Mexicans, to be good citizens since they were only "one-half American."

[5] Interview with José Anguiano, East Chicago, September 14, 1974.

tempted to take advantage of the free transportation did not do so because of their children who knew no other home except the U.S.

The promises to accommodate the repatriates made by Mexican presidents Emilio Portes Gil (1928-1930), Pascual Ortiz Rubio (1930-1932) and Abelardo Rodríguez (1932-1934) did not materialize. These were former revolutionaries, hand-picked by the now-conservative former president, Plutarco Elías Calles, as his yes men. They slowed down social reform such as land redistribution and concessions to labor. The burden of helping the economic refugees from the U.S. was placed on state governments and on private charities. Both sources of aid turned out to be woefully inadequate. For the thousands of Mexicans fleeing the severe crisis in the U.S., the hope that their government would help them, a fantasy promoted by eager Americans in charge of repatriation, turned out to be a cruel hoax.

CHAPTER FOUR

In Defense of *México Lindo*

26. An Alianza Hispano Americana parade in Tucson, Arizona.

Nationalism, with hints of separatism, was a hallmark of the Chicano Movement. Rodolfo "Corky" Gonzales, founder of Denver's Crusade for Justice, advanced Chicano nationalism as the central agenda of the Chicano Movement—it would lead to self-determination, he preached.

> Nationalism exists. . . but until now, it hasn't been formed into an image people can see. Until now it has been a dream. . . . [N]ationalism is the key to our people liberating themselves. I am a revolutionary. . . because erecting life amid death is a revolutionary act. . . . We are an awakening people, an emerging nation, a new breed.[1]

According to the *movimiento* canon, the Mexican American generation of the 1930s, 1940s and 1950s, in league with Anglos bent on cultural genocide, cast Mexican culture aside, roots and all, leaving only a barren field for the Chicano generation. Gonzales once said that his schooling gave him cultural amnesia: it led to his forgetting Spanish and other Mexican attributes. But Gonzales was probably unaware of how intensely cultural nationalism had permeated U.S.-Mexican communities through immigration at the turn of the century. As *movimiento* activists embraced cultural nationalism, they exalted *mestizaje* (Indian and Spanish mixture) and borrowed from the pantheon of Mexican patriotic symbols as did their immigrant grandfathers and grandmothers at the turn of the century.

In his pronouncement Gonzales was correct in stating that nationalism can lead, if not to complete liberation, to defense. The immigrants often employed the unity created by identification with *lo mexicano* to protect themselves. And to the immigrants, nationalism represented more than culture. It was truly based on nationhood: they were Mexicans from Mexico. And they lived in what they called *El México de afuera* (Mexico abroad). To Chicanos, however, the basis for their nationalism remained elusive. How were they to

forge a nation? *Movimiento* participants reconciled themselves to expounding a profuse ethnic pride and cultural affirmation, which was called "cultural nationalism," while still expecting the constitutional rights of U.S. citizens.

THE RISE OF *MÉXICO LINDO*

With massive immigration, the growing presence of Mexicans in the U.S. created large *colonias* (colonies) in urban centers. The Mexican ambiance had been transplanted to such an extent that these little Mexicos came to be seen as *el México de afuera*. Mainly conservative, middle-class refugees fleeing the Revolution engaged in a *México Lindo* (pretty Mexico) identity that was crafted from the chart of homeland nationalism. The ideology spread quickly because it contained symbols with which few Mexicans could quarrel—primarily patriotic icons, the Spanish language and the Catholic religion. These emblems came from a nationalistic surge evident in Mexico during the late Porfiriato, reaching a crescendo in the years after the Revolution. Central to the ideology was a symbolic indigenism that had also evolved during the Porfiriato. The Chicano Movement especially tapped this aspect of the *México Lindo* blueprint.

This nationalism intensified in the immigrant *colonias* that emerged from the 1890s to the 1920s in response to intense deprivation of civil rights, police brutality, segregation, abuse in the workplace and general rejection from the mainstream community. No matter how long the immigrants lived in the U.S., the pain from these violations was not alleviated by initial adaptive postures such as mutual aid, religiosity, cultural reinforcement or the notion that soon they would be back in Mexico. Mexicans mobilized community resources for the purposes of self-defense, but only after an immigrant nationalism became pervasive and cut across regional and class divisions within the *colonias*.

The political power and experience amassed

---

[1] Quoted in Carlos Muñoz, *Youth, Identity, Power: The Chicano Movement* (London: Verso, 1989), p. 52.

27. Officers of the Sociedad Patríotica Juárez (Juárez Patriotic Society) pose for a photo at one of the organization's events in Los Angeles, 1877.

by Southwest Mexicans, if it helped immigrants at all, did so mainly in older Hispanic regions to which few Mexican immigrants were attracted.

Unfortunately, twentieth-century modernization, which reduced the value of the Mexican's utility as brute immigrant labor, also eroded the understanding that had been worked out by both ethnic groups in the nineteenth century.

"Greenhorn" immigrants encountered more difficulty in dealing with the American system than their settled Southwest brethren. As thousands of Mexicans entered the country after the 1890s, generally the only white Americans who tolerated the immigrants were employers who saw them as a necessary evil, to be pressured to return home when they were no longer needed. But by the 1920s the rapidly increasing Mexican population in the U.S. caught Anglo Americans and their institutions off guard.

It became clear to Americans that the system of segregation employed for Blacks was more appropriate for newcomer Mexicans than the arrangement which had evolved with the older Hispanic population. Although the "separate-but-equal" policy used on African Americans to keep them within a rigid web of control did not apply to Mexicans, laws regarding vagrancy, weapons control, alcohol, drug use and smuggling were largely designed to control Mexican immigrant behavior. Mexicans were also marginalized and kept powerless by the use of segregated schools, private-sector housing and labor segmentation (reserving the worst jobs for Mexicans). It rarely

The term *México Lindo* was popularized in the immigrant song, *México Lindo* (Pretty Mexico), which was recorded by Mexico's most cherished popular singer of this century, Jorge Negrete. The song was made all the more poignant because it seemed to be a self-fulfilling prophecy for Negrete, who actually died in the U.S. at a Los Angeles hospital. Note the lyrics.

Voz de la guitarra mía	As the morning awakens
Al despetar la mañana	My guitar beckons to me
Quiero cantar la alegría	I want to sing my joy
¡De mi tierra mexicana!	Of my Mexican land!
México lindo y querido	Pretty and beloved Mexico
Si muero lejos de ti	If I die far from your soil
Que digan que estoy dormido	Say that I am asleep
Y que me traigan aquí	And bring me back to thee

28. Orquesta Típica, Houston, Texas, ca. 1927.

occurred to U.S. citizens that Mexicans might be eligible for the constitutional rights that Americans held so dearly and protected zealously.

THE SPREAD OF *MÉXICO LINDO* NATIONALISM

An extensive interimmigrant network made up of businessmen, editors of newspapers, Mexican consulates and even theatrical companies helped spread the Mexican exile nationalism throughout the U.S. The most central institution of all, however, in solidifying the immigrant community and its identity was the mutual aid society, an association that often offered a center or hall for cultural activities, schooling, health services, insurance and general protection. In order to achieve this exile nationalism, divisions created

by regional origins in Mexico, class and even race had to be bridged. Class discord, for example, blocked immigrant solidarity, usually because the Mexican immigrant upper class often sought to distance itself from poorer compatriots. Sometimes disdain for the lower classes was expressed in racist terms. A middle-class Mexican woman told a researcher in Chicago during the 1920s, "The people from old Mexico here disgrace the real Mexicans. . . . the people that are here were either servants or mountain Indians."[2]

Nevertheless, middle-class refugees who did not fraternize with the working classes back home were moved do so because they witnessed first-hand the mistreatment of poorer compatriots in the U.S. A Chicago Mexican businessman told Paul Schuster Taylor, a University of California economist who researched Mexican *colonias*

[2] F. Arturo Rosales, "Mexicans, Interethnic Violence, and Crime in the Chicago Area During the 1920s and 1930s: The Struggle to Achieve Ethnic Consciousness," *Perspectives in Mexican American Studies* 2 (1989), p. 63.

29. Club Deportivo Azteca, Houston, Texas, ca. 1927.

"Fiestas Patrias" on September 16, the Mexican independence celebration, reaffirmed ties to the homeland and strengthened a mutual ethnic bond in the *colonias*. In Arizona La Junta Patriótica Mexicana in Litchfield held its annual Mexican independence day celebration in 1928. Many young people participated in *desfiles* (parades) made up of *carros alegóricos* (floats), which they had decorated. Mercedes García de Rosales, a girl of fifteen then, remembers riding in one decorated as a ship, called "Ship of Continents." A number of girls rode on the float, each one depicting a continent in a *declamación* (poetic speech). Mercedes was American and still remembers by heart the *declamación* she memorized for the event. "My father was very proud of me. He was very patriotic and wanted to go back to Mexico someday, but he died here."[3] After the parade, the program featured live music, speeches and an allegorical play in which young girls acted out the roles of Mexico, Spain and the pre-Columbian Indian nation.

throughout the country in the 1920s, that he refused a partnership offer from a non-Mexican because of disparaging views of lower-class Mexicans held by the would-be partner. In another Taylor interview, a Mexican said that, during Mexican patriotic celebrations in Chicago, he might be rubbing shoulders with a Mexican prostitute because, on that day, "we forget it."

Immigrants from the same areas in Mexico tended to concentrate in the same immigrant communities in the U.S. and would at first look with some misapprehension at compatriots from other regions. As they duplicated their hometown associations, they created barrios with names like *el michoacanito* (little Michoacán), as a one-block area of East Chicago was known. So many inhabitants in the Argentine, Kansas, *colonia* came from Tangacícuaro, Michoacán, that they were called *Tangas*. The sobriquet *Chihuahuita* graced El Paso, Texas, and Morenci, Arizona, barrios. Because of the number of *sonorenses* that lived there, the barrio on the outskirts of the mining town of Ray, Arizona, became known as Sonora while the neighboring community where Spaniards

[3] Interview with Mercedes García de Rosales by author, Tucson, Arizona, October 15, 1991.

lived was called Barcelona. Residents named one entire hillside barrio in Bisbee, Arizona, a mining town built on hills and crags, Zacatecas, after their home state in Mexico. *México Lindo* ideology, however, helped reduce regional allegiances that were so divisive once immigrants from all over Mexico came together. This was especially true when, as a *México de afuera*, they could act collectively. For example, raising funds to help compatriots victimized by earthquakes or floods was common. During major flooding in the Veracruz-Puebla region in 1919, a campaign in U.S. *colonias* netted $46,539 to aid flood victims. In Miami, Arizona, alone, hard-pressed immigrants raised $2,000 for the campaign.

Mexicans accepted an outsider role in American society, and in this respect they differed from their Mexican American children of later years who resorted to a rhetoric of equal rights under the Constitution. Defense activity was mainly designed to make the *temporary* home of immigrants in the U.S. tolerable. The image of *México Lindo* beckoned to them; indeed, most intended to return to Mexico as soon as they made enough money or when conditions wrought by the bloody revolution back home stabilized. Even if their sojourn was temporary, however, Mexicans wanted to be treated with dignity and respect.

ANTIDEFAMATION

Mexican immigrants built up their own nationalistic infrastructure for mobilization and defense, especially in areas outside of old Southwest Hispanic centers. Many outbreaks of nationalism were often spontaneous responses to specific events. The 1914 Veracruz invasion and the 1916 Pershing Expedition that crossed the Rio Grande into Chihuahua to punish Pancho Villa for the raid on Columbus, New Mexico, elicited protests and talk of armed insurrection among immigrants. At a point when Mexico and the U.S. were on the verge of war, Arizona Senator Henry Ashurd proposed annexing Baja California. Mexican officials as well as immigrants reacted furiously, and organizations and newspapers inveighed against the proposition. An Arizona organization called La Asamblea General (The General Assembly) was even started specifically to protest the incident.

Defamation of Mexico in the nascent cinema during World War I, when Americans suspected Mexico of collaborating with the Axis powers, also drew fire from Mexicans in the U.S. During 1918, Francisco Chapa, publisher of *El Imparcial de Texas*, editorialized against denigrating images in contemporary films and led a delegation to Austin to lodge a protest with Governor W. P. Hobby about the screening of these movies in Texas. In response Hobby proclaimed a ban on films that cast Mexicans in a bad light. In August 1919 Los Angeles's short-lived *La Prensa* editorialized against what it called gross stereotyping of Mexicans in films, newspapers and books. That same year Tucson's *El Mosquito* launched a campaign to ban anti-Mexican films at the Tucson Opera House because respectable Mexican families found them offensive.

The campaign continued into the 1920s as well. San Francisco's *Hispano América* proudly announced in May 1923 that Brazilian customs officials agreed to ban negative movies about Mexico. In 1928 Los Angeles's *La Opinión* endorsed a move by the Mexican government to prohibit these offensive films in Mexico. Such campaigns eventually had a desired effect. The California film industry, in order not to jeopardize expanding Latin American and Mexican markets, toned down negative portrayals of Mexicans. Despite these concessions, negative film portrayals would continue and would be one of the targets of attack during the Chicano Movement.

Immigrant leaders routinely objected to racist literature and negative journalism as well. Former Texas Governor James E. Ferguson penned a particularly vitriolic broadside in his *Ferguson Forum* during November of 1920, in which he charged that Mexicans were inferior to Negroes and that Mexico had contributed nothing to civilization. Alonso L. Perales, who like Chapa was a Mexican American political activist and World War I veteran, wrote Ferguson denouncing his diatribe, saying he defended Texas Mexicans and immigrants alike. *El Imparcial de Texas*, in publishing Perales's letter, characterized him as an "American" who understood and loved Mexican people.

Similar efforts were made outside of Texas. In the fall of 1926 the Los Angeles City Council threatened to exclude businesses from obtaining city contracts if they hired noncitizens. At this point a recession sparked unemployment and anti-Mexican sentiment among white workers. *La Opinión* accused the American Federation of Labor of pressing for this code but added that the sentiment was not representative of all Americans. G. Figueroa del Valle, an official at the Bank of Italy, told the newspaper that employers and Californians in general knew the extent to which the Mexican worker contributed to the state's prosperity. As it turned out, the city council failed to act on the law.

Inversely, Anglo Americans who publicly countered anti-Mexican sentiment were lauded by the immigrant community. When historian Amos Hershey gave a lecture on Mexican history at a local forum in March of 1928, *La Opinión* commended the Indiana University professor for giving a "positive lesson" on Mexico. At this point the Los Angeles *colonia* was miffed over a local white teacher's comment to her Mexican students that Mexican leaders were all thieves. Whether or not these antidefamation campaigns achieved the desired objectives is not relevant here. That immigrant leaders rose up to protest these indignities served to keep Mexicans vigilant and ready to organize defenses against the more concrete abuses shown below.

INFORMAL DEFENSE AGAINST LEGAL ABUSES

Another pressing issue in the early *colonias* was abuse of civil rights in the judicial system. This provoked informal resistance such as withholding information from the police or even intervening directly to prevent arrests of countrymen. In 1908 two Mexicans beat Los Angeles officers to stop them from arresting a drunken female *paisana*. In the Los Angeles *placita* during May of 1914 one hundred Mexicans rioted to foil a compatriot's arrest during a labor rally. That same year in December one hundred fifty Mexicans attacked the Oakville, Texas, jail upon learning that white citizens had threatened to lynch Ysidro González

and Francisco Sánchez. In Elko, Nevada, during March 1925 a mob besieged the local jail in order to lynch Guadalupe Acosta, who had confessed to the shooting death of a policeman. About seventy-five armed Mexicans surrounded the jail and prevented the lynching.

Mexicans also challenged police hegemony by resisting arrest. So intense was police abuse that, in the killing of a policeman by a Mexican during an arrest situation, compatriots generally interpreted the incident as self-defense and stood by the cop killers. Most informal defense efforts by Mexicans in the judicial system were less dramatic, however. Mexicans resorted to spontaneous efforts in *colonias* too small or young to have immigrant organizations. During 1913 the Mexican community in Taylor, Texas, suspecting that the local sheriff had framed and jailed a transient Mexican couple for theft, collected $21.50 for their bail.

FORMAL LEGAL DEFENSE

Irrespective of these informal efforts at defense, only the organizations or Mexican consuls could muster the necessary resources to sustain successful campaigns that protected civil rights. During the Revolution itself when the Mexican diplomatic service did not give much priority to immigrant protection, Mexicans found it difficult to depend on consuls. Immigrant societies—normally oriented towards mutual aid, patriotism and recreation—stepped into the breach and added protection to their agenda. Still other organizations were founded expressly for defense purposes. This process was more apparent in Texas, which by 1910 had more than sixty-five percent of the Mexican immigrant population.

Texas Mexicans had maintained some political and economic self-determination in the nineteenth century, a leverage that weakened as modernization changed the face of Texas economic and race relations. Inability to counter justice abuses such as lynchings sadly demonstrated this lack of influence. For example, in June of 1911 white vigilantes lynched Antonio Gómez, a fourteen-year-old Mexican, after he stabbed a

German-American grocer who tried to evict him from his store. The Orden de Caballeros de Honor (The Order of the Knights of Honor) and a number of other Mexican organizations protested the incident, but to their dismay local authorities did nothing to punish participants in this mob action.

Such mistreatment served to intensify initiatives to defend civil rights. Houston Mexicans organized in January of 1910 "a society for self-protection in the courts," according to the *Houston Chronicle*. Similarly, in San Antonio, one hundred Mexicans started La Agrupación Protectora Mexicana (The Mexican Protective League) in 1911 to provide "legal protection for its members whenever they faced Anglo-perpetuated violence or illegal dispossession of their property."[4]

In Houston such leaders as Mexican school teacher J. J. Mercado started a chapter of the Agrupación. The group often worked with the Mexican consul to ameliorate grievances Mexicans had towards employers, such as not receiving compensation for work-related injuries.

In 1911 one of the first major attempts to organize statewide resulted in El Primer Congreso Mexicanista (The First Mexicanist Congress). A principal organizer of the Congreso was Nicasio Idar, the influential editor of Laredo's *La Crónica*. J. J. Mercado and members of the Houston Agrupación, along with "four-hundred Mexican leaders—journalists, school teachers, and mutual aid society representatives—gathered in Laredo in 1911 to draft some plan of action."[5] Land ownership issues, school segregation, lynchings, police brutality and capital punishment predominated as the major issues of discussion. The Gómez lynching and the questionable death sentencing of another youth, León Cárdenas Martínez, had occurred just a few months before the conference started.

Since two major agenda items at the

30. *La Crónica* newspaper, Laredo, Texas.

Congress were lynchings and unjust sentencing, these recent events fueled the resolve of the participants. It is unclear if the lot of Texas Mexicans changed because of this historic meeting, but certainly it became a building block for future mobilization.

Organizing appears early in Arizona as well because, like Texas, the state absorbed the initial immigration waves from Mexico. Carlos Velasco, editor of *El Fronterizo,* had attempted to start El Centro Radical Mexicano (The Mexican Radical Center) in Tucson as early as the 1880s. The orga-

[4] Arnoldo De León, *Mexican Americans in Texas: A Brief History* (Arlington Heights, Illinois: Harlan Davidson, 1993), p. 38.

[5] David Montejano, *Anglos and Mexicans in the Making of Texas, 1836-1896* (Austin: University of Texas Press, 1987), p. 116.

nization's main objective was to ameliorate problems that Mexicans encountered with the Tucson police. Southern Arizona at this point was attracting thousands of Mexican immigrants to lay track for the Southern Pacific Railroad and to work in the industries spurred by the new transportation system.

La Alianza Hispano Americana (The Hispanic American Alliance), which began in Tucson in 1894 as a mutual aid society and political organization, spread throughout the Southwest and by the 1920s had accumulated a respectable record in protecting civil rights for Mexicans. La Alianza, as it became known, joined other associations in efforts to save Mexicans condemned to the gallows. When one of its members was accused of killing the man who impregnated his daughter, the organization raised funds to defend him.

Organized during 1914 in Phoenix to deal with violations of civil rights and labor abuse, another organization, La Liga Protectora Latina (The Latin Protective League), became a groundbreaking protection organization. Protesting legislation which would prohibit non-English speakers from working in the Arizona mines became a major issue for the group. The Arizona Legislature threatened to institute this prohibition for four years, but opposition from Arizona Mexicans helped prevent the passage of any such law. As in La Alianza, defending Mexicans in the justice system became La Liga's priority as well. Chapters from both organizations were founded in Southern California, where they also became important vehicles for political mobilization.

In Los Angeles, which saw the most rapid increase of Mexicans between 1915 and 1925, defense organizations quickly appeared. La Liga Protectora Mexicana (The Mexican Protective League) and La Confederación de Sociedades Mexicanas (The Federation of Mexican Societies), for example, pursued legal rights issues and kept lawyers on retainer for that purpose. These groups soon articulated an opposition to capital punishment as the number of Mexicans sentenced to the gallows increased.

When the Los Angeles City Council tried to ban Mexicans from city jobs during the 1926

recession, Arturo Chacel, "Supreme Organizer" of La Liga Protectora Latina, boasted that La Liga lawyers would bring suit if the code passed. Los Angeles Protestant-based organizations, besides providing recreation and other services to Mexicans, also extended legal aid.

During the 1920s Dr. E.M. Seen, a Mexican-born and Mexican-educated minister who ran the Plaza Methodist-Episcopal Social Service Center, often visited jails and attempted to help accused Mexicans obtain legal advice.

Houston's Mexican immigrant population increased more during the 1920s than San Antonio's—five times from 1910 to the mid-twenties. As a result, self-defense consciousness proliferated, prompting the formation of the Asamblea Mexicana (Mexican Assembly) in 1924 by businessmen led by Fernando Salas and

31. Carlos Velasco, founder of the Alianza Hispano Americana and editor of *El Fronterizo* newspaper, 1882.

Frank Gibler, a former U.S. consul married to a Mexican woman. Its prime objective was to help immigrants who had been jailed unjustly. During 1928 the group pressured the city to suspend a police sergeant for jailing, without providing medical attention, a young Mexican who had been in an auto accident. At least five Mexicans obtained their releases that same year, thanks to Asamblea efforts.

Systematic justice abuses affected Mexican communities more in the Midwest than in the Southwest because Mexicans were newer there and were made up of a larger proportion of young single men whose lifestyles made them vulnerable to negative contact with the police. Based primarily in Kansas, Missouri, Illinois and Michigan, the *colonias* had a majority of newly arrived inhabitants from central Mexico who lacked experience with the American system. This is evidenced by a belated appearance of immigrant institutions, which as late as 1920 barely began to acquire a maturity evident in Texas and Arizona for a longer time.

In Chicago, where the Mexican arrest rate in the 1920s was higher than in southwestern communities, Mexicans launched the most intensive crusades to help compatriots in trouble with the law. An umbrella organization for thirty-five Chicago mutual aid societies, La Confederación de Sociedades Mexicanas de los Estados Unidos de America (The Federation of Mexican Societies in USA), was founded on March 30, 1925. It had the following aims, according to José Amaro González in his study of Mexican mutual aid societies: 1) helping new arrivals to the cities to find a place to stay, 2) providing job referrals, 3) providing defense funds to help Mexicans before the courts, 4) making available emergency loans from the credit union 5) combating racial discrimination in public places.[6] La Confederación did not survive long, but cooperation between organizations continued.

By the early 1930s the return of unemployed Mexicans to Mexico crippled the ability of Mexican communities in the U.S. to sustain organizations. In addition, a distinct Mexican American (not Mexican national) ideological thrust, reflecting the demographic character of Mexican-origin communities, was replacing the *México Lindo* orientation. Many scholars have pointed to the emergence of the League of United Latin American Citizens (LULAC) in Texas as emblematic of Mexican Americanization, a process that was well underway in Mexican communities elsewhere as well.

DEFENSE OF POLITICAL REFUGEES

Mobilization to defend Mexicans arrested for political activity was frequent in this era. It was an activity that provided experience for erecting barriers against other kinds of abuses. U.S. officials regularly arrested revolutionaries and other activists for violating neutrality laws, for border banditry, for smuggling arms into Mexico and for labor union activity. The most persecuted activists were Partido Liberal Mexicano (PLM) members whom authorities pursued even before the Revolution. In January of 1908, for example, when federal agents in San Antonio jailed PLM organizer Manuel Sarabia for neutrality laws violations, sympathizers in that city clamored for his release. More well-known are the actions taken against Ricardo Flores Magón and his brother, Enrique. The brothers had been in exile from Mexico since 1903 while U.S. federal agents and Pinkerton detectives hired by Porfirian diplomats pursued them hotly. The brothers, the most active of the PLM revolutionaries, published *Regeneración*, a newspaper which delivered a strong radical message of worker liberation to Mexicans in both Mexico and the U.S.

In 1910 when the new Arizona Territorial Prison in Florence opened, officials had transferred most of the prisoners from the old Yuma facility during the previous two years. Among those moved were Partido Liberal Mexicano members Ricardo Flores Magón, Librado Rivera

---

[6] José Amaro González, *Mutual Aid for Survival: The Case of the Mexican American* (Malabar, Florida: Robert E. Krieger Publishing Company, 1983), p. 75.

32. *Regeneración*, the Flores Magón newspaper.

and Antonio Villarreal, who were all convicted in Arizona for violating neutrality laws. The trio was received at Yuma in May of 1909 and immediately taken to the more secure Florence institution. After their release Ricardo and his followers remained in the U.S. and continued to advocate radical unionization measures among Mexican workers; authorities pursued Ricardo until he was again jailed in 1918 at Fort Leavenworth for sedition. At this time Americans were thoroughly convinced that Mexicans were in cahoots with Germans. Ricardo Flores Magón died in prison, allegedly from a heart attack, but his comrades thought he had been strangled by a prison guard.

For years Texas governors were pressured to release *los mártires de Texas* (the Texas martyrs), PLM members led by Jesús Rangel who were jailed at Perry's Landing after killing a deputy sheriff as they crossed border in 1913 to join revolutionary *zapatistas*. The instigation came mainly from immigrant sympathizers, but it included a rare diplomatic foray by Emiliano Zapata, who through the Brazilian Embassy pleaded for Rangel's release, attesting that "he is an honorable man and friend of the Revolution."[7] It was not until 1926 that Governor Miriam "Ma"

Ferguson acceded to granting the *mártires* their freedom. In 1921 La Agrupación Socialista (The Socialist Group) in El Paso pressed for discharge of PLM members imprisoned at Fort Leavenworth, including Ricardo Flores Magón and other stalwarts such as Juan Cabral. Support, centered in San Antonio, succeeded in freeing Emilio Vásquez Gómez, a perennial opponent of numerous revolutionary governments, after he was charged with violation of neutrality laws in 1923. His backers accused President Álvaro Obregón of orchestrating the incident by pressuring U.S. authorities to arrest the political refugees.

The experience gained by helping defend imprisoned exiles was important as immigrants attempted more regular defense activities in the U.S. legal system. In the spring of 1912 Dr. J. B. Ruffo, chief surgeon in Francisco I. Madero's army, defected to Pascual Orozco in the anti-Madero rebellion. When Orozco's fortunes declined, Ruffo fled to the U.S. and in October of 1912 was recruiting support for the rebels in Arizona. At the behest of Phoenix Consul Francisco Olivares, he was arrested in Tucson and jailed. Ruffo's imprisonment prompted the

[7] Cardoso de Oliveira, Brazilian Embassy, to William S. Bryan, secretary of state, January 25, 1915, National Archives, Record Group 59, 311.1221, R16.

founding in Phoenix of La Liga Protectora de Refugiados (The Refugee Protection League) by Pedro de la Lama and others who two years later started La Liga Protectora Latina (The Latin Protective League). The 1912 group, however, which also supported Sonoran anti-Madero rebels, explicitly protected refugees.

Opposition to President Plutarco Elías Calles's anticlericalism was extensive among Mexicans in the U.S. In 1927 Francisco García y Alva, publisher of Los Angeles's *El Heraldo de México*, joined *Hispano América* editor Julio G. Arce in San Francisco and Dr. José I. Trejo of Oakland to help free General Enrique Roque Estrada and his supporters, who had been arrested by U.S. officials in San Diego during September of 1926. Estrada, a former Mexican cabinet member in Álvaro Obregón's administration, was recruiting supporters for the *cristero* movement. In March of 1928 *La Opinión* protested the visit of Moisés Sáenz, Mexico's secretary of education and a Protestant minister. Because he came under YMCA auspices, conservative expatriates felt he served as a Protestant propagandist.

CRUSADES AGAINST CAPITAL PUNISHMENT

The immigrant community was convinced discrimination existed in sentencing Mexicans to capital punishment. As a consequence, saving Mexicans became an emotionally charged issue that provoked U.S. Mexicans to expend prodigious amounts of political energy. There were so many efforts in the early immigrant era to save Mexicans from execution that this period could be classified as the "clemency movement" era. To be sure, not every condemned Mexican received community support. Executions were elevated to a *cause célèbre* if it seemed that an injustice had been committed and if the incident caught the attention of publicists within the immigrant community.

These efforts transcended the single motive of saving a life, however. For *colonia* members, success in these crusades measured its value within a larger community, which constantly rejected them. Even if they lost, forcing officials to pay attention to their plight provided a sense of

empowerment and affirmed their right to live in the U.S. When they succeeded in saving a compatriot from the gallows, this affirmation achieved even greater prominence. This kind of organizing was a precursor to many "class-action" activities in civil rights in later decades and particularly during the Chicano Movement.

At the end of 1926 four Mexicans were sentenced to die at San Quentin. The year had been a most difficult one for Mexicans because of a severe agricultural crisis which threw thousands of Mexicans out of work. Deportations abounded, and in September the air was rife with rumors that the Los Angeles City Council would not allow city contractors to hire foreigners. A spokesman for the Confederación de Sociedes Mexicanas announced that the organization had retained lawyers and was prepared to confront this social affront and economic threat. The city ordinance, which was supported by the California Federation of Labor, was never passed, but the Mexican community was alienated. The threat coincided with elaborate efforts to save the four Mexicans from the gallows, and in the end both issues blended into one.

For each Mexican saved from the death penalty, however, about two were executed, despite the pressure put on state officials to provide commutations. Discrimination in assessing death penalties was not as blatant for Mexicans as it was for Blacks, however. Executions declined considerably after 1925, suggesting that clemency campaigns were successful and that anti-Mexican feelings were not as intensive as during the period of revolution in Mexico. The decline is also attributable to changing demographic patterns—e.g,, in the adult proportion of the Mexican-origin population born in Mexico, which was the most prone to getting into trouble with the law. Nonetheless, Mexicans also became more adept at obtaining clemency as their *colonias* matured.

SPANISH-LANGUAGE PRESS AND DEFENSE

Spanish-language newspapers were in the forefront of the clemency campaigns, and they encouraged readers to help Mexicans in trouble with the law or to obtain commutations for condemned compatriots. At times publications explained immigration laws or warned readers against violating vagrancy laws, carrying weapons or consuming alcohol during Prohibition. A regular feature of *El Imparcial de Texas* was a La Liga Protectora Mexicana column that counseled on legal matters. Veracruz native Santiago Lerdo fled to the U.S. because he was a journalist critic of Díaz. He returned to Mexico to join the Revolution in 1911, only to be jailed and exiled again when Huerta came to power. In 1927 Lerdo was in Nogales, Arizona, where he published a newspaper with a major objective of ameliorating mistreatment of immigrants in the justice system.

Spanish-language newspapers in large cities were the most effective because they linked campaigns nationally and even internationally through informal mail links that publishers kept throughout the U.S. and Mexico. Communication was enhanced because practically all the editors were members of the Congress of the Latin American Press. In Los Angeles, Juan de Heras, editor of *El Heraldo de México*, the first major Spanish-language daily in California, consistently supported celebrated cases such as those of Aurelio Pompa and Juan Reyna. The state of California executed Pompa in 1924 for killing his Anglo foreman in Los Angeles in spite of a rigorous defense campaign by the Mexican government and the immi-

EXECUTIONS IN ARIZONA, CALIFORNIA, NEW MEXICO AND TEXAS
1836-1935

	WHITE	MEXICAN	BLACK	INDIAN	ASIAN	
Before 1871	16	22	16	14	3	
1871-1875	16	8	10	0	0	
1876-1880	21	7	22	0	2	
1881-1885	17	12	19	6	0	
1886-1890	16	13	19	4	1	
1891-1895	22	6	35	0	2	
1896-1900	28	17	35	1	3	
TOTAL	136	85	156	25	11	= 413
PERCENTAGE	32.9	20.6	37.8	6.1	2.6	
1901-1905	27	18	18	3	1	
1906-1910	15	11	32	1	1	
1911-1915	19	11	27	1	1	
1916-1920	17	15	13	1	5	
1921-1925	28	23	33	0	0	
1926-1930	34	7	33	0	0	
1931-1935	43	8	33	0	0	
TOTAL	183	93	189	6	8	= 479
PERCENTAGE	38.2	19.4	39.5	1.3	1.6	

SOURCE: M. Watt Espy and John Ortiz Smykla, *Executions in the United States, 1608-1987: The Espy File* (Ann Arbor: Inter-University Consortium for Political and Social Research, 1990), Machine Readable Data File, 8541.

grant community. Reyna killed a policeman in Los Angeles, but because of extensive efforts, he received a light sentence. When Reyna was found dead in his San Quentin cell, the Mexican community suspected foul play.

One family, the Lozanos, owned newspapers in the two largest Mexican concentrations—*La Prensa* in San Antonio and *La Opinión* in Los Angeles. As a consequence, they shared articles and editorials oriented to justice issues. But one of the most effective editors was *El Imparcial de Texas*'s Francisco Chapa, not because of his militancy, but because he successfully cultivated Anglo connections. More than any of the other leaders discussed here, Chapa symbolized the ability of more settled immigrants to assist the newly arrived. His newspaper advocated that Mexicans vote and become involved in civil rights issues, and Chapa himself served as a broker between Anglo politicians and Texas Mexicans.

As newspaper publishers supported Mexicans facing death, they advanced anti-capital punishment philosophies, a position embraced among the immigrant intelligentsia across the country, regardless of ideology. Jesús Franco, publisher of Phoenix's *El Sol* in the 1930s, was Arizona correspondent for El Paso's *La Patria* in the 1920s. He crusaded on behalf of Mexicans accused of crimes, not only as a journalist but also as a member of the Phoenix Comisión Honorífica Mexicana (Mexican Honorary Commission), La Cruz Azul (Blue Cross) and Woodsmen of the World.

Another Arizona journalist crusader was Pedro de la Lama, a La Liga Protectora Latina founder as well as publisher of numerous newspapers in Phoenix, including the vitriolic *Justicia*. He came from Veracruz during the late nineteenth century, first to Solomonville, a mining community, and then to Phoenix. By his own account, because he opposed the U.S. war with Spain, he was almost lynched. During the Mexican Revolution he sided with the reaction— first with the opportunistic Pascual Orozco when the latter turned against Madero in 1913 and then with various exiled dissidents in the 1920s.

One of the most persistent critics of capital punishment was Julio Arce, publisher of San Francisco's *Hispano América*, also known by his pen name, Jorge Ulica. As editor of two Guadalajara dailies, he had

33. Julio G. Arce, writer and publisher of *Hispano América*.

railed against Madero and his heir, Carranza. He consequently was forced to flee his native Jalisco for San Francisco in 1915. A prolific writer, Arce often satirized American culture and its effects on Mexican immigrants. More importantly he directed his pen at criticizing the justice system's effect on Mexican immigrants.

According to Arce, Mexicans were often framed for capital murder because police, anxious to convict, manipulated trial proceedings. In addition, he charged authorities with not providing competent interpreters for Mexican immigrants. As he put it, "We must exhaust all our resources to assure that Mexicans who are accused of crimes are provided with opportune defense" (trans-

34. Francisco Moreno, publisher of *El Tucsonense*.

lated by author).[8] Arce lamented that crusades began only after accused men were sentenced to death when the only hope became that the indifferent state functionaries would provide clemency. Arce suggested to family members, friends and compatriots of accused Mexicans to contact immediately the Mexican consul and newspapers to ensure a competent and timely defense.

There were other crusading journalists. One was Daniel Venegas, president of Los Angeles's La Confederación de Sociedades Mexicanas. A journalist, a businessman and a novelist, Venegas also served as an articulate figure in defense of Mexicans whom the community felt were unjustly treated. Antonio Redondo, the Los Angeles correspondent for *El Tucsonense*, moved by the inordinate number of 1920s executions of Mexicans in California, employed classic eighteenth- and nineteenth-century

35. Daniel Venegas.

French and English arguments against capital punishment, replete with compelling moralistic arguments against taking someone's life. Another articulate defender was Rodolfo Uranga, who through his *La Opinión* daily column demonstrated marked sympathy for imprisoned Mexicans and the need to defend Mexicans slated for capital punishment. In San Antonio "Las Crónicas de Loreley" (Loreley's Chronicles) a regular feature of *La Prensa* written by María Luisa Garza, also called for compassion for

In 1935 a Tucson judge released two whites, W.A. McGreight and Jeff Viliborghi, after they were convicted of second-degree slayings of two Mexicans. McGreight was charged with killing Alberto López in April of 1933. In the first trial the jury could not reach a verdict, but in a second he was convicted of second-degree murder. The other killer, Viliborghi, was convicted on June 10, 1933 of the second-degree murder of Alfredo Carreón. When both appealed, the county attorney recommended dismissal because it would be too costly to defend the verdicts. An editorial in *El Tucsonense* was indignant, "If the victims had been Americans killed by Mexicans, then the cost would have been no object; but justice for Mexicans is measured in grams" (translated by author).[9]

The editorial implored the community to organize, blaming this treatment of Mexicans on disunity.

36. *El Tucsonense* newspaper building and staff, ca. 1925.

[8] Quote from reprint in *El Tucsonense*, April 3, 1923.

[9] *El Tucsonense*, June 14, 1935.

condemned Mexicans.

When attempts at saving a condemned man ended in failure, the execution itself reminded crusaders that more needed to be done. This happened in the 1926 trial of Mauricio Trinidad, who received a death sentence. According to Los Angeles Mexicans, however, the procedure was a sham. J. Inés Magallanes, chairman of El Comité de Defensa de Mauricio Trinidad (The Defense Committee), wrote a moving account in Ulica's *Hispano Américano* of Trinidad's funeral in October 1926, in which he acknowledged those who had joined in the effort to save his life. He also provided a redeeming message. Unity now existed in the community even though the struggle to save Trinidad failed, Magallanes asserted.

DESEGREGATION EFFORTS IN THE *MÉXICO LINDO* ERA

Challenges to school segregation, either through the courts or through confronting of school boards and administrators, were also mounted by immigrant leaders. During the early years of immigration (1900-1910), many accepted the rationale given by school officials that they separated Mexican children because they did not know English. The school officials were promoting an "Americanization" program designed to socialize immigrant children into the mainstream. But when bilingual children were still being separated from Anglo children in the 1920s, that argument wore thin. It took stability and permanency before the community was ready to mount formal desegregation efforts. But a quality education for their children became more important the longer the Mexican immigrants lived in the U.S. This was an early sign of Mexican Americanization.

During 1924 Mexican parents, mainly from Guanajuato, and the consul protested when white parents petitioned to segregate Mexican students in the Argentine, Kansas, high school. After much protesting, Mexican children were allowed to attend the white high school in Argentine, but segregation was enforced in the elementary schools. This compromise did not sit well with either white or Mexican parents, but at least it did not bar the Mexican children from attending high school, which was the case in many places in Texas. In San Bernardino during the 1929 school year, students, parents and the Mexican government objected to efforts by the school board to segregate Mexicans with Blacks at the De Olivera Elementary School. The community refused to accept the rationale given by Ida Collins, the county superintendent of public instruction, who claimed the purpose for the separation was to help the children learn English.

The first successful desegregation court case of Mexicans took place in Tempe, Arizona, in 1925. Mexican families, many of whose ancestors helped found the city in the 1870s, succeeded in overturning a segregation policy in effect since 1915. Unfortunately, segregation continued for children of the recently arrived or from poorer families until the 1940s. More successful was the 1930 undertaking in Lemon Grove, California, a community near San Diego where Mexican parents resisted, also through the courts, the placing of their children in separate facilities. Despite these efforts, segregation continued in many public schools throughout the Southwest. And even in "desegregated" schools, unequal education for Mexican children persisted through placement of children into "Mexican" rooms and unequal funding of segregated schools.

REPATRIATION AND THE LAST *MÉXICO LINDO* MOBILIZATION EFFORT

Privations suffered by Mexican immigrants during the industrial depression of the 1930s provoked the last major *México Lindo* mobilization. As in the 1921 recession, thousands of Mexicans lost their jobs throughout the U.S. and returned to Mexico either through voluntary or coerced repatriation efforts or they remained stationary and rode out the economic storm as best they could. Many immigrant organizations ceased to exist. Those that survived tailored their efforts to survive these conditions. The resources which had been mustered for other issues were now more narrowly channeled to provide assistance

37. The Queen of Fiestas Patrias, Houston, Texas.

for the destitute and for those wishing repatriation to the homeland.

Mexicans throughout the U.S. responded enthusiastically to the plight of their hungry and homeless compatriots. Organizations in San Antonio, Donna and Laredo, Texas, organized food drives to feed the destitute returnees as they passed through the city on their way south, and in border towns Mexicans from both sides of the border did the same. Specialized Mexican organizations sprang up in various U.S. cities for the express purpose of feeding destitute compatriots and raising funds to send them home. In Los Angeles, the Mexican consul and various immigrant leaders started the Comité Mexicano de Beneficencia (Mexican Welfare Committee) for this purpose. In Houston where in 1931 the Tri-City Relief Committee refused to provide help to Mexicans and Blacks, a group led by Bartolemé Casas organized the Comité Pro-Repatriación (Pro-Repatriation Committee).

CONCLUSION

By the time of the heavy influx of Mexicans to the U.S. in the early twentieth century, Southwest natives had made great strides in adapting to their situation under Anglo rule. The immigrants, on the other hand, had to establish a new home and adapt while fleeing a violent, famine-stricken homeland; they were often greeted with hostility in their unfamiliar new home. There can be no doubt that, as they settled down, their situation was fragile and vulnerable. The sustained abuse of their civil rights provoked some of the first efforts to organize among Mexican immigrants and Mexican Americans. But the circumstances of immigration seem to have presented greater challenges to Mexicans in the U.S. than did the process of adapting to conquest for Hispanic natives of the Southwest.

What I call the *México Lindo* orientation emerged everywhere there were Mexicans and became a unifying umbrella under which Mexicans of different classes and backgrounds organized to defend their civil rights. Nonetheless, in older communities which had already established an orientation not as linked to Mexico, native Southwest Hispanic traits were more crucial in contributing to identity. Significantly, the native-born Hispanics with fewer links to Mexico were in a better position to help immigrants, that is, if they chose to do so. Inversely, in the newer *colonias*, immigrants depended more on their home government for cultural orientation and to serve as brokers for a myriad of problems they encountered in U.S. society. Mexican Americanization—a commitment to living in the U.S. permanently—gained ground among U.S. Mexicans by the late 1920s. The Chicano Movement ideologies of the 1960s, in essence, shared the nationalist ideology of their *México Lindo* grandparents and the passion for equal rights as citizens of the U.S., which their parents had taught them. Curiously, they were able to have it both ways.

CHAPTER FIVE

Organizing *el México de Afuera*

38. Labor contractors, San Antonio, Texas.

Throughout the 1960s Mexico's robust economy promoted confidence in the nation's future. The malaise many thought was a permanent part of Mexican history seemed far behind. More Mexican workers, whose only hope for a better life had been immigration, stayed home to fill a growing number of skilled, technical and even professional jobs. The middle classes grew at a phenomenal rate during this period. To be sure, hundreds of thousands still immigrated. But since the U.S. economy was also healthy, Mexicans who took unattractive but essential work in agriculture and the service sectors were not resented as much as in the past.

The Mexican government, which spent a large part of its diplomatic capital since the Revolution intervening on behalf of its expatriates in the U.S., now rested much easier. Fifteen years had elapsed since Operation Wetback, the last of the massive deportation campaigns that punctuated the history of Mexicans in the U.S.; no threat of this kind seemed to be looming in the near future. Moreover, Mexico did not feel accountable to the Mexican Americans, who made up the majority of the U.S. Mexican-origin population. In the 1960s the ratio of the Mexican-born to Mexican natives of the U.S. was about one to three. This contrasted markedly with the 1920s, when more than half of U.S. Mexicans had either immigrated or were the youthful offspring of the Mexican-born.

Mexican Americans had become an adult majority among Mexican-origin people by the 1940s; they did not require Mexico's attention nor did they expect it. This generation, or at least its ideological spokesmen, saw itself as wholly American. Even when the Chicano Movement loomed forward, *movimiento* activists did not seek inspiration nor help in contemporaneous Mexico. Rather, they borrowed for purposes of Chicano self-definition the abstract symbols of Mexican nationalism: the pre-Columbian past, the revolutionary pantheon of heroes, José Vasconcelos's theory of *mestizaje* and an array of other Mexican traditions.

In the initial stages of the *movimiento*, activists did not even forge a strong fraternal link with the Mexican student movement. In October of 1968, the very year that the Chicano Movement demonstrated its greatest thrust of energy, Mexican President Gustavo Díaz Ordaz ordered the brutal repression of students in Mexico City who were protesting educational neglect and the ignoring of Mexico's poverty. In the 1970s President Luis Echeverría Alvarez, who as minister of governance under Díaz Ordaz was directly responsible for the 1968 student repression, made overtures to Chicano Movement leaders. To some critics it seemed the Mexican government was seeking Chicano acceptance in order to atone for its past sins. This criticism did not deter the New Mexico land-grant crusader, Reies López Tijerina, and some La Raza Unida activists from heeding the Mexican president's beckoning. That the connection between Mexican student radicals and Chicano Movement activists was so tenuous simply reflected the remoteness that had grown between Mexico and Mexican Americans. But what Chicanos probably did not realize was that the Mexican government's extensive intervention in trying to shape *el México de afuera* (Mexico abroad) served to plant strong seeds of nationalism that served the Chicano Movement's ideological formation.

Because of severe mistreatment of its expatriates, Mexico was forced to intervene extensively on their behalf during most of the century. In 1928 the Secretaría de Relaciones Exteriores, Mexico's Foreign Ministry, issued a report outlining the treatment of Mexicans in the U.S. The fifty-two-page study detailed the travails facing immigrants such as abuse by employers, segregation, physical attacks by prejudiced whites, police brutality and inequities in the justice system. The latter was of great concern because, in the words of the report, "it is only with extreme difficulty that initial judgments are reversed of our compatriots who are wrongly convicted of crime" (translated by author).[1]

While the Mexican government usually backed these words with action, the U.S. government rarely afforded full cooperation, making it difficult for efforts to be effective. In 1922 after Mexican Charge D'Affairs Manuel Téllez protested with a strong note an incredible number of atrocities against Mexicans, Secretary of State Charles Hughes chided him for using extreme language. Recent historical assessments of Mexican government attempts to protect immigrants have been largely critical, but immigrants were left unprotected not because of lack of effort by the Mexican government; lack of concern and racist attitudes even in the U.S. government were often insurmountable.

Consuls also served as ethnic brokers for compatriots in trouble with the law. This was especially true during the initial formation of the immigrant communities when their institutions were in a nascent stage or nonexistent. Unfortunately, owing to the turmoil in Mexico, instability often plagued the diplomatic corps. Nonetheless, consuls at times performed intrepidly, considering the hurdles which fell in their path.

From the outset of their existence, Mexican consuls variously attempted protection; consular defense dates to the California Gold Rush. In 1850 the Foreign Miners Tax to keep Mexicans and other Latin Americans out of gold fields prompted protest from the San Francisco Mexican consul. At end of the century, increased emigration required more defined expatriate policy.

Immigrants welcomed Mexican government protection, but assistance did not always come without encumbrances. An important consular function was to maintain *mexicanidad* among immigrants; hence, loyalty to the home government was solicited. In the 1860s San Francisco consuls promoted *juntas patrióticas* (patriotic committees) to support Benito Juárez's Republicanism. Until the 1890s, however, such overtures

reached only a small number of nationalistic expatriates. Increased immigration at the end of the century intensified promotion of Mexico. Dictator Porfirio Díaz's attempts at building a national identity coincided with his efforts to bring economic and political unity. By the 1890s immigration carried nationalistic sentiments across the border, a process aided by consuls.

In addition to maintaining political support, Porfirian diplomats actively assisted destitute compatriots. During the 1907-1908 depression, for example, the Mexican government repatriated workers, appropriating one hundred thousand pesos for that purpose. In Los Angeles and San Francisco, consuls rallied expatriates to provide housing and food for thousands of unemployed compatriots. According to one report, San Francisco alone had close to one thousand destitute Mexicans who could not find food or shelter. The Mexican government then paid for train fare through El Paso for families from various points in California.

39. President Porfirio Díaz of Mexico.

The diplomatic system was also successful in influencing the justice system. As early as 1903 the Mexican consulate in Los Angeles had a special fund "to be used in assisting Mexican subjects, who become involved in difficulty, either through ignorance of the laws of this country or through the mistaken arrest or accusation

---

[1] *La migración y protección del mexicano en el extranjero* (Mexico City: Secretaría de Relaciones Exteriores, 1928), p. 12.

of crimes."[2]

After Díaz's ouster in May of 1911, Francisco León de la Barra's caretaker government was only nominally concerned about immigrants. At that time, however, the consular system was reorganized and governance policy reassessed. Higher salaries were paid, seniority was upheld and consuls had to be Mexican citizens and demonstrate rigid educational qualifications. In addition, they were prohibited from practicing other professions. Added to consular management was the office of visitador general, an inspector. These reforms, which were in the offing before Díaz was defeated, however, did not result in more effective protection.

After Francisco I. Madero ousted Díaz, immigrant leaders—some of them supporters of the exiled Díaz—criticized the lack of consular protection during the interim presidency of Francisco de la Barra. When Madero was elected president in December 1911 he did little to change this shortcoming. In January 1913 Texas Rangers gunned down Juan Reyes as they arrested him for highway robbery and murder, even though he fit only a vague description of the purported killer. San Antonio's La Prensa commented on the lack of protection afforded Mexicans and then added, as if the envoy might not do so unless pressured, "Let's hope that the Mexican Consul in El Paso can look into this matter."[3]

The historian Juan Gómez Quinoñes argues that Madero used consuls primarily to thwart activities of exiles opposed to Madero. This is correct, but no Mexican president in this century contended with as much factionalism as Madero. From his inauguration in October to his bloody ouster in February of 1913, endless plots to overthrow him were hatched both in and outside of Mexico. Undoubtedly, protection for immigrants acquired less priority than political survival.

In February of 1913 General Victoriano Huerta had Madero assassinated and then assumed the presidency. He also attempted to use the consular system to spy on exiled enemies and to instill support among the immigrants, but his efforts met with singular failure. In addition, his consuls did not improve protection of expatriates. The years 1911 and 1912 broke all official emigration records with an influx that by 1913 severely taxed consular resources. Victoriano Huerta's government became more adamant about curtailing the exodus, especially of emigrants from central Mexico who, unlike norteños, were unfamiliar with the American social and economic terrain and thus were at a higher risk. In addition, large landowners feared jeopardizing their own labor needs because of the outflow. As Mexican consular reports of immigrant mistreatment increased, the Foreign Ministry considered restricting emigration by imposing a fine on anyone caught recruiting workers.

Responding to looming government restrictions on immigration, a Mexico City daily, La Nación, scolded the government for impeding the exodus of Mexicans, considering that economic reality dictated the emigration. Besides, the sojourn in the U.S. taught the emigrants practical skills which would be put to good use when they returned. In the United States, said the newspaper, they would soon abandon their country ways of dressing and behaving and return to their patrias chicas to serve as role models. As for American antipathy, it was normal for natives to dislike foreigners, it continued. After all, the Germans disliked the French and vice-versa, continued the piece.[4]

[2] Quoted in Edward J. Escobar, "Race and Law Enforcement: Relations between Chicanos and the Los Angeles Police Department, 1900-1945," unpublished manuscript, p. 19.

[3] La Prensa, January 11, 1913.

[4] Cited in La Prensa, December 4, 1913.

The plan called for individual states to prohibit emigration.

As the Revolution intensified, Huerta's officials became diverted from emigration issues. Besides, some years earlier, in November of 1906, the Mexican supreme court had struck down a Zacatecas decree designed to discourage emigration by imposing an eight-peso levy on each laborer recruited by contractors. The decision was based on article eleven of the 1857 constitution, which gave Mexican citizens the right to enter and leave the territory of Mexico freely and to change residence. After 1913 Huerta's officials did not have to worry about regulating the outflow. Revolutionary battles destroyed railroads, bridges and rolling stock, thus paralyzing transportation. This was propitious because, like Madero, Huerta was preoccupied with political expediency above all else and Venustiano Carranza's growing insurrection did not leave much room for emigrant problems.

In the last months of Huerta's dictatorship, consuls turned to unabashed full-time propagandizing. During the April 1914 invasion of Veracruz, for example, U.S. agents jailed the inspector of consulates and the El Paso consul and vice-consul for recruiting immigrants. Because U.S.-Mexico relations were severed, the Spanish ambassador had to represent Mexico in attempts to save León Cárdenas Martínez, a fifteen-year-old sentenced to die for the murder of a white woman three years earlier.

Venustiano Carranza, who ousted Huerta in 1914, implemented a more vigorous strategy for protecting immigrants. Good intentions notwithstanding, Mexican diplomats found the protection of expatriates extremely difficult during this turbulent era. For Carranza, lack of recognition of his government by the U.S. made it difficult to pursue normal diplomatic relations at the consular level. In 1915 the conspicuous failure by his government to obtain a commutation of the hanging of teenager Federico Sánchez is a case in point. An even greater setback came when Carranza's diplomats embarked on an equally fruitless quest to save four Mexicans executed in Arizona between December of 1915 and July of 1916.

40. Carranza's Cruz Blanca nursing corps members with founder, Leonor Villegas de Magnón (in white hat). The corps was founded in Laredo, Texas.

The U.S. recognized Carranza at the end of 1916, but before the consular corps could function effectively, it needed reforming. A slate of consul posts was announced ceremoniously in the beginning of 1916, but thereafter offices were vacated with dizzying regularity, creating voids detrimental to immigrants who often counted on the consul's ability to provide protection. Some limited victories took place, however. During World War I, local draft boards mistakenly called up Mexican citizens into the U.S. Army, claiming they were Mexican Americans. In cooperation with U.S. officials, Carranza's consuls organized meetings to explain draft rules, helped Mexicans fill out registration forms, obtained release for immigrants jailed for not registering and secured discharges for those mistakenly drafted into the Army.

In 1917 a revolutionary convention led by *carrancistas* formulated the constitution which is the basis for Mexico's legal structure to this day. Although this document helped solidify Carranza's legitimacy, internal threats continued and relations with the U.S. did not improve appreciably. As a consequence, only men loyal to Carranza were appointed to diplomatic posts. But depending on the faithful reduced the number of experienced candidates, and many untested emissaries went north.

When World War I ended, many American investors worried that a revolutionary Mexican government was putting their investments in Mexico at risk. Article 27 of the new constitution called for Mexican control of subsoil rights, such as oil, which were in the hands of American and British companies. Moreover, Carranza seemed unable to control border banditry that was instigated by his domestic enemies, who Americans thought were allied with Germany. Relations became so malignant that the U.S. made plans to invade Mexico and in 1919 consuls throughout the Southwest asked expatriates to prepare for war.

Carranza's program to obtain immigrant support included underwriting the publishing of Spanish-language newspapers and magazines that propagandized on behalf of his regime. In 1918 Carranza's U.S. consuls made a more concerted effort to gather immigrant support by identifying Carranza's government with nationalistic symbols. They organized *juntas patrióticas* "wherever ten or more Mexicans lived to foster support for the true and revolutionary government of Mexico" (translated by author).[5] Carranaza's aggressive foreign policy of putting political survival first resulted in disgruntled immigrants, however, which his exiled opposition abroad used against him. Carranza's efforts to foster nationalism abroad rested on anti-American feelings among the immigrants—an attitude that lasted into the Chicano era.

President Álvaro Obregón, who succeeded Carranza after his ouster and assassination in 1920, had the Foreign Ministry make more resources available to expatriates. In 1920 only fifty-one consulates throughout the U.S. existed to assist close to a million Mexicans who had immigrated between 1910 and 1920. Only eleven more offices were added in the course of the 1920s, but the Foreign Ministry added personnel and funds, assuring better functioning of the corps. In response to the indigence immigrants faced during the 1921 recession, the Department of Repatri-

ation was formed in Mexico in order to relocate, according to Mexican sources, some four hundred thousand workers in the U.S. who were being threatened with deportation or wanted to return to Mexico voluntarily. Obregón's consuls decided at a conference in San Antonio to continue the *juntas patrióticas* concept championed by Carranza by creating *comisiones honoríficas mexicanas* (Mexican honorary associations). The visitor of consuls decided to establish some of the first *comisiones* in San Antonio, Dallas and Austin. Los Angeles had the first one in California and they quickly spread throughout the nation. The main purpose of these organizations was to assist Mexicans with the inordinate number of problems encountered during the 1921 recession.

The *comisiones's* immigrant board of directors maintained nationalism by organizing *fiestas patrias* (patriotic holidays) and supporting immigrant schools to teach Mexican history and "proper" Spanish. The consuls also promoted these initiatives directly. In Phoenix, for example, to offset the Americanization efforts of adult immigrants by the Friendly House, Consul M. G. Prieto offered Spanish literacy lessons during 1923. From Karnes City, Texas, Atilaño Saldaña wrote to President Álvaro Obregón in 1924 asking if the Secretaría de Educación (Education Ministry) could send books, especially math texts, because *comisión honorífica* members had enrolled sixty students in a school bearing the president's name.

President Obregón faced different diplomatic problems from those of Carranza. The U.S. wanted to barter recognition of his government for assurances that Mexico would not tamper with foreign-owned oil properties. In addition, the immigrant problems that had plagued the governments in the previous decade quadrupled because of the record number of Mexicans in the U.S. In 1920 the El Paso consul submitted a report in which he documented the killing, mainly by police, of 391 compatriots during a ten-year period. Almost none of the assailants he named was charged with any crimes. The most difficult prob-

[1] *El Cosmopolita*, June 22, 1910.

41. The Border Patrol, 1920s.

lem facing Obregón's consular envoys sprang from the 1921 depression. Anti-Mexican riots, some extremely violent, ensued as record unemployment brought on white worker resentment against workers from Mexico. So severe was this dilemma, that in July a cabinet-level agency within the Secretaría de Industria y Trabajo (Ministry of Industry and Labor) was created with a threefold purpose—to investigate migration causes, to prevent immigration and to deal with repressive treatment of Mexicans in the U.S.

In April 1921 the San Antonio consul general met with Texas Governor Pat Neff to see if his officials could help ameliorate recession-related immigrant unemployment. The difficulties facing consuls became insurmountable, however, and the Mexican government decided to use the *comisiones* to repatriate jobless workers. Significantly, in 1921 the Foreign Ministry directed consuls to report *atropellos* (violations of civil rights) quickly so that amelioration could proceed through channels. This new posture did help see immigrants through the worst surge of lynchings and anti-Mexican riots during the 1921 recession although it could not prevent atrocities in their entirety. These included hooded night riders invading Mexican neighborhoods and burning their homes. In 1923 the U.S. recognized Mexico's government after negotiators had reached an agreement at the Bucareli meetings which promised that oil properties of Americans would not be expropriated. The recession abated also and tension between both countries declined as did the degree of Mexican immigrant abuse.

The consular service eagerly took credit for the ebb in the attacks on immigrants which had characterized the worst years of the recession. But overrecruiting, even in the more ample labor market of 1924, soon resulted in a labor glut. The large outflow alarmed Mexican officials because previous experience demonstrated the inevitability of recessions when repatriation responsibilities would fall to them. West central Mexicans were the most vulnerable immigrants in the previous crisis and to avoid a repetition, the Ministry of Industry and Labor warned the governors of Guanajuato, Jalisco, Michoacán and San Luis Potosí to discourage recruiter propaganda.

42. Leonor Villegas de Magnón and her *escuelita*, Laredo, Texas.

The prophecy came true. During 1926 economic downturns racked the Southwest and demands for repatriation increased. Minimal repatriation efforts made by the President Plutarco Elías Calles government in 1926 encouraged the belief among immigrants, as Mexican unemployment in the U.S. worsened, that the Mexican government would continue to provide repatriation support. Calles in the meantime refused to use public funds to bring home Mexicans because it did not benefit the country.

That same year Calles threatened to eliminate the immunity from constitutional limitations given in the Obregón era to foreign oil companies. As a consequence, relations between Mexico City and Washington deteriorated to a point not seen since the Carranza era. Secretary of State Frank Kellogg and the insensitive ambassador to Mexico, James Sheffield, responded by bashing Calles in the American press, an action used by immigration foe Texas Representative John C. Box to strengthen his hand in trying to pass legislation to halt immigration from Mexico.

As the U.S. economy and diplomatic conditions deteriorated in 1926, atrocities against Mexicans, accompanied by stepped-up deportations, increased. That was also the year of the Cristero Rebellion, a violent reaction to Calles's attempt at enforcing constitutional provisions curbing the power of the Catholic Church. Calles' policy also provoked a backlash in the U.S. among influential church leaders and Catholic politicians. During the crisis, the tradition of consuls spying on expatriates, this time militant Catholic subversives, was revived in full force.

As had occurred to other presidents before him, it became important to Calles to keep as much of the immigrant population in his camp as possible. He named Moisés Sáenz, a Protestant minister, as sub-secretary of education in 1926.

Saenz initiated a campaign in Mexico to combat rural superstition and backwardness fostered by the Catholic Church—in essence the revolutionary elites wanted to modernize Mexico. Ironically, a similar tact was used for the immigrants in the U.S., done in the name of deterring Americanization of immigrants, whose ideological base was also modernization. In January 1928, Margarita Robles y Mendoza, from the Mexican Ministry of Education, toured the Southwest to promote newly established Mexican schools in the U.S., which became known as *escuelitas*. Most were established in California and Texas.

The Mexican Chamber Deputy from Oaxaca, Alfonso Ramírez, toured various *colonias* in the U.S. to further the *escuelita* movement and to investigate immigrant problems. In February 1928 he assured immigrants that their children were still considered Mexican citizens and said parents should discourage Americanization. The initiative continued into later years. In Phoenix local immigrant leaders and Consul Manuel Payno inaugurated La Escuela Mexicana amidst much fanfare during the 1930 Cinco de Mayo festivities. Payno was so enthusiastic, he obtained certification from the Arizona Department of Education. Thirty children were enrolled during summer vacation and Payno himself taught geography and history while volunteer Rosendo Serna instructed reading and writing in both languages.

How the expatriates measured the success of the consuls in the 1920s was contradictory because they often did not know the extent of the consuls' power. Police mistreatment and court abuses mainly concerned the immigrants. In 1924 as two Mexicans tried to hold up a Chicago speakeasy, they killed a Chicago off-duty policeman. The police responded by indiscriminately arresting scores of Mexicans, an action that provoked condemnations from Spanish-language newspapers and Consul Lorenzo Lupián. But because nothing came of his protests, many Mexicans criticized him for being ineffective. As in the previous decade, politically disgruntled expatriates continued to denounce consuls for being concerned only with spying, especially during the

Calles administration.

When consuls helped Mexicans in trouble with the law, they mostly hired Anglo lawyers because of their availability. Samuel Pereyra, in fact, the Mexican consul in Eagle Pass, reported in the 1930s not using Mexican American lawyers simply because white juries did not respect them. However, they were often the only bilingual attorneys available and so they defended immigrants frequently, although not always under the consular auspices. Many of these attorneys went on to become civil rights leaders in the Mexican American era. Significantly, their exposure to the inequities experienced by immigrants helped politicize them. It is difficult to know if they proffered services to the immigrant community in order to help *la raza* or because Mexicans were their only clients.

Again because consuls had to shift priorities to espionage activity during the Cristero Rebellion, immigrant grievances were neglected. Catholic exiles lost no time in discrediting Plutarco Elías Calles and his emissaries because of this shortcoming. Other immigrants had nothing but praise, especially in successful interventions.

Mexican emissaries themselves suffered indignities at the hands of hostile Anglo Americans. Reports abounded of consuls being segregated in public places, being manhandled for pursuing protection for immigrants and being arrested on trumped-up charges. In April of 1926 José Puig Casauruac, Mexican minister of public instruction, delivered a lecture at the University of Texas where he lambasted U.S. policy towards Mexico. Some Texas officials could not countenance such talk from a Mexican at a time when diplomatic relations were quite sour with Mexico, so they arrested him for libel. He posted bond and then fled the country via California. This disregard for diplomatic privilege was even more evident in a 1931 Chicago incident in which Vice-Consul Adolfo Domínguez was jailed briefly by Judge Thomas Green, who became tired of the envoy's zealous courtroom advocacy on behalf of immigrants. After learning that the Mexican emissary was protected by diplomatic immunity, Green exploded, "It would take nothing short of an act of President Hoover to make him change his mind." Then he added, "I'm an ex-Marine myself and that's the way we Marines handle things. I don't see why people. . . scrape to these consuls and ambassadors. They've got to be put in their place."[6]

THE LAST MAJOR INTERVENTION: THE GREAT DEPRESSION

During the Great Depression, Mexican envoys worked diligently to help compatriots. Consul Rafael de la Colina constantly lodged protests against the raids by the police in Los Angeles, in which Mexicans by the hundreds were rounded up and jailed before it was decided

Prominent among Mexican American lawyers was Manuel González. Early in his career, the World War I veteran became secretary to the U.S. military attaché in Madrid. In the 1920s he participated in fledgling Mexican American organizations such as the Order of the Sons of America and in 1929 became a founding member of the League of United Latin American Citizens (LULAC). The San Antonio consul general often asked him to serve as a friend of the court in trials of policemen who killed Mexicans. In 1931 the young attorney represented the Mexican government at the Oklahoma deliberation of the two deputies who killed two middle-class students from Mexico, one a nephew of the then-president of Mexico. Significantly, González in addressing the court made sure it knew of his war record. In 1928 he also represented Clemente Rodríguez and Eziquiel Servín, two young Mexicans accused of raping a white girl outside San Antonio. The defense effort put up by González failed and the two were convicted and executed.

Frank E. Domínguez, who defended Aurelio Pompa, was another Mexican American lawyer who was very active in helping Mexicans in trouble with the law. Unfortunately, his extensive efforts to appeal Pompa's death sentence for the killing of his supervisor at a Los Angeles construction site in 1922 were to no avail. Domínguez, who was in partnership with an Anglo attorney, also penned essays opposing capital punishment for *La Opinión* and *El Tucsonense*.

Phoenix attorney Gregorio "Greg" García was among the most active Arizona criminal lawyers in

defending Mexicans. For example, García and Alejandro Martínez, the Mexican consul, led the successful 1926 campaign to obtain a commutation for a deranged Ramón Escobar, who was sentenced to hang for killing his wife in a jealous rage. García was also the main lawyer in the case of Alfredo Grijalva, a southern Arizona rancher accused of killing a customs official in 1926. Grijalva was found guilty, but García's defense was vigorous enough to cast some doubt, and the judge sentenced Grijalva to life imprisonment rather than give him the death penalty. García was a member of the Alianza Hispano Americana and in the 1930s went on to become a founding member of the Latin American Club, an organization that supported the Democratic Party and the New Deal. In the 1940s and 1950s he worked with attorney Ralph Estrada in desegregation cases in the Phoenix area.

43. Alfredo Grijalva.

[6] *Chicago Daily Tribune*, July 8, 1931.

if they had entered the country illegally. Historian Francisco Balderrama, however, asserts that

> Colina interpreted his duties narrowly: To keep his superiors informed and to solicit pledges of fair treatment from U.S. officials. He was also handicapped by the lack of support from his superiors in Mexico City. A protest from the Secretary of Foreign Relations might have stopped the massive raids before the immigration agents themselves halted them.[7]

The consuls, however, were at their best in assisting Mexicans in the exodus. De la Colina, for example, helped the Comité Mexicano de Beneficencia (Mexican Welfare Committee) in providing immediate relief to destitute immigrants and in assisting Los Angeles County officials to repatriate as many Mexicans as possible through railroad trains scheduled specifically for that purpose. Los Angeles County was so enthusiastic about ridding the city of Mexicans that it provided train fare on Mexican railroads so that the immigrants would return all the way to homes in central Mexico and not remain at the border.

During the Depression, Chicago and its industrial suburbs in Indiana were hard-hit with severe unemployment among its thousands of industrial workers. The Unión de Sociedades de Caridad (The Social Charities Union) had the help of Consul Rafael Aveleyra in providing train fare for those wanting to return. Like De la Colina in Los Angeles, however, he cooperated with the non-Mexican groups that were enthusiastically pressuring Mexicans to return by organizing repatriation trains. Unlike Los Angeles, where officials sometimes sponsored repatriation all the way to homes in Mexico from Chicago, fares were provided only as far as the border. Then because transportation from the border to central Mexico was not as efficiently organized as in the U.S., the refugees were caught in bottlenecks in Ciudad Juárez and Laredo without food or shelter.

Most of the repatriates were returning to central Mexico, and President Pascual Ortiz Rubio asked state governors from this region to implement programs to accommodate returning workers, a task they did reluctantly. Ortiz Rubio lived in the U.S. after his presidency and continued to work towards persuading Mexicans to return to Mexico. In 1934 he gave a speech in San Diego, stating that Mexico should favor returning Mexicans from the U.S. rather than allowing in Europeans or Asians because the expatriates were of the same blood as Mexico's Indians and mestizos.

When Abelardo Rodríguez assumed the presidency from Ortiz Rubio after the latter resigned in 1932, he formed a Comité Nacional de Repatraición (National Repatriation Committee) to raise half a million pesos in order to found special colonies in the jungle-infested regions of Oaxaca and Guerrero—this effort failed miserably. Otherwise, Ortiz Rubio and Rodríguez adhered to the policy that the federal government should avoid direct involvement in the issue of resettling the returning emigrants.

President Lázaro Cárdenas replaced Rodríguez and implemented a more far-reaching program with federal pesos. His most ambitious project came in 1938 in the state of Tamaulipas with the formation of the 18 de Marzo (March 18) colony, named after the date when American and British oil companies were expropriated. All in all, however, these efforts came too late because the bulk of the repatriates had returned before his presidency. The effort, however, was successful in promoting Cárdenas's image as a man of the people. In 1938 he sent his foreign minister, Ramón Beteta, on a whirlwind tour of the U.S., partially to offset the backlash to oil expropriation but also to assure Mexican immigrants that their government welcomed them home and was willing to help them financially.

The problems immigrants brought before the consuls declined as their numbers fell during the massive repatriation of the 1930s. Many of the young single males, unaccompanied by families, had left; thus a more stable atmosphere emerged in the *colonias* as proportionately more women, young children and older people remained. In the

---

[7] Quoted in Leonardo Macías Jr., "Mexican Immigration and Repatriation," (M.A. thesis, Arizona State University, 1992), p. 28.

44. Braceros leaving from Mexico City for the U.S. Photo by Hermanos Mayo.

1930s the consuls continued to pursue their usual efforts to protect immigrants despite their ranks having thinned out. Interestingly, intervention took place on a large scale in California labor disputes. Nonetheless, the workers were not as dependent on consuls as in previous decades.

Cárdenas handpicked General Manuel Avila Camacho to replace him in 1940; Avila Camacho was a moderate who decided during World War I to curry favor with the U.S. by supporting the war effort. Negotiating the Bracero Program, which provided badly needed workers during World War II, became the most important manifestation of this support. Mexico attempted to shield braceros from the abuse that Mexican workers had always suffered in the U.S. and even forbade their importation to Texas until state officials implemented measures that would reduce mistreatment.

The Mexican government also joined the Mexican American civil rights campaign to further better treatment. The Comité Contra el Racismo (The Committee against Racism) was formed, headed by poet and career diplomat Jaime Torres Bodet. Its purpose was to promote cooperation between the two countries against the fascist threat in Europe and, as Juan Gómez-Quiñones indicates:

> To demand that the U.S. government guarantee the human rights of Mexican nationals and Mexican Americans in the U.S. Action stemming from the Mexican government provided leverage in ameliorating . . . prejudice. This was possible because of the wartime exigencies placed upon Washington and because there was a will among Mexican officials to exert pressure while they still had leverage . . . in regard to discrimination, violence, and wages. Later, however, they lost that leverage.[8]

The Comité reflected the Mexican Americanist perspective on the nature of racism, i.e., that

---

[8] Juan Gómez-Quiñones, *Chicano Politics: Reality and Promise, 1940-1990* (Albuquerque: University of New Mexico Press, 1990), p. 36.

45. Bracero camp, 1940s.

only a minority of racists were responsible for these acts, not the majority of the American people or the U.S. government. This represented a far cry from the stridency shown during Carranza's era.

After World War II, the need for Mexican immigrant labor diminished, but the Korean War, which lasted two years, again raised the demand. A recession followed this latest international altercation, resulting in the predictable decline in Mexican worker desirability. In 1954 the U.S. government initiated Operation Wetback, and Immigration and Naturalization Service officers rounded up thousands of undocumented workers and deported them to Mexico. In many cases, they were sent back in airplanes to southern Mexico to

prevent their return north. President Adolfo Ruiz Cortines protested the methods used but concurred with American authorities that the Bracero Program should be the legitimate conduit by which Mexicans should enter to work in the U.S.

The role the consular service played in the lives of expatriates during the early immigration period has probably never been equaled. It became the only recourse for thousands of penniless immigrants caught in legal predicaments, labor disputes or civil rights abuses. The sociologist Emory Bogardus, who studied Mexican immigration during this era, indicated that "by remaining a citizen of Mexico and by calling on the Mexican consul for assistance, the Mexican can secure justice, whereas if he becomes an American citizen, he feels helpless. He does not understand our courts and is not able to secure as adequate a hearing as if he remains a Mexican citizen."[9]

Indeed, even Mexicans born in the U.S. claimed Mexican citizenship when they wanted help. The South Texas newspaper, *El Defensor,* which had a Mexican American orientation, lamented in 1930 that Mexican immigrants had the lowest record of naturalization and that descendants of Mexicans who lived in Texas before it became part of the U.S. registered with consuls. In 1923 Mauro Parisi, an Italian doomed to hang at San Quentin, claimed to be Mexican in order to sustain his clemency request through the San Francisco Mexican consulate. A consular void in the Kansas City jurisdiction during 1916 prompted A. L. Martin in Springfield, Missouri, to impersonate a consul and fleece Mexicans by charging for services. That he did this demonstrates that Mexicans depended on and used the consuls regularly. Of course, as was shown above, Mexican government emissaries discouraged naturalization and encouraged children born in the U.S. of Mexican parents to remain Mexican citizens and maintain their Mexican identity.

The Mexican government's efforts to protect the civil rights of its expatriates in the U.S. maintained immigrant links with the *patria.* In addition, the *México Lindo* nationalism permeating the *colonias* was partially promoted by the consular service. While in the Mexican American generation this identity thinned out, vestiges of it remained into the Chicano Movement era. Both the Mexican government and immigrant leaders demonstrated a stridency which accelerated in the Chicano era. This occurred in spite of Mexico's having been so foreign and removed from the consciousness of the Mexican Americans who forged the Chicano Movement.

[9] Quoted in Ricardo Romo, *East Los Angeles: History of a Barrio* (Austin: University of Texas Press, 1983), p.155.

CHAPTER SIX

The Mexican American Generation

46. First LULAC convention, Corpus Christi, Texas, May 19, 1929.

By the 1940s and 1950s incidents of abuse that in the past had mainly aroused a *México Lindo* nationalistic response in the U.S. Mexican community now elicited a new approach: Mexican American ideology, with its irrevocable message of permanency, i.e., the right to live in the U.S. and enjoy constitutional guarantees. Mexican Americans no longer saw themselves as visitors being mistreated but as natives who were denied full equality. Mexican Americans now attempted to resolve problems with faith in education, electoral politics, litigation and a claim to being white Americans. By the 1960s Chicano activists categorically rejected the assimilationist and racial identity aspects of this ideology—that "belonging" meant being just another white American—but advanced most of the other ideals. Thus, advocacy for civil rights shifted from a focus on Mexican nationals living in the U.S. to U.S. citizens of Mexican descent.

The concept of permanency and belonging was transformed by Chicanos to claim proprietorship to a lost homeland (Aztlán), wrested away through territorial imperialism by the U.S. Here they also borrowed from the "lost land" ideal—a sentiment that adherents to the Texas Plan de San Diego in 1915 or the Gorras Blancas of northern New Mexico in the 1890s had expressed most stridently (see Chapter One).

Significantly, Chicano-Movement symbolism tapped *México Lindo* nationalism, which included homage to *mestizaje*. But the rest of the *México Lindo* belief system—no will to stay in the U.S. and loyalty to Mexico—was irrelevant to Chicanos. After putting all these past ideological references through the wringer, the Mexican American sense of permanency remained the core of political and ethnic identity for the Chicano Movement.

The common thread that held together all those engaged in Mexican Americanization was the realization, sometimes unconscious, that returning to Mexico was no longer an option. During the 1930s and 1940s Ignacio L. López, publisher of *El Espectador* in Southern California, best applied the rule of thumb in defining Mexican Americanism. His newspaper consistent-ly promoted "permanency." Unlike most other Mexican Americans, however, he insisted on maintaining Spanish, a language he used in his bilingual newspaper.

Two factors arose out of the Great Depression that diminished *México Lindo* ideology. One, immigration came to a halt, thus eliminating for at least a decade the previously constant reinforcing of Mexican culture. Second, Mexicans resisted repatriation; mostly families with growing children committed themselves to staying in the U.S., thus becoming more rooted. During the decade, a generation grew up who had no memories of Mexico. Their only home had been the *barrios* in their immigrant communities.

OVERLAPPING *MÉXICO LINDO* AND MEXICAN AMERICANISM

Mexican Americanism did not appear magically after repatriation. The process, while becoming dominant in the 1930s, was advocated as early as World War I in areas where immigration was not as recent. In Tucson and San Antonio, for example, where Mexicans, primarily from the Mexican north, had come earlier, the penchant for naming businesses, immigrant organizations and newspapers with signatures evoking Mexican symbols was not as intense as in Houston or Chicago. On the contrary, in Arizona the two first major Mexican organizations were called the Alianza Hispano Americana (Hispanic American Alliance) and the Liga Protectora Latina (Latin Protective League), a choice suggesting a desire to put some distance from Mexico and its national symbols. A major challenge during the war years for Liga members was a xenophobic campaign in Arizona that tried to prohibit Mexicans from working in the mines. Liga protests were couched in terms of emphasizing contributions Mexicans had made to Arizona history and arguing that Mexicans had lived in the state since before the Gadsden Purchase. Such a tactic became a major wedge used by Mexican Americans and Chicano Movement activists in later years.

In Texas, San Antonio's Pan American Round Table and the Order of Sons of America (OSA)

47. Order of the Sons of America, Council No. 4, Corpus Christi, Texas, 1927.

existed as early as the 1920s. The OSA was started by Luz Sáenz, a teacher and a World War I veteran—veterans were crucial to the forming of the Sons. The group, whose members were mainly U.S.-born, encouraged naturalization and participation in U.S. institutions for all Mexicans. During 1921 also in San Antonio, Ricardo Arenales organized the Pan American Round Table, which attracted Mexican American and Anglo businessmen. It was dedicated to promoting a positive "Hispanic-American" image and fighting the "anti-Latin American" attitudes which were so salient during 1921, mainly because a severe recession that year intensified antipathy towards Mexicans.

The most influential advocate of this incipient Mexican American generation was druggist Francisco A. Chapa, publisher of *El Imparcial de Texas*. Chapa used his newspaper to promote electoral activism, to celebrate Mexican American exploits during World War I and to mourn their casualties. One reason that Mexicans were deemed disloyal stemmed from the confusion in which local draft boards had called up Mexican nationals, suspecting them of being Mexican Americans pos-

Born into a prominent Matamoros, Tamaluipas, family, Francsico A. Chapa studied pharmacy at Tulane University and then founded a thriving drugstore that included a laboratory in San Antonio during the 1890s. In 1906 Chapa was elected to San Antonio's Board of Education and was named treasurer. Chapa helped deliver San Antonio's Mexican American vote to Oscar Colquitt in the late 1910s to defeat efforts to ban the sale of alcohol in Texas. Consequently, he was commissioned as one of twelve lieutenant colonels on Colquitt's personal staff. Chapa was the only Mexican in the group, which served in an advisory capacity, and as publisher of *El Imparcial de Texas* in San Antonio, he wielded considerable influence among Texas Mexican Americans. In 1911 he was implicated in a plot hatched in Texas to unseat Francisco I. Madero. He was convicted of violating U.S. neutrality laws, but charges were later dropped at the behest of influential Texans.[1]

[1] For biographical data on Chapa, see Charles H. Harris III and Louis Sadler, "The 1911 Reyes Conspiracy: The Texas Side," in Harris and Sadler, (eds.), *Border Revolution* (Las Cruces: Center for Latin American Studies/Joint Border Research Institute, New Mexico State University, 1988), pp. 31-33.

48. Man on donkey promoting payment of poll tax in San Antonio, 1925.

In the *Mexican Voice*, the official publication of California's Mexican American Movement, a youth organization sponsored by the YMCA, editor Félix Gutiérrez disclosed the story of a young Mexican who, in filling out his Social Security card, identified himself as white instead of Mexican. This provoked his fellow Mexican workers to give him the "raspberry." The young man admitted that he was "part white and red," but since he was not a full-blooded Indian, he chose to emphasize the white part of his background. Gutiérrez agreed, adding that Mexicans are not a race but a nationality. "I'm an American of Mexican descent," he wrote and suggested that claiming whiteness would clinch that assertion.[2]

ing as immigrants—a calculation that was probably true in some cases.

Adding to Mexican American insecurity was the passage of the Disloyalty Act by the thirty-fifth legislature of Texas. Immediately, some German Americans were arrested for expressing anti-American feelings, but xenophobia extended towards Mexicans as well. To offset this stigma, Mexican Americans joined in the war efforts on a number of home fronts. In the El Paso Valley, Mexican American farmers pledged to increase agricultural production to meet wartime demands. *El Imparical de Texas* and *La Prensa* continued to emphasize Mexican American loyalty and support for the war effort through weekly listings of Mexicans killed or wounded in European armed actions.

Francisco Chapa also attempted to maintain the Mexican political power that nineteenth-century Tejanos were able to amass (see Chapter One). But because the majority of adult U.S. Mexicans during the *México Lindo* era were immigrants, their numbers could not easily translate into voting blocks. Such an aspiration was not really fulfilled in Texas until after the Chicano Movement. But Chapa still tried. In November of 1918, as he extolled the heroism of Mexicans fighting for the U.S. in World War I, the pharmacist reminded his readers that,

[2] *Mexican Voice*, September 1928, p. 95

49. LULAC Council No. 1 in 1940.

before the war, politicians had abandoned Texas Mexicans. Now they were gaining prestige because of wartime involvement. "Using this new-found force, Mexican Texans have obtained political advantages," (translated by author), editorialized Chapa, urging his fellow ethnics to "go forward" and support Jim Wells for governor.[3]

FULL-FLEDGED MEXICAN AMERICANIZATION

A more complete shift towards Mexican Americanization became apparent in the early 1930s. Mexico as a source of identity, however virulent it seemed in the initial *colonia*-building

stage, did not survive the massive repatriation provoked by the Great Depression. In Texas the League of United Latin American Citizens (LULAC), which has continued to this date as a major civil rights organization, dominated this era. An article by O. Douglas Weeks in the *Southwestern Social Science Quarterly* in 1929, the same year the organization was founded, signaled the emergence of this organization. According to Weeks, LULAC was middle class, accepted only U.S. citizens for membership and tended towards assimilation.

An articulate LULAC spokesman was lawyer and proud World War I veteran Manuel

[3] *El Imparcial de Texas*, November 14, 1918.

González, who often showed unabashed admiration for the Anglo. When elected LULAC president in 1932, he advised Mexican Americans to mix with Anglo Americans, who were "known to be members of a vigorous and masterful race." But Mexican Americans expressed sufficient ethnic pride to prevent cultural amnesia, enough to give the Chicano Movement a jump start. It was crucial, González thought, for Mexicans to strive for U.S. citizenship, but with "dignity and pride in our racial origins." Nonetheless, he exhibited classic ambivalence in confessing "that respect and admiration for the land of my forefathers may grow from day to day—and our love, devotion, and loyalty to America, the land of our birth, may never be surpassed by anyone."[5]

In listing problems that LULAC chose to solve, Weeks identified segregation as paramount, but he also indicated another main concern was the judicial system. Three articles, for example, in the first LULAC constitution directly dealt with the justice system. A constant issue in all of the eras discussed thus far, and a dominant one for LULAC and later the Chicano Movement, was equal treatment under the law. But

Benjamín Márquez, a scholar of LULAC, indicates, "The LULAC membership recognized that they were members of a dark-(rather darker) skinned ethnic group. But to be associated with Blacks or any other dark race was considered 'an insult.'" In 1936 when some Black musicians played at a Mexican gathering in an undetermined Texas city, a LULAC official criticized "illicit relations between these Negroes and certain ignorant and ill-informed Mexican girls." When the band went to Corpus Christi, the LULAC member wrote an official in that city asking him to prevent a similar incident from taking place there. "Let us tell these Negroes that we are not going to permit our manhood and womanhood to mingle with them on an equal social basis."[4]

50. Southern Pacific Railroad workers in Tucson, Arizona, during World War II.

[4] All quotes from Benjamín Márquez, *LULAC: The Evolution of a Mexican American Political Organization* (Austin: University of Texas Press, 1993), p. 33.

[5] Both quotes taken from David G. Gutiérrez, *Walls and Mirrors*, pp. 83-84.

while Mexican Americans always protested blatant police brutality, they also blamed the victim, in a certain sense believing that education of their people would curtail such conflicts. Chicano Movement advocates emphasized more the responsibility of police in such violent actions.

RACIAL AMBIGUITIES: CLAIMING WHITENESS

An essential goal of many Mexican American activists was to be classified as white. Basically, this stemmed from denial of Mexico's racial realities, but other reasons also accounted for this stance. It became obvious to U.S.

51. Soldier Jimmy Gastelum (left) of Amado, Arizona, and an unknown Mexican American soldier from Chicago during World War II.

Mexicans, even in the immigrant era, that if they were to be classified as colored, it could subject them to *de jure* segregation. The strategy employed in the few successful school desegregation efforts, as happened in the Tempe (1925) and Lemon Grove (1930) school cases discussed in Chapter Four, was based on the claim to whiteness.

In spite of accepting their nonwhite *mestizaje, México Lindo* leaders voiced opposition to segregation because they found being treated like Negroes was humiliating. In San Francisco during August of 1919 Consul Gerónimo S. Seguín protested that city authorities forced Mexicans to live in Black neighborhoods and that they had to sit with Blacks in cinemas and other public places. In 1935 Chicago's *El Nacional* inveighed against Mexicans being forced to use Negro undertakers. It urged its readers to use white funeral parlors because intimacy with Blacks only brought them down to that level in the eyes of white society. It can be said that these attitudes demonstrated not so much a desire to be considered white, but that Mexicans, as a brown people, were better than Blacks.

When the U.S. Census Bureau identified Mexicans as colored in 1930, Mexican American activists decided to fight the classification tooth and nail. For example, when in 1935 after Congress passed the Social Security Act, providing a federal retirement plan for the first time in history, its implementation required distributing millions of forms to employers throughout the country to identify the race of their employees. The choices were white, Negro and other—Asian, Indian or Mexican. When LULAC discovered that the Social Security Board had assigned a non white status to Mexicans, the group organized a major

Thousands of Mexicans not serving in the military engaged in "home-front" efforts such as bond drives. In the forefront of this effort were organizations like LULAC. For example, the El Paso Council No. 132 formed civil defense committees that instructed Mexican Americans on what action should be taken if the war ever came to the United States. A special measure of patriotism and endorsement of the war was the selling and buying of war bonds, a task that LULAC members took seriously. They also mustered support for the men in uniform by collecting gift packages and sending them to Mexican American members of the armed forces. In Phoenix middle-class Mexican American women joined a campaign sponsored by local women's clubs to harvest cotton and other crops needed for the war effort that would go unpicked because of labor shortages.

The 1946 LULAC national convention held in Houston focused on continuing discrimination. The honored guest was Macario García, one of five Medal of Honor recipients from Texas. Prior to the meeting, the *LULAC News* had denounced the refusing of service in restaurants and bars and the denial of low-cost veteran's public housing to the Mexican American GIs who had just "finished helping this country defeat countries . . . who would impose upon the world a superior culture." The reason they deserved better treatment was that, "we have proven ourselves true and loyal Americans by every test that has confronted us." The piece went on to demand "social, political and economic equality and the opportunity to practice that equality . . . not as a favor, but as a delegated right guaranteed by our Constitution and as a reward for our faithful service."[6]

campaign to reassign Mexicans to the white category. That same year in El Paso, Alex Powell, the county registrar, decided to record all Mexican births as non white, ostensibly to promote a healthful image to attract white tourists. The county had heretofore registered Mexicans, who suffered disproportionately from diseases such as tuberculosis, as whites, thus spoiling the image of health. Mexican Americans, however, raised enough of a protest to change Powell's mind.

WORLD WAR II AND THE MEXICAN-AMERICAN GENERATION

The U.S. declaration of war against the Axis powers in 1941 elicited enthusiastic support from Mexican Americans. In spite of continuing discrimination, patriotism among Mexican Americans ran high; in this optimistic era they felt more accepted than their parents. Also, unlike their parents, their ties to Mexico were weak or nonexistent. At least three hundred thousand young Mexican Americans joined soldiers from different backgrounds in all branches of the armed forces.

When the war ended, Mexican American GIs came back by the thousands to urban, small town and agricultural camp barrios. Many young people who had postponed wedding plans during the years of strife now married and had babies. The soldiers came back more assertive, ready to take their place in a society which by any reckoning they had fought to preserve. After the war, many young married Mexican American couples moved to the growing suburbs and were further acculturated.

52. Unknown Mexican American sailor from Houston during World War II.

53. Wedding photo of Roberto Colores and Juanita García in 1945. Colores, from Eloy, Arizona, was wounded during his service in the Air Corps.

[6] Quoted in Rosales, "Shifting Self-Perceptions and Ethnic Consciousness among Mexicans in Houston, 1908-1946," *Aztlán* 16 (1985), p. 89.

54. Guadalupe School in Austin, Texas, March 12, 1932.

LULAC leaders saw in Mexican wartime involvement an embodiment of their hopes and aspirations. The *LULAC News*, for example, editorialized in 1945 that World War II had accelerated the general objectives of the organization by teaching Mexican Americans to be better and more loyal citizens.

Mexican war veterans, angered by the continued discrimination that greeted them after the war, strove to achieve political power and status by making good use of their war record. Mexicans were still subjected to segregation or barred from public facilities in schools, theaters, swimming pools, restaurants and housing tracts. In Phoenix city officials tried to block Mexican American veterans from living in federally funded housing for veterans. Macario García, a Medal of Honor recipient, was denied service at a Texas roadhouse and then unceremoniously thrown out.

A dynamic organization that zealously sought the protection of civil rights for veterans was the American GI Forum. Mexican American veterans organized it in response to the refusal of a funeral director in Three Rivers, Texas, to bury Félix Longoria, a soldier killed in the Pacific theater. Key figures in the group were Dr. Héctor García, a former army medical officer who saw action in Europe, and civil rights lawyer Gus García. Longoria's remains were finally buried at Arlington Cemetery with full honors after Congressman Lyndon Baines Johnson intervened. The organization, nonetheless, became permanent, opened up its membership to veterans and went on to become a leading advocate for civil rights. Unlike LULAC, whose avowed policy was not to involve itself directly in electoral politics, the Forum openly advocated getting out the vote and endorsing candidates.

Mexican American veterans also founded American Legion Posts and, although their main purpose was social, members used them as vehicles to achieve civil rights. When Frank Fuentes and Ray Martínez organized the first American Legion Post for Mexican Americans in Phoenix, Arizona, they successfully integrated GI housing over the fervent protests of white veterans.

Ironically, in East Chicago, Indiana, the American Legion Post that some fifteen years earlier had led the campaign to repatriate Mexicans now welcomed the Mexican American veterans and even had a "Latin American night."

Mexican American politics of the postwar period did not produce radically new objectives or ideology. The main strategy pursued during the 1930s and the war itself continued. Mainly middle-class organizations focused on the obstacles to social and economic mobility, such as racism and segregation, in order to achieve higher status and greater prestige both as individuals and as an ethnic group. A good example of how this goal was undertaken is the formation of Club Vesta in Arizona during 1954, which admitted only college graduates at a time when few Mexican Americans went to college. Interestingly, the group took its name from the mythical Roman goddess Vesta, who symbolized purity, exclusivity and perpetuity. The organization provided its members with a status which they found so diffi-cult to obtain from Anglo Americans. Many *México Lindo* organizations pursued similar objectives; the difference is that Club Vesta prized Anglo symbols of success such as an American college degree and fluency in English.

YOUTH AND THE MEXICAN-AMERICAN GENERATION

The youth of the Mexican American era had the most in common with Chicano Movement activists—the generations almost overlapped. Certainly some of the leaders, such as "Corky" Gonzales, Luis Valdez and César Chávez, strad-dled both eras. It is no coincidence that, in spite of the clean-cut, "happy days" image projected by Mexican American youth, their thinking greatly influenced the more rebellious Chicano era.

The difference in the cultural and political outlook of young Mexicans growing up in the 1930s and 1940s with middle-class aspirations and the youth of the *México Lindo* era was that

Félix Tijerina came from a family of farm workers. He grew up in Sugar Land, an agricultural community adjacent to Houston. His life fulfilled the Horatio Alger ideal which inspired Mexican Americans. As a boy he moved to Houston, where he worked in restaurants and, by his account, learned to read English from menus. He opened up his own restaurant, which went broke after the Crash of 1929. With economic recovery, he modi-fied Mexican food to make it palatable to Anglos and "opened up a Mexican restaurant in the stylish Montrose area of Houston. Its success led eventually to establishing a chain, all displaying the familiar 'Felix's' signs throughout the city."[7]

55. Texas Governor Price Daniels signing Little School of 400 documents, with Félix Tijerina standing to his right.

[7] Rosales, "Mexicans in Houston: The Struggle to Survive, 1908-1975," *Houston Review* 3 (Summer 1981), p. 241.

56. Mexican American teenagers in Houston during the 1930s.

the leaders they admired most were not immigrants who intended to return to Mexico. They were a new generation who either had been born in the U.S. or who had been very young upon arriving from Mexico. Increasingly, more young people graduated from high school, giving them greater expectations in the larger society than those held by their parents. They could not identify with the symbolism perpetuated in previous decades by immigrant leaders. Instead, they leaned more towards Americanization. A great influence, for example, was Ignacio López, the publisher of *El Espectador*, who, although born in Mexico, championed these ideals.

Houston's Félix Tijerina was another salient Mexican American figure who also embodied the kind of leadership that greatly influenced young Mexican Americans. Tijerina served as national president of LULAC in the 1950s. Under his watch, the influential "Little School of 400," which sought to teach preschool Mexican Americans four hundred English words, was established in Texas.

In addition, in the 1930s young Mexican Americans were exposed to the greater Anglo society through such New Deal agencies as the Civilian Conservation Corps (CCC) and the National Youth Administration (NYA), both

designed to enroll young people and keep them off the streets during this era of massive unemployment. But the program reached into many parts of Mexican society. In Amado, Arizona, for example, a small village near the border made up of Southern Pacific Railroad workers and some Mexican farmers and farm workers, young men from local families were recruited into the CCC and taken out of this very remote and enclosed region. Some never returned to the old way of life after having been exposed to a broader society; they chose to make lives in Tucson and Los Angeles or, during World War II, become soldiers.

The clarion call for the ambitious young was education and self-improvement. The apotheosis of this formula made it a guiding principle that conceivably could eradicate discrimination and mistreatment in proportion to the degree of education Mexicans achieved. Youth clubs such as Houston's El Club Chapultepec, made up of young Mexican American girls, followed this ethos. They strove for education and mobility. When a young Mexican had been killed in his Houston city jail cell by his incarcerators, the group protested in writing. Its letter condemned police misconduct, but a major cause of such injustices, the statement read, stemmed from the difficulty Mexicans had in speaking English. It was crucial for Mexicans to learn to speak and write good English, a goal the club established for itself.

The quintessential Mexican youth organization emerged in Southern California during the 1930s under the auspices of the YMCA. It was called the Mexican American Movement (MAM). The members were made up of upwardly mobile youth, mostly college students who had committed themselves "to improve our conditions among our Mexican American and Mexican people living in the U.S." and to pursue "citizenship, higher education . . . and a more active participation in civic and cultural activities by those of our national descent." [8]

[8] Quoted in Gutiérrez, *Walls and Mirrors*, p. 136.

Mexican Voice editor Félix Gutiérrez Sr. penned a column entitled "Nosotros" in almost every issue. In one anecdote Gutiérrez recounted attending a meeting where the Mexican consul spoke and encouraged *paisanos* not to naturalize because "once a Mexican, always a Mexican." Apparently the consul went so far as to say that, if Mexican immigrants became U.S. citizens, they might as well "drain their blood and dye their hair blond." This affront and challenge prompted Guitiérrez to write one of his strongest appeals to Americanism, wishing that, the consul could "see young students of our national descent—gay, carefree, thinking of success, interested in American activities, playing American games, speaking and using American terms, having the same ideas and ideals, using American sportsmanship, enjoying American customs, loving American food."[9]

Then, Gutiérrez concluded, the consul would see that Mexicans who were born and live in this country have become Americans.

57. Southgate School in Corpus Christi, Texas, 1939-40.

The organization propagated these views through its newspaper, the *Mexican Voice*. Issue after issue of the newspaper bombarded its readers with the ideal of progress through education and hard work. It minimized racism as the main detriment to success. But cultural pride that recognized pre-Columbian roots was part of their ideological kit, possibly as a link between the mestizo identity of the *México Lindo* era and the Chicano position of the 1960s.

In a July 1938 issue of the *Mexican Voice,* Manuel Ceja wrote a piece entitled, "Are We Proud of Being Mexicans?" It comes very close to the rhetoric of identity used by Chicanos in the 1960s. An exemplar of MAM's professed ideals, Ceja was born in Los Angeles in 1920 of immigrant parents. He attended Compton Junior College and graduated from the Spanish American Institute, a leadership tank for Mexican Americans. He was also a volunteer coach at the local chapter of the Mexican American Pioneer Club, a boys club within the MAM.

In the article Ceja claims to have overheard a boy respond to a query about his ethnicity by saying he was Spanish. He asks, "Why are we so afraid to tell people that we are Mexicans? Are we ashamed of the color of our skin, and the shape and build of our bodies, or the background from which we have descended?" He emphasized that the bilingual and bicultural attributes of Mexican Americans could open innumerable doors. "Then why is it that we as Mexicans do not com-

[9] *Mexican Voice,* July 1938.

mand respect as a nation? Are we doing justice to our race when we do not endeavor to change this attitude?"[10]

While they extolled the virtues of *mexicanidad*, when confronted with a situation where they had to choose between Mexicaness and being American, they chose the latter. MAM ideology equated white with Americanism, the same assessment held by the older Mexican American leadership. Moreover, MAM organizers accepted a prevalent notion that Mexicans in the U.S. inherited traits that were shaped by Mexican history and were incompatible with modern society.

The *Mexican Voice* continuously posited the belief that Mexicans needed to improve themselves in order to be accepted and to succeed in the U.S. Paul Coronel, in an "Analysis of Our People," said that Mexico's poverty and its corrupt and weak political leadership created a deficient culture, but education was the solution to this problem. In another article Coronel observed that Mexican girls married whites who had better jobs and could provide a better life. He then chided a friend who angrily derided the women for turning their backs on fellow Mexicans and saying, "We are not good enough for them." Coronel did not blame the women because Mexican Americans need to wake up and work harder so they can also make good husbands.[11]

Some of MAM's most dynamic leadership came from its female members. Like their male counterparts, they also held strong beliefs of progress through self-improvement. Importantly, they advised this for women also. Particularly active was Dora Ibáñez. Born in Mexico, she attended public schools in Texas and worked her way through college in Iowa and Arizona, where she received a teacher's certificate from the Arizona Normal School (now Arizona State University) in Tempe. In a 1939 *Mexican Voice* essay entitled "A Challenge to the American Girl of Mexican Parentage," she praised the direction MAM males took towards education and Americanization. But she feared that the group aimed this message mainly at men and did not encourage women. She also encouraged Mexican American females to strive for education and professional careers; that was why they should participate more in MAM activities.

Just as Chicano Movement activity in Los Angeles influenced other areas, MAM was an important vehicle for spreading the message of Mexican Americanization from Los Angeles to New Mexico and Arizona. Its appeal reached especially into Arizona, where Félix Gutiérrez met his wife, Rebecca Muñoz. Members of a club called Los Conquistadores (The Conquistadors) at Arizona Normal School, they attended a conference sponsored by the MAM in Los Angeles and returned to Tempe, excitedly propagating lessons learned at the confer-

A MAM activist, Consuelo Espinoza, in an essay entitled "The Constitution and the Fourteenth Amendment," discussed constitutional rights and how they should be respected, especially at that time when a war had been fought against dictators. "I am not afraid to say that some parents teach their children not to talk or play with a Negro or a Mexican. This is un-Christian and un-American. We say that we have to teach the youth of Germany the way of Democracy. Let me tell you, Americans, we still have a great job ahead of us, especially against the same racial prejudice."[12]

[10] *Mexican Voice*, October-November 1938.

[11] *Mexican Voice*, October-November 1938.

[12] *Forward*, May 12, 1946.

In the 1942 Sleepy Lagoon case, twenty-two teenagers were tried for killing a Mexican teenager at a party. The group was convicted on some very weak evidence and sentenced on charges ranging from assault to first-degree murder. In 1944 an appeal resulted in reversal of charges because of the bias which permeated the first trial. But the event clearly demonstrated that exaggerated hostility existed towards Mexican American youth. According to Manuel Ruiz,

> Instead of arresting two or three trouble-makers for disturbing the peace at some dance, authorities arrested, on one occasion, as many as seventy-two young boys. . . . Whenever a group of young boys, even on slight pretext, could be rounded up, they were arrested. . . . Naturally, the wholesale arrest procedure gave a distorted picture. Although the rate of juvenile delinquency convictions did not rise over any other similar period of time among youngsters of Mexican extraction . . . the press continued to lay emphasis on group apprehensions . . . . the public received a picture of roving gangs of bloodthirsty, marijuana-crazed young men, committing arson, rape and robbery.[13]

58. *Pachuco* defendants in the infamous Sleepy Lagoon case, 1944.

The position of the Sleepy Lagoon Defense Committee is clearly made by the following statement:

> It wasn't only seventeen boys who were on trial. It was the whole of the Mexican people, and their children and grandchildren. It was the whole of Latin America with its 130,000,000 people. It was the Good Neighbor Policy. It was the United Nations and all for which they fight.[14]

ence. Links from the Mexican American generation to the Chicano Movement can be seen within a family context as well. A member of the Los Conquistadores in Arizona was Rosalío Muñoz, whose son, Rosalío Jr., became a stalwart of the Chicano Movement. This older generation, represented by Rosalío Sr., in its own way was a precursor of the kind of activism that their children would participate in later.

YOUTH REPRESSION: *PACHUCOS* AND THE CHALLENGE TO OPTIMISM

The gang activity of *pachucos* (zoot-suited street youth) provoked a severe police crackdown and an onslaught of negative media coverage that inflamed a widespread public backlash against Mexicans. Some observers even linked this youth culture to Mexican *sinarquistas* (fascists). In the atmosphere of World War II, this was enough to paint all Mexican Americans, who were either children of immigrants or immigrants themselves, with the brush of disloyalty. Lawyer Manuel Ruiz, a youth worker, said that, if the negative newspaper coverage about *pachucos* were not enough to unnerve the public, "the stage was set for international intrigue. Three prominent officials in Los Angeles County were directly misquoted to the effect that these boy

---

[13] Manuel Ruiz, "Latin American Juvenile Delinquency in Los Angeles: Bomb or Bubble," typescript in Carey McWilliams Papers, Special Collections, University of California, Los Angeles Research Library, p. 2.

[14] Quoted in Gutiérrez, *Walls and Mirrors*, p. 128.

gangs were inspired by Nazi and Fascist agents."

Blatant repression of Mexican American youth threatened the gains civil rights activists secured within the American system. But instead of distancing themselves from the issue, many California Mexican American activists came to their defense by forming the Citizen's Committee for Latin American Youth, with Manuel Ruiz as chairman. But the strategies employed were carefully crafted in order to not exacerbate an already intense xenophobia aimed at Mexicans during the war.

In fact, Mexican American leaders quickly attempted to turn this dilemma to their advantage. Wartime rhetoric was manipulated to publicize the plight of young, isolated Mexican Americans whom mainstream society ignored at a time when all Americans should be promoting unity. Ruiz promoted bilingual education as a "means to teach any curricular subject, whether it be Americanization, hygiene or anything else." He lamented the contradictory policy that "Spanish may be taught but the Spanish language cannot be used to teach."[15]

Other Californians, besides Mexican Americans, considered this treatment unjust. A committee was formed to provide legal support for the Sleepy Lagoon defendants who were accused of killing another Mexican American teenager at a party in 1942. It included journalist-crusader Carey McWilliams, labor organizer Bert Corona, Josefina Fierro Bright from the Congress of Spanish-Speaking People, Anthony Quinn and an array of other Hollywood actors and moviemakers. Curiously, because the activist group contained well-known socialists—McWilliams, Fierro Bright and Corona—the effort tried not to be seen as un-American.

It was the infamous Zoot Suit Riots that elicited the greatest amount of hand-wringing among Mexican American leaders. In the spring of 1943 with the tacit support of the press and their superiors, servicemen stationed in the Los Angeles area commandeered taxi cabs and spilled out into the streets of East Los Angeles, beating up every Mexican teenager who crossed

their path. The immediate cause of the riot was conflict between young Mexican Americans and equally young American soldiers in East Los Angeles. Under proper discipline, the servicemen would not have been allowed such behavior—in essence, permission was given to carry out the persecution of Mexican American youths. And police, rather than stopping or arresting the soldiers, took the Mexican American youths into custody.

DESEGREGATION EFFORTS

Although prejudice and rejection persisted after the war, Mexican Americans were now more integrated into mainstream society, and they displayed stronger capabilities in breaking down obstacles to economic and social mobility. In the 1950s Mexican Americans saw school segregation as the most formidable barrier blocking their progress. In the 1930s the Bliss Bill, designed to segregate Mexicans using a "separate-but-equal" foundation, was defeated in the

59. A youth stripped of his zoot suit by servicemen in Los Angeles, June 7, 1943.

---

[15] Last two quotes, Ruiz, "Latin American Juvenile Delinquency in Los Angeles: Bomb or Bubble," pp. 2, 4-5.

In San Antonio Judge Albert Peña remembers how, in 1950, the GI Forum asked him to investigate school segregation in Hondo, Texas. Peña went to the superintendent and asked him to persuade the board to end segregation because it was unconstitutional. Mexican children could go only as high as seventh grade, after which there was no school for them. When he was turned down by the school board and the Department of Education at the state level, he and some members of the GI Forum persuaded all of the Mexican American parents in Hondo to attend the school board meeting and complain. Eventually the board capitulated.

Another case demonstrates the injustice of segregation. Roberto Villarreal did not start high school in Karnes City, Texas, until he was twenty years old, when the school was finally integrated in the 1950s. Upon his high school graduation, Villarreal went on to the University of Texas at Austin, received a BA and an MA, and then went to the University of Oklahoma, where he earned a Ph.D. in political science. Today he is a professor of government at the University of Texas at El Paso.

60. A Mexican school less than two blocks away from an Anglo school in Austin, Texas.

California legislature. Lawmakers recognized the difficulty of separating Mexicans, who were considered white after precedence set by the Lemon Grove decision (see Chapter Four). Still, school boards maintained segregation in a different guise, emphasizing the necessity to give Mexican Americans a separate education because of cultural and language differences. Certainly if this had been the real reason, few Mexican Americans would have objected, knowing that their children would eventually join the mainstream. But seeing that it was really racism that motivated these policies, they strove to eliminate school segregation.

For example, in a LULAC-sponsored initiative, attorneys from the Lawyer's Guild succeeded in 1946 in desegregating a number of Southern California schools in the landmark *Westminster v. Méndez* case by arguing that segregation violated constitutional rights of Mexican children guaranteed by the

61. A Mexican school in a former church building. White children of the district were transported to city schools.

Fourteenth Amendment. At least five thousand Mexican American children were affected. As expected, the Westminster decision had a momentous effect on the future efforts to segregate Mexican children. And, in fact, the case set a precedent for NAACP lawyers, arguing *Brown v. Board of Education* in 1964.

Texas and Arizona Mexican American leaders waged the most intense efforts to desegregate schools because it was in those states that the policies were most stringent. In Texas LULAC was in the forefront of this campaign and could point to successes even before the war. During the 1930s schools in Del Rio, Goliad and Beeville were integrated, but the bulk of the battle remained for later years. In 1948 lawyers commissioned by LULAC used the historic *Westminster* decision as precedence to challenge segregation in Bastrop, Texas, schools. The court ruled in favor of prohibiting segregation either in separate schools or in separate rooms within the same school.

In Arizona, because of the 1952 *Sheely v. González* decision, segregation was abolished in Tolleson, a town near Phoenix. The successful integration decision came about because of the resolve parents demonstrated by organizing into the Tolleson Civic League. Also essential in this endeavor was Ralph Estrada, a lawyer and president of the Alianza Hispano Americana. Two years later in nearby Peoria, the school board voluntarily ended segregation of Mexicans in local schools —this was the last holdout in the state. The initiative foiled the desires of school officials who stubbornly clung to the idea that Mexican Americans required separation because of their different culture. As in the Texas cases, the *Westminster* decision played a crucial part in the Tolleson case.

But these court victories were only as good as the desire of school administrators to carry out the judicial mandates. In Texas officials did not act promptly in issuing desegregation orders, and it took continuous prodding from the Mexican community to bring about true integration.

SEE-SAW SUCCESS AND USING THE BALLOT BOX

After the war, status-conscious Mexican American *políticos* turned increasingly to the ballot box in order to achieve objectives. The tactic was not new. It was expressed as early as the 1890s by Arizona's Alianza Hispano Americana and El Partido del Pueblo (The People's Party) in New Mexico.[16] By World War I, the number of potential Mexican voters increased, especially in Texas, and Mexican American leaders began to savor the leverage they could wield by controlling a bloc vote (see the case of Francisco Chapa, pp. 91-92). In Los Angeles and other large cities with *colonias* made up mainly of recent immigrants, electoral power was not even a remote option until the 1940s when the immi-

The Elpidio Cortés incident, which involved a Mexican who was killed in his Houston jail cell by policemen in 1937, demonstrates how the Mexican American generation used any issue to promote its political agenda. Manuel González, the LULAC stalwart, pressured city officials to prosecute the officers and then monitored the proceedings closely. But González also interpreted the whole episode from within the canon of Mexican Americanism. Such incidents would not occur if the Houston Mexicans voted in greater numbers, he and LULAC members reasoned. González used the incident to rally the community to pay poll taxes and vote.

In Arizona the issue of registering and voting was the core purpose of the Latin American Club as the club's spokesperson Laura Rodríguez demonstrated when she read the following founding principles on a 1934 radio program: "Mexican people of Arizona, for many years our race has been dormant in the affairs of governmental policies. . . . The Latin American Club, now

---

[16] I am not including nineteenth-century machine politics of New Mexico and Texas, in which Mexicans participated at a significant level, but their leaders did not express a desire for reform or to recoup lost ethnic power.

organized throughout the State of Arizona, is the best means by which the Mexican people. . . can take a leading part in the. . . government."[17]

Using tactics employed in Los Angeles, in 1952 Adam Díaz became the first Mexican American to serve on the Phoenix, Arizona, city council. Later, former Chicano Movement activists, such as Ed Pastor, Mary Rose Garrido-Wilcox and Saúl Leija, continued the tradition of running for city and county positions in Maricopa County—an activity that before the *movimiento* was exclusively the domain of Mexican American style politicians. Ed Pastor is now the first and only Hispanic member of Congress from Arizona.

62. Edward Roybal today.

grants' children matured into adults.

While few Southwest Mexicans voted during the immigrant era, electoral participation in the Midwest in this period was virtually nonexistent. But by the early 1930s signs appeared that Mexicans who survived repatriation realized the need to use the ballot box and change the *México Lindo* orientation of Chicago Mexicans. In 1932 the newspaper *El Nacional* supported Russell J. Alvarez, son of a Spanish father and a German mother, for municipal court judge, indicating that Mexicans and other Latins should vote for him because "he is familiar with our customs and . . . will impart justice to our race with less prejudice than any other judge."[18]

In East Chicago the first Mexican American Political Club was formed by a group of naturalized immigrants with the goal of uniting the *colonia* as a voting bloc. The generation of potential voters had not yet matured, however, and East Chicago *políticos* would have to wait until the 1960s before they became a dominant force in the Democratic Party of Lake County.

Elsewhere electoral politics yielded successes earlier. After a major voter registration drive by the Community Service Organization (CSO) in Los Angeles that enrolled fifteen thousand Mexican Americans, Edward Roybal won a seat on the city council in 1949. After Roybal had lost his first bid for the city council in 1947, his Mexican American supporters, many of them veterans, established the CSO with the help of Fred Ross, an organizer for Saul Alisky's Chicago-based Industrial Areas Foundation (IAF). The success-oriented IAF had a solid history of empowering poor neighborhoods through political organizing, a tactic which suited the aspirations of Los Angeles's Mexican Americans.

In California Mexican Americans felt confident that their political acumen was now highly polished, and they proceeded to seek political offices with a great amount of optimism. But the results were not heartening. Edward Roybal in 1954 raised his sights from representing his community on the Los Angeles City Council and unsuccessfully sought the Democratic nomination for lieutenant governor. Four years later, he ran for a slot on the County Board of Supervisors and lost. That same year, 1958, Hank López, a Harvard-educated lawyer, won the Democratic Party nomination for California secretary of state but lost in the general election. Both candidates lost by narrow margins, and many Mexican American politicians resented that the Democratic Party

[17] Harvey Wilson and Laura Rodríguez, "Aims of the Latin American Club," *Latino Americano* 1 (April 1934), p. 12.

[18] *El Nacional*, April 9, 1932, Chicago Historical Society, Reel 62, Chicago Foreign Language Press Survey.

structure provided only lukewarm support to Mexican American candidates.

In New Mexico, where Mexican Americans comprised a very large portion of the population, they had the greatest amount of twentieth-century success. In 1919, for example, the Mexican-born Octaviano Larrazolo served as governor. Dennis Chávez occupied a U.S. Senate seat from the 1930s until his death in 1962. His successor, Joseph Montoya, elected in 1964, stayed in the Senate until the 1970s. More importantly, in New Mexico Hispanics controlled numerous local positions as would be seen in Tierra Amarilla, where Chicano Movement leader Reies López Tijerina was opposed by the Mexican American establishment.

Similarly, in South Texas where La Raza Unida's greatest stronghold existed, mainstream Mexican American *políticos*, always Democrats, enjoyed some success before the emergence of La Raza Unida. During the immigration era, for example, constituents had elected native Tejanos to local positions in the machine-dominated Laredo area and throughout the Lower Rio Grande Valley. Powerful Anglos dominated the machines, but at least one *político*, José Canales, managed to break away from the Jim Wells Machine in the early 1900s. Elected repeatedly to the state legislature, he was successful in deterring Texas Ranger abuses during the period of the Mexican Revolution. Others, Eligio "Kika" de la Garza and Henry B. González, were elected in the 1960s to the U.S. Congress.

The most encouraging electoral gain for Mexican Americans was the 1957 election to mayor of Raymond Telles, who had served as El Paso county clerk since 1948. Telles's victory also demonstrated that Mexican Americans would vote in bloc if the candidate was one of their own. Half of El Paso's population of 250,000 was Mexican, but they were outnumbered by non-Mexican registered voters by a considerable margin. To win, Telles needed to carry a sizable percentage of the white vote, which he did by waging a campaign in which ethnic and race differences were minimized. In addition, Telles did not dwell on the impoverishment affecting a large portion of El Paso's Mexican working class. Instead, Telles struck a more general populist cord that emphasized curbing the power of the professional politicians who had run city hall for years.

Owing to this strategy, he did not scare away potential white supporters who wanted to see city politics cleaned up. At the same time, he did not appear too tame to a large Mexican electorate that was predisposed to support him because of his ethnic appeal. Moreover, Telles's tenure as an efficient county clerk completed his image as a tested and trusted official. To Chicano Movement politicians, essentially those in La Raza Unida Party, such a strategy required too many com-

The shift to accepting and even claiming nonwhite status did not come easy for some Mexican Americans, who themselves held racist views. In an interchange with another retired judge in Edinburg, Judge Juan Carlos Cadena commented that Mexicans are Mongoloid, according to anthropologists, and that they came across the Bering Straits. His friend indignantly replied, "'You're going to make a Chinaman out of me.' And I said, 'Well, would you rather be a Chinaman with full rights . . . or a white person with no rights?'" The judge's friend replied that he would rather be subjected to discrimination than give up his claim to whiteness. Also in the 1950s Cadena told another acquaintance that he planned to enroll a Black girl into San Antonio's all-Mexican Sidney Lanier High School because she lived in the barrio and had to travel miles to another school. When his friend objected to this, Cadena queried, "Don't you believe in civil rights?" His friend replied in the affirmative, but said, "Only for humans."[19]

[19] Interview with Judge Carlos Cadena by Jesús Treviño, n.d., NLCC-GP.

promises for their ambitious reform objectives.

EMULATING THE BLACK CIVIL RIGHTS MOVEMENT

By the 1950s Mexican Americans began to see the success of Black civil rights activists that was garnered by leaders insisting that racism was responsible for many of their people's problems. The integration of the armed forces and the entry of Black athletes into major league professional sports, for example, demonstrated that concessions could be wrested from the white establishment by pricking their conscience. This encouraged Mexican Americans to abandon the claim of being white Americans of ethnic descent—like Italian Americans or Polish Americans—and to start identifying with the course favored by Blacks.

Another reason for abandoning the white ethnic identity is that, at times, this status backfired. For example, demands for a jury of peers, when the defendant was Mexican, were met with retorts that seating all-Anglo juries did not exclude the Mexican race since it was supposedly white. This changed when in 1953 lawyer Juan Carlos Cadena, later a judge in San Antonio, with partner Gus García successfully argued before the U.S. Supreme Court that Pete Hernández's rights to a jury of peers had been violated because no Mexican Americans were on the panel that convicted him of murder. Mexican Americans were beginning to think of themselves as ethnic and racial beings.

By the late 1950s Mexican Americans, more than ever impressed with the success of the Black civil rights movement, consciously or unconsciously emulated many of its strategies. Determined to obtain political agency, in 1959 Edward Roybal, Bert Corona and Eduardo Quevedo met in Fresno and formed the Mexican American Political Association (MAPA). MAPA's goals varied because militant and moderate members differed on strategies. But the group's loose organizational structure allowed it to function effectively in spite of divisions. Soon the organization spread throughout the Southwest.

The new organizations, especially the ones in California, departed from traditional Mexican Americanism in two ways. One, they diluted the notion that mainly a lack of education made Mexicans vulnerable and, two, they regularly employed the rhetoric of racism as a source of problems. Both of these were immediate precursors to Chicano Movement beliefs. By 1966 after the success of Martin Luther King's civil rights campaigns, Mexican Americans were even more encouraged to emulate his tactics. At an Equal Employment Opportunity Commission meeting in Albuquerque, New Mexico, in March of 1966, the watchdog group heard grievances from members of such organizations as Political Association of Spanish-speaking Organizations (PASO) and LULAC, who walked out after demanding that EEOC put Mexican Americans on the commission's board and punish large southwestern corporate employers who discriminated in hiring Mexican Americans. Judge Albert Peña, a San Antonio politician, explained after the walkout why Mexican Americans were now using these tactics. Government officials told them, he said, "the trouble with you [Mexicans] is, you don't make enough noise, you don't demonstrate, you don't raise Cain enough." Joan Moore and Ralph Guzmán, scholars from the Mexican American Study Project at UCLA, observed in an article in the *Nation* after an Albuquerque walkout, "The New Mexican leader studies Negro civil rights techniques with a degree of attention approaching the Pentagon's study of Chinese guerillas."[20]

At the end of the 1950s Mexican Americans felt ready to transcend regional political aspirations and obtain political saliency and power at the national level. The ability to head in that direction was manifested during the 1960 campaign by the Democratic Party to elect the charismatic John F. Kennedy to the presidency. The cards were stacked against his winning, primarily because of his Catholic Irish background. But

---

[20] Both quotes in Peter Skerry, *Mexican Americans: The Ambivilant Minority* (New York: The Free Press, 1993), pp. 253-254.

Mexican Americans identified with his Catholicism and to a degree with his ethnicity. Moreover, at the 1960 convention, the Democratic Party selected as Kennedy's running mate, Lyndon Baines Johnson, a Texas politician who early on recognized the importance of the emerging Mexican American vote in his home state. Johnson urged Kennedy to be responsive to this constituency.

Mexican American leaders Edward Roybal and Dennis Chávez, the GI Forum, MAPA and the Alianza Hispano Americana responded to Johnson's call and formed the Viva Kennedy clubs to deliver the Mexican American vote for the Kennedy-Johnson ticket. Prior to this, as one historian stated, "Mexicans were not widely recognized electorally as a significant factor in national presidential elections. Mexican American voters were taken for granted as a known but modest part of the Democratic Party constituency."[21]

In the Kennedy-Nixon contest for the presidency, it was widely held that the Mexican American vote was crucial in delivering Texas, a state with a significant wealth of electoral votes. Texas could provide the margin of victory that Kennedy needed. For the thousands of Mexican American volunteers who worked on the campaign, Kennedy's success also became an ethnic victory. Their leaders, who forged heretofore unseen national-level alliances, were buoyant about their political future in the U.S. The wealth of experience acquired in the Kennedy campaign was subsequently parlayed into political action that would help Mexican American candidates locally. One clear result was the formation of PASO, which successfully overturned the city council in Crystal City in 1963.

CONCLUSION

As seen, Mexican Americanization was in large part dominated by middle-class reformers who advocated assimilation and working within the system as the solution to problems facing Mexicans in the U.S. But by the end of the 1950s middle-class prescriptions began to change as Mexican Americans witnessed the successes Blacks were registering by using demonstrations and picketing and charging white America with racism. As the bolder Mexican American leaders turned to these tactics, they undoubtedly served as examples to the young Chicano generation which was coming of age during this period. In addition, Mexican American politicians began to see themselves as major players in national politics by the end of this era. This was a factor that left the legacy of the ballot box option to Chicano Movement activists, as will be seen in the rise of La Raza Unida Party.

---

[21] Juan Gómez-Quiñones, *Chicano Politics*, p. 89.

CHAPTER SEVEN

In Defense of the Workplace

63. "La Marcha," marching for minimum wage in Corpus Christi, Texas, in 1966. Dr. Clotilde P. García (far left) and Dr. Héctor P. García (far right).

In this chapter the role of Mexican Americanism in fostering labor unions is examined. Using permanency as a core prerequisite, a working class alternative to LULAC and its similar organizations emerged that was truly in the Mexican American mode. But unlike the Mexican American civil rights strategy, Mexican American union efforts emphasized bread-and-butter objectives and radical goals. This aspect of Mexican Americanism was an important precursor to the Chicano Movement, but it was not as crucial as fighting for civil rights and ending job discrimination. Except for supporting labor organizing in general and the farm-worker movement of César Chávez in particular, Chicano Movement activists did not make labor organizing or rectifying workplace exploitation direct objectives. Perhaps because recent immigration, both undocumented and legal, did not initially attract the attention of *movimiento* activists, the most dramatic examples of severe labor exploitation failed to enter their field of vision. *Movimiento* participants continued to be concerned with the middle-class Mexican American vision of educational attainment and social mobility more than bread-and-butter concerns of Mexican workers. This is understandable. Like their Mexican American predecessors, they were the children of workers, and removing the racist obstacles that prevented them equal opportunity in jobs outside the working class was more important.

In addition, *movimiento* participants did not dwell on unionization because its success depended on a working-class consciousness that required collaboration with white workers—an unattractive option during these very nationalistic times. Moreover, in the late 1960s thousands of Mexican Americans in California, Arizona and the Midwest already belonged to established unions such as the United Automobile Workers, the United Mine Workers and the International Brotherhood of Machinists. These well-paid Mexican American workers saw their struggles behind them or separate from the Chicano Movement.

But mainstream unions, which led a significant proportion of American working people down the path of an "elite blue-collar" nirvana, did not accept many Mexican workers within their ranks. The reason? Labor unions usually established their successful drives in industrial sectors located in areas of the country where few Mexicans worked. Then, too, benign or outright racist neglect by unions ignored the plight of many sectors that employed Mexicans, serving to keep them subordinated socially and economically. This chapter examines why U.S. Mexicans did not share equally with white workers in their empowerment and economic advancement and how Mexican Americans struggled for change and thus set the stage for the later activism of the Chicano Movement.

With the rise of industrialism and modernization in the U.S. during the nineteenth century, Mexican workers were inexorably drawn into meeting a significant portion of the labor needs of this process—with lamentable results. Since the early 1900s the dream of all Mexican immigrants was to find a job, but once working, they labored under the most arduous of conditions, usually in labor sectors designated for Mexicans only. They also remained extremely vulnerable to job insecurity because the "last-hired, first-fired" syndrome particularly applied to Mexicans, especially during severe economic slumps.

During the downturn of these cycles, Mexicans confronted long-term unemployment and destitution, a worse predicament than the most laborious of jobs. Daniel Venegas, in *Las aventuras de Don Chipote*, a humorous novel written in the 1920s, casts the immigrant protagonist, Don Chipote, in one disagreeable job after another. The tasks at a Los Angeles cement factory are so oppressive that he quits the same day he is hired. Generally, the most distasteful job experiences stemmed from having "*patrones que eran muy perros* (bosses that were mean dogs)."[1] Anglos,

---

[1] This was a pat aphorism of my uncle, Roberto Rosales, who, like the character Don Chipote, worked as a sharecropper, on railroad maintenance crews, as a construction laborer and in a cotton compress and finally retired from his janitor job at Catalina High School in Tucson. Being a janitor was for him the easiest work he had ever done.

and even Mexican Americans, who supervised Mexican workers sometimes leveraged power by resorting to demeaning force. At times these bosses even severely injured or killed their charges during altercations.

Mainstream labor unions often felt Mexicans were unorganizable, a posture that produced chauvinistic attitudes among rank-and-file white workers. Indeed, many Mexican immigrants were used as strikebreakers in various industries. In addition, both white and Black American workers disliked Mexicans because they saw them as competitors for jobs and because they lowered wages.

The most severe backlash towards Mexicans occurred during the recession of 1921 in Texas. As unemployment rocked the Texas oil industry, citizens of Eastland, a town near Temple, attempted in February to expel Mexicans hired during World War I. In nearby Ranger, mounted, masked men ravaged the frame shacks of Mexican work-

White workers were not the only ones who resented Mexicans during the recession. Black leaders during the 1920s often railed against the threat Mexicans posed to workers, ". . . taking bread from the mouths of colored people."[2] Early in 1921 ninety percent of the Fort Worth Mexican work force was jobless after Black and white workers coerced employers into firing Mexicans. The Blacks and whites had marched on city hall after city officials received an anonymous letter threatening to blow up the building unless Mexicans were discharged from city construction projects.

Unemployment in the 1930s, as had been the case in 1921, encouraged antagonism towards Mexicans, manifested through threats and violence. On January 12, 1931, one hundred fifty Anglo workers in Knickerbocker, Texas, signed a petition and presented it to E.E. Foster, the Tom Greene county commissioner, demanding that Mexican workers be fired from highway construction jobs. Foster replied that only Americans would be hired from that point on. In June Sheriff Haynes of San Angelo received a letter threatening Mexicans, signed "The Unemployed, South with Mexicans." It indicated, "We are making raids on all Mexicans in and around San Angelo in the near future. This is the First Warning. We are prepared for trouble, so keep yourself out of it." The San Angelo *Evening Standard* received one from the "Darts and Others," which said, "We are forming a club known as the Darts and our aim is to clean up this city making working conditions better for Americans. You will hear from us from time to time as our good work progresses (sic) each member will work separately not knowing any other member. All Mexicans must leave." [3]

In May disgruntled workers in Malakoff, an oil company town near Dallas, took more concrete action. On May 19 the "Mexican Hall," a gathering place for Mexicans who worked for the Malakoff Fuel Company, was dynamited. After the blast, placards attached to the wrecked hall read, "LEAVE TOWN, DAMN PRONTO."[4] The Dallas *Dispatch* attributed the violence to the hiring of Mexicans during the economic crisis. The terrorized Mexicans appealed to Dallas Consul Juan E. Achondo, who asked County Sheriff C. G. Pharris to protect the workers. The sheriff did not seem too enthusiastic, so Achondo appealed to the Malakoff Fuel Company. The incident prompted the fuel company's director to come to Malakoff from Dallas and confer with local managers. After assuring the consul that the company would protect Mexicans, he called Governor Ross Sterling, who dispatched Texas Rangers to the area to keep the peace.

[2] Quoted in Arnold Shankman, "The Image of Mexico and the Mexican American in the Black Press, 1890-1935," *Journal of Ethnic Studies* 3 (Summer 1975), pp. 43-56.

[3] *El Defensor*, June 12, 1931.

[4] Juan E. Achondo, Dallas consul, to Lorenzo Lupián, consul general, San Antonio, May 20, 1931, Archivo Histórico de la Secretaría de Relaciones Exteriores, IV-325-68.

ers and warned them not to compete with American labor. The beleaguered Mexicans sought help from local authorities, who told them to leave town. About one hundred refugees fled to Fort Worth and told the grisly story to the Mexican consul. They had come with a petition asking the Mexican government to help in curtailing hostilities and providing repatriation funds.

The refugees disclosed that at least five hundred of their countrymen were still in Ranger, unable to leave. Consul Francisco Pérez then sought funds to transport the besieged Mexicans to the border so that from there they could return to homes in the Mexican interior. Following the Ranger assaults, others occurred in Cisco, Texas, where white attackers threw rocks at Mexicans and threatened their lives if they did not vacate the town.

While competition provoked white worker vengeance, white elites—influential employers and officials—protected Mexicans for financial as well as humanitarian reasons. Oil company executives moved quickly to pressure newly elected Governor Pat Neff to send Texas Rangers into troubled areas to quell the violence once again in January. By the end of February 1921 Ranger and the surrounding areas were pacified. But depredations continued in North Texas during the course of the year. Americans continued to attack Mexicans, primarily because of the backlash and fear created by unemployment.

Anti-Mexican violence subsided when the recession ended, but during another downturn in 1926 outbreaks returned, especially in Texas. The Mexican consul in Houston complained in December that hooded Klu Klux Klan members had attacked and ejected Mexicans and Black workers from Sugar Land. Most of the Mexicans were humble peons, said the consul, and whites had targeted them because they accepted low wages. Indeed, Mexican Consul Humberto Valenzuela in San Antonio warned earlier in the year that this could happen because Mexicans worked for $1.25 a day, a wage so low that even Blacks would not accept it.

INFORMAL DEFENSE IN THE WORKPLACE

The crucial question here is, did Mexicans

64. Mexican women working at a tortilla factory in San Antonio in the 1930s.

defend themselves against these abuses? Mexican workers at times had organized unions at the risk of life and limb, but they also defended their interests without taking such formal avenues. For example, a common strategy for farm workers was to travel in groups and insist on being hired as such. These independent work crews, usually made up of families, close friends or *compadres,* were less vulnerable to exploitation.

The consular service also served as a broker for Mexicans with their employers. Consuls were supposed to maintain distance when labor conflicts involved compatriots, but they monitored procedures to prevent legal violations. When Cochise County officials jailed four thousand Mexican participants in the 1917 Arizona copper mine strikes, the Mexican consul in Douglas, Ives Levelier, helped get hundreds of strikers released. Consuls also objected to dangerous and unhealthy working conditions. Miner's consump-

tion, the dreaded "black lung," affected Mexican miners so disproportionately that the Mexican consul in Globe, Arizona, Gustavo G. Hernández, wrote in May of 1918 to the Arizona State Federation of Labor and to Governor George W. P. Hunt asking for an end to the conditions which caused this disease. "It strikes me that the number of Mexicans who are sick [are more] than any other nationality," the consul wrote Governor Hunt. Mexicans were more susceptible to black lung because they operated "pluggers," from which most of the deadly dust was inhaled. "As everybody knows . . .," Hernández lamented, "Mexican laborer[s] . . . always accept any kind of condition without any protest, and I think this is where the whole trou-

ble lies." He also asked management to comply with state regulations requiring ventilation of mining shafts.[5]

FORMAL DEFENSE— STRIKES AND UNIONIZATION

Unionization of Mexican workers, while extensive in the *México Lindo* era (1910-1930s), was not commensurate to the degree of exploitation that immigrants encountered. Most often the methods used by Mexicans to deal with workplace abuse were informal such as stoppages, walkouts, sabotage and personal violence. Up to now, the history of organizing by Mexicans has been presented by scholars within a context of establishing and joining unions. Little is known, for example, about "wildcat" strikes which did not leave a well-defined paper trail.

Because of the industrial nature of mining, the most intensive institutional union efforts involving Mexicans took place in Arizona. In 1903 a number of strikes rocked the mining regions of the southeastern part of the state. The most important one, involving Mexican and Italian miners, was led by Mexicans William Wenceslado Laustenneau and A. F. Salcido and Frank Colombo, an Italian. The three were convicted of inciting a riot in the three-day work

In the late 1920s near Hamilton, Texas, a group of Mexicans refused to pick cotton because Johnson grass overran the fields. The infuriated farmer summoned other ranchers, who charged on horseback into the frightened group of men, women and children, beating them. The farmers then prepared to lynch all the men but stopped after one of the farm workers claimed the local Catholic priest knew exactly where they had gone to work that day.

At times, Mexicans beat the boss to the punch in inflicting real physical damage. In Los Angeles Aurelio Pompa, who killed his boss on a construction job, achieved legendary status for defending himself; he was later executed for the crime. In July 1916 José González, a Kansas labor contractor, was killed by a worker whom he was mistreating unmercifully. *El Cosmopolita,* which carried the story, warned contractors to treat their workers more humanely.

[5] Gustavo G. Hernández, consul in Globe, to Thomas J. Croaff, president, Arizona State Federation of Labor, May 10, 1918, Archivo General de la Nación, Trabajo, 137-20.

stoppage, during which armed workers milled through Morenci occupying company buildings and making demands. They were sentenced to two years at the infamous Arizona Territorial Penitentiary in Yuma.

After serving four months, Laustenneau and four other Mexican convicts tried unsuccessfully to escape in 1904. That earned Laustenneau another ten years, but he died in prison on August 20, 1906. This rather enigmatic figure became an Arizona folk hero among Mexicans and unionists alike. Salcido served his time and after his release became instrumental in the Cananea Strike in Sonora, Mexico, during 1906 against the American-owned Consolidated Copper Company. Colombo's whereabouts after his imprisonment are unknown.

During extensive labor organizing activity in 1914 by the Western Federation of Miners, employers and local officials conducted harassment campaigns to intimidate workers. In August a posse of Americans fought a pitched battle with Mexican unionists after they were accused of stealing a horse near Ray, Arizona. Four Americans and two Mexicans were killed after the Mexican bandits took refuge in a canyon cabin and the Americans assaulted the building. "After the first brush between horse thieves and posse, Ray citizens drove all the Mexicans out of town," said *The New York Times*. The dead Americans were two law officers and two employees at the Ray Consolidated Company.[6] The *Arizona Republican* identified the Mexicans as wood cutters and unionists who hauled wood for mining operations.

Mining company officials considered Pedro Smith, one of the dead Mexicans, and Ramón Villalobos, the only survivor of the shootout, to be union agitators. The Mexican community suspected that the "horse stealing" charge was trumped-up in order to jail these alleged "troublemakers." Villalobos, hanged two years later for his part in this killing, became a *cause célèbre* as compatriots tried to save him from the gallows. This episode was played out within the context of the 1914 recession, which had thrown hundreds of Mexicans out of work throughout central Arizona,

One of the most violent reactions to Mexican efforts to organize and obtain higher wages took place during November 1897 at a coaling and water depot near Yuma, Arizona, called Mammoth Tank. In the midst of a "wildcat strike" against the Southern Pacific, José Rodríguez killed strikebreaker Francisco Cuevas. San Diego County deputies and Arizona officers were called to the scene because, although Rodríguez had fled, the atmosphere remained explosive. When the deputies arrived in a railroad car, they arrested a number of protesting Mexicans and detained them with their hands tied behind their backs. The other workers, who were unarmed, threw rocks at the officers. The deputies fell back to the train and then fired at the mob, killing six of the angry workers. The strikers managed to confiscate a gun from the retreating officers and wounded one of the deputies. The officers subsequently arrested eighteen of the Mexicans, but the rest, about two hundred fifty, fled.

In January 1919 a lumber company owner, Almond Robinson, personally crushed a stoppage of Mexican workers in Thorndale, Texas, by killing the leader. As he spoke to the strike leader, Jesús Navarrete, Robinson lost his temper and hit him with a stick. Navarrete wrested the stick away from Robinson and started hitting back whereupon the owner took out his gun, shot and mortally wounded the Mexican. The other workers were prevented from helping their fallen comrade by white foremen wielding guns. A grand jury exonerated Robinson and his foremen, basing their verdict on a self-defense claim.

[6] *The New York Times*, August 21, 1914.

a factor which worried officials because they were playing into the hands of labor radicals.

Strikes with a large Mexican following, led by the International Workers of the World (IWW), also known as the Wobblies, continued throughout World War I in the Arizona mines. Aware of the huge wartime profits being made by the owners, workers demanded better wages. But the mining companies fought any concessions tooth and nail. They employed the tactic of accusing the Wobblies of un-American activities and sabotaging the war effort. During the Clifton strike of 1918, two thousand Mexicans went out on strike but became so destitute that Consul C. Emilio Martínez Preciat attempted to repatriate them to northern Mexico. Strike leaders, however, accused him of attempting to provide labor to Sonoran and Chihuahuan mines, which were just as exploitative. Mine labor unrest among Mexicans declined in the 1920s, and it was not until the 1940s that unionization was resurrected.

In 1900 California had fewer Mexicans than Arizona, but their numbers increased dramatically in the state during the next twenty years. Mexicans in California worked primarily in agriculture, augmenting the Asian work force that had begun to decline because of restrictive immigration policy. The first known effort to organize Mexican farm workers took place in April 1903. Mexican and Japanese beet workers, aided by the American Federation of Labor (AFL), struck in Oxnard for better wages and for the right to deal directly with farmers, independent of middlemen or contractors. The strike was relatively successful because the contractors were eliminated. Mexicans found common cause with their Japanese coworkers, refusing to sign unless the Japanese were also included in the contract. Another documented Mexican farm-worker union effort took place on New Year's Day in 1915 in Santa Paula. Lemon harvesters refused to work at the Limonería Ranch on this holiday. In 1922 during the *Fiestas Patrias* celebrations, Mexicans launched another agricultural strike in Fresno after grape pickers were inspired by a three-day celebration of Mexican Independence Day in September of 1922. Major agricultural union activity, however, would not appear in the state until the end of the 1920s.

In Texas labor organizing activity had been evident since the early part of the century. Nicasio Idar and his son worked closely with the Texas Socialist Party in an effort to organize the tens of thousands of Mexicans entering the state between 1900 and 1930. Much of this incipient unionizing activity was performed through the auspices of mutual aid societies which had a *México Lindo* orientation. Until the 1930s, most Mexicans involved in union activities still maintained this nationalist outlook based on allegiance to the mother country. Their own leaders, and even radical white organizers, appealed to their Mexican nationalism rather than trying to form an international workers' identity.

MEXICAN-AMERICAN PRECIPICE— UNIONIZATION IN THE 1930S

Mexicans became more union-minded after acquiring a degree of permanency—in essence, when they reached the Mexican Americanization precipice. As historian Mario García indicates,

> Increased participation in unions symbolized the coming of age of Americans of Mexican descent, who, like their middle-class contemporaries, were now sufficiently acculturated to recognize and demand their rights as U.S. citizens.[7]

The most extensive organizing efforts took place in California agriculture from the late 1920s and through the entire 1930s. By then, longer residence in the U.S. had given Mexican farm workers more willingness to struggle against workplace exploitation.[8]

Before this era, however, a Federal Writers

---

[7] Mario T. García, *Mexican American Leadership: Ideology and Identity, 1930-1960* (New Haven: Yale University Press, 1990), p. 176.

[8] It is not a coincidence that one of the most robust symbols of the Chicano Movement, the American Farm Workers of America, emerged in California.

66. Farm workers in the 1930s.

Project writer painted a dismal picture of the conditions under which Mexican agricultural workers lived:

> It is sad, yet true, commentary that to the average landowner and grower in California the Mexican was to be placed much in the same category with ranch cattle, with this exception—the cattle were for the most part provided with comparatively better food and water and immeasurably better living accommodations.

Up until the 1930s the Mexican worker was attractive to farmers because he "did not organize troublesome labor unions, and it was held that he was not educated to the level of unionism." A fruit grower put it more forcefully:

> We want the Mexican because we can treat them as we cannot treat any other living man. . . . We can control them by keeping them at night behind bolted gates, within a stockade eight feet high, surrounded by barbed wire. . . . We can make them work under armed guards in the fields.[9]

In addition to farmer exploitation, *enganchistas* (contractors) also gouged Mexican farm workers. For example, they stole part of the advance farmers gave the contractor in trust to relay to individual workers once they hired on. For every three dollars paid in wages to each worker, the contractor kept one dollar. Farmers also withheld twenty-five percent of wages until the end of the harvest; this assured that workers would stay on. He depended on the *enganchista* to give the sum to the workers, but often dishonest middlemen absconded with the whole amount.

Mexicans tolerated such conditions more in their "greenhorn" stage. But by the end of the 1920s, judging by the spate of efforts to organize

[9] Last three quotes from "Organization Efforts of Mexican Agricultural Workers," typescript in Works Progress Administration, Federal Writer's Project File, CR2, Box 37, Bancroft Library, University of California, Berkeley, p. 2.

that had begun then, they were fed up. Leading off unionization efforts in March 1928 was the Confederación de Uniones Obreras (Federation of Labor Unions) in Los Angeles. In quick fashion, twenty-one chapters extended throughout Southern California. Its total membership as of May 1929 was between two and three thousand. But because its members were migrants who lacked a stable residential base, the union had major difficulties in staying afloat.

From the Confederación effort in April of 1928 came La Unión de Trabajadores del Valle Imperial (Imperial Valley Workers' Union), a union supported by the local Mexican consul. A year after its formation, Mexican cantaloupe workers belonging to the organization in the Imperial Valley decided to demand better working conditions and higher wages for the number of melons picked. The growers refused to budge and, as became a pattern, local authorities sided with the farmers and through harassment broke the strike. One good thing came out of this ignominious defeat: the workers wrested from the employers a contract that promised to reform the issue of contractor abuses. Moreover, following the strike, the union set up offices in key areas throughout the Valley.

After the cantaloupe strike, a series of labor disputes in which Mexicans were the main actors followed. During 1930 two major outbreaks took place in the Imperial Valley among lettuce packers and trimmers led by an all-Mexican union, the Asociación Mutua del Valle Imperial (The Imperial Valley Mutualist Association). The Communist-led Agricultural Workers Industrial League supported the undertaking, but this doomed the organization. By using red-baiting techniques, the growers successfully defeated this effort.

Between 1931 and 1941 Mexican agricultural workers struck at least thirty-two times in California, all the way from Santa Clara in the north to the Imperial Valley in the south. The workers walked out of canneries and from harvests of peas, berries, beets, cantaloupes, cotton, citrus fruits, beans, lettuce and celery. A roll call of these commodities tells us how extensively California depended on Mexican workers and also shows the wide range of products coming out of

the Golden State.

In California, Mexican working women showed the greatest tendency to organize during the 1930s; this too was a reflection of the general Mexican Americanization tendency evident in this era. The Los Angeles garment industry, which before the 1930s had used a multiethnic work force, increasingly turned towards Mexican women, who migrated into the city from agricultural towns during the Depression, and paid them substandard wages. The International Ladies Garment Workers Union (ILGWU), led by Rose Pessota, recruited heavily and in 1933 launched a massive strike that brought garment production to a halt. The strike was sustained despite city officials constantly harassing the workers at the behest of the industry owners. Eventually, the union signed a contract with a number of shops and its members received better wages but not before internal divisions between militant Communists and bread-and-butter leaders of the ILGWU almost wrecked the effort.

The Bracero Program, a government-funded program that recruited workers from Mexico, hindered unionization efforts during World War II. One of the last strikes before the arrival of braceros began on January 31, 1941, in Ventura County. AFL organizers persuaded lemon pickers, packers and cannery workers to strike across the whole county. The stoppage lasted six months, during which the growers, led by Charles C. Teague, refused to bargain with the umbrella negotiating team established by the AFL. Rather than capitulate, the growers allowed the citrus to rot. The strikers were just as resolute, which explains the extraordinary length of the stoppage. The strikers received support from the AFL and mutual aid societies in Los Angeles, but the growers used every strategy they could to prevent success. The adamant posture of their leadership looked beyond this dispute. They knew that unions would destroy the ability to obtain cheap labor. To break the strike, the growers recruited hundreds of "Okies" (dust-bowl refugees) and then evicted the strikers from company-provided camps.

In the mid 1940s writer and scholar Dr. Ernesto Galarza started the National Farm Workers Union (NFWU), an offshoot of the Southern

67. Bracero at the U.S. border. Photo by Hermanos Mayo.

Tenant Farmers Union. Because the Bracero Program had brought thousands of workers to California, the NFWU expended its energy in opposing the program because it would deflate wages to such a degree that domestic workers could not make a living. Some two decades later, César Chávez's movement would also oppose Mexican immigrants on the same basis—a position that influenced the Chicano Movement leaders initially to ignore the specific plight that undocumented immigrants encountered in this country.

The most significant strike initiated by the NFWU occurred in October of 1947 against the powerful Di Giorgio Fruit Company in Arvin, California. Hundreds of Mexican, Filipino and white workers walked out, demanding higher wages. The strike was broken by the usual methods. With local authorities on the side of the Di Giorgio company, strikers were evicted and undocumented workers brought in as strikebreakers. The union, in league with a Hollywood film company,

produced a documentary, *Poverty in the Land of Plenty*, which Di Giorgio lawyers claimed was libelous. Galarza spent an inordinate amount of time defending the suit, only to lose. The financial strain was too much for the struggling union and it folded. This organization, however, served as a precursor to the United Farm Workers Union of César Chávez.

UNIONIZATION OUTSIDE CALIFORNIA

In contrast to California, limited unionization took place among Mexican farm workers in Texas and Arizona during the 1930s and 1940s even though large-scale agriculture also characterized their economies. During 1930 Pedro de la Lama tried to organize Los Agricultores Mexicanos (Mexican Agriculturalists) in the Phoenix area. The Mexican consulate, who opposed De la Lama's leadership because he was a major critic of the Mexican government, accused him of defrauding

68. Pecan shellers in San Antonio in the 1930s.

the members of the union. This triggered an investigation by postal inspectors that led to the group's demise. In Texas Mexicans formed La Asociación de Jornaleros (The Journeymen's Association) in 1933, which represented everything from hatmakers to farm workers. The union was too diverse to be effective and it died after Texas Rangers arrested the leaders of an onion harvester strike in Laredo during 1934. Reasons for the difficulty in organizing in Texas were identified by one historian: "Tradition of paternalistic labor relations, a comparatively repressive political atmosphere, and the huge distances ethnic Mexicans traveled in the migratory labor stream combined to militate against the level of labor unionism that evolved in California."[10]

In the 1930s Texas did produce one of the most well-known labor crusaders in Emma Tenayuca, a member of the American Communist Party and an activist in unionism since she was in high school. She brought to her work a fervor born out of her dedication to the class struggle and an interpretation that Mexican workers in the Southwest were part of this conflict. Tenayuca helped organize the well-known San Antonio Pecan Shellers' Strike against the Southern Pecan Shelling Company in 1938.

San Antonio's pecan industry, which began during the Civil War, employed about ten thousand Mexican workers who cracked and divested the nut of its meat by hand. At one point, the owners introduced mechanization, but they removed the equipment because it was cheaper to use the hand labor of Mexicans, who were paid five to six cents per pound and earned as little as two dollars per week. Such conditions forced the Mexicans to organize El Nogal (The Pecan Tree), a union that attracted as many as four thousand members.

[10] Gutiérrez, *Walls and Mirrors*, p. 107.

At the peak of the shelling season, on February 1, 1938, the Mexican union became affiliated with the Congress of Industrial Organizations (CIO) packing-house union and walked out of one hundred thirty shops after the owners had cut their wages by one cent per pound. In San Antonio the pecan processors were influential, and the police quickly embarked on a harassment campaign to break the strike. At this point, Tenayuca became a strike leader but had to resign because of her Communist affiliation. Nonetheless, she continued to support the effort and remained dedicated to the cause. Tenayuca gave such fiery speeches to animate the striking workers that she earned the nickname *La Pasionaria* (The Passionate One). The strike, which lasted one month, succeeded in obtaining higher wages for the pecan shellers although, soon after that, the industry mechanized. When the dispute began in 1938, ten thousand shellers toiled in the Southern Pecan Shelling Company; by 1941 the company employed only six hundred workers.

A major reason Mexicans found it so difficult to organize enduring unions in the 1930s is that sectors in which they toiled lacked government support given other workers. Workers' provisions in the 1933 National Recovery Act (NRA), initiated by Franklin D. Roosevelt, showed this Democratic administration to be sympathetic to organized labor aspirations. The act was declared unconstitutional, but a compliant Congress quickly passed the National Labor Relations Act (NLRA) in 1935, a crucial law that allowed for the relatively unencumbered unionization of industrial, mining and construction workers.

The NLRA facilitated the formation of the powerful giant that eventually put under its umbrella dozens of unions. The act, however, which obliged employers to bargain in good faith, did not include agricultural and packing house workers—sectors that contained almost half of the Mexican work force in the U.S. But thousands of Mexicans worked in mining, steel and automobile plants, areas which the CIO rapidly organized under the auspices of the new law.

When automobile manufacturing and urban building booms expanded to California, thousands of Mexican workers joined the unions under the CIO. In the Chicago area some of the most militant members of the Steel Workers Organizing Committee (SWOC) were Mexicans who were either born in the U.S. or had no intention of returning to Mexico. To these workers, ethnically mixed unions seemed a better solution to dealing with workplace issues than the *México Lindo* mutual aid societies used earlier by Mexican workers. As a consequence, Mexicans participated significantly in the "Little Steel Strike" of 1937, one of the most famous events in U.S. labor history.

The dispute began after the Roosevelt administration had pressured large steel makers such as U.S. Steel to allow unions, but smaller steel companies such as Republic, Youngstown and Inland resisted. SWOC then focused its efforts on these smaller companies. A bitter struggle ensued when scores of workers, including thousands of Mexicans, walked out of these plants throughout the Midwest. The family-owned businesses swore they would destroy the effort. On May 30, 1937, striking workers at Republic Steel held a rally at a commons next to the plant and the police ruthlessly shot into the crowd, killing ten workers. The "Republic Steel Massacre" became legendary union lore, but until the 1970s few people knew the extent to which Mexicans participated in this effort. In the Chicago area almost half of the strikers were Mexicans, according to Mike Patterson, a SWOC organizer in this period.

The National Labor Relations Act was instrumental in prompting mine and smelter workers to unionize, which affected Mexicans as well. Mexican participation in unions representing workers employed by such companies as Phelps Dodge, Anaconda, American Smelting and Refining and Nevada Consolidated was extensive. In Gallup, New Mexico, for example, Mexican coal miners became entangled in the political struggle between John L. Lewis's United Mine Workers (UMW) and the Communist-led National Miner's Union (NMU). Jesús Pallares and other Mexicans started the Liga Obrera de Habla Española (Spanish-Speaking Labor League), which eventually organized eight thousand workers. But because the workers opted for the Communist NMU, they were persecuted, jailed and eventually deported.

The most successful undertaking by Mexican miners came in the International Union of Mine,

69. The National LULAC Convention in Houston, 1937.

Mill and Smelter Workers (Mine Mill), a union based in El Paso. The association sprang from the earlier Western Federation of Miners, a union which since the turn of the century had organized Mexicans in mines and smelters throughout the Southwest. It became affiliated with the CIO in 1936 and, although multiethnic, it soon had a large proportion of Mexican American workers. The union was symbolic of the new kind of union that sought to unify all workers regardless of ethnic background or race. The union attracted minorities because it promised to address dual wage systems and the labor segmentation which had been the bane of Mexican miners.

Most Mexican unionists in the 1930s were interested only in bread-and-butter issues. But some Mexicans in the U.S., such as Emma Tenayuca, strove for civil rights, using the class struggle as an ideological foundation. Hence they aimed their appeal at the workers, unlike middle-class groups such as LULAC, who were more concerned with class mobility for Mexicans. During the late 1930s the Communist Party in its "Popular Front" stage cooperated with Democratic bourgeoisie groups, which stood up to the fascist threat. It thus supported U.S. Mexican workers with bread-and-butter objectives and middle-class

Mexican Americans in their struggle for civil rights. In other words, it supported progressive organizations dedicated to reform within the capitalist system.

The organization that stands out the most in this respect is the California-based El Congreso del Pueblo de Habla Española (Spanish-Speaking People's Congress) started in 1938 by Luisa Moreno, a Guatemalan, and Josefina Fierro Bright, a Los Angeles Mexican American. Moreno became radicalized while organizing New York's Latino garment workers and, upon moving to California, she became a member of the United Cannery, Agricultural, Packing and Allied Workers of America (UCAPAWA). She also helped in other Southwest organizing activities among Mexicans, including the pecan shellers' in San Antonio.

Moreno formed a coalition by forging contacts with a variety of Mexican American organizations and involving well-known personalities. In April 1938 the first meeting of El Congreso was held in Los Angeles. Supporters included Hollywood actors Anthony Quinn and Rita Hayworth along with Bert Corona, who remained a lifelong civil rights and labor leader. Her coleader, Fierro de Bright, was the wife of screenwriter John

Bright, who was instrumental in politicizing the union to radical stances.

The Congreso meeting attracted over one thousand delegates from 128 organizations, whose combined membership was seventy thousand people. The main agenda confronted problems affecting Latinos such as education, housing, health, job discrimination and segregation. Congreso goals, while complementing those of middle-class organizations such as LULAC, hesitated in the emphasis on acquisition of American values. The group did demand the civil rights for Mexican Americans guaranteed by the Constitution in addition to espousing unity among all Latinos in the U.S., including Mexican immigrants, a group that LULAC had distanced from its organizational objectives. A meeting scheduled for March of 1939 never materialized, and the organization dissipated after this.

In 1949 an organization similar to the Congreso emerged: the Asociación Nacional México-Americana (The National Mexican American Association). It grew out of the Mine Mill union, which was later ousted from the CIO in 1950 because of Communist affiliation. Union members, predominantly Mexican Americans, recognized that the problems of working Mexicans transcended workplace issues and organized this civil rights entity to deal "with the plight of Mexican undocumented workers, housing needs in the Southwest, education, Mexican American political representation, youth work, the promotion of Mexican American culture and police brutality."[11] Congreso veterans such as Josefina Fierro were involved in this organization as well. The "Red Scare" atmosphere of the 1950s, however, did not allow the group the opportunity to succeed.

Although these two organizations did not survive, they left another legacy which was carried through its members in providing another ideological strand for the Chicano Movement. In the mid-1970s after Chicano cultural nationalism failed to provide a structured course of revolutionary action, many activists resurrected some of

the Marxist features of these groups. Bert Corona, in fact, continued to organize alongside young *movimiento* activists well into the 1980s.

EARLY AFFIRMATIVE ACTION DEMANDS

Unionization helped Mexican Americans in employment sectors where they had no trouble getting jobs. But they also hungered for the work reserved for whites—because it was better paying and not as backbreaking and it conferred more status. Mexicans could not get jobs as store clerks, for example, except in places that catered to Mexicans. Many a young Mexican would look at the crisp white uniform of a Texaco service-station attendant or the technological skills needed to drive an urban bus with a degree of longing. Obtaining such a job was a mark of mobility. Again, this longing became an integral feature within the Chicano Movement. Many of the *movimiento* objectives, irrespective of the separatist rhetoric and emphasis on cultural pride, stemmed from a hunger for job status.

Mexicans also looked to government employ-

70. Members of the Ladies LULAC Council, Houston, Texas, 1954.

[11] García, *Mexican Americans*, p. 200.

ment as way of "getting ahead." To get "un trabajo del citi" (a municipal job), even in street maintenance, offered security and fringe benefits. Convincing the city council to put Mexican American employees on permanent status rather than being "temporary" became one of the first issues of Houston's Latin American Club (LAC). In reality, the Mexicans worked full-time for the city; they just did not get the fringe benefits. The dispute came to the forefront during May 1938 after the city did not pay their Mexican workers for taking off on April 22, the commemoration of the Battle of San Jacinto (in which General Antonio López de Santa Anna was defeated in 1836).

LAC then became a LULAC chapter and forced the issue. In response, city councilman S.A. Starsky retorted that he did not understand why Mexicans should get a paid day off to celebrate their own defeat. This insensitive retort further incensed the LULAC council, and it doggedly pursued the issue until Starsky apologized. More importantly, the Mexican workers were given permanent status.

The Works Progress Administration (WPA) served to integrate Mexicans into an occupational structure which had eluded them in the past. Even the Federal Writers Project, a section within the WPA with the smallest number of minority workers, provided writing jobs to Mexican Americans such as Isaac Aceves and Ramón Welch in California and Ernest Mendívil and José del Castillo in Arizona. Mexicans mainly obtained jobs as construction workers although in 1937 noncitizens were taken off the rolls, mainly because of pressure from nativists and employers who found the WPA competed for laborers.

One of the most noteworthy spokesmen for the ideals that are akin to today's affirmative action programs was university professor George I. Sánchez. As president of LULAC in 1941, he explored ways by which the federal government in this wartime atmosphere could guarantee Mexican Americans full civil rights. According to Dr. Sánchez, they were

> Without benefit of lobby because of the very nature of their social and economic status. . . . They are. . . segregated and demeaned. Even the descendants of the Spanish colonials, who have belonged here for three centuries and more, are "forgotten on the other side of the railroad tracks." "Mexican" has become a term of opprobrium, applied indiscriminately to citizen and alien alike, and associated with discriminatory practices in wage scales and employment procedures, in education, in the exercise of civil rights and the like. In effect, many of these people live in a veritable concentration camp.[12]

Sánchez attempted to lobby Nelson Rockefeller, who was coordinator of inter-American affairs, to use his authority to encourage federal policy that would benefit Mexican Americans by emphasizing how important this would be during the war years.

Concepción González, who was born in Texas, was repatriated with her Mexican-born husband from East Chicago, Indiana, against her will in 1932. Her husband abandoned her, pregnant and penurious, in Monterrey. After much suffering, she returned to Indiana with her young son, José, who had been born in Mexico. Barely subsisting, she was hired at Inland Steel Company during the war as a tool specialist and she was finally able to make a decent living for herself and her son.

---

[12] Gutiérrez, *Walls and Mirrors*, p. 131.

World War II for many Mexican Americans became a major source of upward mobility. Just in the military service alone, some rose high in the ranks as enlisted men, fewer as officers, and were given supervisory duties over other men, including whites. Employment in the more highly technological manufacturing sector, spurred mainly by the defense industry, became the bailiwick of white workers, but Blacks and Mexican Americans wanted access as well. In 1941 the President's Committee on Fair Employment Practices (FEPC) was established in order to stem discrimination in projects financed by the federal government. The FEPC's effectiveness was stymied by opposition from southern politicians and the resistance of war industries to hire minorities in skilled positions. Mexican American politicians and civil right activists tried to make the agency accountable, but for the most part the policy of keeping out Mexicans from other than menial jobs continued during the war.

Most Mexican women stayed behind although many moved to other industrial areas in the boom years of the war and worked in places where Mexicans had never been allowed. In cities in the Midwest and Southwest that had wartime industries, hundreds of daughters of immigrants, who had first settled in the *colonias* earlier in the century, obtained industrial jobs that were normally done by men. They became "Rosita, the Riveter."

CONCLUSION

The organizing of Mexican workers in the first four decades of the twentieth century cut across many labor sectors, but it concentrated mainly in mining and agriculture. The breadth of its activity was extensive, but victories were few, primarily because employers had the support of officialdom—local police, judges, city councils, and such. A report done for the Works Progress Administration indicated,

> While some gains have been made by the Mexicans as the result of organization, both through their own racial unions and as members of others of mixed racial makeup, these have been won at the cost of considerable violence and economic loss due to time spent in carrying on their struggles, during which income stopped.[13]

In addition, agricultural and service sectors were not accorded the protection of the National Labor Relations Act. That crucial legislation provided industrial sectors struggle-free unionization by removing many of the obstacles that had stood in their way. Certainly when Mexicans participated in work sectors that unionized, the tide of worker prosperity carried them into the suburbs and material well-being. In Ari-

Felisa Ruiz, of Kansas City, Missouri, relates her memories of how the war affected her life: "During the Depression, the only jobs available to young Mexican American women were limited primarily to sewing and laundry work, hotel maids, and as domestics. These jobs were both physically demanding and paid very little. When the war broke out, defense jobs were all of a sudden open to us because of the labor shortage with the men off to war. Many of us left these menial jobs into highly-skilled occupations with good to excellent pay with overtime. Despite changing our jobs, we were still required to turn over our checks to our parents."[14]

[13] "Organization Efforts of Mexican Agricultural Workers," p. 28.

[14] In Richard Santillán, "Rosita the Riveter: Midwest Mexican American Women During World War II, 1941-1945," *Perspectives in Mexican American Studies* 2 (1989), pp. 124, 125.

zona for example, at the time of the Chicano Movement a great sociological divide based on material attainment existed between Mexicans in mining communities and their *paisanos* in agricultural towns. It was the continued poverty of farm workers, who were not necessarily new arrivals from Mexico, that prompted Chicano activists to support the farm-worker movement, at times volunteering their time to picket at the strike lines or to leaflet at supermarkets in support of the continuous boycotts of grapes and lettuce called for by César Chávez.

But the unfinished work of acquiring "affirmative action" served as a vertebra for the *movimiento*. Confronting the systematic exclusion of Chicanos from educational institutions and desirable jobs that continued even after the Mexican American generation gave it "its best shot" became the primary target of the Chicano Movement. To be sure, other issues were in the forefront, including cultural pride, police brutality, the Vietnam War. But all of these really revolved around the core concern: gaining access to the proverbial piece of the pie.

CHAPTER EIGHT

The Struggle in the Fields

71. Picketers promoting the boycott of agricultural products for the United Farm Workers.

This chapter studies two basic dynamics within the Chicano Movement: one, the actual beginning of the California-based United Farm Workers (UFW) before a defined *movimiento* emerged, and two, how the Chicano Movement and the farm-worker struggle became inexorably linked. Interestingly, the leader of the farm workers, César Chávez, contrasted sharply with other Chicano leaders. The former farm worker, who had worked in California agriculture since his birth into an Arizona migrant-worker family, did not possess an imposing figure; he did not swagger or project a tough persona as did many militant activists of the era. Chávez's short stature and soft-spoken, quiet

Eliseo Medina devoted many years of his young life to the United Farm Workers (UFW) after hearing Cásar Chávez speak on the occasion of the first big strike meeting called in Delano on September 16, 1965. He remembers attending as a nineteen-year-old, "And people started talking about how unfair what the growers were doing and why we needed to fight back, and then this guy gets up and starts talking. I said, 'Oh that must be César.' And he was tall with a mustache, very distinguished looking. I was very impressed. And then he says, 'Now I want to introduce you to César Chávez.' And then, so César gets up and he's this little guy. . . very soft spoken. I say, 'That's César?' You know, I wasn't very impressed. . . but the more he talked, the more I thought that not only could we fight, but we could win."[1]

César Chávez was born in Yuma, Arizona, in 1927 to poor farm-worker parents who followed the migrant stream to California, where Chávez grew up. This background sensitized him to the plight of these workers—especially those who were Mexican like himself. In their migrant years, both Chávez and his father were exposed to union efforts, but an early influence shaping Chávez's dedication to helping people was family behavior. He recalled that the Chávezes were known for helping others out.

As he put it, "My mom and dad were. . . especially my mother was like . . . the CSO [Community Services Organization] . . .. We were migrants but we were a service center. We did all kinds of work for people." He remembered his folks interpreting for monolingual farm workers and taking farm workers they found stranded out of gas on the highway to a service station. On other occasions he remembered being awakened at midnight because a woman about to give birth needed to be taken to the hospital. "We were known as the people—but it was my mother, not us. Sometimes we got very mad at her, but she would commit us and we would do it. So I learned—seeing her doing that is what got me in the CSO."[2]

72. César Chávez, March 28, 1968, the day he broke his first fast.

[1] On-camera interview with Eliseo Medina by Sylvia Morales, November 18, 1995, NLCC-GP.

[2] Last two quotes from interview with César Chávez by Luis Torres, April 20, 1992, NLCC-GP.

73. First National Farm Workers Association Convention, in Fresno, California, September 1962. (Left to right) José Martínez, Dolores Huerta, Tony Orendáin and César Chávez.

demeanor was often mistaken for the stereotypical look of passivity rather than forceful leadership.

Chávez received his formal training as an organizer with the Community Services Organization (CSO) in 1950 at a time when the group came under the sway of the Industrial Areas Foundation (IAF), an advocacy organization founded by the radical populist Saul Alinsky. Its strategy required house-by-house visitations to persuade families to join whatever cause needed mobilization. Chávez had come to the attention of Fred Ross, a CSO trainer who recruited him in San Jose through Father Donald McDonnell. The priest, who preached from the *Rerum Novarum*, an encyclical issued by Pope Leo XIII advocating labor unions to eradicate poverty, influenced the young farm worker tremendously.

In the late 1950s CSO officials sent Chávez to Oxnard to help with the United Packing House Workers of America's efforts to organize packing-shed workers. But while the CSO wanted this effort to succeed, it did not provide sufficient support and prevented Chávez from joining another effort to organize the workers in the fields under the Agricultural Workers Organizing Committee (AWOC), a union financed by the United Auto Workers (UAW) but spearheaded by Ernesto Galarza. During this period Chávez met another farm worker, Gil Padilla, who until he retired in 1982 was one of the most ardent leaders of the UFW. In 1960 when Chávez became national director of the CSO, he was already thinking of directing the energies of the organization towards farm workers. It was then that he encouraged Padilla to work as a volunteer. But so impressed was Chávez with Padilla that a few months later Chávez recruited him to work full-time on a CSO project that helped farm workers. Padilla, then a manager of a dry-cleaning franchise, agreed reluctantly. With a grant from the Bishop's Committee on Farm Labor, Padilla went to Stockton and opened an assistance center.

At this point, CSO objectives did not clearly prescribe union organizing, but from previous experiences Padilla knew that was the only avenue to get the farm workers to help themselves. "All my work there for a year and eight months was basically done with farm workers, migrants, *braceros* taking the jobs of the locals. The locals got upset about that. There was no unemployment [insurance]; there was no minimum wage at the time," he recalled. Lack of protection for farm workers or "lack of agencies that would get excited for doing something for farm labor" brought the greatest frustrations to Padilla.[3]

By 1962 Chávez was anxious to implement his "dream" of organizing farm workers but met resistance from the CSO leadership:

Doctors, lawyers and politicians began joining.

They would get elected to some office in the organization and then, for all practical purposes, leave. Intent on using the CSO for their own prestige purposes, these "leaders," many of them, lacked the urgency we had to have.[4]

In 1962 at an organization meeting in Calexico, CSO president Tony Ríos opposed involvement in unions because the Agricultural Workers Organizing Committee (AWOC), Galarza's old group now affiliated with the AFL, had been organizing for about three years in Northern California. So Chávez resigned, closed his office at 4th and Mott Streets in Los Angeles and moved to Delano. Now on his own, Chávez convinced Padilla also to bolt the CSO and join him in Kern County.

Dolores Huerta, another CSO staff member who was assigned to lobbying the California Legislature for pro-migrant worker legislation,

Born in Los Baños, a labor camp in Merced County, Gil Padilla worked in agriculture all his life except for a brief stint in the army during World War II. After being discharged in 1947, he returned to the fields only to find that the wartime expediency of importing Mexican contract laborers (*braceros*) had lowered wages, and he had to work for less than when he had enlisted. "I was very bitter about that," he revealed, "and joined, in 1948, Ernesto Galarza's group," the union that the Mexican American intellectual Ernesto Galarza was organizing through the National Farm Workers Union (NFWU)—later the Agricultural Workers Organizing Committee (AWOC). When the union failed, Padilla hired on with a dry-cleaning business. But in 1955 when he returned to the fields, Padilla noted, "Things were worse than when I left in 1948. The *braceros* were there and they used to pay $1.00 an hour, there was no water, there was no rest periods, there was nothing. I worked there

maybe a month or so in the melons and had a big fight with the employers there and left. I moved to Kern County from Merced County, back into the cleaning business."

Fate intervened and César Chávez's CSO house-to-house organizing led him to knock at Padilla's house one evening in 1956. As Padilla put it, "He talked the same thing as I was talking and the same thing that I was thinking in those days about discrimination in jobs. . . about bringing some laws to the farm workers." When he met Chávez, Padilla remembers he had just gone to the California Labor Commission to complain about a dispute that had driven him out of the fields the previous year and led him to discover that farm workers were not protected under any labor relations regulation either at the state or federal levels. "We talked and talked about that. We talked about what can be done to bring them into the mainstream," stated Padilla.[5]

---

[3] Interview with Gil Padilla by Myléne Moreno, January 14, 1994, NLCC-GP.

[4] César Chávez, "The Organizer's Tale," in Livie Isuaro Durán and H. Russell Bernard (eds.), *Introduction to Chicano Studies* (New York: Macmillan Publishing Co., Inc., 1982), p. 341.

[5] Last two quotes from interview with Gil Padilla.

Born in New Mexico, Dolores Huerta moved to Northern California with her family. But unlike most other future farm-worker leaders, she did not labor in the fields. In explaining why she dedicated her life to service, first in the CSO and then in the farm-workers union, Huerta stated:

> My background is a little different than most people [farm workers]. My mother was a business woman and she was born here [in the U.S.] . . . I was always active in organizations. I was. . . in the Girl Scouts for ten years. I was active in all the Catholic groups. I started a couple of teen-age centers. I always liked to organize. Even when I was really young . . I liked to join things.[6]

74. Dolores Huerta, UFW vice president.

capped off what became the original "*los tres*" of the union—Chávez and Padilla being the other two. Compatible because of their mutual training, the three shared the CSO will to win. According to Huerta, her lobbying efforts succeeded because the CSO proved to the politicians time and again that the organization could deliver votes. As was seen in Chapter Six, the CSO acquired clout by registering and organizing Mexican Americans to vote in a bloc, a feat leading to the election of Edward Roybal to the Los Angeles City Council.

As Huerta tells it, her major accomplishment as a lobbyist was persuading the legislature to eliminate the citizenship requirement for public-assistance programs. Before serving as a lobbyist, she was assigned by the CSO in 1957 as an unpaid volunteer to help organize AWOC in Stockton. This CSO assignment came from the same initiative that sent Chávez to help packing-house workers in Oxnard. Dissatisfied with the methods being used by Galarza and his followers, she withdrew from the effort. But like Padilla and Chávez, her overall experiences convinced her that farm workers needed effective labor unions.

When Chávez and Padilla resigned from the CSO, Huerta at first continued as a lobbyist but helped the two organize on a part-time basis. "I would work in Sacramento and then had meetings with the farm workers up in Stockton, Merced, all of that area," Huerta recollects. She accuses self-seeking professionals who dominated the CSO of castigating her for union activities and refusing to pay her wages. "I had no money," she recalls. "Luckily my mother owned the house where I lived, but it got to where they shut off my lights, shut off my gas."

As he did with Padilla, in 1961 Chávez asked Huerta, now running the Los Angeles CSO office, to join him on a full-time basis with the union. By now he recognized that using outside groups, in this case the CSO, as a backup to union organizing was superfluous. In Huerta's words,

> César, after studying everything. . . knew that it wasn't going to work unless people owned the union. . . the only way we are going to do it is to organize the union ourselves. And I thought he was kidding. . . .That's how it started.[7]

[6] Interview with Dolores Huerta by Sylvia Morales, January 13, 1995, NLCC-GP.

[7] Last two quotes from interview with Dolores Huerta by Luis Torres, March 19, 1992, NLCC-GP.

Chávez began the organizing effort by drawing a map with all the towns and labor camps between Arvin and Stockton—eighty-six in all. Employing IAF techniques, he and his associates canvassed each town and camp, signing up small groups in each community. As he arrived in each town, Chávez recalled,

> I would go to the last house, the last house on the way out...and knock on every door. Twenty houses would turn me down. One would listen. And then I would talk to them about the union and they would look at me, either afraid or disbelieving. . . . And then after I explained, I would get them. . . I would say why don't you call your friends and let me come back next weekend.[8]

He did this for six months. The small group of organizers did not even discuss labor unions outside their meetings with the recruits so as not to tip off employers. They called themselves the National Farm Workers Association (NFWA), avoiding the word union. According to Dolores Huerta,

> We set up our little chapters all over. . . we did the stuff. We put out the program. We had dances at Delano. . . . We charged members $3.50 a month dues and part we used to pay death-benefit insurance [$1,000 for any family member that died]. We finally got a little office and we had to pay rent. . . about $30.00 a week.[9]

The organizers collected some eighty thousand pledge cards from potential union members, many with scribbled messages like "I hope to God we win" or "Do you think we can win?" or "I'd like to know more." Chávez separated the cards containing these messages and made sure he paid a personal visit to those who wrote them. The tactic paid off because some of the scribblers became the core of the union. Cognizant of the value of historical symbols, they conducted a ninety-day drive in Cocoran, where in 1936 a bloody battle took place between striking farm workers and local law officials. Through dues the union built up $25,000 in the credit union which was run by Chávez's wife, Helen. "I had gone without pay the whole of 1963. The next year, the members voted me a $40 a week salary," Chávez recalled. By 1964 the movement had one thousand members.

While Chávez felt that an effective union could only be built slowly and quietly through methodical organization, a series of unexpected events forced the NFWA to reveal itself sooner than expected. In April of 1965 a farm worker named Epifanio Camacho traveled to Delano to discuss with Chávez a dispute that rose grafters were having with the flower growers in McFarland, California. Camacho told Chávez that "he was sick and tired of how people working the roses were being treated and he was willing to 'go the limit.'" Chávez sent his cousin

The organizers and the fledgling union survived on their wits but also by relying on family members for loans and food. César's wife, Helen Favela, worked full-time outside the union while César, Dolores and Gil, sometimes assisted by family members, went into the fields and organized. César's brother Richard, who worked for the telephone company, wrangled phone service for the fledgling office; another brother, Manuel, who sold used cars, provided vehicles for the hundreds of miles which the organizers traversed weekly. Between Chávez and Huerta, they had fifteen children.

[8] Interview with César Chávez.

[9] Interview with Dolores Huerta.

Manuel and Gilbert Padilla to McFarland, where the two conducted a meeting at Camacho's house.

The workers wanted a union, but more immediately, wages were the main issue. Apparently, to entice workers, farmers promised up to nine dollars for every thousand roses grafted, but once in the gardens, cutters received only about seven dollars. The disgruntled workers signed pledge cards and then the NFWA targeted the biggest flower farm, which employed eighty-five workers. After a series of meetings, the union set the date. On the assigned morning, strike leaders cruised the workers' neighborhoods to remind them of their pledge not to break the strike; Dolores Huerta even blocked the driveway of one family who was preparing to go to the fields and cut flowers.

For two days, the rose plots remained untouched, but the company imported Filipino strikebreakers; they walked out after half a day. The strike succeeded and the company negotiated a one hundred twenty percent pay increase, but did not concede a contract, which was what the union wanted. "We wanted to hold out for a contract and

more benefits, but the majority of the rose workers wanted to accept the offer and go back," Chávez lamented. He also recalled that the victory "was a small one, but it prepared us for the big one."

A few months later in August, an independent walkout of Mexican and Filipino grape workers at Rancho Blanco in Delano also caught the attention of the Chávez's NFWA because "the people were getting a raw deal there and being pushed around pretty badly." Chávez felt compelled to help out. "So Padilla went to the ranch, climbed on top of a car and took a strike vote." The workers, many who had previously signed pledge cards with the NFWA, voted unanimously to strike. Contractors immediately brought in strikebreakers. According to Padilla, they accused one, Luis Campos, of separating the women from the men in order to harass them sexually. The union attack on this individual intimidated him into pulling all his workers from the field, and the strike was then a success. Said Chávez, "The grower kept saying, 'I can't pay. I just haven't got the money.' I guess he must have found the money somewhere, because we were asking for

César Chávez recalled how his fledgling union got into the grape strike. On the morning of September 8, a family, all union members, came to the union office proclaiming excitedly to an organizer named Esther that there was a strike. Just as excitedly, Esther went to Chávez and announced,

"There's a strike, there's a strike, the Filipinos are striking, but they're not asking us to go out!" I said, "Well what do you want to do?" They said, "Well, we don't know, we don't feel good working. . . ." So I immediately called Dolores and we began to set up. I called the leadership. . . . We had a meeting that night. We said, "What are we going to do?

No, we are not ready, but we got to support them. It would look bad if we didn't." See, we worked all that week and called a meeting on September 16, at the church hall. We were astounded, we had like six thousand workers. We were ready to strike and we took a vote and we struck. And we said, "God will provide," and we struck. That's how it started.

When asked why he relied on God providing, Chávez replied, "There was absolutely no way that I could. . . . I had no money. I had no idea. All I knew was. . . they wanted to strike. . . we couldn't work while others were striking. That was more important to me than the [lack of] money."[10]

[10] Interview with César Chávez.

$1.40 and we got it."[11]

A larger strike that same year drew the NFWA into an unexpected and unwanted confrontation with all the grape companies in the Delano area. Significantly, this premature encounter became the pivotal event in the fledgling union's history. On September 5, 1965, Filipino workers belonging to AWOC—by now Galarza had resigned—refused to leave their company-provided living quarters to pick grapes at the Marcos Zaninovich farm. The AWOC felt confident it would win because earlier that year a walkout in the hot Coachella Valley west of Los Angeles resulted in a victory. But in the temperate San Joaquin Valley, where grapes would not ripen as fast, the farmers refused to budge. According to the union's lawyer, Jerry Cohen, AWOC head Larry Itlong at first tried to discourage Fred Abod, a Filipino leader in the sit-in, from striking, but Abod said, "The hell with you guys. I asked Marcos Zaninovich for one lousy dime last year and he wouldn't give it to us."[12] The AWOC then encouraged sit-ins in the rest of Kern County, which included striking at the giant Di Giorgio and Schenley Liquors farms.

The dispute, right in César Chávez's back yard, pressured Chávez and his associates to join, mainly in a show of solidarity. The previous

There are various versions of how Luis Valdez came to the union movement. This is César Chávez's version. In 1965 on an occasion when Chávez happened to be in Berkeley attending to union business, Valdez introduced himself. Chávez replied, 'Look, okay, why don't you follow me right now.' So the poor guy followed me all night, and we're going to meetings and raising money. Finally. . . it was almost midnight, he said, 'I'm sorry, I'm just graduating and I'd like to come to Delano and do a teatro.' I said, 'Great! Come on! When? Right now.' So he came."

The Teatro Campesino's and Luis Valdez's tremendous contributions to the formation of a Chicano art movement are legendary. But in its initial years, Valdez only wanted the genre to serve the farm-worker cause. In Chávez's own words,

Well, it helped with the workers. . . . It was street theater. . . . it was able to deal with three important things. One was just deal with. . . like we're here to stay. You know, he came out and sang, "Viva la Huelga" [Long Live the Strike] and "No nos moverán" [We will not be moved] and all that stuff—great!

75. El Teatro Campesino (Luis Valdez at center).

The other thing he was able to ridicule. . . growers. . . which was great. Not attack them. But ridicule. . . . Then deal with the internal problems we had about the strikebreakers or being afraid. . . . Oh, the Friday night meetings would be jammed with people. . . because even though we were losing the strike. . . they're still coming because the teatro was there.[13]

[11] Last seven quotes in main text from Chávez, "The Organizer's Tale," pp. 343-344.

[12] Interview with Jerry Cohen by Myléne Moreno, January 20, 1994, NLCC-GP.

[13] Interview with César Chávez.

smaller efforts served to build confidence, but this challenge seemed insurmountable. Chávez, after all, was committed to the slow but sure strategy mapped out some years earlier with his CSO associates. Besides, he felt constrained by other factors. The union could count on three thousand members to support the AWOC walkout, but with only eighty-seven dollars in the strike fund. He knew that, as soon as the initial fervor and excitement dissipated, strikers would need support to see them through the ordeal.

> Well, see, we're led into it, we didn't have any money. See, I told my wife, I said, "I can organize a huge organization of workers, but I don't know if I can take them into contract. And it is going to take ten years this early in the game.". . . . my ambition was that I would get a grower and just stick with a grower.[14]

After much agonizing, Chávez and his associates decided to take a strike vote to the rank and file on September 16, which was Mexican Independence Day. Imbued with the fervor of celebrating the *Fiestas Patrias,* NFWA members voted overwhelmingly to support the Filipinos. As expected, most of the strikers did not stay on the pickets lines. Some returned to work while others went elsewhere to find work. In addition, thousands of strikebreakers were hired—many were undocumented workers from Mexico. The farmers also recruited Arabs from Yemen, Japanese-American students and local Mexican Americans. Even so, the union enticed some of the strikebreakers to walk out of the fields. "Some of those Arabs became leaders in the strike," recalled Gil Padilla.[15]

But the stark reality was that the union could not maintain pressure on the growers with the strike alone. Chávez remembered, "We got a lot of food first and. . . money [donations]. . . . But our ranks began to deplete by December."[16] A core group remained with the strike, however, for the entire fifty-nine months that it lasted. The NFWA decided at the outset not to take money from outside sources so as not to compromise its goals. Chávez, for example, balked at accepting funding from well-meaning groups, even with no-strings-attached provisos, because this would pressure the union into producing premature results. Once he even rejected a fifty thousand dollar grant, despite his union needing the money to stay afloat.

With the strike impending, however, Chávez says he "asked the membership to release us from not accepting outside money, because we'd need it now, a lot of it."[17] Help came from various sources, especially the California Migrant Ministry, a loose confederation of clergy

Gilbert Padilla responded to a query as to why the movement had such religious overtones:

"Yeah, that was planned. . . . We knew from history that strike brings violence. We knew that when that happens, the sheriff and the police department side up with the employer. . . . One of the things we did during those meetings [planning the strike] was that we were gonna do it non-violently...and that anyone that used violence would have to leave the strike. . . . We talked about bringing. . . in religion and bringing in priests. We knew, from past experience, in Mexico and in here, that the Mexicanos especially respect. . . the Vatican, and most of the time we had mass or a prayer when we were out on strikes and stuff.

"And the Church responded. Not everybody. . . not the Catholics at the beginning. Like the local. . . priests were scared and didn't want to get involved. Local ministers in Delano were against it because their parish-

---

[14] Interview with César Chávez.

[15] Interview with Gil Padilla.

[16] Interview with César Chávez.

[17] Chávez, "The Organizer's Tale," p. 341.

ioners. . . were growers. In Delano there was St. Mary's Church for the growers and the Guadalupe Church for the Chicanos, across the freeway"[18]

76. César Chávez. Photo by Oscar Castillo.

pledged to help farm workers.

Fortunately for the union, at this point the nation, more than at any time since the Great Depression, was receptive to social reform. Chávez cultivated a Ghandi-King image that fascinated Americans, many of whom viewed with misgiving the rough-and-tough mainstream unions like the Teamsters. In addition, the Bracero Program ended in 1965 and, as one historian indicates, "That took a lethal weapon from the growers."[19]

When the strike could not shut down work in the fields, the farmers charged publicly that the unions did not enjoy support among workers. Chávez then envisioned a march to Sacramento, California's state capital, for April of 1966. Such a march would associate the farm workers' struggle with social causes which Blacks in the American South had done so much to advance. Besides, Chávez knew that a large turnout for the march would counter the accusations leveled by the growers—he was determined to make this more than a grubby union-management fight. To give the march a set of objectives, Luis Valdez, a budding playwright and founder of El Teatro Campesino, wrote the Plan de Delano, "a ringing call for justice with echoes from past plans in Mexico. . . and in Catholic pietism."[20]

El Teatro Campesino, which serves as an excellent example of the *movimiento* intersecting with the union, was an important source of consciousness-raising for union members. Crucial in shoring up morale during the march, it was started in 1965 by Luis Valdez, a recent graduate from San Jose State University. Originally from Tulare, Valdez was

[18] Interview with Gil Padilla.

[19] Rodolfo Acuña, *Occupied America: A History of Chicanos* (New York: Harper and Row, Publishers, 1988), p. 326.

[20] Gómez-Quiñones, *Chicano Politics*, p. 106.

77. Robert Kennedy with César Chávez when the union leader broke his fast.

a student activist in college who had traveled to Cuba as a member of the Progressive Labor Party. Upon his return, he joined the San Francisco Mime Troupe, a foremost exponent of guerrilla protest theater emerging in the turbulent 1960s' atmosphere of the Bay Area.

The NFWA's detractors constantly accused the union of being Communist-run. Valdez, for example, supported Fidel Castro and the Cuban Revolution. In addition, other union supporters were sympathetic to socialism. But Chávez was careful never to endorse any radical ideas that opposed capitalism, primarily because he himself did not espouse revolution. To counter any allegations of radicalism, NFWA organizers decided to emphasize the religiosity of its membership. "We wanted them to see that first of all we had numbers, that we were organized. . . and we had the Virgin with us," said Chávez.[21]

Indeed, Chávez obtained support from a dazzling interdenominational array of religious groups. This helped sustain the union through its most difficult times, but it would have been impossible if the union had projected a radical image. The rallying cry became simply, "*¡Justicia para los campesinos y viva la Virgen de Guadalupe! (Justice for the farmworkers and long live the Virgin of Guadalupe!)*" Such symbol manipulation was deliberate but not cynical. First, most of the leadership, including Chávez, were observant Catholics. The farm-worker theme song, for example, was "De Colores," the theme song of the Catholic *cursillo* movement, a charismatic prayer and study association to which Chávez and many union members belonged.

In one eventful testimony, Senator Robert Kennedy chided Kern County Sheriff Gaylen for violating the rights of farm-worker organizers. Later at a press conference with Chávez at his side, Kennedy proclaimed, "We have come clearly to the conclusion that an ignored part of our population has been the farm workers. The farm workers have suffered over the last thirty years, and that has to be changed. It's not just a question of wages. It's a question of housing. It's a question of living conditions. It's a question of hope for the future."[22]

[21] Interview with César Chávez.

[22] From film clip, NLCC-GP.

78. United Farm Workers praying. Photo by George Rodríguez.

In the marches of the Black civil rights struggle throughout the early sixties, television news programs beamed images across the country showing a liberal sprinkling of white clergymen conspicuously interspersed among Black demonstrators. This sanctioned even further the notion that the movement was not just among Black Americans. Chávez wanted to project the same vision. While many religious leaders responded, others needed convincing, especially those from the Catholic Church. Because the union membership was predominantly Catholic, the leaders saw Catholic clergy as indispensable in maintaining spirituality and the moral high ground during the upcoming Sacramento march. After prodding the Church, the NFWA finally obtained Catholic support.

The 250-mile march to Sacramento that emphasized religiosity—with Chávez's emulation of Ghandi and Dr. King—proved to be highly successful in getting national attention. As Chávez put it,

> Dr. King had been very successful with that [marches]. So anyway, it was a great experience for us. Oh, it was very difficult to march for 21 days, but it was like God-sent, it was fantastic, it helped us a lot.

At this time, thousands of Mexican American students and youths enrolled in southwestern universities were consuming the gospel of social justice from their liberal professors. Many flocked to Sacramento to join the marchers and received a hearty dose of inspiration. The march served as the underpinning for them of future involvement

79. César Chávez with picketers during the grape boycott. Photo by Oscar Castillo.

in the Chicano Movement that was in its infancy.

Chávez mainly wanted the march to inspire farm workers to join the union. Significantly, he recognized that getting a farm worker to participate in an activity bound him to the union.

> So we have the teatro, the Virgin, we had the flags, but see people marching and their participating. They're committing themselves because their compadre. . .[or the boss] in the car sees them in the march, they can't deny it. Now they're committed, now they have to support it.

The march had served as a vehicle to get public support for the union and to inspire workers, but Chávez knew that neither it nor the strike would bring the grape producers to the negotiating table. Prior to the march, the NFWA had decided to call a boycott of the Schenley Liquor Company, which owned extensive vineyards in the San Joaquin Valley. NFWA planners recognized that a nationwide campaign against table grapes required time they did not have and an infrastructure that did not exist yet. So the union decided to concentrate on boycotting the liquor products of one company by targeting its Los Angeles market. The idea was devised by Fred Ross, who continued helping the NFWA, in order to get a quick boycott victory during the march.

The boycott succeeded. The Sacramento marchers were resting in Stockton when a call came from Schenley's lawyers, who wanted to negotiate a contract. At first Chávez, who thought this was a bribe attempt, hung up, but a second call convinced him the request was genuine. He and two associates drove all night to Beverly Hills (about eight hours), where the company granted all of the union's requests. "You got it," Chávez

Union activist Jessica Govea remembers that, while many working for the union disagreed with the fast, "The majority of us were, like, concerned about César, but at the same time respected his decision. . . . what we did. . . . was to say. . . . what can we do now to support César? With every passing day of the fast, more and more supporters gathered around Chávez, some fasting themselves, while priests said mass in his presence and gave him communion." The upshot, according to Govea, was that it forced supporters to ponder, "whether or not they were willing to continue sacrificing in order to build a union."[24]

80. National Farm Workers Association headquarters in Delano, California, 1965.

claims Schenley's negotiators to have said, "but take the. . . wine boycott off." The next day the unionists were back in Stockton asking the membership to vote on the contract. Because the victory came as the march was underway, the unionists simply crossed out "Boycott Schenley's" from their placards and "by the time we got to Sacramento, a miracle happened."[25] Other wine grape producers—Gallo, Christian Brothers, Paul Masson, Almaden, Franzia Brothers and Noviate—soon signed contracts. The ten thousand NFWA workers and supporters who gathered at the capitol steps on April 11, 1966, were

Eliseo Medina, who joined the union at the historic September meeting in 1965, was sent to Chicago to coordinate activities there.

[For the] longest time [I] was in Chicago. I went there. . . in '67 and I stayed until 1970. That's how long it took the boycott to end. Now, César didn't tell me that's how long it'd take. He told me, oh well, you just got to stop the grapes, and then you can come home. I didn't know what that meant. . . . I was twenty-one years old, never been to any big city by myself, had no idea where Chicago was. And they gave me a bag of buttons. . . one name of a supporter. . . and fifteen dollars. . . . Remember, Delano's a very little town. . . and all of a sudden you go in a city. . . . My whole world had been a Spanish-speaking world. . . a farm worker world, and all of a sudden I had to go out and meet church people and unions, and white people, and all kinds of people. It was a big experience.[23]

[23] On-camera interview with Eliseo Medina, NLCC-GP.

[24] Interview with César Chávez.

[25] On-camera interview with Jessica Govea by Sylvia Morales, December 5, 1994, NLCC-GP.

81. Grape
boycotters,
1968.

euphoric. To many it seemed that the battle had ended. Unfortunately it had not.

Chávez did not stick to the traditional union tactics of using the strike as the main tool. His critics accused him of not having a dependable member base that would honor picket lines. Chávez, however, knew that farm-worker organizing had failed with traditional techniques. Even Chávez's supporters criticized him for spending too much time appealing to public support rather than sticking to the gritty, day-to-day efforts necessary to build a union that could intimidate growers with the old-fashioned strike. But as Chávez so often explained, his hand was forced by the events of 1965.

So he continued using the unorthodox tactic of winning favorable publicity and intimidating employers by demonizing them. As part of this strategy, he asked for a hearing before the U.S. Senate Migratory Subcommittee to air grievances held by farm workers. The committee came out to Delano in the spring of 1966, an event that brought a

Dolores Huerta explained her negotiating style in the following manner: "I guess the growers complained. . . they weren't used to dealing with women. . . . People like Jerry Cohen [also a negotiator] would say, 'You have to be polite.' And my thinking is, Why do we need to be polite to people who are making racist. . . [and] sexist comments? You have to call them at it."[26]

[26] On-camera interview with Dolores Huerta by Sylvia Morales, January 13, 1995, NLCC-GP.

tremendous amount of publicity, primarily because Senator Robert Kennedy was a member. Millions of people watched news reports of the hearings on national television, which both Kennedy and the union used as a forum to denounce the deplorable conditions of farm work.

The event bolstered morale and provided hope, but the NFWA still needed to win against a more formidable opponent if they were to succeed: the gigantic table grape industry. The NFWA was born as a massive social movement which had won the hearts and souls of the public. But grassroots farm worker support was extremely uneven. As a consequence, and because of grower support, the Teamsters Union started to undercut NFWA strength.

One of the most recalcitrant members of the table grape companies was the Di Giorgio Corporation, which had already brought Galarza's union to its knees. Company executives did not take the union seriously until the Sacramento march and the capitulation of their wine grape counterparts. In April of 1966 Di Giorgio announced the company would allow elections. But NFWA representatives charged the company was intimidating its workers into voting for Jimmy Hoffa's Teamsters Union, whom the San Joaquin Valley growers considered less threatening. The NFWA, claiming that Di Giorgio management rushed the elections to prevent NFWA organizers from recruiting members, urged the grape workers to boycott the election. Those who did vote, about half of the work force of 732, voted overwhelmingly for Teamster representation.

Chávez's union charged fraud and demanded that state officials conduct an investigation. NFWA supporters put such pressure on Governor Pat Brown, a personal friend of the Di Giorgio family, that the governor persuaded the grower to allow another election on August 30, 1966. In the campaign to win votes, the Teamsters and the

The most replicated and powerful symbol of *el movimiento* came out of the farm-worker movement. In one of the few pieces ever written by Chávez, he describes how the by-now familiar and striking union flag with its cubistic Black eagle patched on a white circle with a bright red background came to be:

> I thought it would take ten years before we got that first contract. I wanted desperately to get some color into the movement, to give people something they could identify with, like a flag. I was reading some books about how various leaders discovered what colors contrasted and stood out the best. The Egyptians had found that a red field with a white circle and a Black emblem in the center crashed into your eyes like nothing else. I wanted to use the Aztec eagle in the center, as on the Mexican flag. So I told my cousin Manuel, "Draw an Aztec Eagle." Manuel had a little trouble with it, so we modified it to make it easier for people to draw.

At the first meeting of the National Farm Workers Association (NFWA) in Fresno on September 30, 1962, Manuel pulled off the butcher paper covering the "huge flag on the wall. . . and all of a sudden it hit people." The impact was not entirely what Chávez had expected. Some farm workers walked out of the meeting, which attracted 287 people, because they thought it to be communistic while others just wanted an explanation. Manuel then got up and shouted, "When that damn eagle flies—that's when the farm workers' problems are going to be solved."[27]

[27] Last two quotes from César Chávez, "The Organizer's Tale," pp. 341-342.

growers again accused the NFWA of harboring Communists, a charge that prompted a state senate investigation. The inquiry found the accusations unfounded. Chávez and his associates struck back by emphasizing the criminal nature of the Teamsters under its shady leader, Jimmy Hoffa.

In August 1966 the necessity of winning the votes of workers forced Chávez to merge his union with the Filipino-dominated AWOC into a group now called the United Farm Workers Organizing Committee (UFWOC). The NFWA had opposed such an affiliation because it meant coming under the auspices of the AFL-CIO giant and the relinquishment of autonomy. But the effort paid off, and the UFWOC won almost two-thirds of the vote in the August election. DiGiorgio executives signed a contract, but this type of resistance became the first in a series of what became a frustrating trend. Each victory simply unleashed new and tougher battles.

The union continued the tactic of "one grower at a time" and decided to target the biggest table grape producer in the country, the Guimarra Vineyards Corporation. The owner, according to union lawyer Jerry Cohen, was "a feisty Sicilian" who swore his farms would never be unionized. By now, UFWOC publicity had helped build a far-reaching network of sympathy among Americans who associated repressive treatment of Blacks with the plight of Mexican farm workers. César Chávez and his organizers were canonized as civil rights leaders—not just simple unionists—by the liberal-minded population who had elected John F. Kennedy and Lyndon Baines Johnson on a social-reform platform.

As the UFWOC leaders prepared to fight against the Guimarra interests, they realized that this sympathy rather than a strike was the key to their success. So the largest boycott campaign in history was organized and dispatched throughout the country. While the union depended on local cadres of boycott leaders made up of sympathetic influentials, Chávez sent farm-worker representatives out to coordinate boycott activity throughout the country. In every large city in the nation, boycott meetings and fundraising parties were attended by well-dressed students, professors, lawyers, mainstream union leaders and other professionals who contrasted in appearance with the humble farm-worker representatives. At really important events, Chávez himself made appearances.

The Guimarra grape boycott became very difficult to sustain, however. Other table grape companies illegally lent the targeted corporation their labels so that the company's grapes could be shipped clandestinely into grocery stores. Upon discovering this, the UFWOC decided to boycott all table grapes, ushering in a four-year era during which many Americans forgot what a grape tasted like.

The boycott expansion, however, deflected scarce union resources needed to support day-to-day strike-level activity. While some unionists assigned to boycotting in large cities hobnobbed with liberal supporters, on the California strike front, picket captains had to contend with thinning ranks, scarce reserves to support the picketers and, most galling of all, a constant supply of strikebreakers from Mexico. Many of the UFWOC members in the fields wanted to use violence against the "scabs." In the fall of 1967 the California table grape crop was completely harvested. Morale was at an all-time low. Some unionists took out their frustrations by engaging in unsanctioned sabotage, such as the burning of farm buildings.

Chávez's commitment to nonviolence, according to Cohen, was fundamental, and he would not tolerate such tactics. More crucial, the injudicious acts resulted in contempt charges against the union that could land Chávez and other UFWOC officials in jail. At ranch committee meetings (small cadres at each individual farm), Chávez again and again emphasized the necessity to reject destructiveness which some union members were engaging in. At some gatherings, "there were some guys laughing at this. . . so basically, he said. . . 'Hell with you. You want to see who has got the guts? We'll see.'" On March 12, 1968, Chávez decided to use a hunger strike, a la Ghandi, to bring his people into line. The fast was also designed to enhance his image, which the violence had begun to tarnish among supporters outside of the union.

As Chávez fasted, Democratic Party candidates made preparations for the California presi-

82. Signing the union contract ending the grape strike in 1970, with John Guimarra (hands raised).

dential primary. Senator Robert Kennedy, one of the contenders, joined Chávez at Delano on the twenty-fourth day of the fast, the day Chávez announced it would end. Was the sacrifice worth it? It was not the last time Chávez resorted to this tactic, and it certainly took a toll on his body, probably hastening his untimely death. In fact, numerous supporters abandoned the cause because of Chávez's fast, thinking it romantic and ineffectual. Jerry Cohen, however, felt that the fast provided focus to an organization that seemed to be falling apart.

The day the fast ended turned into one of the most memorable events in the history of the union. The image of Chávez, with Kennedy supporting his emaciated body and breaking bread with the union leader, was televised across the country. Thousands of farm workers turned out for the occasion, and many who had given up on the

faltering union now reconsidered their commitment. But more crucial, throughout the country and in Canada, the spectacle persuaded millions not to eat grapes—the fast had revitalized the boycott. It also magnified the Chávez mystique, but many supporters were still asking, was this the best way to organize a union?

Obviously, Chávez and his inner group thought so. They pursued the boycott with renewed vigor. Success depended on the receptive atmosphere of a sympathetic public, but more importantly, activists with as much commitment to the union as its members were needed to keep the boycott alive. The UFWOC continued to send out agents from Delano to large cities to recruit local supporters to form boycott committees, usually called "Friends of the Farm Workers." The committees were multiethnic, but they also served to politicize Chicanos into the *movimiento*, providing them with their first experiences of militancy. The boycott committees demonstrated in front of grocery stores, disrupted their business by intimidating customers and sometimes created chaos inside the stores. All this drove away shoppers, even if they did not sympathize. Cancellation orders for grapes poured into California from throughout the country.

The Coachella Valley farmers relented first because their grapes ripened faster under the hot desert sun. Lionel Steinberg, the owner of Freedman Farms, who signed one of the first contracts in the spring of 1970, recollected the pressure that forced him to capitulate: "They had hundreds and hundreds of people scattered in at least fifty cities. . . . So they gradually closed down our outlet for fruit. . . it was the most successful boycott in American history." The union sanctioned Steinberg products and a union label was put on his table grape crates. As a consequence, he sold all of his produce, even at a higher price than nonunion grapes. In the meantime, the fruit of the holdouts rotted in warehouses. "We had a temporary. . . advantage," Steinberg said. "Of course. . . competitors were very bitter." Nonetheless, other growers, while resentful, also eventually relented, saying, "This is too good, we better get in on the act."[28]

The Guimarras and other San Joaquin growers soon followed the lead of their associates to the south. The boycott accomplished what traditional tactics such as strikes could not. For Chávez, the sweetest moment came when John Guimarra Sr. called Cohen asking to negotiate—the first one to do so in the San Joaquin Valley. Later the "feisty Sicilian" told Chávez, "Okay, I give up, you won.... I am a tough Italian, but I got to admit you beat us."[29] Despite this major victory, the union was not about to sign a contract with just one company and call the boycott off. Guimarra arranged for all San Joaquin Valley table grape companies to meet with Chávez and his associates to negotiate a settlement. Chávez assigned Dolores Huerta to negotiate, and by all accounts she drove the hardest bargain. The signing of contracts with the Guimarras took place on July 29, 1970, in Delano with a lot of fanfare and media coverage. This was the most significant victory in the long history of farm-worker organizing; never had any union delivered such significant benefits to as many workers.

As the UFWOC acquired experience, it sadly realized the magnitude and difficulty of building an industrywide agricultural union. While now-reconciled foes were signing contracts in the joyous ceremony, Salinas Valley lettuce farmers such as Bud Antle, whom the UFWOC targeted next for a boycott, were negotiating "sweetheart" contracts with the Teamsters. These agreements provided lettuce pickers with half-a-cent increase a year on their piecework over a five-year period. The contracts, one historian asserts, "were worse than sweetheart contracts: they provided no job security, no seniority rights, no hiring hall, and no protection against insecticides."[30]

The Teamsters were not new in the area. The Antle farms, for example, had allowed the union to represent many of their shed workers and drivers since the 1950s. The UFWOC decided to compete with the Teamsters, anyway, sending hundreds of organizers to woo away farm workers covered by the "sweetheart" contracts. This move precipitated an arduous and sometimes bloody battle between the two unions. At the Salinas lettuce fields, the UFWOC established pickets, and the familiar red flags were everywhere. The effort convinced thousands of farm workers to walk out. Some estimates indicate that ten thousand farm workers went on strike. Lettuce shipments from the Valley declined from two hundred carloads a day to seventy-five, imposing losses on the growers of as much as half a million dollars daily.

In spite of the show of strength, enough

[28] Two previous quotes from the on-camera interview with Lionel Steinberg by Sylvia Morales, December 7, 1994, NLCC-GP.

[29] Interview with Dolores Huerta.

[30] Acuña, *Occupied America*, p. 327.

83. Farm Workers Union organizing meeting. Photo by Oscar Castillo.

workers remained in the fields, or the Teamsters recruited others to continue the harvest, that the UFWOC decided to employ a boycott as it had with grapes. But the Teamsters, no strangers to violence, used strong bullying tactics to intimidate UFWOC members. During the picketing, unknown enforcers beat Jerry Cohen senseless. In addition, local officials continued to side with the growers and the Teamsters. On December 4, 1970, Monterey Judge Gordon Campbell jailed Chávez when he did not comply with a picketing injunction. This worked in favor of the union because of the nationwide publicity it received. When Chávez was released on Christmas Eve, supporters ladened with presents and reporters surrounded the jailhouse.

The campaign to persuade Americans not to buy head lettuce was more difficult to execute than the previous grape boycott. Lettuce, after all, was a staple which few consumers could do without. Moreover, retail outlets claimed that union labor harvested the lettuce because of the contracts with the Teamsters—an explanation that confused the public. Moreover, by 1970, the sympathetic liberal atmosphere had begun to wane. Richard Nixon, a foe of the union, who had once

eaten grapes publicly to goad the union during the boycott, was now president.

More setbacks were in store. Heartened by Teamster-grower collusion to destroy the union, table grape growers, who had reluctantly signed with the UFWOC earlier in the year, announced that when contracts expired, they too would turn to the Teamsters. By all indications, however, the bulk of the farm workers sympathized with the farm-worker's union.

As the lettuce strike continued in the ensuing months, unsympathetic law officials arrested 3,500 workers. By the spring of 1971 high-level leaders of the AFL recognized that the strenuous feuding was wreaking havoc in the U.S. labor movement and urged an agreement that gave the United Farm Workers (UFW, no longer an organizing committee) sole union representation of lettuce workers. But even if the Teamsters agreed, the growers made it clear they would not bargain with César Chávez. So the strike continued.

In 1973 the strike was still on in California, but as had happened in 1965, wildcat walkouts not called by Chávez in Arizona and Florida drew away UFWOC resources, diluting its effectiveness in the California lettuce fields. While this conflict plagued the union, the growers launched a California state initiative, called Proposition 22, that would outlaw the secondary boycott. This effort jeopardized Chávez's most potent weapon, and so the union had no choice but to fight at the risk of straining its capacity. The grower campaign, financed by half a million dollars, used extensive television advertisements. The union resorted to door-to-door campaigning and using "human billboards" on major traffic thoroughfares, urging Californians to vote against Proposition 22. The union was successful: 4.3 million people voted against the initiative while 3 million voted for it. But fighting this campaign created still another front which drained the energy and money of the UFW.

Fortunately for Chávez, the struggle wearied the other side as well. Relying on the Teamsters backfired on the growers. They were now easier to demonize because they had affiliated with a union that Americans considered to be the shadiest in the nation. The Teamsters also realized that the boycott threatened the well-being of their other agriculture-related unions—i.e., cannery workers, truck drivers, etc. Again national union leaders from the AFL-CIO and the Teamsters decided to mediate the dispute, but Chávez was determined not to give in to the truckers' union and vowed to "break them" rather than compromise.

To this end, the UFW focused on Julio Gallo Wineries, the biggest business to sign a Teamsters contract, and initiated a national boycott of Gallo products. Remembering the successful Sacramento march, a similar tactic was employed on the giant liquor company to publicize this latest venture. On February 22, 1975, about three thousand marchers trekked 110 miles from San Francisco's union square to Gallo's Modesto headquarters. The undertaking provided the union needed publicity and sympathy for its boycott.

In addition, by 1975 a liberal Jerry Brown had replaced the hostile Ronald Reagan as California governor. This assured an improved political climate in Sacramento for the UFW. The strike had taken a tremendous toll on everyone involved. It had devastated the California agricultural industry, the most important source of revenue for the

84. El Teatro Campesino's depiction of Gallo Wineries as a strutting cock.

state. Enlisting the support of California legislators who wanted an end to the turmoil, Brown introduced a bill called the Agricultural Labor Relations Act to provide California farm workers protection from which they were excluded when the U.S. Congress passed the National Labor Relations Act in 1935.

The legislation passed, becoming a crowning achievement for the UFW. At times, though, it hurt the movement because it did not allow for secondary boycotts—the union's constant recourse. In addition, the years of extraneous disputes deflected the UFW's ability to conserve the few gains it had achieved through great sacrifice. Unfortunately for the union, after Jerry Brown's

term, a conservative George Deukmajian succeeded as governor. He appointed Agricultural
Labor Relations Board members who favored the
growers' interests. Dolores Huerta complained
that, because of this arrangement, "the growers
disobey the law and get away with it." As an
example, she reeled off a number of instances in
which the UFW won elections, but it took years
to get certification from the board.

Unionization of agricultural workers was con-
centrated in California. But because of César
Chávez's influence, efforts to organize farm workers were made in Arizona, Texas, Florida and the
Midwest. During 1966 Eugene Nelson, a former
Chávez organizer, along with Margil Sánchez and
Lucio Galván, formed the Independent Workers'
Association (IWA) in Texas's Lower Rio Grande
Valley. They called a strike of farm workers that
was met with enthusiasm, but the use of undocumented workers by the growers prevented its success. The union even attempted to block them
from crossing the border. When IWA members
elected to become an affiliate of the Chávez's
NFWA, division ensued. Galván and Sánchez
opposed the California union and even resorted to
discrediting it by using right-wing propaganda
that claimed the NFWA was Communist. Under
the auspices of Chávez's union, the Texas
UFWOC pursued a California strategy that included a march to Austin to present its grievances.
Antonio Orendáin, the UFWOC national treasurer, became the de facto leader of the Texas effort.
Ultimately, Cesár Chávez had to withdraw efforts
from Texas because the odds against succeeding
seemed insurmountable, but he left Orendáin in
charge of a shoe-string operation. Eventually, the
miffed Orendáin resigned and started a new
union called the Texas Farm Workers, which lasted only a few years.

UFW successes in California during 1968
inspired Gustavo Gutiérrez to resign his position
with the Arizona Migrant Opportunity Program
(MOP), a Baptist-financed project, and start a
union in Arizona. Gutiérrez encouraged Mel
Hewey and Carolina Rosales, two other MOP
employees, to quit the organization and help him
with his work. Chávez sanctioned the effort, but
Gutiérrez financed the union, named the Arizona

Farm Workers Organizing Committee (AFWOC),
with local funds. It was centered in Tolleson, an
agricultural community located a few miles west of
Phoenix—a base of previous efforts to organize during the 1940s. By 1969 the AFWOC struck local
grape growers and obtained contracts, primarily
because the national boycott threatened all grape
producers, not just those in California. The fortunes
of the Arizona farm workers followed those in
California, except that political opposition was
more formidable in this very conservative state.

The Farm Labor Organizing Committee
(FLOC) was formed in Ohio during 1968 to organize Texas migrant workers who trekked annually
to the Midwest to harvest vegetables for farmers
who contracted with major food-processing giants
such as Campbell, Heinz and Vlasic. As in
California, they employed the boycott to obtain
favorable contracts. When they targeted each
company individually, as they did with
Campbell's Foods, they enjoyed some success.

By the late seventies, internal dissent had
weakened the California-based UFW, and the
rank and file began to challenge the leadership in
the decision-making process. In fact, many members questioned Chávez's ironclad hold on union
policymaking. A third grape boycott was issued in
1984, mainly to protest pesticide use as harmful
to the workers. The boycott was a far cry from the
dynamic effort made in the 1960s. To bring attention to the flagging campaign, in 1988 Chávez
embarked on still another fast. Although it was
publicized, it seemed to have little impact.

Recently, the union has continued to fall on
hard times. It has lost many contracts signed in
the 1960s and 1970s. In the early 1990s, no
more than one hundred contracts covered about
ten thousand farm workers. A bane for the union
has been the ability of agricultural interests to use
undocumented workers. From the very outset, the
UFW opposed immigration because it built up
labor surpluses that lowered wages and made it
difficult to organize.

Chávez has always felt that the union should
obtain benefits for U.S. citizens and permanent
residents. Not surprisingly, he argued as had
Ernesto Galarza, for a restrictive immigration policy to reduce immigration. Chávez and his sup-

porters also believed that union enticements were less appealing to immigrants than to more settled Mexican American farm workers. As a consequence, the union opposed the Bracero Program and in 1970 even supported from behind the scenes the California Arnett Bill, which imposed criminal charges against employers who consciously hired undocumented workers.

The farm-worker movement seems to have lost its symbolic appeal for Chicanos, and indeed until César Chávez's tragic death in 1993 at age 65, the struggle was not as public as in previous years. The grape boycott was still in place at the time of his death, for example, but few people knew about it.

CONCLUSION

Collectively, the organizers of the farm-worker union differed from other *movimiento* activists in many respects. Many of them were Anglos, for example, such as Fred Ross and Jim Drake. Moreover, Chicano unionists did not wrestle with goals such as reconciling Chicano identity and promoting affirmative action. Attaining civil rights played an indirect role whereas it was the *sine qua non* of the mainstream *movimiento*. For farm workers, bread-and-butter objectives remained paramount. Their goals emphasized the lack of economic justice for a generic farm-worker class—although Chicanos more than other ethnic farm workers would benefit if the union were successful.

Ironically, at times activists could be heard grumbling that Chávez hogged the movement. This criticism was gratuitous because the union did not actively seek identification with the *movimiento*—Chicano activists drew it into the pantheon. And once in the cauldron, the UFW did not shy away from identification with the movement if it could benefit. While many whites worked in the trenches of the UFW, the aura of the struggle also attracted thousands of young Chicano Movement activists, such as Luis Valdez, who were instrumental in helping with union work.

Chávez and his followers also appealed to young *movimiento* participants because of their seemingly antiestablishment bent. The unionists defied convention by their simple dress while at the same time eschewing material comforts that mainstream unionists and older Mexican American civil rights activists took for granted: suits and ties, expense accounts, conventions in luxury hotels, and the like. They relied on the meager resources at hand, living simply, even before the counterculture movement extolled such a lifestyle. Supporters provided organizers their homes and fed them and soon the union organizers established a reliable network across the breadth of the U.S. and even Canada.

In addition, the UFW leaders often criticized well-heeled Mexican Americans whose commitment to change was not as complete as theirs. Also, the genesis of Chicano theater, a hallmark of the *movimiento*, is in the farm-worker movement. Finally the farm-worker flag, whose origins are described earlier, became the main symbol of the Chicano Movement, whether or not activists were associated directly with the UFW.

CHAPTER NINE

In Quest of a Homeland

85. Reies López Tijerina. Photo by Oscar Castillo.

The rise of the Chicano Movement had no greater symbol of defying the Establishment than Reies López Tijerina. While César Chávez evoked a Ghandi-like image, the aggressive exploits of Tijerina and members of his Alianza Federal de las Mercedes (Federal Alliance of Land Grants) provided Chicanos vicarious gratification. The tactics used by his northern New Mexico movement to regain land lost to Anglos or to the federal government were dramatic and audacious. As a consequence, Tijerina earned the designation, "The Tiger" (an obvious play on his name).

The basis of the Alianza crusade was the 1848 Treaty of Guadalupe Hidalgo, which guaranteed Mexicans all the rights of citizens, the right to their property and the right to maintain cultural institutions, i.e. the Spanish language and Mexican traditions. Indeed, the treaty and the perception that Anglo-America had violated its stipulations became a *raison d'etre* for the Chicano Movement. Every Tijerina proclamation, even if untenable, helped to fix ideological goals for the *movimiento*. The following statement, for example, expressed sentiments that would become dear to *movimiento* activists:

> We have been forced by destiny to adopt two languages; we will be the future ambassadors and envoys to Latin America. At home, I believe that the Southwest is breeding a special kind of people that will bridge the color gap between Black and white. . . We are the people the Indians call their lost brothers.[2]

Besides the Alianza's militancy and boldness, the goal of establishing a free, independent community appealed to the emerging Chicano nationalists and separatists. Young militants, in the throes of rejecting the "politics as usual" posture pursued by mainstream Mexican American politicians and civil rights activists, saw in the Alianza the closest and most concrete manifestation of separatism—a notion they only expressed in vague terms.

The stated objective of the Alianza movement was regaining lost lands, but the *hispano* villager, embittered from grinding poverty, isolation and neglect, supported this movement regardless of his or her own land claims. As explained by David Cargo, a sympathetic New Mexico governor during the era when much of the Alianza activity took place,

> Most of what they call the land-grant movement didn't have a great deal to do with land grants. It had to do with all kinds of political problems, not all of them connected even with the land grants. Unemploy-

Carlos Montes, a founder of the militant Brown Berets in Los Angeles, saw firsthand on a trip to New Mexico that Tijerina was trying to establish a separate state: "The whole concept of an alliance of Free City States. . . we had a meeting with them, they had their own mayor . . . their own sheriff. . . apart from the so-called U.S. government. . . . We tripped out. . . the grazing rights, communal lands, we want our land back. . . . We said, 'Shit, these people want their own land, they all got their own government structure.'"[1]

---

[1] Interview with Carlos Montes by Enrique Berumen, February 6, 1994, NLCC-GP. Without exception, movement leaders who traveled to see the Alianza in action tell similar stories.

[2] Quoted in Chávez, *The Lost Land*, p.141.

ment, welfare. . . no roads, poverty, no medical care, all kinds of things. The area is a kind of Hispanic Appalachia.[3]

Potential Chicano Movement activists first heard of Tijerina at different points in their politicization, but his existence could not escape their attention after June 6, 1967. On that day Tijerina led an armed group of Alianza members in storming the Rio Arriba County courthouse in Tierra Amarilla to free eight jailed comrades. The background story to this event is just as remarkable as the raid itself—perhaps even more. It revolves as much around the charismatic Tijerina as it does around the New Mexico *hispano's* dream of regaining traditions anchored by land ownership. From their perspective, conspiratorial forces led by the federal government but supported by Anglo-American and Hispanic elites had destroyed their ability to remain rooted to the land, a process that allowed for keeping family and culture intact. Under Tijerina, this *hispano* aspiration coalesced in the Alianza.

Tijerina's was not the only land-grant movement in the history of this area—it was just the latest and largest. After the unsuccessful Taos Revolt of Padre Antonio José Martínez in 1847, which cost the first Anglo governor of New Mexico his life, *hispanos* have often confronted authorities over the issue of land loss. U.S. political hegemomy in New Mexico did not create a clear Anglo-Mexican dichotomy as was the case in Texas. *Hispano* discontent over erosion of their land base stems from a class collaboration between wealthy Mexicans and Anglos, a process predating the U.S. period.

In the early nineteenth century, New Mexico village farmers and ranchers north of Santa Fe raised foodstuffs—corn, wheat and chilies—which they bartered mainly in local markets. The only cash endeavor was the raising of sheep for wool. Richer landowners monopolized the fertile, well-watered properties along the Upper Rio Grande Valley south of Santa Fe, where on large haciendas they raised foodstuffs for local markets. But

86. Father Antonio José Martínez.

access from the Camino Real into Chihuahua's large markets allowed handsome profits for sheep and livestock ranches. The opening of the Santa Fe Trail after Mexico's independence allowed for Anglo merchants and trappers to enter regions formerly closed to outsiders. Wealthier *hispanos* soon discovered the advantage of tapping the Anglo economy to the east. Farmers with small ancestral lands had a diminished capacity to enter the incipient capitalist market and remained traditional in their way of life, producing only enough to live on. The meager surplus was sold for cash to obtain essential consumer goods and to buy more land.

The property-owning system was based on Spanish land law. The crown issued *mercedes* (land grants) to colonizing groups, who divided them among themselves. The petitioners then lived in villages and walked or rode to their assigned plots to plant, irrigate and harvest. Land use was governed collectively, utilizing a system called *ejidos*. The villages were organized around a *plaza*, where inhabitants gathered to establish policy and settle disputes.

With the changeover after the U.S. acquired New Mexico, villagers continued using "public domain" lands as they had for centuries, but in the twentieth century the U.S. Forest Service took control of these grounds. Now economic growth fostered land antagonisms, and although the vil-

---

[3] Interview with David Cargo by Claire Jones, February 3, 1994, NLCC-GP.

87. *Hispano* farm family in the Mora Valley, New Mexico, September, 1895.

lagers participated in the new ventures and competed with newcomers, lack of capital prevented their full integration. According to some interpretations, the collective approach that evolved among the small farmers did not engender the keen competitive spirit that was common among Anglos and their rich Hispanic collaborators. This notion also holds that *hispanos* pursued a traditional way of life that put less emphasis on profits and more on family. This assumption can be put to debate, but if true, such fealty must have blunted their competitive edge.

The assault on the villager's way of life provoked endemic poverty, debt and vulnerability to land usurpation by developers such as the wealthy Anglos and Hispanics who belonged to the infamous Santa Fe Ring in the nineteenth century. Those who held on to their property into this century struggled with taxes and a constant battle to obtain favorable water and grazing rights.

The result was continuing tension that often erupted into violence. In 1928, a full eighty years after the annexation, Isuaro Pacheco, a native New Mexican envisioning a revolution of *neomexicanos* to end what he considered Anglo oppression, wrote to Mexican President Plutarco Elías Calles to obtain support. The main problem, Pacheco stated, was that his people's lack of education made them vulnerable. They had lost their land and culture to the *yanqui* invaders. But he did not trust the Anglo educational institutions, so he asked the Mexican government to provide Spanish-language schools to elevate his people from ignorance. The writer claimed to represent an Albuquerque organization devoted to stemming the tide of American encroachment.

Obviously, the conditions for such movements to regain land were always present in northern New Mexico; all that was required was a catalyst. This is the void which Reies López Tijerina filled and played to perfection. Tijerina was born into a farm-working family in Fall City,

Texas, on September 10, 1926. He spent the better part of his youth migrating with his widowed father and twelve brothers in a stream typical to Tejano farm workers: West Texas, Arizona and up to the Midwest. His formal education was sparse: neither he nor his siblings ever stayed long enough in any one area to finish school terms, so he did not even graduate from the eighth grade. He did possess a probing mind, however, and became literate in both Spanish and English at an early age.

Tijerina eventually became a minister in the Assembly of God Church after studying at a seminary in Isleta, outside of El Paso. He traces his desire to become a preacher to his youth. At age fifteen, while the family labored in Michigan agriculture, the young Reies obtained a copy of the Bible and read it incessantly during the rest periods in the fields and at night. After ordination, he held a number of permanent posts, ministering to the Spanish-speaking in New Mexico and Texas. A sedentary post did not suit Tijerina, who was used to an itinerant life, and so he went out on the road as a Pentecostal revivalist. With tents in tow, he and a coterie of followers, including many of his brothers, preached their way throughout the Southwest. Family cohesiveness, a crucial trait among migrant farm workers, stayed with Tijerina even after he became the Alianza leader and a self-proclaimed revolutionary. Before settling in Tierra Amarilla, Tijerina and some followers from Texas and New Mexico had bought eighty acres and established a religious commune in the middle of the Arizona desert. After being accused of a crime and jailed there, he jumped bail and, with his group, fled the court's jurisdiction to northern New Mexico. Tijerina's wife, Patsy, was a native of this region.

88. Reies López Tijerina.

At this point, Tijerina's remarkable land-grant venture began. Even before he arrived in Rio Arriba County, he was aware of the bitterness that Hispanic farmers harbored. He quickly learned more as he moved up and down the mountain valleys, preaching to the predominantly Catholic *hispanos*. Although Tijerina was not a native New Mexican, his Texas roots were similar to those of the New Mexican villagers. His great-grandfather, he often recounted, was killed by an Anglo who robbed him of his land. The Arizona dispute in which his commune wound up losing its property also moved him closer to the issue.

How did Reies López Tijerina, a Texas-born Mexican with no roots in northern New Mexico, become the leader of a uniquely New Mexican movement? Three personality traits account for this: oratorical flair, a piercing intelligence and, most importantly, the ability to understand the resentment that village-dwelling farmers held towards those who

Sabine Ulibarrí, writer, poet and scholar from northern New Mexico, does not doubt the intimate link that his people have chosen of family, community and the land over "progress." He puts it thus: "The land was sacred because your parents and their parents were buried there, some of your children were buried there and you would be buried there. So the sweat, blood and tears have filtered into the land. So it is holy, it is sacred, it is sacrosanct."[4]

[4] On-camera interview with Sabine Ulibarrí by Myléne Moreno, April 18, 1995, NLCC-GP.

usurped their lands—Anglo farmers, developers and the federal government. The poet and novelist Sabine Ulibarrí, who is from Tierra Amarilla, provides the following powerful explanation: "He was speaking the magic words, the issue. . . The struggle had been alive for all these generations and here was a man on a white horse, a man with tremendous charisma, who plugged into deep-felt passion."[5]

It is probable that Tijerina did not introduce militancy to the villagers; they introduced it to him. Sabotage and violence by the Spanish-speaking farmers was a well established tradition before Tijerina's arrival. As the geographer Clark Knowlton puts it, "For more than fifty years, intruding Anglo American ranchers had their buildings burnt, their fences cut and their livestock killed." [6]

The Anglo farmers retaliated by forming secret societies and shooting or beating up *hispano* leaders.

In the 1950s, as New Mexico acquired more people, land competition fostered a crescendo of tension. With the purpose of stemming further erosion of their economic situation, villagers formed the Corporation of Abiquiu. Tijerina, by then in New Mexico, moved around the villages with freedom because local *penitentes* (religious lay brotherhoods) trusted him and shielded him from authorities. An arrest warrant was still pending in Arizona, where authorities wanted him for jumping bail. It is not known, however, what role he played in the founding of Abiquiu, the forerunner to the Alianza.

A main reason for the increased unrest was that the U.S. Forest Service had issued stricter codes regulating grazing, wood cutting and water use on federal lands. The new decrees presented new problems to the villagers. Before, it had been a matter of individual families recouping property lost, perhaps generations earlier. The federal government incursion perniciously and suddenly affected the struggling farmers all at once.

Worse yet, it appeared to the *hispanos* that the policy discriminated against them. For example, in 1965 the U.S. Forest Service, using the new edicts, banned the grazing of the milk cows and draught horses of the *hispanos* at Kit Carson National Forest but allowed Anglo owners of riding horses and beef cattle to continue using park land. Poverty followed for many small farmers—practically all *hispano* villagers. Some began to brace for possible loss of lands because they could not pay their taxes. Adding to their resentment, the villagers saw that the Forest Service had improved hiking trails and campsites for the recreation of outsiders from the cities. The *hispanos*, however, were banned from land that had supported their way of life for generations, if not for centuries. In 1963 the Area Redevelopment Report, in a study of Mora County, illustrates that the villagers were being driven out:

> The U.S. Forest Service is limiting the grazing permits to an unreasonable degree. Our U.S. Department of Agriculture is encouraging all farmers and ranchers to raise more livestock, to stay on farms and ranches. On the other hand, one of its departments, the U.S. Forest Service, is telling them to get out and get out fast.[7]

By 1962 the statute of limitations for Tijerina's arrest in Arizona had expired, leaving him unencumbered to pursue his crusade. As the movement grew and attracted public attention, its headquarters was moved from Tierra Amarilla, in 1963, to a two-story building in Albuquerque. The Corporation of Abiquiu became incorporated as a nonprofit group; it now called itself La Alianza Federal de las Mercedes (The Federal Land-Grant Alliance). The organization broadened its aspiration base to include bilingual education, civil rights, economic equality and an end to mistreatment by law-enforcement authorities.

Tijerina then turned to a strategy never before attempted by the *hispanos*; he attracted

[5] On-camera Interview with Sabine Ulibarrí.

[6] Clark S. Knowlton, "Reies L. Tijerina and the Alianza Federal de Mercedes: Seekers After Justice," unpublished manuscript in author's files, p. 4.

[7] Quoted in Ibid., p. 5.

attention to the cause by emulating the Black civil rights movement. Rather than projecting an image of simply disaffected farmers, the Alianza hosted conferences that had the air of civil rights rallies. Tijerina invited to his gatherings Chicano Movement activists, Native American leaders and white liberal supporters. His stated goals were simple. The greedy actions of the U.S. government and rich Anglos and *hispanos* violated the God-derived guarantees of the Treaty of Guadalupe Hidalgo; therefore, a holy crusade was appropriate to rectify these wrongs.

When asked recently what drew him to the movement, Tijerina replied,

> Our land was stolen, we wanted it back. Our towns were alive and now they're dead, they're frozen, and the common lands that belonged to the towns were taken away, just like we see now in Palestine. Just like Zapata's towns in his days. . . . That's what pulled me into that area.[8]

But the most important work accomplished by Tijerina was to provide hope to the villagers, who had an eternal optimism that they could somehow recover their lands. Tijerina; his wife, Patsy; his brothers and a cadre of faithful organizers traveled across the breadth of village country, persuading disgruntled *paisanos* to join the Alianza. A 1960 court ruling, however, placed arbitration of Treaty of Guadalupe Hidalgo issues in the hands of Congress, not the courts. The ruling made this perennial hope more futile.

Tijerina had researched the status of New Mexico land grants in Mexico City archives and concluded that the U.S. had violated the terms of the treaty. Irrespective of the quality of his legal analysis, the *aliancistas'* hopes were buoyed by this proclamation. Tijerina's message resonated among the villagers, whose economic condition was deteriorating on a daily basis. As Tijerina's nemesis, Alfonso Sánchez, the Tierra Amarilla

county attorney, put it, "Reies is very, very convincing, fiery, and I would listen to him too, very fiery. . . he can motivate."[9] Or as Clark Knowlton observed,

> Tijerina and those around him were engaged in a profound crusade to raise the level of consciousness among the Spanish American people, to teach them their history as interpreted by the Alianza, and to stress the importance of the Alianza as a defender of the Spanish American rights.[10]

Between 1964 and 1966 Tijerina purchased time on the radio for a daily show that was broadcast to every remote region in northern New Mexico. Mustering his considerable oratorical skills, every program exploded with charges of mistreatment against *hispanos* by Anglo Americans and the need to establish a civil rights movement. This effective tool tapped a groundswell of anger and bitterness among thousands of *hispanos* who never met Tijerina or his devotees in person.

At first, the solution envisioned by the Alianza was to work within the system, and Tijerina expounded a nonviolent approach. He insisted on the establishment of a government commission to study, as he had already done, the whole land grant issue to determine if villager claims of land theft were true. To highlight its cause, the Alianza resorted to a maneuver similar to César Chávez's Sacramento march. Alianza members decided to trek from Albuquerque to the steps of the state capitol in Santa Fe on July 2, 1966, a distance of fifty miles. Tijerina and a committee of his group met with Governor Jack Campbell on July 11, 1966. The group explained its purpose, stating, "We do not demand anything. We just want a full investigation."

The governor asked Myra Allen Jenkins, state archivist and a historian with expertise on land grants, to research the claims. Her findings were devastating to the hopeful *aliancistas*. "There is lit-

[8] Interview with Reies López Tijerina by Luis Torres, December 29, 1989, NLCC-GP.

[9] Interview with Alfonso Sánchez by Jesús Treviño, July 24, 1992, NLCC-GP.

[10] Knowlton, "Reies L. Tijerina and the Alianza Federal de Mercedes," p. 6.

tle historical validity to any of their claims," the report stated, and it went on to say, "Many members of the so-called Alianza were not descendants of any Spanish or land grantees. I feel there are outside influences which are reopening this old issue for pecuniary gain."[11] Jenkins's conclusions discredited the movement and, significantly, the media refused to accord Tijerina the same respect given Martin Luther King and César Chávez. Instead, he was portrayed as a confidence man who manipulated ignorant *hispano* villagers to enrich himself personally. It is doubtful that Tijerina or his immediate family profited by their involvement in this cash-strapped organization whose membership dues barely paid for its upkeep. More importantly, Tijerina did not lose the allegiance of most rank-and-file Alianza members, and thousands of other *hispanos* and white Americans continued to sympathize with the cause.

His opponents in government, especially Governor Campbell, were anxious to discredit Tijerina and forgot to consider the truly meritorious issues brought out by the Alianza movement. In addition, many influential Hispanics could not abide Reies López Tijerina or his movement—such class antagonism characterized New Mexico even before its incorporation into the U.S. One of his biggest opponents was Emilio Naranjo, the political boss in Rio Arriba County, where Tierra Amarilla is located. David Cargo, however, when he ran for governor against Campbell, courted support from the Alianza, a factor that helped his election in November of 1966. Cargo, a Republican, ran the campaign on a shoestring budget with very little help from party coffers, and campaigned on his own throughout the north. "They'd say old Lonesome Dave is off by himself. . . I traveled all by myself and I would go to those areas and go to the little towns. . . and campaign." When the Alianza had its 1966 convention at the Civic Auditorium in Albuquerque, Cargo

addressed the gathering: "I went up and addressed them and said I didn't know if they were right or wrong, but I would certainly listen.... I told them I'd try to straighten things out."[12] Married to an Hispanic woman who actually belonged to the Alianza, Cargo was not just acting politically. Campbell, on the other hand, was from Roswell, an area renowned for its antipathy towards Mexicans and known in New Mexico as "Little Texas."

Cargo's sympathy notwithstanding, Campbell remained governor until 1967, and after the Jenkins report was issued, he would have nothing to do with *aliancistas*. As Clark Knowlton aptly explains,

> If the governor, the state legislature, the U.S. Forest Service, and local officials of federal departments had taken the Alianza and its request seriously and opened a dialogue. . . it is possible that none of the subsequent violence would have taken place. . . . the failure of government and mass media to properly understand the reasons for the existence of the Alianza and of the deeply-rooted grievances of the rural Spanish American people...can be traced to a fundamental lack of concern or knowledge.[13]

At the very conference where Cargo delivered his genial speech, Tijerina announced plans for occupying a disputed land grant and set up a security council to resist any government actions to evict his group. Alianza activists chose Echo Amphitheater, a campground in the Kit Carson National Forest which had been an original *merced* (land grant) called San Joaquín del Río Chama, granted by the Spanish crown in the eighteenth century. On October 16, 1966, a large contingent of *aliancistas* converged on the campground. The government ignored the takeover for about a week. This gave land-grant activists time to establish the Republic of San Joaquín del Río Chama and serve eviction papers on William D. Hurst, the forest ranger supervisor for Kit Carson.

[11] Two previous quotes from Ibid., pp. 7-8.

[12] Interview with David Cargo.

[13] Knowlton, "Reies L. Tijerina and the Alianza Federal de Mercedes," p. 17.

During the occupation of the campground, Tijerina declared, "Fidel Castro had what he has because of his guts. . . . Castro put the gringos off his island and we can do the same."[14]

The group then quietly vacated the campground but vowed to come back. To prevent this, Hurst sealed off the entrance with two rangers, reinforced by state police, and announced that anyone entering would have to register and buy a dollar permit. Tijerina and a large body of armed *aliancistas* broke through the barricade, captured the rangers and escorted them out of the park. Tijerina then held a press conference, proclaiming that now it was the federal government's turn to defend its claim. But since the Department of Agriculture (the agency which runs the federal parks) had the greater power to enforce its claim to sovereignty, Tijerina and five other *aliancistas* were arrested for conspiring to prevent forest rangers from conducting their duties. The group was arraigned and released on bond. This was the beginning of the more militant phase of Alianza politics during the next year.

With the arrival of winter and snow, the group did not engage in any major protest, except perhaps to set forest fires and intimidate tourists and sportsmen. Anglo-American families on private lands and in lodges built on government-leased land feared race war and withdrew to the safety of towns. Others armed themselves, thinking an uprising of *hispanos* was imminent. When the snows melted, the Alianza announced a renewed campaign to occupy former land grants. On May 14, 1967, the group chose the old Tierra Amarilla land grant, now divided among private landholdings belonging primarily to Anglos. Simultaneous with the announcement of plans for the Tierra Amarilla takeover, sabotage increased—arson of farm buildings, fence demolition and other acts of destruction—that were blamed on Tijerina and his followers. This galvanized even more the opposition to his movement. The investigations ordered by Governor Cargo came up emptyhanded and only increased the antagonism of Alianza foes, who blamed Cargo's lack of zeal for this failure.

Verbal warfare ensued during the summer months with *aliancistas* constantly threatening to occupy former land-grant properties. The main spokesman for their enemies was Tierra Amarilla county attorney, Alfonso Sánchez. Governor Cargo attempted to steer a middle course, not wanting to alienate his Alianza friends completely, but still followed the letter of the law. The result was that he pleased neither group. As the news of sabotage spread, the severity of these incidents became exaggerated and soon stories were spread of assassination squads and Cuban aircraft drops of guerrilla experts and heavy weapons. Some New Mexicans thought a major rebellion was near. Fueling these beliefs were the pronouncements of politicians and some newspapers.

Establishment New Mexicans and the media attempted to censure Governor Cargo. In his words, "Oh boy, they really went after me. . . and the newspapers did too. Because they said I was too pro-Hispanic. . . and I was some kind of revolutionary. Oh man, it was just awful. I mean the whole world was going to collapse."[15]

[14] Quoted in Chávez, *The Lost Land*, p. 140.

[15] Interview with David Cargo.

The *aliancistas* remained on good terms with Governor Cargo, however. After meeting with him, Tijerina announced on May 19, 1967, that the Alianza would again occupy the San Joaquín del Río de Chama land grant and invited his followers to meet at the village of Coyote on June 3 to formulate plans. The pronouncement was so well known that authorities immediately moved to prevent the meeting by resorting to illegal and even unconstitutional methods. For example, U.S. District Court Judge H. Verle Perle in Albuquerque authorized U.S. Attorney John Quinn to confiscate the Alianza membership list so that the Internal Revenue Service could investigate the organization. To counter this gambit, Alianza leaders dissolved the group and started another one called La Confederación de Pueblos Libres (The Federation of Free Peoples). Federal authorities still sought compliance; therefore, Tijerina and other Alianza officers secluded themselves. The Coyote meeting was not called off.

Complicating matters on the weekend of the Coyote meeting, Governor Cargo flew to Michigan to attend a Republican Party fundraiser given by Governor George Romney. At home, authorities were not communicating with each other effectively. This gave Alfonso Sánchez and his mentor, Emilio Naranjo, carte blanche to impede the *aliancistas* from convening in Coyote because Cargo's absence prevented countering their actions. The night before the meeting, Sánchez ordered the state police to block all state roads into Coyote and to threaten Alianza partisans with conspiracy charges if they participated in the meeting. Governor Cargo maintained a less alarmist assessment of the Alianza movement's nature. Looking back to May 1967, Cargo recalls that Alianza members

> contacted me and wanted to know if they could have a public meeting in Coyote. Well, why not? I thought we had freedom of assembly. I thought we had freedom of speech. . . . So I told them, I don't know any reason why you can't meet. . . . As soon as that hap-

pened. . . Alfonso Sánchez got on the radio and said they were a bunch of Communists; actually a lot of them were Republicans. . . . He was very abusive. . . and tried to get the American Legion into it. . . . He claimed they were subversives. They were being trained by Cuba. Oh, it went on and on.[16]

The former governor claims that, on the night he left, it seemed that all was well because he himself had broadcast a radio appeal to the *aliancistas*, asking them not to convene because of the danger of being arrested. "I thought maybe that would pretty much resolve it."

He was wrong. Sánchez succeeded in disrupting the meeting. *Aliancistas* heading in the direction of the village in their dilapidated cars and pickup trucks were intimidated into turning back. Then the Sánchez-marshaled forces entered town to gather Alianza partisans who had eluded the blockade and arrested eight for unlawful assembly, which Sánchez defined as "three or more persons assembling with intent to take over lands of the U.S. government by force and violence." And those "not charged with unlawful assembly would likely be charged with extortion, and an extortion charge promised a sentence of up to ten years in the penitentiary and a fine of up to $5,000."[17] Throughout New Mexico, the media supported this roundup without mentioning the obvious violation of civil rights.

After gaining assurances from Cargo, the *aliancistas* did not expect such harsh repercussions. They felt betrayed by the governor, whom they did not know had left the state before the arrests. Their eight comrades in the county jail, incarcerated for unlawful assembly, symbolized this deception. They decided to free them. The band also wanted to conduct a citizen's arrest of Alfonso Sánchez and jail him in their own community of Abiquiu. Sánchez, Tijerina reasoned, had violated the civil rights of the imprisoned men; therefore, he was subject to a citizen's arrest. In a frenzied June 5 attack by the Alianza, two officers were wounded—Nick Saiz, a state

---

[16] Interview with David Cargo.

[17] Quoted in Knowlton, "Reies L. Tijerina and the Alianza Federal de Mercedes," p. 14.

policeman, was injured critically in the chest and Eligio Salazar, a deputy sheriff, sustained a superficial head wound.

Former Sheriff Benny Naranjo remembers the events vividly:

> I heard a shot in the hallway. . . . My jailer ran into the hallway and said, "Get the hell out of here, Benny!". . . And he jumped out the window and they started shooting at me through the door. So I lay down on the floor, but I heard them say, "Reies said not to hurt nobody, all we want is Alfonso Sánchez."[18]

Unknown to the raiders, Judge James M. Scarborough had released their cohorts on bond before the attack because Sánchez had failed to appear—he was laying low. Not finding their comrades in the courthouse, the band herded everyone they could find into the County Commission room. Among the hostages was Associated Press reporter Larry Calloway, who was phoning his office in Albuquerque. The raiders spotted him in the booth crouching down and forced him in with the rest of the hostages.

For a while it seemed that the raiders were going to retreat without any further incidents. But two "accomplices," Baltazar Martínez and an older *aliancista* Baltazar Apodaca, decided to take hostages. This was unknown to Tijerina and the others, who had already left. They chose as hostages the reporter Calloway and a deputy, Pete Jaramillo. Apparently the two stragglers did not want to leave empty-handed. Martínez and Apodaca, hostages in hand, sped off in Deputy Jaramillo's high-powered GTO.

Spotting a road block, the fugitives abandoned the car and set out in different directions. Apodaca guarded Calloway, and Martínez, Jaramillo. Calloway managed to disarm his elderly guard and escaped; the deputy was released unharmed. The two kidnappers then fled into the mountains. Within hours, acting governor L. C. Francis mobilized the National Guard, which embarked on one of the most massive manhunts in New Mexico history. Four hundred and fifty guardsmen and several trucks, jeeps, tanks and helicopters under the command of General John Jolly were rushed to the pristine Sangre de Cristo mountain range. Cargo probably would not have ordered such drastic measures, but he was still out of town visiting with Michigan Congressman Gerald Ford and Governor George Romney. Recalls Cargo,

> We were both in a receiving line in a hotel in Grand Rapids. And Jerry Ford leans over to me and says, "I've got a message for you. . . .you've got a civil war going on in New Mexico". . . . And I said, "No kidding?" And he said, "They said that some people raided a courthouse in Northern New Mexico and shot the judge and killed several people. . . . I think you better call home.". . . That's how I found out about it.[19]

Alfonso Sánchez filed a criminal case "against Tijerina and those that were responsible for killing deer out of season. . . for butchering cattle. . . those warrants were outstanding at the time of the Coyote meeting." These charges stemmed from allegations that, during the previous year's meeting at Echo Amphitheater, where about one thousand people converged, the assembly augmented their food supplies by living off the land by hunting. According to Sánchez, the butchered carcasses of deer and cattle were found at Echo Amphitheater after the *aliancistas* had withdrawn. "Well, how is Tijerina going to feed all of those people?" he asked. "He butchered cattle that had grazing permits. . . he butchered deer out of season. . . . They used to hang people for stealing cattle. . . and that can still be done. Those laws are still in effect." The eight men arrested in Coyote were charged with that crime as well.[20]

---

[18] From voice clip of Benny Naranjo, NLCC-GP.

[19] Interview with David Cargo.

[20] Interview with Alfonso Sánchez.

The National Guard officers, mostly *hispanos*, were reluctant to conduct an aggressive pursuit for fear of killing their own people. The responsibility of the search for Tijerina and the other fugitives fell to Captain Joe Black of the State Police, who sent eighty men with patrol cars into the mountains and about thirty-five mounted officers. The U.S. Forest Service and other federal agencies also provided personnel. The police, without warrants, searched the homes of Alianza members and their sympathizers. The National Guard gathered Alianza family members who were encamped in Coyote and put them in a corral—some say to draw the fugitives into a snare. Responding to a *New York Times* reporter's question about the legality of holding the families without arresting them, General Jolly responded, "Let's not get involved in civil rights. None of them are complaining."

Sánchez charged Cargo with "holding hands with members of the Alianza, feeding them a misleading impression as to their rights under the law." Retaliating, the governor accused Sánchez of issuing "warrants based on flimsy charges to arrest the leaders of land claimants prior to the Coyote raid."[22]

Cargo also alleged that Sánchez's aggressive tactics were used to break up the Coyote meeting and that he provoked the *aliancista* courthouse raid at a time when he, the governor, was on the verge of reaching a peaceful solution.

With no success in finding the raiders, Governor Cargo demobilized the National Guard, insisting that the troops only succeeded in terrorizing innocent people. Sergeant Joe Fernández remembers, "After we got home. . . it really turned out to be something comical. . . . We talked and laughed about it afterwards. . . . I didn't see any reason to call the Guard up."[23]

In another accusation, Sánchez alleges Cargo was in contact with Tijerina the whole time the police searched for him:

> I wanted my troops to. . . arrest Cargo because he was in indirect contact with Reies López Tijerina—that's after the T.A. raid, and here the Albuquerque *General* comes out that Cargo was in direct contact with him, negotiating this and other bullshit, you know, headlines!. . . So the next morning. . . I called the person...that wrote the article and he said, "Yeah, I was present when he dialed for Reyes and he knows where he's at."[24]

Sánchez remembers being incensed, especially since the fugitives had wounded two officers; one was in the hospital in critical condition. He went to Governor Cargo and threatened to arrest him unless

On his kidnapping, reporter Larry Calloway remembers, "It wasn't planned, I think Baltazar [Martínez] just lingered around town. . . enjoying himself. . . shooting from the hip at police cars. . . strutting around and showing me off as a hostage. . . . Then he decided he better get out. . . and drag me along. . . . It was safe passage for him. He could have picked anybody."[21]

[21] Interview with Larry Calloway by Jesús Treviño, July 23, 1992, NLCC-GP.

[22] Last three quotes in main text from Knowlton, "Reies L. Tijerina and the Alianza Federal de Mercedes," p. 15.

[23] Interview with Joe Fernández by Jesús Treviño, July 27, 1992, NLCC-GP.

[24] Interview with Alfonso Sánchez.

he told him where to find Tijerina. The fugitive raiders turned themselves in individually. Tijerina was picked up at a roadblock, prompting Captain Black to say, "Tijerina was a Jewel that dropped out of his setting and we picked him up."[25]

After the courthouse raid, Tijerina and his movement became mired down in court cases. The raiders were charged with second-degree kidnapping, assault to commit murder and an unlawful assault on a jail. Hoping to destroy the movement by embroiling it in a legal quagmire, Sánchez filed lesser charges against other Alianza members and Tijerina's family, including a nineteen-year-old daughter and a fourteen-year-old son who lived in Denver. Colorado authorities refused to extradite the boy, however. Sánchez's zeal and extralegal procedures did not make him very popular in Rio Arriba County, and he lost his reelection in 1968. During the campaign he alleged that the Cuban government had trained Alianza members in guerrilla warfare tactics at a Taos ranch and that Mexican Communists had joined the Tijerina movement.

A total of twenty *aliancistas* were tried in the Las Vegas District Court of Judge José Angel, who dismissed all charges against nine of the defendants and dismissed kidnapping charges against the others. All *aliancistas* indicted were given bail. Unhappy with this seemingly indulgent treatment, the state supreme court reassigned the case to the court of Judge Paul Larrazolo, the son of the former governor Octavian Larrazolo. To the dismay of Sánchez and other Rio Arriba officials, the new judge upheld Angel's rulings. At this trial, Tijerina put to use the self-taught legal knowledge he had acquired over the years. He fired his lawyer and defended himself brilliantly, prompting Sánchez to comment publicly, "He could have been a great man if he had just understood and carried out what he believed in within the framework of the American system instead of inventing his own." The jury, made up of *hispanos*, found all of the defendants not guilty.

Then came the federal government's turn to prosecute the *aliancistas*. Federal attorney John Quinn charged Tijerina and four others, chosen from among the three hundred Alianza members present at the Echo Amphitheater confrontation, with obstructing federal officials and converting government property to private use. Aware of the sympathy that the defendants enjoyed in Tierra Amarilla, Quinn successfully had the trial changed to Albuquerque, where the jury was made up almost entirely of Anglos. But Alianza lawyers asked for a change of venue because of the jury's makeup. This request backfired on the *aliancistas* because the case wound up in the Las Cruces court of Anglo-American Judge Joseph Bratten, who selected an Anglo-American jury from a district where antipathy towards Mexicans was high. Governor Cargo testified on behalf of the *aliancistas*, telling the court,

Sergeant Joe Fernández, then a private in the New Mexico National Guard, remembers the day he was mobilized: "I was working for a finance company. . . and I got the call from the first sergeant from my unit, and he says we've been mobilized. . . You know, I thought it was some kind of war. . . . He says, 'No. We're going up to Tierra Amarilla.' I said, 'For what!?' 'Well I guess Tijerina and his gang went in there and they shot up the courthouse and they want us to go in there and look for them.' I closed the office down. . . packed all my equipment and reported to the armory b. It was a surprise really for everyone. . . . When you're told to report to the armory, you're really not given too many details. . . so after they talked to us and briefed us, it was kind of shocking. . . . You say, you know, this isn't. . . happening, not in this period of time, not in New Mexico."[26]

---

[25] Quoted in Knowlton, "Reies L. Tijerina and the Alianza Federal de Mercedes," p. 15.

[26] Interview with Joe Fernández.

89. President
Lyndon (back
right) Johnson
at swearing in
ceremonies of
Vicente
Ximenes.

The people of the north tend to view all government with hostility. They are not violent by nature; they are very patient. But when they lose their water rights and their grazing rights, they become bitter. They feel that no one cares and they take it out on whoever is closest.[27]

Cargo's support notwithstanding, the jury found Tijerina guilty on two counts of assault against forest rangers. Bratton sentenced him to two years in prison.

With every act of defiance shown by Tijerina, Chicano Movement participants exalted him as their leader in the struggle against not only the Establishment, but also the Mexican American old guard, which many activists considered *vendidos* (sell-outs). The older leadership had acquired a new vitality when President Johnson in his 1965 "Great Society" inaugural address declared a "War on Poverty," which promised to eradicate Mexican American poverty. This augured both solutions and jobs. However, their optimism was dashed when Johnson's Great Society set its sights

more directly on America's Black population.

Traditional Mexican American leaders showed militancy when they walked out of the 1966 Equal Employment Opportunity Commission meeting in Albuquerque, and it reverberated among Mexican American organizations throughout the country (see Chapter Six). But most Mexican American conservatives saw their dignity disparaged by these tactics and their positions endangered. For younger, less-compromised Chicanos, however, and for some from the Mexican American generation, this paved the way to using confrontation. Now there was no turning back.

In response to the protests, President Johnson named Vicente Ximenes to the Equal Employment Opportunity Commission, which in turn established the Inter-Agency Cabinet Committee on Mexican American Affairs. In October of 1967 Ximenes scheduled hearings at El Paso that coincided with the much-heralded ceremony in which the U.S. returned to Mexico the disputed Chamizal territory. President Johnson would be there along

---

[27] Last two quotes in main text from Knowlton, "Reies L. Tijerina and the Alianza Federal de Mercedes," p. 17.

with Mexican president Gustavo Díaz Ordaz. The Mexican Americans invited were from the old guard, and most were unlikely to replicate the boldness shown in Albuquerque. After all, they seemed to have obtained the recognition they wanted from the Johnson administration. But some of them, including Bert Corona of MAPA and Rodolfo "Corky" Gonzales, a former Democratic Party stalwart from Colorado, went to El Paso but boycotted the meeting. They joined young activists from the emerging Chicano Movement, led by Reies López Tijerina, in a protest that accused the invited guests of not representing the "grass-roots" community; the old guard accused the young Chicanos of being interested only in their own advancement. Tijerina, from now on, was the undisputed leader of the *movimiento*, a mantle acquired not through design but through demonstration of sheer daring.

After the courthouse raid, however, extreme violence characterized all activities surrounding the land-grant movement, a situation that began to erode Tijerina's hold on the leadership. On January 2, 1968, for example, Eulogio Salazar, one of the deputies wounded in the courthouse raid and a star witness for the prosecution, was shot to death as he drove down a quiet country road fifteen miles from Tierra Amarilla. Suspicion fell immediately on the *aliancistas*, and Tijerina and his associates were jailed but, with the exception of Tijerina, released because of insufficient evidence. Tijerina was released the following month. The murder of Eulogio Salazar has never been solved. Rumors circulated that his killing might have been the work of Tijerina's enemies in order to discredit the Alianza movement.

The *aliancistas* themselves became the target of violence. Their headquarters was peppered with rifle fire on many occasions. From 1968 to 1969, the building sustained four bombings. In one, a former Bernalillo County deputy sheriff, William Fellion, lost his right arm when a bomb detonated prematurely—he was planting the explosive. Arrested on bombing charges, he disappeared after his hospital recovery while still in custody. Albuquerque police never charged anyone for these hostilities.

In the midst of the uproar over the Salazar murder, Dr. Martin Luther King invited Tijerina and a contingent of *aliancistas* to join the Poor People's March on Washington, a development that angered Alianza enemies. To prevent him from going, Tijerina was arrested, but pressure from Mexican American and Native-American civil rights leaders convinced state police chief, Captain Joe Black, to intervene with local authorities to release Tijerina. By the time *aliancistas* joined the Poor People's March as it came through Albuquerque, the Rev. King had been assassinated. The *aliancistas* spent sixty days at the nation's capital, making friends among civil rights leaders from the Native-American and African-American communities. Tijerina decided to make

Ernesto Vigil, who accompanied "Corky" González, explains what troubled the demonstrators outside of the hearings called by Vicente Ximenes: "It was felt on the part of the protesters that the people inside the conference were people with government jobs, people who could be controlled by the government, people who would not jeopardize their connections, their prestige or their positions. So they were like Uncle Sam's boys. They were not the leadership of the Chicano communities."[28]

---

[28] On-camera interview with Ernesto Vigil by Myléne Moreno, February 14, 1995, NLCC-GP.

The Alianza became an integral part of the Poor People's March, which continued under the Reverends Ralph Abernathy and Jesse Jackson after the Reverend King's murder. Tijerina recently recounted the occasion: "Dr. King invited me to participate in the Poor People's March, and I agreed on one condition, that the treaty of Guadalupe Hidalgo be used and mentioned. And I demanded that it be complied with. And it was done, although he was shot and killed before the march, but Jesse Jackson said it once or twice [evoked the demands by *aliancistas* based on the Treaty]."[29]

cause with New Mexico's Native Americans. Today, he claims that his movement influenced President Richard Nixon to decree in 1970 the repartition of eighteen thousand acres to the Taos Pueblo Indians.

While in Washington, Tijerina announced his intention to conduct a citizen's arrest of Chief Justice Earl Warren—an action that by now was a routine part of his political theater tactics. Before and after going to Washington, amid much media hoopla, Tijerina had attempted to arrest a number of state officials for committing crimes against the people. These included his erstwhile friend Governor Cargo and an official at the Los Alamos Atomic Laboratory. When asked what he expected to gain from these antics, he replied, "To destroy fear and intimidation [held by] our people. . . . And then the opposition knew that they were up against men who knew no fear, who could not be bought, they had to be destroyed, they had to be sent to prison."[30]

Not knowing what his next act would be, Tijerina's wild maneuvers kept New Mexico officials on tenterhooks. News-media members maintained close tabs on Alianza activity because at any moment something newsworthy could occur. By the same token, law-enforcement agencies had Tijerina and the group under constant surveillance. On June 6, 1969, *aliancistas* again converged on Coyote and set up a tent city on private land to camp out while they held their annual conference. In attendance were Chicano Movement activists from different parts of the U.S. Tijerina was at the height of his fame and prestige among Chicano militants. They heard what they came for. Speaker after speaker denounced land usurpation and how the rights of Mexicans under the Treaty of Guadalupe Hidalgo had been violated.

During this conference, authorities fully expected another act of defiance—perhaps occupation of park land or violence against National Forest personnel. The defiance came from an unexpected source. In the final session of the conference, Patsy Tijerina announced she planned to burn National Forest Park signs the following day. Tijerina acted surprised that his wife would take such a step; she had never showed such independent political interest, he swore. Patsy Tijerina explained that she intended to carry out this symbolic protest because Tijerina was on probation and would be immediately jailed if he did it.

The next day a motley caravan of cars and trucks carrying *aliancistas*, media staff, Students for Nonviolence Coordinating Committee (SNCC) members, Chicano Movement activists, television equipment and police followed Tijerina's vehicle with Patsy inside. When they came to some National Forest signs, Patsy proceeded to burn them. When a Forest Service employee tried to stop her, Tijerina came to her aid, was beaten and almost shot. The police dispersed the crowd, but arrested both Patsy and Reies Tijerina—again they were released on

---

[29] Interview with Reies López Tijerina.

[30] Ibid.

bond.

A few days later, Tijerina attempted to arrest the chief of National Forest Service inspectors, James H. Evans, at his office, but he was not there. Tijerina did file charges of assault and attempted murder against him and other personnel, whom he alleged had attacked him. With this latest gambit, Tijerina provoked Judge Bratton to revoke his bond, and the innovative crusader wound up in jail. Albuquerque police confiscated $4,241 that Tijerina had on his person, which he said was his life savings—he never saw that money again. Eventually, all of the accumulated charges against Tijerina resulted in his imprisonment. For federal offenses, Tijerina received a five-year sentence; the state of New Mexico judges also sentenced him to five years. For her part in the sign burning, Federal Judge Bratton gave Patsy Tijerina probation.

While Tijerina was incarcerated, to the dismay of New Mexico's establishment press and many of the New Mexican people who had grown weary of his campaign, the Episcopalian Executive Council endowed the Alianza with a $40,000 grant to conduct its work. For the group it seemed possible to continue its agenda without Tijerina at the helm. It even attempted to enter electoral politics, but with very little success.

Tijerina was released from prison on July 26, 1971, contingent on his not associating with the militant stance of the Alianza. Significantly, he emerged with a new philosophy: to work towards brotherly love between all races and ethnic groups and to better relations between the police and minorities. Not all Alianza activists supported Tijerina in this latest shift, especially those who had been involved in violent confrontations encouraged by Tijerina. A breakaway group calling itself Los Herederos de Nuevo México (The Inheritors of New Mexico) continued the original goals of land-grant recognition. Eventually, even the *aliancistas* who remained loyal grew weary of Tijerina's new tact, which seemed opportunistic and zany. Under its new guise, the Alianza continued to function until the 1980s when the weakened organization finally collapsed.

Tijerina's turnaround could be related to his jail experiences, which were not only sobering but totally unnerving. No other major Chicano Movement leader spent as much time incarcerated, and while many were harassed by the police, it was not to the same degree. While Tijerina languished in prison, his wife, Patsy, was allegedly molested sexually by men believed to be associated with the Albuquerque police. His life savings, impounded after the sign burning arrest, were never recovered. Then in March 1973 a state policeman sexually molested his adolescent son. The officer was arrested and given a suspended sentence. Finally, because of the strange behavior he exhibited after being released, rumors were rife that he had been given mind-altering drugs to control his behavior while in jail. In a recent interview, he claimed that being put into prison was a plot to destroy him: "as if psycho. . . I was in prison with ninety-five psycho patients in Springfield, Missouri."[31]

New Mexico authorities were not forgiving. In June 1974 they again incarcerated Tijerina, this time for charges stemming from the courthouse raid. The now frail "Tiger" still had friends in high places. The Albuquerque archbishop, the Board of Pardons and an array of influentials tried to intervene to have him pardoned. He had served only a few months when Governor Bruce King released him in response to constant pressure from New Mexico influentials. Some observers believe that King was prompted to free the aging land-grant crusader because he knew that incoming Governor Jerry Apodaca, the first Hispanic governor of New Mexico since Octaviano Larrazolo, intended to release Tijerina.

In the 1970s Tijerina returned to his land-grant activity only in token fashion. Becoming obsessed with achieving heroic recognition, he lead a caravan of adherents to Mexico City in 1972 and ingratiated himself with Mexican government officials, including President Luis Eche-

---

[31] Interview with Reies López Tijerina.

verría, himself bent on projecting a populist image among his people. Tijerina also captivated the Mexican intelligentsia and artistic community; consequently, a full-length film of the crusader's life was produced and El Fondo de Cultura Económica, one of Mexico's most prestigious presses (government run), published a rambling autobiography of his life.

By then, the much-strained relationship with state officials had eased. The city of Albuquerque funded his Brotherhood Awareness Center, the new name for the Alianza. But Tijerina still had a few antics up his sleeve. During his trip to Mexico, he asked President Echeverría to investigate the land question in New Mexico. The Mexican leader responded by establishing an agency charged with helping protect Mexican Americans in the U.S. and a commission to investigate land claims. This latest gambit again alienated him from the New Mexico establishment. After a press outcry, Albuquerque officials revoked funding for his project.

CONCLUSION

The pivotal event that changed the course of the Alianza movement was the courthouse raid. Until then, all indications point to a less militant, more legalistic thrust to regain land grants. But by all accounts, an overzealous reaction to the occupation of Echo Amphitheater had led the Alianza to escalate its efforts. Former sheriff Benny Naranjo said some ten years after the Tierra Amarilla courthouse raid, "I believe that the Alianza should have been allowed to hold its meeting in Coyote back in 1967. . . . If they had been allowed to meet, the raid would never have happened."[32] Governor Cargo maintains to this day that other government officials, notably Alfonso Sánchez, had outmaneuvered him. The raid also broke the stereotype of Chicano passivity and demonstrated that Chicanos were capable of using violence as a political act.

Reies "The Tiger" López Tijerina has managed to survive to this day as the subject of a personality cult. In the 1980s college lecture fees, usually at the bequest of Chicano students who saw him as an inspiration, provided him with a modest income. As time went by, these invitations waned as they have for other formerly lionized Chicano Movement leaders. The fanfare surrounding the Alianza movement and the justness of its cause cannot mask its failure to achieve its objectives as elaborated in 1963 when the organization first emerged. It might be that, legally, the task of restoring the grants is impossible. This gives credence to allegations by critics that Tijerina was providing hopeful land grantees with unrealistic goals. Certainly wild and meandering tactics, a reflection of Tijerina's state of mind, invited repression at the most inappropriate moments, thus impeding the ability of his group to obtain a real power base.

This assessment can be made for other sectors of the Chicano Movement that will be discussed below. But the Alianza experience symbolizes how sacrifice by Chicano activists provided a wider power base for Mexican Americans, most of whom did not participate in or agree with the tactics of the Movement—at least not when it was in its throes. Tijerina is the quintessential "shock trooper." It is easy to portray him as traveling down the proverbial primrose path without pausing to measure the effectiveness of his tactics. But one can also ask if the twelve hundred days he spent imprisoned was a sacrifice that most people would make.

Despite *aliancista* activity having divided many New Mexicans—not necessarily along ethnic lines—it also brought attention to the plight of the poor in one of the most impoverished areas of the U.S. A partial response was that of Alex Mecure, who administered New Mexico's Home and Livelihood Program (HELP): the agency provided half a million dollars in aid for the northern part of the state soon after the courthouse raid. At the 1967 cost of living, that was a significant amount. In addition, Alianza activity also energized other Hispanics in New Mexico and throughout the country into joining in civil rights activities and pushing for educational reform.

---

[32] Quoted in Knowlton, "Reies Tijerina and the Alianza Federal de Mercedes," p.18.

CHAPTER TEN

The Fight for Educational Reform

90. High-school student picketers. Photo by Oscar Castillo.

At the end of the 1950s Mexican American attempts to end the educational neglect affecting their people seemed to be making headway. No Mexicans were segregated by *de jure* methods anywhere in the country—not even in Texas, where as recently as the previous decade school authorities had segregation codes for Mexican children. Certainly by the 1960s more U.S. Mexicans than ever were entering the work force with a high school education or were attending college. Despite these advances, the perception of inadequate education served as one of the most crucial forces motivating the 1960s Chicano Movement. Why was this so at this time when conditions were seemingly improving?

In large cities like Los Angeles, an underlying and partial explanation for this is that whites and a small number of minority families had abandoned the inner cities for the suburbs (white flight), leaving minorities behind. Except in border communities or in towns with large, long-standing Mexican populations such as Santa Fe, San Antonio or Tucson, Mexicans lived in mixed neighborhoods in the larger southwestern cities. In the 1950s this ethnic heterogeneity started changing and, by the 1960s the shift resulted in the division of metropolitan areas—with whites living in more affluent peripheries and the minorities in the central cities. Black ghettos and Mexican barrios were now islands in a complex of freeways, tacky industrial parks, auto repair shops, sporting complexes, small office buildings and expanded airport areas. The large Asian communities that are in inner cities now had not yet emerged except in California. And even there, they were not as large as today.

In cities like Los Angeles, Denver, Phoenix, San Jose and Houston, large-scale de facto school segregation of Mexicans and Blacks took hold as never before. Before, their populations were rarely large enough to dominate elementary, middle- and high-school enrollments, as they did by the 1960s and thereafter. Moreover, with white flight, educational funding was diverted to institutions in the suburbs at the expense of urban core schools, which by now were stigmatized as minority institutions.

In addition, the creation of new and better-paying jobs took place mainly in the suburbs, a factor compounding the inner-city woes. With whites gone, law-enforcement attitudes toward inner-city residents became uniformly less tolerant and, too often, police and media overreacted to minority crime. All in all, tension and resentment were on the rise. Their increasing ghettoization made Chicanos feel betrayed by the American Dream. The optimism that in the U.S. anything was possible, proclaimed so often by the Mexican American generation, came into question. This generation had chased an all-American status, but

The Chicano historian, Rodolfo Acuña, recalling his earliest memories in the Boyle Heights area of Los Angeles in the 1940s, said, "I remember as a kid probably Yiddish being used as much as Spanish. . . . My next-door neighbor was Flora, and she was married to a bookie, who was Jewish, and the neighbors across the street were Filipino, the neighbors were Italians down the [street]. . . . it was more multi-ethnic at that time."[1]

Today it is almost completely made up of racial minorities.

[1] Interview with Rodolfo Acuña, March 6, 1992.

the real white society, it seemed, had left them behind in the barrios, perceiving them simply as "Mexicans."

As a result, like Blacks, many Mexicans gave up on the dream and became more conscious of their own lost identity. Thus, as Chicano intellectuals reconciled themselves to remaining Mexican, they formulated a catharsis to build a positive self-image. But where to start? In their haste to Americanize, their predecessors (Mexican Americans) had seemingly misplaced Mexican identity—not just the leaders and intellectuals but regular folks who did not speak Spanish to their kids and had named them Brenda and Mark, a sign that they wanted their children to Americanize.

It is no small wonder that an impassioned searching for roots—in *lo mexicano*—dominated the beginning of the Chicano Movement. Incipient issues discussed by fledgling Chicanos revolved around cultural nationalism. Mainly Chicanos in institutions of higher education, with access to information about the state of their communities, were stimulated to treat these themes. Then, the degree to which they influenced the folks back in the community was in proportion to the distance of barrios from their universities.

NASCENT YOUTH RUMBLINGS

The first major rumblings of the Chicano youth movement were heard in California in 1967. Although the Alianza movement of Reies López Tijerina and César Chávez's farm-worker movement came first, they did not have a conscious Chicano orientation. The Crusade for Justice of "Corky" Gonzales in Denver, while showing early signs of a *movimiento*, was too small to have an immediate widespread influence. In Texas only conceptual stages characterized the Mexican American Youth Organization while in Arizona middle-class Mexicans and the majority of students throughout 1967 still practiced Mexican Americanism. But in California the Brown Berets were coalescing rapidly. The organization was a militant youth group that protested educational neglect and police brutality; it had strong links to the community and local East Los Angeles high-school students.

That year at California college campuses, a social revolution of sorts affected the first large contingent of Chicano Movement participants. Throughout the decade of the 1960s, more Mexican Americans attended college than ever before; they formed part of the college-age population created by the baby boom. A sheer weight of numbers put them on campus. In addition, the Educational Opportunity Programs (EOP), funded by President Johnson's War on Poverty, recruited thousands of Mexican Americans throughout the Southwest, but more so in California. Arizona State University did not make EOP available until 1969, for example. The Vietnam-era GI Bill, instituted in 1966, also

Carlos Montes, an original member of the militant Brown Berets, recalls why he became a movement activist: "I was buying into this whole thing about the American Dream. Get an education. You can be whatever you want to be and, you know, read all these books and listen to the teachers. Even though at the back of my mind I was saying, 'Something is going on here, you know, the reality that I see here is different from what you're saying.'"[2]

[2] On-camera Interview with Carlos Montes by Susan Racho, December 1, 1994, NLCC-GP.

91. Ricardo Sánchez reading his poetry.

Poet Ricardo Sánchez, in "Three Days to Go," from *Selected Poems* (Arte Público Press, 1985), captured the enthusiasm for the early Chicano Movement and some of its leaders:

I've also heard
of movimiento,
the shout Chicano
    Chicano POWER,

viva la huelga
viva la raza
qué vivan Chávez y Tijerina
y el poeta Lalo Delgado. . .

it is good to know
that things might now be different,
and if so
I will pick up a gun
or a typewriter
for this cosa called movimiento.
I'm ready, raza, to join you,

if we have to burn
or shout or sing
or act or whatever
we have to do
to make our freedom real,
I am ready,

—and I
mean to embrace you, raza chicana,
and tell you that it's good
we're finally together
to fight our common enemy.
I'll trust you, you'll trust me,
and we'll build a new nación. . .

brought many Chicanos to campuses. A large number of new student organizations started appearing in the mid-1960s, with an orientation only slightly different from that of the 1940s, Mexican American Movement (MAM, see Chapter Six). But the Mexican American student enrollment grew at the precise moment when colleges were radicalizing.

A vital example of this process is the story of Luis Valdez and Roberto Rubalcava, students at San Jose State College in the mid-1960s. Their experience provides an early example of how Mexican Americans became radicalized in the heady college atmosphere of the Bay Area, in contrast to the conservative atmosphere at universities in other southwestern states. Mexican American-era organizations such as Mexican American Political Association (MAPA) and the Viva Kennedy Clubs provided Valdez's initial political socialization. But while in college, members of the Progressive Labor Party (PLP) influenced his political formation and Valdez's ideas quickly changed. Under the auspices of the PLP, he and Rubalcava traveled to Cuba as part of the *Venceremos* Brigades—young American volunteers invited to Cuba to harvest sugar cane. The experience radicalized the young Valdez and Rubalcava even further. On returning, Valdez sported a Che Guevara beret and perennially smoked Black Cuban cigars and preached vague notions of revolution.

But the Valdez-Rubalcava tact was not yet quickly embraced by other Mexican American students, who continued to follow the trajectory set by leaders intent on accomodationist politics. Even when young Chicanos began challenging the Mexican American old guard, they did so within a relatively conservative milieu. Few Chicano participants showed the early radical precociousness of a Luis Valdez. At UCLA in the mid-1960s, for example, about a dozen students led by Luis Ortiz met regularly to discuss issues dealing with their community. Basically, they rejected the mainstream politics of MAPA and the Viva Kennedy stalwarts, but few at this point incorporated Marxist or ultranationalist prescriptions.

Their mentor was Dr. Ralph Guzmán, who with Joan Moore and Leo Grebler conducted the Mexican American Study Project, which revealed a disturbing profile of the the socioeconomic position of U.S. Mexicans. Guzmán, while supporting the group's nascent critique of the older political generation, was himself still steeped in Mexican Americanism. Certainly he did not toe a strong nationalist line nor did he hold the same Marxist ideas that white radical professors were imparting elsewhere in Los Angeles, California— e.g., Donald Bray and Timothy Brading at California State University (CSU), Los Angeles or Maurice Zeitlin at CSU, San Francisco.

Young *Chicanismo* showed the most vital signs of growth in Southern California. At the end of 1967, thirty-five Mexican American student organizations existed with almost two thousand members. The following year, according to Professor Juan Gómez-Quiñones, thousands

92. Luis Valdez today.

With his comrade Roberto Rubalcava, Luis Valdez produced one of the first radical assessments of the conditions under which their people lived in the United States:

> The Mexican in the United States has been. . . no less a victim of American imperialism than his impoverished brothers in Latin America. In the words of the Second Declaration of Havana, tell him of 'misery, feudal exploitation, illiteracy, starvation wages,' and he will tell you that you speak of Texas; tell him of 'unemployment, the policy of repression against the workers, discrimination. . . oppression by the oligarchies,' and he will tell you that you speak of California; tell him of U.S. domination in Latin America, and he will tell you that he knows that Shark and what he devours, because he has lived in its very entrails. The history of the American Southwest provides a brutal panorama of nascent imperialism.[3]

---

[3] Quoted in Muñoz, *Youth, Identity, Power*, 1989, p. 52.

Carlos Montes, who became a Brown Beret leader, was a nineteen-year-old student at East Los Angeles College in 1967. He had nothing more than a simple aspiration to succeed in America by going to college. But joining MASA (Mexican American Student Association) represented a departure from this path: "I was a student. . . involved in student government. . . I was student body parliamentarian. . . Associate Student Vice President and saw a sign announcing. . .an organizational meeting that said MASA meeting. . . . So I went to one of the first meetings . . . organized by older, GI Chicanos. . . going to college on the GI Bill. Al Juárez was there. Carlos Hunter was there."[4]

Quickly, the restive Montes found MASA's main mission to tutor younger Mexican American students and provide them scholarships too tame. He soon encountered greater action in the rapidly politicizing East Los Angeles atmosphere—Montes discovered the Brown Berets.

more participated as the organizations multiplied to about fifty. By 1968 they were making a greater commitment to confrontationist strategy—white radicals and Black civil rights activists were in the throes of adopting these tactics as well.

As indicated in the last chapter, the Alianza Federal de las Mercedes of Reies López Tijerina served the nationalist agenda by providing a living example of how instrumental objectives could be obtained and ethnic pride could be asserted through militancy. Consequently, the Alianza movement became a magnet for activists throughout the country. The students trekked to northern New Mexico to see this motivational phenomenon in the flesh. As a consequence, the Alianza served to link Chicano Movement people across the Southwest, standardizing the styles of expression Chicano activists would use.

Eleazar Risco, a founder of Los Angeles's Barrio Communication Project, tells of being so impressed by the Alianza's militancy that he was delighted when Tijerina put out a call to young Chicano activists throughout the country to meet in Albuquerque on October 21, 1967. Young Mexican American organizers from Chicago, Colorado, New Mexico, California and Texas, many of them students, responded to the invitation. Among these were some of the pioneers in the California Chicano Movement: David Sánchez, Moctezuma Esparza, Carlos Montes, Carlos Muñoz, Henry Gómez and Armando Valdez. Risco remembers meeting for the first time activists who formed the Texas Mexican American Youth Organization (MAYO) and others from Denver's Crusade for Justice. At that meeting, José Angel Gutiérrez from Texas asserted that *la raza* was the best term to identify Mexican American people—*Chicano* was not yet that widespread. At this meeting, also, the idea of holding a mass national meeting of Mexican American youth was bandied around—this led to the historical National Chicano Liberation Youth Conference of March 1969. And finally, the concept of a Chicano political party emerged at this meeting, an idea that came to fruition with the formation of La Raza Unida Party in 1970.

That same year, a pivotal student meeting sponsored by the University of Southern California's United Mexican American Students (UMAS) attracted two hundred Mexican American students from throughout Southern California on December 16 and 17. This was one of the first occasions Chicano students from both Southern and Northern California met within a movement context. A contingent from the Mexican American Student Confederation (MASC), a group with chapters in the San Francisco Bay Area, and staff from Berkeley's Quinto Sol Publications drove down in a bus. Generally, students from Northern California expressed a Third-World alignment. They adhered to a sketchy

---

[4] Interview with Carlos Montes by Enrique Berumen, February 6, 1994, NLCC-GP.

form of socialism and identified their cause not just with oppressed Chicanos, but with other racial minorities in the U.S. and colonized peoples throughout the world; Communist Cuba and China served as inspirations. In 1967 Chicanos in Southern California were barely beginning to identify their ideology but generally they emphasized the problems of Chicanos along the lines of Chicano nationalism. The Chicanos from both areas of the state found they had much in common. As will be seen in Chapter Twelve, Chicano Movement activists outside of California, especially in Texas, elaborated a unique Chicanismo.

In session after session, forceful speakers exposed the dire conditions affecting their communities—data they had garnered from the Guzmán project. The students mapped out a "leadership revolution" for their communities which advocated political militancy as a means of wresting from the Establishment resources to resolve social and educational problems. The conference participants also envisioned interracial cooperation and invited students from the Black Student Union.

Incipient forms of nationalism permeated the gathering, especially when students heard about Alianza feats from those who had been at the Albuquerque meeting in October. The group then voted to support the release of Reies López Tijerina because he had been unjustly imprisoned for "trying to recover lands that had been stolen from Mexican Americans in the Southwest by Anglos." At this point, Tijerina was incarcerated for the courthouse raid. The students also decided to promote the grape boycott that César Chávez's union was using to force the DiGiorgio table grape firm to negotiate.

In spite of the rhetoric, however, the meeting was basically reformist. An indication of this was a session on how gerrymandering broke up solid Mexican American voting areas—a sign that faith still existed in the system. As the Chicano Movement became radicalized, the strategy of using the ballot would lose the significance it had had for the older Mexican American generation—until the rise of La Raza Unida Party, that is. Even then, except for movement activists in Texas, winning office was not seen as a serious objective. Instead, the electoral campaigns were used for raising consciousness and publicizing Chicano Movement goals.

By 1969 a network of *movimiento* participants spread across the Southwest and even reached into the Chicago area. As stated above, the publicity generated by Tijerina's exploits in New Mexico served as a catalyst to bring people together beyond California. But another nexus emerged in the course of the previous year—the Crusade for Justice in Denver. It was led by "Corky" Gonzales, a former professional boxer, bail bondsman, Democratic Party leader and a major protagonist in Denver's War on Poverty. The Crusade achieved prominence after Gonzales co-chaired, with Reies López Tijerina, the Mexican American contingent of the Poor People's March in the spring of 1968. The main role of the Crusade in the Chicano Movement was establishing cultural nationalism and a vague notion of separatism.

Gonzales became disenchanted with mainstream politics in 1966

At the USC UMAS conference, presenters provided empirical data to make their case. One speaker told the group that Santa Anna schools assigned sixty-five percent of the Mexican students to mentally retarded programs. This occurred, said the speaker, because of an inadequate educational system that did not consider bilingual and cultural needs of these children. Another disturbing issue for the conferees was the pre-college attrition rate. Sixty percent of Mexican Americans dropped out before graduating from the twelfth grade. In the summations, conference participants emphasized that problems facing Mexican Americans should be blamed on an oppressive system, not on the victims.

Mexican Vietnam causalities were by now a prominent issue. The mostly young audience was distressed to learn that the military conscripted forty-five percent of the Mexican Americans eligible for the draft in contrast to nineteen percent of white Americans. More galling, they thought, was that twenty percent of all Vietnam casualties were Mexicans, who made up only five percent of the total population.

93. Rodolfo "Corky" Gonzales.

and, with a group called Los Voluntarios (The Volunteers) that he had formed in 1963, he began protesting Denver's policy toward its impoverished Mexican American population. The group then took on police brutality issues and earned the enmity of Denver's law-enforcement establishment. In a 1966 speech, Gonzales declared "that on that day a new crusade for justice had been born."[5] The name stuck and his informal group coalesced into the Crusade for Justice. While in the Poor People's March, the efforts by the Blacks to gain civil rights and achieve self-sufficiency greatly impressed Gonzales.

At the nation's capital, Gonzales issued "El Plan del Barrio" (The Barrio Plan), a proclamation that mapped out separate public housing for Chicanos, bilingual education, barrio economic development and restitution of land that had been taken from *hispanos* in Colorado and New Mexico. After the Washington trip, the energized crusaders bought an old church building in downtown Denver and converted it into the Crusade headquarters. From there, Gonzales engaged in a series of militant actions that drew attention to Denver's Mexicans. Gonzales also wrote an epic poem, "I Am Joaquín," that became the anthem for the *movimiento*. But more importantly, as the Black Muslims had done, Gonzales envisioned an array of self-sufficient barrio businesses controlled by his organization.

Like Tijerina and Chávez, Gonzales's ability

---

[5] Christine Marín, *A Spokesman of the Mexican American Movement: Rodolfo "Corky" Gonzales and the Fight for Chicano Liberation, 1966-1972* (San Francisco: R and E Research Associates, 1977), p. 10.

to capture headlines increased his prominence outside his state. When he called the National Chicano Liberation Youth Conference for March 1969 in Denver, Chicanos throughout the country knew who he was. More than one thousand young people attended and engaged in the most intense celebration of Chicanismo to date—most were from California. The most enduring concept that came out of this meeting was contained in the document *El Plan Espiritual de Aztlán* (The Spiritual Plan of Aztlán), which posited separatism, a position justified because of the

> Brutal "Gringo" invasion of our territories: We the Chicano inhabitants and civilizers of the northern land of Aztlán, from whence came our forefathers, reclaim the land of their birth and concentrating the determination of our people declare that. . . . Aztlán belongs to those who plant the seeds, water the fields, and gather the crops, and not to the foreign

Europeans.... We declare the Independence of our Mestizo Nation. We are a Bronze People with a Bronze Culture.... We are a Nation, We are a union of free pueblos, We are Aztlán.[6]

The conference was more a celebration than a strategic planning meeting, but no other event had so energized Chicanos for continued commitment. The idea of a national protest day against the Vietnam War emerged and indeed it became a reality, as shall be seen below. In addition, the assembly also provided one of the earliest attempts to deal with the role of women in Chicano society. It was not planned, but the white women's liberation movement had brought the issue to the forefront, and many of the Chicanas did not want to leave without addressing their concerns. The *movimiento* had been dominated by males, many who asserted that the prior-

94. Rodolfo "Corky" Gonzales at a rally.

On March 20, 1968, students walked out of classes at Denver's West Side High School to demand the resignation of teacher Harry Schaffer, who reportedly said in class, "All Mexicans are stupid because their parents were stupid and their parents were stupid. . . if you eat Mexican food, you'll look like a Mexican." The protest grew, lasting three days, and then street riots broke out in which the police attacked the participants with clubs and tear gas. Twenty-five people were arrested, including "Corky" Gonzales. After his release, the Crusade for Justice leader told a young audience,

> What took place. . . was a battle between the West Side liberation forces and the occupying army. You kids don't realize you have made history. We just talk about revolution, but you act it by facing the shotguns, the billies, the mace. You are the real revolutionaries.[7]

[6] Quoted in Armando Navarro, *Mexican American Youth Organization: Avant-Garde of the Chicano Movement in Texas* (Austin: University of Texas Press, 1995), p. 67.

[7] Quoted in Marín, *A Spokesman of the Mexican American Movement*, p. 10.

The poet known as Alurista recounts the circumstances that led to his going to Denver for the youth conference that March. He was a college student at the time.

By that time, the student organizations up and down the state at the campus level. . . were pretty much in touch. . . either directly or by watching the news. . . . Everybody adimired Tijerina because of the court-house raid. He was sort of like a hero. . . . Chávez was talking campesino, so that was very attractive to me. . . . Then came "Corky" Gonzales. . . he was talking nation. He was a nationalist. So we took our contingent, a bus full of people. . . to Denver, Colorado.[9]

95. Alurista in 1982. Photo by Francisco Blasco.

María Varela, a pioneer activist, observed at the time: "'Conference' is a poor word to describe those five days. . . . It was in reality a fiesta: days of celebrating what sings in the blood of a people taught to believe they are ugly, discovering the true beauty in their souls during the years of occupation and intimidation. . . . Coca-Cola, Doris Day, Breck Shampoo, the Playboy Bunny, The Arrow Shirt man, the Marlboro heroes, are lies. 'We are beautiful. . . .' This affirmation grew into a grito, a roar, among the people gathered in the auditorium of the Crusade's Center."[8]

ity of the Chicano Movement was to liberate the males first. Ex-Brown Beret leader Chris Cebada related in a recent interview what was perhaps the most extreme manifestation of rejecting feminism among activists: "I think the CIA. . . pushed feminism. . . . They felt that if they pushed feminism, you could divide them [Chicanos]." Cebada goes on to say that Gloria Steinem, whom he thinks was an FBI agent, was pushing feminism to destroy nationalist Chicano and Black liberation movements. Cebada was not alone in espousing this notion, but may be one of the few ex-Chicano leaders who has not repented.

Many of the women at the Denver conference were aware of oppression within the culture and they decided to hold an impromptu workshop, which issued a statement that condemned chauvinism within the Chicano Movement. Unfortunately when workshop leaders read the results of their particular sessions, Crusade for Justice women hushed up the women's complaints and concurred with the prevailing male idea—that women were not ready for liberation. Many Chicanas,

[8] Quoted in Muñoz, *Youth, Identity, Power*, p. 78.

[9] Interview with Alurista by Enrique Berumen, March 2, 1995, NLCC-GP.

needless to say, were not deterred from pursuing the issue. La Raza Unida Party activist Marta Cotera, for example, organized Chicano feminist meetings in Houston during 1971 and 1972 that started an initative which has put Chicanas in the forefront of today's international feminist movement.

Less than one month after the Denver meeting, California students met at the University of California, Santa Barbara, in a conference that became one of the most crucial Chicano events in California. It was sponsored by the Coordinating Council on Higher Education, a network of students and professors, many of whom had attended the Denver Youth Conference and had returned full of enthusiasm and energy. By now the Chicano student community was ready to implement a higher education plan that would go beyond previous pronouncements. A major objective was to create college curricula that were relevant and useful to the community. Higher education, the students reasoned, was a publicly funded superstructure that enhanced the business community and other white bastions of power; very little was expended on the needs of the taxpaying Chicano community.

The students at the Santa Barbara meeting incorporated *El Plan Espiritual de Aztlán* into the ultimate ideological expression that would be used by future Chicano studies programs and students. As such, the group decided to bring all California Chicano student groups under one standard called El Movimiento Estudiantil de Aztlán (MECHA—Aztlán Student Movement). The term *Chicano* became canonized after this meeting, especially among the Mexican-origin intelligentsia. Curiously, while the term has at times almost disappeared as a self-reference term, it is as strong as ever at universities.

More importantly, at the conference *El Plan de Santa Bárbara* (The Santa Barbara Plan) was formulated and written as a design for implementing Chicano studies programs throughout the University of California system. The *Plan* eschewed assimilation and produced the most resounding rejection of Mexican American ideology to date. According to the *Plan*,

> *Chicanismo* involves a crucial distinction in

Referring to the 1969 Denver Youth Conference, Enriqueta Longauex y Vásquez, a Los Angeles community activist and a single mother who was raising small children in a housing project, wrote in *La Raza* in July 1969,

> While attending a Raza conference in Colorado this year, I went to one of the workshops that were held to discuss the role of the Chicana woman. When the time came for the women to make their presentation to the full conference, the only thing that the workshop representatives said was this: "It was the consensus of the group that the Chicana woman does not want to be liberated." This was quite a blow—I could have cried. Surely we could have come up with something to add to that.... I understood why the statement had been made...that going along with the men at the convention was perhaps the best thing to do at the time.

> She then discussed the role of Mexican women in history to show their contribution, including their participation as *soldaderas* during the Mexican Revolution. The article then shifted its mode and the author appealed for men to understand that "the woman must help liberate the man, and the man must look upon this liberation with the woman at his side, not behind him. . . . When we talk of equality in the Mexican American movement, we better be talking about total equality, beginning right where it starts. AT HOME. . . ."[10]

[10] *La Raza*, July 1969, clipping from files of Edward Escobar.

political consciousness between a Mexican American and a Chicano mentality. The Mexican American is a person who lacks respect for his culture and ethnic heritage. Unsure of himself, he seeks assimilation as a way out of his 'degraded' social status. Consequently, he remains politically ineffective. In contrast, *Chicanismo* reflects self-respect and pride in one's ethnic and cultural background. . . . The Chicano acts with confidence and with a range of alternatives in the political world.

These programs contained a curriculum intended to train a vanguard of future Chicano leaders who understood how American capitalism and racism had colonized their people. A future leader had to know that

The liberation of his people from prejudice and oppression is in his hand and this responsibility is greater than personal achievement and more meaningful than degrees, especially if they are earned at the expense of his identity and cultural integrity.[11]

The *Plan* did not ask for specific commitment to physical action—e.g., to unionizing or to striving for a separate country. Nor did it ask students to drop out of school. The Mexican American emphasis on getting a good education remained integral to the Chicano Movement, but not if one had to become an Anglo and had to forget about the community in order to do so. The *Plan* also asked that students control Chicano studies programs—e.g., the power to select and fire professors in accordance with criteria established by Chicanos, not the university administration.

LOS ANGELES WALKOUTS: SHOCK WAVES THROUGH THE COMMUNITY

Irrespective of student mobilization, the key event that ushered in the *movimiento* in Los Angeles, and to a great degree elsewhere, was the East Los Angeles high-school walkout. But this action cannot be separated from the student movement. Because college organizations joined a combination of nonstudent activists to organize the protest, it is likely that college student mobilization served as a necessary precursor to the events.

On March 1, 1968, three hundred high-school students walked out of their Friday morning classes upon discovering that Wilson High School Principal Donald Skinner had canceled production of "Barefoot in the Park" because it "was an inappropriate play to be showing the student body." The cancellation was only a surface reason for the walkout. Underneath, discontent and anger stemming from more profound issues had been brewing in the predominantly Mexican American school. This resentment became evident at other schools as well. On Monday, Lin-

El Plan Espiritual de Aztlán summed up the nationalistic feelings of the time that became some of the basic tenets of *Chicanismo:*

"In the spirit of a new people that is conscious not only of its proud historical heritage, but also of the brutal 'gringo' invasion of our territories, we, the Chicano inhabitants and civilizers of the northern land of Aztlán, from whence came our forefathers, reclaiming the land of their birth and consecrating the determination of our people of the sun, declare that the call of our blood is our power, our responsibility, and our inevitable destiny."

[11] Two previous quotes in main text from Muñoz, *Youth, Identity, Power,* pp. 80, 82.

96. Students walking out of Roosevelt High School, East Los Angeles. Photo by Oscar Castillo.

coln High students walked out. On Tuesday, two thousand students evacuated Garfield High School, another predominantly Mexican American high school. By Wednesday, the walkouts, or blowouts, as the students called them, had extended to Roosevelt High School. Some forty-five hundred students marched out of classes that day. In the ensuing two days, thousands of Mexican American students reported to school only to trek out the front doors once inside the buildings. By Friday, more than fifteen thousand students had left their classes throughout the Los Angeles area.

Chicano youths used the walkouts to dramatize what they considered the abysmally poor educational conditions affecting their schools. But the walkout organizers were not the first Mexican Americans to take a critical view of the educational system. It had certainly been a major issue among Mexican American civil rights leaders for

at least four decades. In this case, however, the planners were all young people, many not yet out of their teens; none was over thirty, except Lincoln High School teacher Sal Castro.

In themselves, the events were significant because they affected so many schools, students, teachers and parents. But more crucial was that the publicity created by the walkouts reminded the Mexican-origin community throughout the U.S. to examine educational conditions in their own communities. The sight of high-school kids on picket lines, carrying placards emblazoned with "Chicano Power!" "¡Viva la Raza!" and "Viva la Revolución," prompted a *Los Angeles Times* reporter to dub the walkouts as "The Birth of Brown Power"—this was an accurate prognosis.[12]

The genesis of these events is found at Camp Hess Kramer, a four-hundred-acre spread in the rolling hills just east of Malibu. Significantly, here too were the elements that linked previous Mexi-

---

[12] Ibid., p. 64.

97. Students boycotting high schools, Los Angeles. Photo by Oscar Castillo.

can American politics and their ideological orientation to Los Angeles *Chicanismo*. In April 1966 in an effort to tackle Mexican American youth issues such as gangs, school dropout rates and access to college education, the Los Angeles County Human Relations Council invited adults in community leadership positions to meet with about two hundred teenagers from various backgrounds in roundtable discussions.

The next year, many of the same young people attended a follow-up meeting at the camp. As one of them, David Sánchez, began to stand out, adult camp organizers decided to mentor his progress. Since age fifteen, Sánchez had worked as a youth counselor for the Social Training Center at the Episcopalian Church of the Epiphany under Father John Luce. The Episcopal priest introduced Sánchez to one of Los Angeles's busiest political activists of the time, Richard Ala-

torre, then a staff member of the Los Angeles Community Services Program, an associate of the NAACP Legal Defense Fund and a Democratic Party activist. Alatorre's connections earned Sánchez a place on the Mayor's Youth Council, which elected him chairman. But according to Sánchez, the Young Republicans did not want a Mexican in that position and tried to oust him. Moctezuma Esparza, however, another council member and an articulate Camp Hess Kramer veteran versed in parliamentary procedure, scuttled their plans.

By his own admission, Sánchez was clean-cut and not a *cholo* (street tough). When he was chairperson, no inkling existed as to the future of this precocious teenager, except that he might be headed for a successful college career. But most young, Mexican American males growing up in East Los Angeles, regardless of their orientation, eventually butted heads with policemen. At one point, Sánchez had been "slapped around by the police," an experience that convinced him that police brutality was a community problem. When he tried to bring up the issue to the youth council, it was ignored because the adult politicians did not wish to air the problem.

In Los Angeles, most Mexican boys his age worked in grocery stores, movie theaters and car washes to make spending money. Richard Alatorre, however, obtained for Sánchez a winter job with the Boy's Club while Father Luce used him as youth counselor in the summer under the auspices of Volunteers In Service to America (VISTA). In the summer of 1967, at age seventeen, Sánchez wrote a successful proposal to the Southern California Council of Churches for funding to start the Piranya coffee house—envisioned as a teenager hangout to keep them out of trouble. The grant provided rent and other expenses for one year, enough time for a social revolution to emerge. Sánchez recruited Vickie Castro, Ralph Ramírez and other friends from Camp Hess Kramer, and they formed the Young Citizens for Community Action (YCCA). The Pirayna became the headquarters of the YCCA. This upward-bound, clean-cut youthful group became the foundation of one of the most militant, sometimes violence-prone, Chicano organizations in the country: the Brown Berets.

Initially the group worked within the system, but the social ferment which characterized East Los Angeles during this time radicalized the YCCA. Eleazar Risco, for example, a Cuban acculturated to Mexicans (he spoke Spanish with a Mexican accent), began publishing La Raza, a tabloid specializing in exposing police brutality and educational inadequacies, issues that resonated among East Los Angeles Mexican Americans.

The crudely printed, passionately written, if not-too-well-researched, La Raza, which Risco regularly left at the Piranya clubhouse, excited the young patrons who read not only about police brutality, but also blistering attacks on the school system. This latter issue was close to a group more interested in college than gang life. In 1967, for example, when Julián Nava, the Harvard-educated historian, successfully ran for the Los Angeles County School Board, members of the YCCA worked enthusiastically on his campaign. He became the first Mexican member ever to serve in that capacity.

Eleazar Risco came to Kansas from Cuba in the 1960s as a ministry student and eventually studied at Sacramento State University. From there, he enrolled at Stanford University, where he studied under Ronald Hilton, a self-styled radical who published a journal that exposed CIA ties to anti-Castro Cubans training in the U.S. before the Bay of Pigs invasion. Luis Valdez, another Chicano Movement pioneer and founder of El Teatro Campesino, whom Risco met in the Bay Area, convinced him to go to Delano. Risco dropped out of Stanford to help publish the National Farm Workers Association's El Malcriado.

Sent by Chávez to East Los Angeles in 1967 to help organize the grape boycott, Risco soon ventured into other activities. At first, he worked on a U.S. Department of Justice-financed project to prevent juvenile delinquency and remembers encountering community dissatisfaction with President Johnson's War on Poverty programs. Another source of discontent in the community was police harassment and violence. "This discontent, related in private conversations, in parrandas, needed a voice—they needed to be aired," recalled Risco. The realization led to the formation of the Barrio Communications Project, which published La Raza.[13]

[13] Telephone interview with Eleazar Risco by author, September 21, 1995.

Sánchez remembers how the Brown Berets established their visual identity: "We needed to make things more colorful. . . . We were up in San Francisco and we saw some people who had some blue berets. . . and we thought that was kinda nice. . . . I says, 'Well, hell with blue berets, let's get some brown berets'. . . . I purchased some brown berets from the General Hat Company, a dozen of 'em, and gave 'em to the people at the coffee house, and said, 'Let's wear these. . . . Though we were the Young Chicanos for Community Action, people started calling us the Brown Berets."[14]

But *La Raza* also appealed to the *cholo* (street tough) element of East Los Angeles. Risco and his helpers shaped the tabloid's content to appeal to this marginalized element, chronicling *la vida loca* (the crazy life), as life in LA's mean streets was known. Police bashing was particularly attractive to this group. To their delight, the first issue of *La Raza* led off with a banner headline attacking Los Angeles Police Department (LAPD) Chief Thomas Redding, "*Jefe Placa, tu abuela en mole*" (Fuzz Chief, your grandmother in chili sauce)." But the LAPD

98. *El Popo* newspaper.

and the Sheriff's Department, noting the critical police stance of persons connected with Father Luce's operation, harassed Piranya club members by enforcing a curfew law for teenagers. David Sánchez's sister, for instance, was detained because she was in the coffee house after 10 p.m. The group decided to protest. For many YCCA members who picketed the sheriff's substation located across the street, it was their first militant act. Not all of the coffee house members agreed with the gradual radicalization of the group, however, and many walked out as a consequence.

About this time, Carlos Montes, who also played a crucial role in the rise of the Brown Berets, entered the scene. As a student at East Los Angeles City College, he had obtained a job as a teen post director for the Lincoln Heights area. This was a federal program sponsored by Father Luce's center and the CSO that Tony Ríos, César Chávez's former boss, ran out of Los Angeles. The YCCA members spent a great deal of time at the Church of the Epiphany, and soon Montes blended in with them. At Father Luce's center, Montes also met the passionate Risco, who produced *La Raza* in the church basement.

[14] Interview with David Sánchez by Enrique Berumen, January 22, 1994, NLCC-GP.

While it is difficult to trace the idea of the walkouts to any one group or individual, it is certain that Camp Hess Kramer veterans, some who became Brown Berets, were the core planners. But certainly many activists participated from other groups; some were members of one, or more than one, organization. For example, Vicky Castro, Carlos Muñoz and Gil Cárdenas from United Mexican American Students (UMAS) from California State College, Los Angeles, and Moctezuma Esparza from UCLA were crucial in organizing the effort. They devoted numerous hours to discussing educational inadequacies and how they could be changed. Perhaps influenced by the Black cultural movement, they all agreed that education of Mexican Americans lacked cultural relevancy.

Soon the planners favored the idea of a walkout as a means of dramatizing their issues. They then printed propaganda broadsides designed to persuade students to abandon their classes. Their activities became so overt that weeks before the strike, students, teachers, and administrators knew about the impending walkout. In fact, one month before the incident, teachers openly debated the issue and started taking sides. Meanwhile, Chicano newspapers *La Raza, Inside Eastside* and *The Chicano Student* helped fuel the passions of students and boycott supporters by spreading an "awareness" among students and non-students alike. A few days before the walkouts, for example, *La Raza* blasted the shortcomings of the school system and encouraged students to leave their classes.

The decision as to when to begin the protest did not come easily, however. The Brown Berets, who dominated the planning group, apparently wanted immediate action, but some of the university students argued for a more cautious approach, according to Brown Beret, Chris Cebada. Because the Brown Berets counted many high-school students in their numbers, they won out and the strike was slated for March. In addition, high-school students not in the Brown Berets provided leadership. The editors of *La Raza*, Eleazar Risco and Joe Razo, enthusiastically supported the effort and, indeed, they were later indicted by a grand jury for their role in a "conspiracy to disrupt public schools."

The college students and Brown Berets must have possessed a precise rationale as to why the walkouts were necessary. But only a few of the ten thousand high-school students who participated in the boycott were as politicized; they did not have the same ideological motives for their action. As John Ortiz, one of the college leaders, indicated,

> It was happening at Berkeley. . . the media reported strikes occurring throughout the country. So many kids got caught in the climate of protest, they were products of their time. Others felt it was the right thing to do. And others because they wanted to "party."

This motivation would be true in other Chicano student activities,

Joe McKnight, a Lincoln High School teacher, published an article entitled, "Can Anglo Education Survive in a Mexican American School," in the faculty newspaper in February, 1968. The essay stated that teachers, instead of reacting negatively to student and parental discontent, should be introspective and consider the legitimate concerns voiced by Mexican Americans. Otherwise, he wrote, "We teachers here at Lincoln must be prepared to face prospects of student walkouts, picketing, charges of ethnic and race discrimination, and civil disobedience." The piece brought an angry rebuttal from Richard Davis, another teacher, who, in essence, blamed the Mexicans and their cultural deficiencies for their problems.[15]

---

[15] *Chicano Student*, February 1968. Clipping from the files of Edward Escobar.

whatever their character. But in the same statement, Ortiz explains the outcome for the uncommitted who just followed the crowd:

But one thing is for sure; as the strike intensified and people were getting arrested, the students became politically aware. The events politicized the students. And that's why they walked out of their classes![16]

Mexican American teachers antagonistic to

the protest came under much criticism. Sal Castro became a hero, according to embittered Roosevelt High School teacher Rudolph Chávez, while administrators ignored his loyalty by publicly criticizing the renegade teacher. A more vocal boycott foe was Roosevelt teacher Carmen Terrazas, who urged the administration to punish the student strikers. Walkout supporters denounced this stance as selling out. But such tension reflected a general split in the Los Angeles Mexican commu-

Vicky Castro, now the school principal of Belvedere Junior. High School in Los Angeles, recalls her participation in the first walkout:

My job. . . the day of the walkouts at Lincoln. . . I was being interviewed for a teaching assistant assignment, but my thing was to stall the principal. We had already planned it, and who was gonna be in the hall and everything, so at the exact time I was there trying to stall the principal, so all. . . the other players could get in and start yelling, 'walkout.' And then he had to excuse himself, and then I disappeared.

Paula Crisóstomo, a high-school leader, was not equivocal about why she walked out.

Our schools. . . on the Eastside were in such poor condition as compared to other schools. We had taken this [trip] to. . . Paley High. And just the physical appearance was appalling to all of us. And I know for myself, never having ventured very far from my own neighborhood. . . just traveling out and seeing how other people lived and how other kids went to school. . . . And there was the building of the

new high shool, Wilson [in East Los Angeles], which was taking an awfully long time. . . . And again schools in the Valley and West LA, brand new schools, were being put up right away with swimming pools.[17]

At a press conference held by Garfield administrators, a teenager rose to the podium to declare nervously,

The majority of the student body is most definitely in favor of some of its proposals [made by walkout leaders and sympathizers]...but I must also add in the same token, that...the majority of students at Garfield High School do not, do not condone or accept the method which has been used.[18]

Another then high-school student who participated recalled more recently,

For me it was kind of a sad time. It was a time when I felt embarassed about the way people were behaving. . . acting rudely, loudly, treating people with disrespect. . . The problem I had was not so much with identification of. . . issues but with. . . proposed solutions.[19]

[16] Quoted in Marguerite V. Marín, *Social Protest in an Urban Barrio: A Study of the Chicano Movement, 1966-1974* (Lanham, Massachusetts: University Press of America 1991), p. 81.

[17] Interview with Paula Crisóstomo by Jesús Treviño, February 15, 1993, NLCC-GP.

[18] Transcript, Rough Cut, Episode 3, "Blowouts - The Struggle for Educational Reform," NLCC-GP.

[19] On-camera interview with Joe Aguerrebere by Susan Racho, January 18, 1995, NLCC-GP.

nity, a fissure symbolized to some degree by those who used the term *Chicano* as a self-identifier and those who did not.

The rift over involvement in the movement existed within families as well. Joe Razo, co-editor of *La Raza*, recalled an incident during the walkouts:

> I saw a man over in one of the East L.A. parks slapping his daughter around because she had walked out. . . . she was crying but still arguing with him about the necessity for fighting for some of her rights and for changing the curriculum. . . . I still remember this vividly. . . . It was a family that at least a man had the interest enough to get involved with his kid. . . . there were going to be a lot of long discussions in that family. . . as to why she walked out of school. . . . It was not a matter "of it's nice and sunny, I think I'll go to the park." They were political. They really knew what they were fighting for.[20]

But wherever they stood on the boycott, the event forced the adult community to think more urgently about educational issues they did not know existed or which they had ignored. The American Federation of Teachers, for example, sponsored a forum featuring walkout student leaders, who explained why the strike took place. Police conduct also politicized those who were neutral. During the demonstrations, the LAPD often overreacted, angering adults who watched students being hit with billy clubs when they refused to move from the front of the schools.

Ultimately, a large portion of the Mexican American adult community rose to support the student participants. The Reverend Vahac Mardirosian, a Baptist minister born in Mexico of Armenian heritage, became one of their most articulate leaders. On Tuesday morning, while at a breakfast meeting with other Baptist ministers, he heard that students had left their classes at Garfield High and were milling around in the streets. Fearing for their safety, the minister drove to the school and sought out the leaders. After about three hours, he gained their confidence and they allowed him to mediate with school administrators.

Mardirosian did not think twice about joining a small group called the Emergency Support Committee (ESC), consisting of about twenty-five parents. At first the group busied itself with raising bail money for students arrested during the strikes. They met in different public buildings, wherever space was available: the Cleland House, The Plaza Community, the Euclid Center, the International Institute. An offshoot of this incipient effort was the formation of the Chicano Legal Defense Fund. Rapidly, ESC assemblies grew in size. As many as two hundred or more people—students, men in work clothes, professionals, elderly women—gathered to hear fiery denunciations of the schools and other institutions. Enthusiasm was at an all-time high, but the group lacked direction.

Less than a month after the first walkout, the ESC changed its name to the Educational Issues Coordinating Committee (EICC) and the group formally elected Mardirosian chairman, but not by acclamation. The openness of the committee curtailed its effectiveness because the meetings attracted a volatile mix of militant activists with long-range Chicano Movement goals and community people who wanted simple reforms on an immediate issue. At first, parents were leery of the college students, thinking they might entice high-school teenagers into violence while the college students felt parents were overly conservative. So many ideas and conflicts arose that consensus was difficult, but eventually the group was divided into committees and more was done.

After about three meetings, Mardirosian and other leaders mollified the divisions, and the group drafted a set of demands that were presented at a packed school board meeting on March 26. The wish list contained items that were eventually incorporated: a relevant cultural curriculum, teacher training that reflected local conditions, hiring of more Mexican American adminis-

---

[20] Interview with Joe Razo, March 4, 1992, NLCC-GP.

On the night of his arrest, David Sánchez says he was at the Brown Beret office on Brooklyn and Soto Streets when some Black men walked in claiming they belonged to SNCC. "They. . . checked everything out. . . so they could get their plan together. . . . So, I thought they were from SNCC. They had ID's from SNCC. . . and this one guy gave me some papers. . . about. . . how to make Molotav cocktails." Sánchez and some of the other Berets thought the SNCC activists had forgotten the materials and would return to re- trieve them, so they put them on a filing cabinet. Two hours later, the police arrested the Berets who were in the office. Sánchez did not want to miss the prom, so he jumped out the bathroom window and ran home, where the police were waiting.[21]

trators and teachers, upgrading of facilities, more community input and a more liberal approach to the rights of students. On April 4 the EICC decided that the school board was not responding to the demands pre- sented two weeks earlier so a group of about eight hundred-strong crowded into the school board chambers to demand action—this was the same day that Martin Luther King was shot, an event lending solem- nity to the protest. A few weeks later, the EICC used a "walk-through" where committee members marched through the schools because they had heard the school board was asking for reprisals against student walkout leaders and sympathetic teachers.

As emotions escalated, Julián Nava, who had just been elected to the school board the previous year to the accolades of the community, now became suspect. Increasingly, Chicano militants ritualisti- cally hurled the *vendido* (sellout) epithet at Mexicans in power and retaliated harshly if they did not comply to their demands. Whether or not they believed their own rhetoric, the tactic became an effective tool in forcing Mexican Ameri- cans wielding a modicum of power into compliance. Ironically, these "establish- ment" Mexicans were rarely driven from power. Most were astute enough to co- opt the militants or move sufficiently towards their position to effect a silent compromise.

99. Julián Nava.

Unexpectedly, the actions of law enforcement forced the EICC away from their original objectives. On June 2 the Los Angeles Grand Jury, at the behest of District Attorney Evelle Younger, returned secret indictments against fifteen persons—most of them EICC members—of criminally conspiring to create riots, disrupt the functioning of public schools and disturb the peace. Only thirteen were arrested and they became known as the LA Thirteen. The most prominent of this group was Lincoln High School teacher Sal Castro. As he dressed at his home to chaperone the Lincoln High School Prom on Friday, June 6, the police came and took him into custody. David Sánchez's arrest also came as he got ready to go to the prom; he had a rented tuxedo in his car trunk when police came to the Brown Beret Headquarters. Sánchez fled but was arrested at his home.

Another indicted Brown Beret leader, Carlos Montes, was on the Poor People's March to Washington, DC. Police arrested him when he returned. Other Brown Berets arrested included Minister of Defense Ralph Ramírez and Fred López. The rest of the Thirteen were UMAS

---

[21] Interview with David Sánchez by Jesús Treviño, July 22, 1992, NLCC-GP.

100. Brown Berets. Photo by Oscar Castillo.

activists Carlos Muñoz and Henry Gómez; Moctezuma Esparza from UCLA; Eleazar Risco and Joe Razo, publishers of *La Raza*; MAPA member Patricio Sánchez; and community organizers Gilberto Olmeda and Richard Vigil.

The EICC immediately mobilized community support for the prisoners and on Saturday, June 12, at least three hundred picketers protested in front of the Los Angeles Police Department. The next day, two thousand demonstrated in front of the city jail and then marched to La Placita, the old center of Los Angeles, to hear speeches condemning the police. Castro escaped being discharged for his role in the walkouts, but the indictment presented school administrators with the opportunity to oust him. When Castro called his supervisor from jail to inform him he would not be able to teach his classes the following Monday, he was told to report to the district personnel office. The administration fired him, and the school board refused to counter the decision.

Now Castro's reinstatement became the EICC's key issue. Mardirosian and the committee members mounted nine straight fruitless days of protest in front of Lincoln High School to persuade the school board to rescind the decision. So the EICC decided to take the demonstration to the school board chambers. On September 26, while EICC members waited, the board voted four to three not to reinstate the fired teacher. The protesters responded by sitting in. The sit-in served to forge bonds between the activists; they slept, sang and discussed plans for continuing the *movimiento*. Father Luce even said an Episcopalian Mass, which was close enough to the ritual the predominantly Catholic

Carlos Muñoz recounts his arrest after the police knocked on his door at 2:30 a.m. when he was writing a term paper on Communism for a political science course: "I had two young children. . . they were upstairs. . . . And the cops ran all the way up there, terrorized my family, looking for weapons. . . . 'You're a Brown Beret,' they were telling me. . . you gotta have weapons . . . . They look at these books [sources for his term paper]. I remember one of the sergeants saying . . . 'Here it is! He's a damm Communist!'. . . They put the cuffs on me. I'll never forget this as long as I live. . . . They took them off again. . . . They say. . . 'We're going to give you ten steps so that you can make a run for it.' I knew what they wanted to do. . . . I was scared for my life. . . . I put my hands back up again—'You better cuff me and take me in.'"[22]

[22] Interview with Carlos Muñoz by Jesús Treviño, October 7, 1995, NLCC-GP.

Católicos por la Raza
continued its protests
into the following year as
seen in the following
excerpt from an article in
its publication: "On Sep-
tember 13, 1970, Pedro
Arias and his family will
burn their baptism certifi-
cates to symbolically
protest the Chicano dis-
gust for the institution
called the Catholic
Church. As a member of
CPLR, Pedro has made
it clear that he is not
renouncing the Catholic
Faith or the Christian
dogma. His act on that
day is instead a renunci-
ation of Catholic Church
hypocricy and racism, as
we in Los Angeles are
only beginning to under-
stand."[23]

activists were used to.

Since at least three of the board members voted to reinstate, the
EICC knew just one more vote was needed. According to the Rev.
Mardirosian, he "sweet-talked" a recalcitrant board member into
changing his mind. Mardirosian urged ending the sit-in based on this
pledge, but the verbal promise did not assure the thirty-five demonstrators, who stayed only to be arrested for failure to leave a public
building. Two days later, the new alignment of votes resulted in Castro's rehiring. The jubilant crowd then carried the vindicated teacher
out of the chambers on their shoulders.

Because the grand jury indictment of the LA Thirteen was still
pending, the issue came to dominate Chicano activism. The Chicano
Legal Defense Fund initiated a campaign to raise funds for legal
expenses and received donations from prominent Californians such as
Governor Edmund Brown and city council member Tom Bradley.
Attorneys from the Civil Liberties and the Chicano Legal Defense Fund
joined to defend the LA Thirteen. The team filed a number of motions.
One questioned the lack of Mexican Americans on the grand jury and
found precedence indicating that demonstrating at a school was not a
felony. Eventually, charges were dropped for the LA Thirteen.

The rise of the student movement in California and the walkouts
were only the beginning of a continued Chicano militancy that spread
throughout the state and even into other areas of the Southwest. In Los
Angeles, for example, between 1968 and 1970 a dazzling array of
incidents testified to this new awareness. But education remained the
core issue and walkouts occurred when students felt that progress was
too slow. The EICC did not sanction these, and they never equaled the
intensity of the March demonstrations. But in April 1969 the California
Association of Mexican American Educators sponsored the Nuevas
Vistas Conference at the behest of State Superintendent of Public
Instruction Max Rafferty, an appointee of Governor Ronald Reagan.
The conference, designed to reveal the latest pedagogical research on
teaching Mexican Americans, raised the ire of Chicano activists
because Governor Reagan was the keynote speaker. Students, including Moctezuma Esparza and Brown Beret Carlos Montes, decided to
disrupt his speech. As the Chicano demonstrators were doing just that,
fires broke out mysteriously throughout the Biltmore Hotel, where the
event was taking place, and the police arrested ten participants. These
arrests prompted another crusade, this time to free the LA Ten. It
turned out that a police infiltrator, Fernando Sumaya, had been
responsible for setting the fires.

Even the Catholic Church came under severe scrutiny. On Christmas Eve, 1969, a group calling itself Católicos por la Raza (CPLR—

[23] *Católicos por la Raza*, undated clipping from the files of Edward Escobar.

Catholics for the People) tried to disrupt midnight Mass at St. Basil's and were beaten up by plain-clothes police. One demonstrator, Dave Domínguez, almost died. The CPLR explained that, in Los Angeles, the Church spent four million dollars in churches for the rich and owned at least one billion dollars in real estate. The CPLR demanded that the Church be more responsive to the needs of its Mexican parishioners and use its money to promote not just spiritual help but material help. The chief villains were Bishop Manning and Cardinal Mcyntire, who once allegedly had said, "I was here before there were even any Mexicans. I came to Los Angeles 21 years ago."[24]

CONCLUSION

The Mexican American generation had a far greater influence on the Chicano Movement than ever imagined. In sensitizing their children, using an ideology that had changed little since the MAM days, it succeeded in instilling a strong reformist agenda, if not notions of identity. This meant that, as young U.S. Mexicans coalesced into a definable Chicano Movement, their core social objectives rarely differed from the older generation's. Except for a brief Marxist era in the 1970s, what distinguished the two eras was that the younger group turned to cultural nationalism instead of assimilation to define identity and freely used shock or militant tactics to pursue almost purely reformist objectives.

The militancy and cultural nationalism served the expressive goals of a culturally alienated generation. Anthropologist John Aguilar has demonstrated how expressive symbols provided catharsis for the activists when he compares the Chicano Movement to the striving for political identity of Mayan Indians in Chiapas:

> Clearly the instrumental functions [i.e., gaining material objectives] of ethnicity are often part of their *raison d'etre*. As long as ethnic minorities are deprived of political and economic power, ethnic movements will have instrumental aims. But it is also the case that as long as such minorities are also deprived of self-determination and social dignity, such movements will serve expressive functions.... In addition, the use of symbolic resources [militancy and nationalism] for their value in mobilizing groups for political and economic competition, the value of symbolic resources also derives from their expressive significance. In such cases ethnicity claims are made not only for the utilitarian ends they may facilitate but as ends in themselves—that is to say, because it simply feels good to make them.[25]

But it is also important to understand why the Chicano youth rebellions took place precisely when it seemed Mexican Americans were making progress. Many students of revolution and social unrest see the frustrations of rising expectations as responsible for such dissatisfaction. James C. Davis in *When Men Revolt and Why*, puts it this way:

> With rising expectations, people redefine themselves and feel that they deserve more than they have. When people feel that they are treated unfairly, they become outraged. And if outraged people see a possibility of gaining justice, they self-righteously join forces in an effort to get what they believe they deserve.[26]

[24] Undated clipping from *La Raza* in the files of Edward Escobar.

[25] John L. Aguilar, "Expressive Ethnicity and Ethnic Identity in Mexico and Mexican America," in *Mexican American Identity*, ed. by Marta E. Bernal and Phylis I. Martinelli (Encino, California: Floricanto Press, 1993), p. 59.

[26] Quoted in Marín, *Social Protest in an Urban Barrio*, p. 75.

CHAPTER ELEVEN

The Chicano Moratorium

101. Chicano Moratorium marchers. Photo by George Rodríguez.

As the antiwar movement grew because Americans despaired over the course of U.S. involvement in Vietnam, the sentiment resonated among *movimiento* activists. In August of 1970 the National Chicano Moratorium march was held in Los Angeles to protest the war. The event became one of the largest and most significant political demonstrations in Mexican American history. The antiwar mood reflected the general disenchantment affecting the whole nation in 1970. During 1968 two major assassinations—of Martin Luther King and Robert Kennedy—left Americans in the throes of bewilderment. At the same time, U.S. troops in Vietnam were miring down in a war that few people understood. As Americans watched in their own living rooms television coverage of their young boys being killed, they realized that defeating the Viet Cong would not be easy; their support for the war waned. The 1968 Tet Offensive, in which the Viet Cong pushed into Da Nang Air Force Base in Saigon, discouraged even the most enthusiastic advocates of helping the South Vietnamese through limited war. The choices, it seemed, were either to escalate the struggle by invading North Vietnam and win or to pull out. In reality, Americans were in no mood to continue. Many who tired of the war were, nevertheless, angry at the antiwar demonstrators whom they saw as disloyal to their country. President Johnson was so beset by the divisions in the country that he decided not to run for reelection.

Most Mexican Americans, like other Americans reluctantly supported their government but had little enthusiasm for the armed conflict. Unlike their actions during previous wars, they did not proudly brandish the heroism of their boys nor did they see a noble sacrifice in Mexican casualties. In fact, many felt resentful because, while twenty-three percent of the casualties of soldiers from the Southwest was Hispanic, only ten percent of the general population in the Southwest was of Hispanic origin. Before 1970 only a few specific antiwar protests were aimed at attracting Mexican American sentiment. In April of 1967, for example, a group known as El Comité Pro-Paz (Pro-Peace Committee) invited the East Los Angeles public to a *Mitin al Aire Libre Para Protestar por la Guerra en Viet Nam* (An Outside Protest Meeting against the War in Vietnam) at Lincoln Park. Later that year, the group opened a draft-counseling center in East Los Angeles. For Chicano Movement activists, however, antiwar expression and sentiment, while always an important issue, did not become a main concern until the final months of 1969. Steering the Chicano Movement in the direction of antiwar protest was mainly the work of the Brown Berets and a former UCLA student-body president, Rosalío Muñoz.

Muñoz was elected UCLA student president in the spring of 1968 as a protest candidate against fraternities which had always controlled student government. In 1968 one of the fraternities was involved in a racist incident against minorities. The mainly liberal UCLA student body, in no mood to tolerate fraternity shenanigans, elected an antiracist ticket on which Muñoz was the presidential candidate. As Muñoz puts it, he was not particularly *movimiento*-oriented when he became involved in student government. He had attended a few UMAS meetings without making much of a commitment. But *movimiento* activists such as Moctezuma Esparza were aware of his usefulness in funding Chicano activities and pressured him to pledge to the movement.

Researcher Ronald López hired Muñoz after he graduated in 1969 to help him organize a Mexican American studies program at the Claremont Colleges. By then, Muñoz's antiwar stance had become more defined. He had attended the funeral of a friend who died after serving in the war and saw other friends being inducted. Muñoz remembers saying to his friend, Ramses Noriega, "We need somebody like Ali [Mohammed Ali], who had an impact on African Americans when he said, 'Hey, you know, no Viet Cong called me nigger'. . . or Martin Luther King, who came out against the war. Although it was generally felt César was against the war, he was not making any proclamations."

Then Muñoz received his own notice to appear at the induction center on September 16, and his reluctance to serve in the military turned

102. Brown Berets at the Chicano Moratorium. Photo by Oscar Castillo.

to outright defiance. Like many other young men of his era, he sought advice on how to avoid induction. When he discussed the issue with Noriega, it was then that Muñoz decided to become a symbol against the war and to provide a message for Chicanos—hundreds of other white boys had already made the gesture. But Chicano Movement leaders, such as Ernesto Vigil in Denver and Salomón Baldenegro in Tucson, also had refused the draft. He decided to make a statement by rejecting his draft notice ceremoniously at the induction center. He and Ron López created as much publicity as possible and linked it to the commemoration of Mexico's independence anniversary, *el diez y seis de septiembre*, which coincidentally was celebrated on the same

day as the induction. "Mexican Americans everywhere were going to be getting together for that, and Chicanos were going to have a lot of special things all around," Muñoz thought.

The two drove to Delano in a rickety Volkswagen bug to get support from César Chávez, who refused to make a public endorsement but gave his moral support. "César had a nice way of saying no, but it was inspiration," recalled Muñoz.[1]

Then they traveled to Fresno, San Jose, Stockton, Sacramento and the Bay Area, gathering support for the fateful day. As it turned out, Muñoz's induction was postponed, so he conducted the ceremony in November. His non-induction had given him more time to organize, and now Muñoz and Noriega vied for national support by crisscrossing the Southwest. The idea had jelled into organizing the first national Chicano peace protest.

The Brown Berets had also come back from the Chicano Youth Conference in Denver during the spring of 1969 with the idea of mounting a massive antiwar demonstration. One of the many topics discussed at the meeting was the war and its effect on Chicanos. On December 19, 1969, the first Chicano Moratorium Committee (CMC) rally at Obregon Park was attended by about two thousand people; it had been organized by Brown Berets. Before this event, Sánchez said he had attended Rosalío Muñoz's demonstration at the induction center, where he had asked him if he wanted to cochair the committee.

The December rally was so successful from the organizers' point of view that Sánchez remembers thinking, "We'll do another one." Many Chicano activists felt alienated from the more general national antiwar movement, which by 1970 was enormous, "because it mainly helped the white and middle-class from going to war." But *movimento* activists seeking their own issues to push Chicano agendas did not necessarily want to share the spotlight. Sánchez remembers, "The trend was there. . . of being against

[1] Last three quotes from interview with Rosalío Muñoz by Jesús Treviño, December 30, 1993, NLCC-GP.

Vietnam. . . but now was time for the Chicano."

On February 28, 1970, the CMC, of which Muñoz was now cochairman, organized a second rally at Salazar Park; five thousand people marched in the rain. This second event brought the committee so much attention within the movement that the group decided on a Chicano national protest day for August 29. Muñoz turned to full-time moratorium organizing. The Southwest Council of La Raza provided him with funds and office space. Now the group started to call itself the National Chicano Moratorium Committee (NCMC). Muñoz traveled to Houston and other cities, where he spoke at the meetings of any organization that would have him and persuaded many to pledge their support—including older Mexican American organizations such as the CSO and MAPA. If Muñoz, with his clean-cut UCLA background, had not joined in the effort, the Brown Berets, who made cautious Mexican Americans uneasy, would have never attained this backing by themselves.

In the spring Muñoz attended the second youth conference in Denver, and Crusade for Justice leaders "Corky" Gonzales and Ernesto Vigil and all of the other participants enthusiastically supported the efforts to organize the antiwar meeting. It was also decided at that meeting to announce at the moratorium rally plans for a national Chicano political party.

The reasons for opposition to the war among the diverse organizations that pledged support were not all the same. The Congress of Mexican American Unity, a Los Angeles coalition of more than three hundred groups—few of which possessed a core Chicano Movement ideology—drew up an antiwar resolution and sent it to President Nixon. Primarily, the letter lamented the burden the war had put on Mexican Americans and the divisions that the struggle created in the country. El Movimiento Chicano Estudiantil de Aztlán, (MECHA) issued a statement condemning U.S. aggression that used Mexican Americans to wage an unjust war. The Brown Berets in their

newspaper, *La Causa*, gave the most radical justification for antiwar sentiments by actually siding with the Viet Cong. But as the NCMC grew to include interests other than those represented by the Brown Berets and Muñoz, its size invited so many ideas that it was wracked by divisions. On the eve of the demonstration, the steering committee had about one hundred fifty people.

As the time drew nearer to the August 29 protest, David Sánchez decided to resign because, as he pointed out in a recent interview, there were so many people coming from across the country and some, it was rumored, wanted a riot. Already under an indictment, Sánchez claims another arrest would have sent him to prison, so the effort was deferred to Muñoz. Other Berets joined Sánchez's abdication, according to an article in *La Causa*, "because there were too many ego-trippers and opportunists."[2]

Members of the steering committee, however, considered the Berets essential and convinced them to return to the fold—Sánchez stayed away, nevertheless.

On the day of the protest, thousands of out-of-town protesters arrived to take their place in the march alongside the local Chicanos. Delighted, NCMC members made their final preparations and fully expected a peaceful march. They recruited hundreds of monitor-volunteers to assure just that. About 10 a.m. the procession advanced on Whittier Boulevard, headed for Laguna Park in the heart of the East Los Angeles business district, where they expected to gather in a monster rally. City officials marshaled hundreds of riot gun-equipped county sheriff deputies and LAPD officers to monitor the event. The officers were conspicuous on every street corner and behind barricades along the whole length of the route.

As the marchers walked, their mood was festive and nonviolent. At the corner of Eastern Avenue and Whittier, a young man was immediately reprimanded by parade monitors after he threw a bottle at a police car; he was sternly

---

[2] Quoted in Marín, *Social Protest in an Urban Barrio*, p. 207.

103. Chicano Moratorium marchers. Photo by George Rodríguez.

warned not to cause any more problems. Hundreds of onlookers along the route succumbed to marchers' entreaties, and the parade of protesters swelled even more. The first ones to reach the park spread out and sat on blankets and lawn chairs or milled around waiting for speakers and entertainers to mount the platform, which was on the back of a flatbed truck. Finally, the stragglers brought in the end of the procession. At least another ten thousand people who did not march crowded into the park as well. By 3 p.m. the park was teeming with as many as thirty thousand demonstrators, most of them under twenty-five years of age. Some were caught up in the festive mood and drank wine and beer or smoked pot, creating some concern among families with children. Sadly, the peace march was destined for trouble.

About a block away, marchers, hot from their long trek, crowded into the Green Mill Liquor store to quench their thirst and overwhelmed the owner, Morris Maroko. Some left without paying for their soda and beer. Maroko locked the store and called the police. "I tried to close the door to the store because they were stealing," he complained. "Then they said, 'If you close the door, you are against us.' Another person threatened me with a knife." Immediately, a number of squad cars arrived. The police gave chase to the suspected shoplifters, and by the time reinforcements arrived, the problem had been resolved. The crowd quieted down, paid for their purchases and had been let out of the store by the shop owner. Everything was back to normal. But prior to this incident the police were prepared to put down a riot, even though they had every indication that the demonstration was peaceful.

After this incident, the police decided to put

104. Marchers bearing crosses to symbolize soldiers fallen in the Vietnam War, at the Chicano Moratorium. Photo by Oscar Castillo.

When the police decided to stop the rally, they forced the crowd to the front, which was cordoned off by trucks and cars so marchers could not come in from the back. Rosalío Muñoz recalls. "People were trapped there, and I thought of these soccer riots. . . and kids were climbing out through the stage. . . . People were climbing and tossing babies over to the other side. . . . Then you saw the monitors coming around and trying to stop the cops . . . . Then the cops started throwing tear gas, making it worse. And so then the people started throwing things back."³

an end to the rally and started to force the participants to leave. Dr. James Koopman, a professor at the UCLA School of Medicine and a participant in the moratorium, recalls,

> My wife and I sat on the grass amongst the diverse people. Immediately around us were little children playing with a puppy, an older woman with a cane, a pregnant woman with a small baby and a family eating hamburgers and french fries. The program began and after two speeches a Puerto Rican rhythm group was providing entertainment. The first sign of any disturbance I saw was when people in the distance began to stand up. . . . I saw a row of gold helmets marching across the park, forcing everyone toward the high fences. The exit was too small for everyone to leave quickly. I, along with everyone else, panicked.⁴

As a police phalanx plowed in on the crowd, some of the demonstrators decided to resist. A battle ensued. Three people were killed, including Rubén Salazar, a columnist for the *Los Angeles Times* and manager of a local TV station, who had exposed police brutality in the *barrios* and had demonstrated sympathy for some Chicano Movement goals. His death led to suspicions that Salazar was targeted for extermination by resentful police. It was well known—he wrote about it—that

³ Interview with Rosalío Muñoz.

⁴ Last two quotes in main text from "Chicano: A History of the Civil Rights Movement," proposal to the National Endowment for the Humanities, submitted by the National Latino Communications Center, p. 14.

police had asked him to tone down his reports because of their incendiary effect on the Los Angeles Mexican community.

Hundreds of others were arrested, including "Corky" Gonzales, who had hitched a ride with his family on the flatbed truck that served as a stage. The police stopped the vehicle and found a gun. Because Gonzales was carrying more than five hundred dollars on his person, he became a potential suspect in an unknown robbery—a normal procedure, the police said. The money was apparently for travel expenses. The abrupt end to the rally prevented the announcement of a national political party. In addition, attending to his arrest distracted Gonzales from organizing the party immediately after the moratorium as he had planned.

Needless to say, the East Los Angeles community was outraged at the way the police had handled the rally. The Congress of Mexican American Unity established a complaint center so it could document police overreaction. Hundreds of people who were gassed charged the police with using anti-crowd control tactics even before some of the demonstrators started resisting.

THE DEATH OF RUBÉN SALAZAR

The issue that most angered the community was the unnecessary killing of the popular journalist Rubén Salazar by a tear gas projectile fired by a deputy sheriff indiscriminately into the Silver Dollar Cafe, where the journalist was sipping a beer. After his death, an editorial in the *Los Angeles Times* eulogized its former reporter by stating, "Rubén Salazar was a most uncommon man who fought mightily for the cause of the economically deprived Mexican American Community." Congressman Ed Roybal echoed this feeling in his tribute to the slain journalist. "Violence has deprived us of the man who best articulated the necessity for the peaceful pursuit of long overdue social reforms for the Spanish-speaking community in the U.S."[5]

105. Rubén Salazar.

Although Salazar had sympathized with the reformist goals of the Chicano Movement, by no stretch of the imagination was he a *movimiento* activist. Ironically, one of the Chicano Movement's most important martyrs and symbols was at the time of his death only peripherally involved.

In fact, the slain reporter's life story fits quintessentially into the middle-class, Mexican American generation mode. Born in the border town of Ciudad Juárez on March 3, 1928, Salazar, along with his family crossed the border into El Paso, where he was raised. Serving in the military after the war, Salazar used his GI Bill benefits to pursue a journalism degree at Texas Western College, today's University of Texas at El Paso. His first job was at the El Paso *Herald Post*. Throughout his early journalistic career, which spanned about fifteen years, he did his job competently and quietly, remaining a dedicated husband and father to his Anglo wife and three children. Except for his journalistic subjects, he stayed aloof from direct political or civil rights commitments.

---

[5] Last two quotes, in Pete Dimas, "Perspectives on the Career and Life of Rubén Salazar," (M.A. thesis, Arizona State University, 1980), pp. 2-3. Much of the story on Salazar is derived from this study.

Salazar's forte became investigative reporting. During his stint with the *Herald Post*, for example, he had had himself arrested and then wrote an exposé of drug trafficking and substandard conditions in the El Paso County Jail. The ambitious reporter's star rose even further when he wrote a series of articles on border drug trade outlets, known as "shooting galleries," after pretending to be a customer. For professional reasons, in 1956 he moved to the California Bay Area and reported for the *Santa Rosa Press Democrat*, but eventually he landed a job with the *San Francisco News*. Although he was considered a good reporter, the newspaper laid him off when it merged with another daily.

Losing this position prompted his move to Los Angeles, where Salazar landed a job with the *Los Angeles Times* in 1959. But unlike the star status he enjoyed in El Paso, assignments in this huge metropolitan daily were mundane and unspectacular. In 1961 Salazar wrote articles on the attempts by Mexican American *políticos* to incorporate East Los Angeles, truly a political activity that preceded *Chicanismo*. Salazar discovered that covering events in the Los Angeles Mexican American community brought him more frequent bylines.

Salazar's growing prestige within the *Times* earned him a position as a foreign correspondent in Latin America, where he covered the 1965 invasion of the Dominican Republic. His reporting was conventional and not critical of American involvement. Certainly, his writing did not demonstrate the anti-imperialistic tinge which was an important part of the Chicano Moratorium, where he perished. His next assignment was in Vietnam. The dispatches he sent home demonstrated a conviction that the U.S. could bring peace; nonetheless, Salazar recognized that South Vietnamese leaders were ineffective. He returned home disillusioned and anxious to cover the racial discontent that was raging in U.S. cities during 1966.

But the *Times* sent him to Mexico City as bureau chief for Central America, Mexico and the Caribbean. Again, his reporting was objective, but somewhat critical of the antidemocratic character of Castro's Cuba and the one-party system in Mexico. He covered the violent suppression of the student demonstrations in Mexico during 1968 without betraying indignation over the harshness the government had used to quell the unrest.

Salazar finally returned to Los Angeles in January 1969, ready to resume the Mexican community beat. During his absence, the *movimiento* had arrived. To cover the intense political scene in the Mexican community dispassionately without incurring the wrath of unforgiving militants would require a deft pen. Significantly, he managed just that. He did not alienate the activists, who appreciated sympathetic coverage, even though he often castigated them for what he considered unnecessary tactics. More importantly, his writings were sufficiently impartial for the *Times* chief, Otis Chandler, to support his work.

Salazar left the *Times* to manage the Spanish-language station KMEX in February of 1970, but continued writing a weekly editorial for the newspaper in which he expressed more subjective opinions. At this point, Salazar tried to make sense of the Chicano Movement to satisfy his own intellectual needs and those of his readers. But even in writing opinion, Salazar did not resort to the angry rhetoric typically used by Chicano Movement journalists such as Joe Razo, Raúl Ruiz or Eleazar Risco, the *La Raza* writers. The conditions he targeted, however, often merited editorial admonition, crafted as they were in careful language. It was not long before the now influential Mexican American journalist began to make establishment enemies—especially in the LAPD.

While Salazar continued to highlight educational and political issues in Los Angeles's Mexican community, law-enforcement abuses increasingly came to dominate the bulk of his commentary. He concentrated on exposing illegal procedures and police brutality, lack of Mexicans on juries and unwarranted spying on legitimate social service organizations. Salazar's scrutiny threatened law-enforcement agencies who had never been under such an intense media magnifying glass. In one case, he revealed that a policeman who shot a Mexican American had been suspended twice before, once because he threatened another boy with a cocked pistol. In another incident Salazar criticized policemen who, in looking for a murder suspect, had killed two Mexican nationals after they sprayed an apartment with gunfire. The police tried to explain the incident away as a possible ambush. Five men were in the flat, but Salazar revealed that the police found no arms and that the suspect the police sought was not there.

Rubén Salazar's death transformed him into the most powerful martyr of the *movimiento*. The inquest, like the walkouts, entered the defense of the LA Thirteen and the moratorium into the *movimiento* pantheon of memorable events. Chicanos hoped the investigation would reveal their worst suspicions, that the LAPD had conspired to murder Salazar to end the pillaring of the department. But more realistically, they wanted to use the inquest to corroborate accusations that the police overreacted in dealing with unrest at the August 29 demonstration.

The Mexican community was soon disappointed, however. In cooperation with the Los Angeles county coroner's office, a "blue ribbon committee" made up of civilians, including Mexican Americans, monitored the proceedings. Their report accused the investigative body of skirting the particulars leading to Salazar's death. Instead, as one member said,

> This inquest was supposed to be confined to the circumstances directly surrounding Rubén Salazar's death. Instead an attempt is being made to inculcate the public with the idea that the sheriff's deputies were justified in all their actions.[6]

The coroner's jury decided that there was no cause for criminal action against the deputy who fired into the Silver Dollar. The decision outraged not only the community, but also many Anglos who saw Salazar as a mediating force between angry militants and a recalcitrant establishment.

Most activists would not have seen Salazar as the prime martyr of the Chicano Movement a few months earlier. Other activists had been killed in Chicano Movement-related events, but few peo-

ple knew their names or the circumstances of their deaths. During 1972 Ricardo Falcón, a member of Denver's Crusade for Justice, was shot on a trip with fellow Crusaders to El Paso to attend the first national La Raza Unida convention. He had argued with a service-station attendant in Oro Grande, New Mexico. The attendant and the rest of the townspeople refused to allow Falcón's friends to call for an ambulance. During 1973 in the Imperial Valley where the UFWA and the Teamsters competed violently to organize lettuce workers, two organizers had been killed. An unknown assailant had shot and killed Juan de la Cruz on the picket line while he lunched with his wife, and Nadgi Difoala, another organizer, had died from injuries sustained in a police beating.

In spite of sharing with *movimiento* activists a desire for reform, Salazar did not identify himself as one of them any more than did Representative Edward Roybal or school board member Julián Nava. Like them, Salazar was an influential from the Mexican American generation who, because of *movimiento* influence, had intensified both his zeal for reform and pride in being Mexican. In essence, this happened to all activists from the previous era—even if they despised the militants.

Yet Salazar became the quintessential martyr of the Chicano Movement. Why? Undoubtedly his death was tragic, but his life's contributions loomed larger after his death. This, after all, is the usual path to martyrdom. But it is unlikely that any of the most salient of *movimiento* leaders—with the exception of César Chávez—would have been eulogized by all Mexican Americans, not just Chicano Movement activists, to the same degree as Salazar. More than anything else, Salazar symbolizes the ability of all U.S. Mexicans who considered themselves in a struggle for civil rights to agree that reform was necessary. Salazar's death was the perfect symbol, and it allowed the old guard to reenter the fold.

Relations between activists and the police worsened after the tragic events of August 29,

---

[6] Quoted in Marín, *Social Protest in an Urban Barrio*, p. 215.

106. Chicano Moratorium. Photo by Oscar Castillo.

1970. The LAPD and other law-enforcement agencies used *agent provocateurs*, spys, rumors and red-baiting to disrupt the *movimiento* and to discredit it. Chief Edward Davis targeted the NCMC. The most notorious infiltrator was Frank Martínez, who egged on members of the committee to commit acts of violence. Martínez admitted later that "agents of the Treasury Department's Bureau of Alcohol, Tobacco and Firearms, working in collaboration with the LAPD, ordered him 'to cause confusion. . . to provoke incidents' in order 'to eliminate' the Brown Berets and the NCMC."[7]

The police tactics accomplished their goals. Harassment of the NCMC and its Brown Beret core eventually led to its dissolution. On at least two occasions the LAPD raided the committee offices, intimidating its members, causing many to leave. The NCMC attempted to counter police intimidation with a series of protests, all of which ended in violence. The most lamentable occurred on January 31, 1971, when the LAPD fired at a crowd of rioting Chicanos, killing one and wounding thirty-five. By now, sympathizers such as the *Los Angeles Times* and the Mexican American Community Council, called for an end to NCMC activities.

Other organizations such as the Brown Berets, the Barrio Defense League and the Chicano Communications Project ceased to exist, but not before a segment of the frustrated Chicano

---

[7] Edward J. Escobar, "The Dialetics of Repression: The Los Angeles Police Department and the Chicano Movement, 1968-1971," *The Journal of American History* 79 (March 1993), p. 1505.

activist community tried terrorist tactics of its own. During 1971 a group called the Chicano Liberation Front (CLF) claimed responsibility for bombings at various Los Angeles sites. On January 31 a bomb detonated at the U.S. federal building; one person was killed. Another explosion at City Hall did not hurt anyone. The terrorist activity was relegated to a lunatic fringe by most Mexican Americans, including *movimiento* activists, and soon the wave of terror came to an end.

CONCLUSION

Rubén Salazar did not live to see the ignoble end to this first phase of the Los Angeles Chicano Movement that had started with the walkouts and ended with desperate tactics of the CLF. More than likely, he would have echoed the pleas of Esteban Torres and the Council on Mexican American Unity and even his own newspaper. Certainly, he would have been aghast at the adventurist tactics of the CLF.

The uncoordinated NCMC activities that many activists, in retrospect, saw as inviting unnecessary repression led to a maturing of the *movimiento*. Out of this process came La Raza Unida Party, which had its origins in Texas in the Mexican American Youth Organization and in Colorado's Crusade for Justice. The idea of the party was born as early as 1967 in the Albuquerque meeting attended by *movimiento* pioneers (see Chapter Ten). The only major successes in winning elections came in Texas, but the party spread to every state with a significant number of Chicanos. In Washington, D.C. and Chicago, the party also made some modest gains. When that third party died out, Marxist principles influenced the Chicano Movement, albeit among a small number, to be sure. But during its brief appearance, the issue of whether to turn to long-term revolutionary goals became a subject of great controversy.

CHAPTER TWELVE

The Youth of Aztlán

107. Denver Chicano Youth Convention. Photo by Oscar Castillo.

Chicanismo was propagated throughout the U.S. by the convening of national meetings (as shown in previous chapters), by touring theater ensembles patterned after El Teatro Campesino (see Chapter Fourteen) and through Chicano newspapers. At its apogee, the Chicano Press Association (CPA), which was established in 1969, had twenty-two members across the country; most were located in California. According to its founding document,

> The CPA is a confederation of community newspapers dedicated to promoting the movement of La Raza for self-determination and unity among our people. The CPA affirms that the time has come for the liberation of the Chicano and other oppressed people. We want the existing social order to dissolve. We want a new social order. The CPA supports the struggle against exploitation and all forms of oppression with the goal of building a new society in which human dignity, justice and brotherhood will prevail.[1]

Even though Chicanos reached out across state lines, the Chicano Movement exhibited differences that were manifested geographically, which at times created divisions. As was shown in Chapter Ten, notions of *Chicanismo* differed even between Northern and Southern California. But when *movimiento* goals expressed in Texas and Arizona are contrasted with those of California and Colorado, the variations were even greater. The *Chicanismo* of California and the Crusade for Justice in Colorado became intertwined since the first National Chicano Youth Liberation Conference was held in Denver in 1969. At the meeting, which attracted mainly California participants, the rhetoric and pronouncements resonated among students and alienated urban youth.

Among activists who received inspiration from the Denver Conference, which elaborated nationalist sentiments and ideological options and envisioned a national movement were the members of the Mexican American Youth Organization (MAYO) in Texas and Chicano organizations in Arizona. But the latter groups put more emphasis on provincial initiatives. Many of the leading Chicano Movement leaders from Texas and Arizona did not attend the Denver meeting because local issues took up all their time. José Angel Gutiérrez, who was in the midst of organizing a regional power base in South Texas, could not attend. Few of the Chicano Movement leaders from Arizona went to the meeting. In Phoenix they were busy organizing Chicanos por la Causa (CPLC—Chicanos for the Cause). This does not mean that Chicanos in these latter areas rejected such precepts as *El Plan Espirtitual de Aztlán*. More than anything, they paid it lip service and did not allow it to deter them from pursuing goals that were defined by local conditions.

THE *MOVIMIENTO* IN ARIZONA

Nonetheless, a good portion of the stimulus for the vibrant

---

[1] *La Raza*, July, 1969, clipping from the files of Edward Escobar.

movimiento activity in Texas and Arizona came through local Chicanos bringing the message from California. At the University of Arizona in Tucson, the Mexican American Student Association (MASA) was founded in 1967. One of its first members was Salomón "Sal" Baldenegro, who soon after became Tucson's most well known *movimiento* leader and a founder of a La Raza Unida Party chapter. Baldenegro learned of the Chicano Movement in Los Angeles, where his mother lived. During 1967 he stayed with her for a short time while he attended El Camino Community College. Baldenegro recalled that while there, "I came across a copy of *La Raza* and I found the address—a little storefront with this guy [Eleazar Risco as editor] who I found later was a Cubano." Baldenegro did not become involved in Los Angeles, but on his return to Tucson, the energized Baldenegro helped found MASA at the University of Arizona. He was disappointed, however, because

> Most of the kids that came to the university were middle class. . . . I'd say, "Let's do something with the [grape] boycott." They'd say, "No, the best thing that we can do is go tutoring in the community, or raise money for scholarships."[2]

It did not take long for the dissatisfied Baldenegro to influence a cadre of activists such as Raúl Grijalva and Lupe Castillo as well as other University of Arizona students with strong barrio roots. They took the *movimiento* out of the university into the Tucson streets and formed the Mexican American Liberation Committee (MALC). Their main objective became the organizing of walkouts at Pueblo and Tucson High Schools, which were predominantly Mexican American. The main grievance was the deterioration of these inner-city schools as they became increasingly Mexican in enrollment because of white flight. The walkouts did not succeed as they had in Los Angeles, i.e., in persuading large

108. Salomón "Sal" Baldenegro.

numbers of students to abandon the classroom. But the MALC-directed effort brought attention to such issues as overcrowding and the need for bilingual education and Chicano culture courses.

In the spring of 1970 the group turned to pressuring Tucson officials to convert the city-run Del Rio Golf Course, located adjacent to a west-side barrio called El Hollywood, into a people's park. This remained an issue until a community center was established in that area. The almost-daily demonstrations held to dramatize the goal of obtaining the people's park attracted hundreds of community people. Some of the MALC members were arrested in these incidents by overzealous police. Out of MALC was born the short-lived La Raza Unida Party in Tucson, which unsuccessfully ran Sal Baldenegro for a city council seat.

One of the main legacies left by MALC was a new-found cultural activism in the barrios, which

---

[2] Last two quotes from the interview with Salomón Baldenegro by Jesús Treviño, February 25, 1992, NLCC-GP.

elevated the Mexican identity of Tucson Chicanos. Barrio residents with little or no former political involvement attempted to renew their ties to their past. Isabel Dalton Urías, for example, led campaigns such as the one to declare as a national shrine "El Tiradito," a religious symbol of longstanding that had been maintained by the people.

In the Phoenix area, the California *movimiento* served as inspiration for future activists as well. In the spring of 1968 students at Tempe's Arizona State University (ASU) led by Alfredo Gutiérrez, who became enthused about the Chicano Movement after visiting Los Angeles and working with the farm-worker movement, invited San Francisco area leader Armando Valdez to speak at the campus. Without a doubt, Valdez's speech sowed the seeds of the movement at the Arizona campus. Valdez acknowledges being a "movement missionary," traveling to various areas of the Southwest, giving a "Chicano liberation" speech that became one of the icons of the movement.[3]

But as Gutiérrez said recently, "I just couldn't relate completely to his notion that Ho Chi Min was a figure that we should emulate."[4]

Despite this, planning meetings were held that summer at the apartment of Miguel Montiel, a graduate student, and as soon as fall classes convened in 1968, the core group—by then I had joined—spread leaflets throughout the campus and talked to other students to instill the ideas of *Chicanismo* and militancy in them.

Subsequently, these *movimiento* activists took over the Liga Pan Americana, a group whose origins in the 1940s lay with followers of Félix Gutiérrez's Southern California-based Mexican American Movement (MAM). The new activists changed the organization's name to the Mexican American Student Organization (MASO), which later became MECHA. The advisor of La Liga, Spanish professor María Escudero, in fact had been a MAM member when she studied at the Claremont Colleges. But she never agreed with the group's new orientation and resigned as advisor.

Before much was said about issues of identity or ideology, MASO students engaged in their first militant action. They were joined by white radical students from the Young Socialist Alliance (YSA) and Students for a Democratic Society (SDS) in occupying the president's office at ASU. The group demanded that the university sever a contract with a linen service that employed Mexicans only in menial positions. Not one Mexican American worker at this laundry was in a management or a clerical job, but all the shop-floor workers were Mexicans, Blacks or Native Americans.

The MASO students decided to tackle this issue because of their close ties to farm-worker organizer Gustavo Gutiérrez, who founded the Arizona chapter of César Chávez's UFWOC. Gutiérrez (no relation to Alfredo) also assisted Ted Caldes, a tough and weathered AFL-CIO union veteran who was in the process of organizing laundry workers in Phoenix. Caldes, whom the students met through Gutiérrez, talked them into supporting his project and also into sitting in the ASU president's office. After two days of the sit-in, university officials promised not to renew the contract. MASO became an overnight sensation after this event because no one expected such drastic action from ASU students. But many of the politically conservative Chicano students questioned a continued coalition with radical white groups. After much debate, MASO voted to break off this association.

The MASO students, like the Mexican American Liberation Committee in Tucson, quickly took the movement out of the university and united with community activists such as Joe "Eddy" López and his wife, Rosie López. Manuel Domínguez and farm-worker organizer Gustavo Gutiérrez then joined in founding a community development organization, Chicanos por La Causa (CPLC), funded by the Ford Foundation through the Southwest Council of La Raza. The

---

[3] Telephone interview with Armando Valdez by author, September 17, 1995.

[4] Interview with Alfredo Gutiérrez by author, November 12, 1995.

initial activity of the group, founded in 1969, dealt with educational issues and politics. In the summer of that year the CPLC ran a slate for an inner-city school board election consisting of an activist parish priest of Basque descent, Frank Yoldi, and other community people. The CPLC slate lost, but it provided the first electoral experience for many activists who today form the core of Chicano political leadership in Maricopa County.

The following year the CPLC organized walkouts at Phoenix Union High School. Alfredo Gutiérrez, one of the three cochairmen of MASO, had studied the 1968 Los Angeles high-school walkouts and had been impressed enough with the strategy that he helped in organizing the walkouts, which also included forming a local Brown Beret chapter. Phoenix Union High School had been a premier institution just a few years earlier when it was thoroughly integrated. By 1970, however, the student body was primarily Black and Mexican American. The main issues that provoked the walkouts were inadequate education and interracial violence.

At the university, MASO students attempted to establish Chicano studies, but conservative administrators resisted and provided an American studies program instead with Dr. Manuel Servín as director. A major cultural concern of the Chicanos at Tempe was that the Spanish they spoke be given respect. Most students, who came from nearby mining communities, agricultural towns and a sprinkling from South Phoenix, were thoroughly bilingual. But Spanish-department professors openly and derisively criticized their language usage as inferior because they used archaic terms and lacked standard Spanish writing and speaking skills. After much protest, a graduate student, Justo Alarcón, who was born in Spain, led a campaign to have courses designed for Chicano Spanish-speakers. After obtaining his Ph.D. at the University of Arizona, Alarcón returned to ASU and instituted some of the first Chicano Studies classes on the campus.

The Chicano Movement did not take hold outside of urban Arizona to the same degree that it did in California rural areas. Even the farmworker movement was limited to the Phoenix area. In October 1971 after a full four years of Chicano Movement activity, David Sánchez, one of the founders of the Brown Berets, launched la Caravana de la Reconquista (The Reconquest Caravan), a campaign which entailed traveling throughout the Southwest to create Brown Beret chapters beyond California. The caravan came to Arizona in November. In Phoenix, where the *movimiento* had made the greatest inroads, the caravan was given a lukewarm reception. Outside of Phoenix, Mexicans ignored the caravan, considered it bizarre or showed it extreme hostility.

In the semirural mining towns of Globe, Miami and Superior, Arizona (all within a seventeen-mile radius), the Brown Berets attempted to organize school walkouts using at least one native of the area who had joined the group as a liaison. According to historian Christine Marín, "In Miami. . . the Berets were creating distrust and anger among the Mexican American students" after the Mexican American principal had evicted them from the school premises.

At the Brown Beret rallies, Sánchez found that the rhetoric which had excited crowds in California fell on deaf ears. At a meeting in the Superior city park, Sánchez spoke of Raza pride and Aztlán, railed against police brutality in the mining towns and lambasted California Governor Ronald Reagan and President Richard Nixon. In a union town where Mexicans certainly had pride in La Raza, where historical protest against police mistreatment was extensive and where the anti-labor policies of Republicans were unwelcome, Sánchez's oratory did not resonate. His audience was sparse, made up of school children at play in the park, plus a few high-school students.

Later local police ejected the group from town with nary a sign of protest from the town's Mexicans. The community response to the Beret "invasion" varied from an oft-repeated Mexican American denial that racism existed to more profound ruminations of why this particular California-created manifestation did not echo local feelings. Miguel Rojo, who wrote one of many letters from Mexicans to the *Superior Sun,* proclaimed,

> The one thing we don't need. . . is. . . outsiders telling us how to think. . . . Through a

virtuous education, our own endeavors and the blessings of God, we stamped out discrimination [here]. . . . GO HOME CHICANOS! The only thing that you can do here is destroy the heritage which we have proudly built for our children and the mutual respect that exists [here] between Anglo-Saxons and Mexican Americans.[5]

THE *MOVIMIENTO* IN NEW MEXICO

New Mexico *movimiento* activity revolved around the Alianza Federal de las Mercedes, but other individuals and movements stand apart

109. *Voz Fronteriza* newspaper.

from this group which captured most of the attention. One individual was María Varela, who came to New Mexico after working with SNCC in the American South and Chicago. Her Black civil rights activity took her to California and New Mexico, where she forged links with the Chicano Movement for SNCC. On those trips, Varela met Chicano activists such as Luis Valdez and Reies López Tijerina and decided that her own people needed her energies more. Settling in New Mexico in 1968, she joined the Alianza and over the years helped found the Ganados del Valle Cooperative and the Tierra Amarilla Free Clinic. In New Mexico another out-of-state activist was Elizabeth "Betita" Martínez, who published the famous movement newspaper, *El Grito del Norte* (The Northern Call). Although many people felt this newspaper was connected to the Alianza, in reality, it attempted to run an independent course.

In Albuquerque the Black Berets were formed to work in conjunction with the publishers of *El Grito,* and the Chicano Youth Association (CYA) was started by José Armas, another newcomer to New Mexico. Reies López Tijerina's renown is one of the reasons that New Mexico attracted so many Chicano activists from outside the state. The Black Berets and the CYA however, were among the few organizations that engaged in urban-style protests, especially against police brutality. One of their most militant acts was to force their way into Governor Bruce King's office to lodge a number of grievances. They were arrested.

A more home-grown leader was Tomás Atencio. A native of Dixon, New Mexico, and a Korean war veteran who studied philosophy in California and then worked in various organizing efforts in California and Texas, Atencio returned to New Mexico in the late 1960s. By then he had acquired a great amount of Chicano Movement influence outside of the state. Once back, he organized La Academia de la Nueva Raza (The Academy of the New Race) in Santa Fe. This grassroots institute emphasized gathering knowledge

[5] Christine Marín, "Go Home, Chicanos: A Study of the Brown Berets in California and Arizona," in Manuel Servín (ed.) *An Awakened Minority: The Mexican Americans* (Beverly Hills: Glencoe Press, 1974), p. 239.

from village elders through a process called *la resolona*—informal discussions held by elders in village plazas warmed by the sun. The knowledge which Atencio and his group collected was called *oro del barrio* (barrio gold). Atencio's project demonstrated that New Mexico Chicano intellectuals used regional influences to promote cultural identity.

La Raza Unida Party chapters also sprang up in New Mexico. The main leader in this impetus was Juan José Peña, an instructor at Highlands University in Las Vegas. As in Arizona, the political activity of New Mexico's activists reflected local conditions. But in New Mexico, since many Mexican Americans were elected to political positions, the *raison d'etre* for the Chicano party, to elect Mexicans, did not seem as urgent in this state. The Alianza of Tijerina remained the premier political organization of the New Mexico Chicano Movement and, apart from the homage paid to its activities by outsiders, it had little in common with Chicano Movement ideals in California or anywhere else. In fact, Tijerina refused to use the word *Chicano*.

THE RISE OF MAYO IN TEXAS

In San Antonio, Texas, the most significant style of Chicano politics which contrasted to the California *movimiento* emerged. During the spring of 1967 in San Antonio, five young men—José Angel Gutiérrez, Mario Compeán, Nacho Pérez, Willie Velásquez and Juan Patlán—met regularly at the Fountain Room, a bar near St. Mary's University, to discuss Texas "politics, the California Chicano Movement, and conditions of Mexican Americans in general." [6]

They eventually founded the Mexican American Youth Organization (MAYO), the forerunner of the Texas La Raza Unida Party.

A political science professor at St. Mary's, Charles Cotrell, guided their politicization and provided them with non-mainstream ideas. Cotrell recalls,

> José Angel Gutiérrez, Willie Velásquez and others who were here in the late sixties were serious about the ideas they were studying because they were in a constant state of transferring and applying those ideas to their own situation, expanding them, changing them.[7]

It was under Cotrell's direction that Gutiérrez produced a master's thesis entitled "La Raza and Revolution: The Empirical Conditions of Revolution in Four South Texas Counties," which became the basis for the Winter Garden Project (WGP), an initiative that led to the founding of La Raza Unida Party in later years.

The five fledgling activists at first held informal rap sessions, then

One of the first consciousness-raising experiences for the future MAYO activists was the farm-worker march to Austin in 1966 by a Texas chapter of César Chávez's union. At that time, student José Angel Gutiérrez belonged to the Mexican American-oriented Political Association of Spanish-Speaking Organizations (PASO) at Kingsville's Texas A&I University.

"Toward the latter part of the sixties. . . the farm-workers began organizing in Rio Grande . . . . I remember first hearing about the farm workers and their plight. There was talk about a march that was going to come by Kingsville. So we organized. . . we had a PASO chapter. . . . And when the farm-worker march came through there [Kingsville], we raised funds and food and accompanied them. Mexicans just didn't march in the streets. That was the first demonstration and march that I was involved in."[8]

---

[6] Ignacio M. García, *United We Win: The Rise and Fall of La Raza Unida Party* (Tucson: MASRC, University of Arizona, 1989), p. 15. Much of the information presented on the early rise of MAYO is derived from this source.

[7] On-camera Interview with Charles Cotrell by Ray Santiesteban, October 14, 1994, NLCC-GP.

[8] On-camera interview with José Angel Gutiérrez by Hector Galán, December 12, 1994, NLCC-GP.

graduated into formal study groups and read the works of Black nationalists Stokely Carmichael, Eldridge Cleaver and Malcom X. But Chicano Movement activity elsewhere also influenced the group—Reies López Tijerina, the Crusade for Justice and, of course, events unfolding in California.

The cadre of five, of course, rejected the existing Mexican American political philosophy and strategies. Gutiérrez explained in 1969 the reasons for this rejection:

> We feel that such groups as PASO [Political Association of Spanish-speaking Organizations], GI Forum, and LULAC are too traditional in their approach to problem solving. . . . They rely heavily on the passing of resolutions, signing petitions, holding of conferences, voter registration and social activities. These tactics are ineffective and the results obtained through them are too meager.[9]

In addition, members of the group visited Black civil rights leaders in the South and other Chicano Movement leaders outside of Texas. In the process, issues that needed remedies were identified: police brutality, labor exploitation and, above all, educational problems, especially mistreatment in the schools. According to a historian of La Raza Unida Party,

> By late summer of 1967, the five had recruited other adherents, mostly high school drop outs. . . . these teen-agers had little regard for society around them and were in fact considered its failures. In the second year a third layer of youth joined. . . teen-agers in school, mostly from the poorest districts deep in the west side of San Antonio. At the same time, the five began to contact other young men around the state. . . . These men, too, came in for extensive study sessions.[10]

The result of these sessions was the development of an ideology derived from cultural nationalism. This identity-building, however, differed in

110. José Angel Gutiérrez and "Corky" Gonzales. Photo by Oscar Castillo.

significant ways from the concepts being formulated in California and in Denver. It was based more on the study of Mexican history, family values, Tejano music and on use of the Spanish language. In essence, these Texas activists did not wrestle as much with an identity crisis as the formulators of *El Plan Espiritual de Aztlán* but basically derived their ideology from their own reality and that of their parents. Hence, while they paid attention and gave lip service to the concepts that motivated the writing of the *Plan*, they chose a more pragmatic nationalism. Significantly, when MAYO activists turned to organizing La Raza Unida Party, they had fewer ideological conflicts in moving outside mainstream Chicano Movement circles.

While less likely to use the expressive symbolism of Chicanos elsewhere, the Texas activists did not eschew militancy and employed confrontational tactics to educate and obtain publicity. As Carlos Guerra, an advocate who joined the

[9] Quoted in Navarro, *Mexican American Youth Organization*, p. 81.

[10] García, *United We Win*, p. 18.

emerging group, said, the message they tried to convey was, "Hey, this is not an organization for everyone. If you can't risk everything, don't bother joining."[11]

Before they had actually adopted the MAYO name, Gutiérrez and Compeán mounted a demonstration at the Fourth of July festivities held at the Alamo Mission in 1967 and tested their strategy. Amid patriotic speeches, the two carried picket signs with the message, "What About Independence for La Raza?" The response from both Mexican Americans and Anglos celebrating the holiday was mainly apathetic, but the local media did cover the event. One of their objectives was met and the activists confidently continued to use the tactic.

During this time, organizers from César Chávez's UFWOC were unionizing farm workers in South Texas, which instantly attracted the budding MAYO activists. They joined the picket lines but also confronted the Texas Rangers, who openly harassed the pro-union workers and sympathizers. But the farm-worker struggle served the small cadre more as a source of inspiration than a permanent objective, so the group turned to other issues. By now Willie Velásquez had joined the group and organized Raza Unida conferences that attracted activists and Chicano scholars involved in the growing *movimiento* from other parts of the Southwest. These meetings were crucial in promoting José Angel Gutiérrez and the other San Antonio-based activists as the avant garde of the Chicano struggle in Texas.

Increasingly, all these ventures gave the group a sense of identity and mission and so they decided they needed to organize a formal group for themselves. After considering a number of monikers, they decided on the Mexican American Youth Organization (MAYO). A planning board was formed that met twice a year. The new organization, whose officers were elected, seemed democratic, but in reality the core leaders remained the pioneer activists who selected confi-

dants as chapter officers. This *personalismo* was common among many Chicano Movement groups and eventually the authority of many a leader was challenged.

By the time MAYO was formed officially, the group's orientation was firmly established:

> Members were expected to "put La Raza first and foremost"; to be alert. . . to have a desire to study. . . and yet be ready to articulate. . . . [It] had the aim of developing a cadre of fiercely loyal members with. . . an obsession with cultural pride. . . militant against the gringo and respectful towards La Raza.[12]

At first, established organizations such as LULAC and the GI Forum helped finance the group's efforts. A rent-free headquarters was lent to it above a drugstore. Mario Compeán became a trainer for the federally funded Volunteers in Service to America (VISTA) and used that position to recruit MAYO members to work in South Texas's poverty-stricken areas. With VISTA as a subterfuge, MAYO indirectly acquired transportation, telephones and travel funds and quickly grew to thirty chapters. Unlike the student-oriented movement in California, MAYO chapters were not as intimately linked to universities.

José Angel Gutiérrez's dream went beyond educational reform and perfecting the notion of *Chicanismo*. He and his cohorts wanted community economic development. As a consequence, the group turned to Willie Velásquez, who wrote a successful proposal to the Southwest Council of La Raza, a Ford Foundation project in order to fund the Mexican American Unity Council (MAUC). The organization, designed to help small business owners provide job training and even buy businesses outright, eventually became one of the largest Chicano economic development collectives in the country. MAUC was similar to Phoenix's Chicanos por la Causa (CPLC), an organization that still exists.

Ignacio Pérez, another of the original cadre, began an organization called the Texas Institute

[11] On-camera interview with Carlos Guerra by Robert Cozens, October 15, 1994, NLCC-GP.

[12] García, *United We Win*, p. 21.

for Educational Development (TIED). Capitalized by federal and state funds, it dedicated itself to providing health care to farm workers throughout South Texas. In later years the organization trained health professionals rather than dealing directly with the health care issues of the public.

These organizations were not greatly endowed, but in tandem with each other, they provided individual MAYO leaders the financial support to conduct their political business and a modest payroll from which MAYO organizers were paid. Subsequently, MAYO advanced the clearest objectives and strategy of any Chicano effort in the country. Devoid of torturous ideological equivocation, its simple policy was to polarize the community between Gringos and Mexicans as the fastest and best way to get quick results. Confrontational tactics, MAYO members thought, would bring repression, which in turn would politicize Mexican American fence sitters and force the accommodationist *políticos* either to relinquish their leadership mantle or to move further to the left.

The MAYO activists started *El Degüello* (The Chopping Off of Heads) in San Antonio, a newspaper that railed against gringo injustice. The choice of the term "El Degüello" was designed to antagonize Anglos because this was the bugle call (no quarter) given by Antonio López de Santa Anna when his soldiers killed all the defenders at the Alamo. Militancy against the Anglo establishment demonstrated to Texas Mexicans, whom MAYO members considered cowed, that the gringo was vulnerable. This would help eliminate fear of the gringo. Besides, in Texas, the Anglo/Mexican dichotomy was more clearly drawn, based on a longer historical relationship of antagonism than in California or Colorado, where most Mexicans and Anglos were newcomers.

In December of 1968 MAYO took on the most brutal symbol of Texas oppression by engaging in a public quarrel with Captain Y. Allee of the Texas Rangers. The U.S. Commission on Civil Rights held hearings on Texas Ranger behavior in San Antonio. The commission subpoenaed Allee to account to charges by the Mexican community of having brutally suppressed a farm-worker strike in 1967 in which a young boy was killed. The captain declined to appear, claiming MAYO members threatened his life. But José Angel Gutiérrez mocked him for not having any courage. After this gauntlet was thrown, Allee appeared at the hearing surrounded by Texas Rangers. There were so many demonstrators outside the hearing rooms, however, that the Ranger officer and his escorts had to enter the building by a side door. Regardless of how Texans viewed this episode, it was clear that some Mexicans were willing to stand up to the Rangers.

The limelight which MAYO so assiduously sought, however, also

Marta Cotera, a founder of the Jacinto Treviño Alternative College, recalled her husband's impressions in 1968 after he met José Angel Gutiérrez at a Chicano function on the University of Texas. "He said, 'I met this really crazy kid, he's worse than we are, he's talking real revolution and he's talking about a lot of political changes.'"[13]

---

[13] On-camera interview with Martha Cotera by Robert Cozens, January 18, 1995, NLCC-GP.

made the group a highly visible target. The Anglo establishment responded to the challenge posed by the new radicals by eradicating their financial base and by accusing them of threatening security. In 1969 Governor Preston Smith expelled VISTA workers from parts of South Texas, and other politicians blamed Gutiérrez and his associates of provoking the violence during the 1967 farm-worker strike.

MAYO's highly publicized antics also provoked the ire of established Mexican American *políticos,* whose support the activists did not particularly court. San Antonio's Congressman, Henry B. González, a highly successful Texas politician, lambasted the Ford Foundation on the floor of Congress in April 1969 for funding "militant groups like MAYO [who] regularly distribute literature that I can only describe as hate sheets designed to inflate passions. . . . The practice is defended as one that will build race pride, but I have never heard of pride being built on spleen."[14]

González was particularly incensed over a metaphoric "Kill-the-Gringo" speech which Gutiérrez had given to gain attention to his cause.

González's clout proved decisive in neutralizing or alienating support for MAYO from liberal funding sources and political leaders throughout Texas. In June of 1969 the Ford Foundation threatened to cut off funds from both the Mexican American Legal Defense Fund (MALDEF) and the Mexican American Unity Council (MAUC), if they continued to employ MAYO members. The organizations complied, and Gutiérrez, in fact, was fired from a research position he held with MALDEF. In spite of this setback, MAYO continued its tactics. Besides, throughout this turbulent period, the group had conducted activities that were not as dependent on outside funding. Unlike the goals formulated by student organizations in California, MAYO founders did not initially opt for reforming or rev-

olutionizing the educational system as a primary objective. In 1968 they now turned to that issue. But rather than use the courts to end segregation or friendly persuasion, as did older Mexican American groups, they employed militant tactics.

Inspired by the student strikes in Los Angeles, MAYO traveled throughout Texas, persuading students to boycott their schools. Absenteeism, they understood well, reduced federal and state funds for schools and provided boycotters with leverage. Early in 1968 the first walkout took place in San Antonio's Lanier High School, located in the west side barrio. MAYO agitation forced the west side Mexican community to express its long-held grievances, regardless of whether the community supported MAYO. After the student walkout, the philosophy towards bilingual education changed among school officials and faculty, many of whom were Mexican Americans. The educators also acknowledged that the curriculum lacked relevancy. MAYO members Mario Compeán and Ignacio Pérez served only as advisors in this protest in order to offset charges of outside agitation, but their initial efforts had sparked the incident.

Other boycotts ensued in Texas schools. The most important occurred in the Edcouch-Elsa school system in South Texas in November 1968. This one was more directly attributed to MAYO students from Pan American University. The main demands were to eradicate the no-Spanish-use rule and to introduce Mexican American content courses. Significantly, the language provision was not part of the Los Angeles walkout demands— either they were allowed to speak Spanish in Los Angeles or the students routinely spoke English. The Edcouch-Elsa effort did not succeed. School board officials refused to implement any of the demands. But according to MAYO historian Armando Navarro, "With this boycott MAYO made its debut and successfully gained a foothold in the Rio Grande Valley."[15]

The most famous Texas school boycott

---

[14] Henry B. González, "The Hate Issue," in Durán and Russell, eds., *Introduction to Chicano Studies*, pp. 561-567.

[15] Navarro, *Mexican American Youth Organization*, p. 119.

111. José Angel Gutiérrez addressing boycotters at Crystal City High School. Photo by Oscar Castillo.

occurred in Crystal City after an intensive organizing campaign by MAYO. In the spring of 1969 group members decided to return to their respective home communities and organize along Chicano Movement lines. This notion was part of the Winter Garden Project (WPG) that José Angel Gutiérrez had designed in his master's thesis. Gutiérrez and his wife, Luz, returned to their hometown of Crystal City with the conscious objective of leading Mexican Americans in taking over the community.

Besides being Gutiérrez's hometown, the community fit perfectly into what Marxist academicians at the time were calling an "internal colony." Like other agricultural areas of South Texas, the population was more than eighty percent Mexican, but the power structure in both the county and municipal governments, small businesses and the large food-processing plants was completely Anglo-American. The subordinated work force was totally Mexican, and most Mexican Americans lived in dire poverty. A small middle class of Mexicans Americans, mainly small merchants and civil servants, was the only concession allowed by the system.

Prior to José Angel Gutiérrez's transformation into a Chicano Movement advocate, a slate of five Mexican Americans, under the auspices of the Teamster's Union and the Political Association of Spanish-speaking Organizations (PASO), had run for city government and won in 1963. The Anglo establishment had underestimated the ability of Mexicans to organize and was shocked. The Anglo leaders fought back, however, first by threatening the jobs of the newly elected city council members and then by hindering day-to-day city government business. This episode left a lasting impression on a young José Angel Gutiérrez, who was then a student at a nearby community college and had participated in the campaign of this initial Mexican takeover. Gutiérrez remembers, "They began trying to indict one of the members of the council for a check that had bounced, they tried to remove two others for being late on payments of utilities—I never forgot those kind of dynamics."[16]

Soon the inexperienced Mexican council members were beleaguered and discredited. At the next election, the Anglo old guard, with its Mexican American minions, returned to power and established an almost all-Anglo municipal government. For Gutiérrez, this failure was proba-

bly the most important single event leading to the development of his particular brand of politics.

In Crystal City, then, Gutiérrez's MAYO-WGP project was aimed precisely at recovering the elusive gains of 1963. But other events intervened which brought the WGP activists into the educational realm. Over the years, as the number of Mexican American students increased at Crystal City High School, their aspirations to participate in extracurricular activities also rose. School administrators, however, through various forms of manipulation, assured that white students would dominate in these exercises. Resentment built up. In the spring of 1969 a cheerleading aspirant, Diane Palacios, aware of high-school protests in other parts of Texas, led her friends in confronting school administrators on the cheerleader selection process. "It was the one issue that. . . opened our eyes to all the discrimination that we had been living with," recalled Palacios recently.[17] Not satisfied with Principal John B. Lair's response, the

---

Severita Lara has recalled the feelings that provoked her and her student companions to walk out of Crystal City High School:

"Eighty-five percent of the [student] population was Mexican American, yet in all of our activities, like for example, cheerleaders. . . there's always three Anglos and one mexicana. . . . We started questioning. Why should it be like that?"

But the discontent went beyond extracurricular activities:

"[We] started looking at other things . . . what we're called in class . . . that *mexicanos* are just *bandidos*. . . . Whenever there were fights, it was always the *mexi-*

cano that got spanked and the Anglos never did. . . . We looked at our books. There's not a nice thing about *mexicanos*. In class, a lot of our teachers, not all of them, would tell us we would never amount to anything. . . . And we didn't have any *mexicano* teachers."

On a family visit to relatives in San Jose, California, her cousins told her about the blowouts in Los Angeles. The idea stuck with Lara. Other Crystal City students also received the same inspiration in California. Again Lara speaks: "Marcos Treviño . . . one of the seniors at the time, and his sister . . . were working over there [California] in the summer. We all got together and talked: 'When we get back, we're going to do this and we're going to do that.'"[18]

---

[16] On-camera interview with José Angel Gutiérrez by Hector Galán, December 12, 1994, NLCC-GP.

[17] On-camera interview with Diane Palacios by Robert Cozens, October 15, 1994, NLCC-GP.

[18] Interview with Severita Lara by Jesús Treviño, January 31, 1992, NLCC-GP.

girls and their supporters were ready to take more militant action. Summer came, however, so all was put on hold.

When school resumed in the fall, the issue surfaced again during the October homecoming queen elections by the Ex-Students Association. Chicano students, frustrated because of a policy that put a grade requirement on the students eligible to be candidates, decided to protest after Severita Lara, a high school leader who belonged to the WGP, wrote a pamphlet criticizing the process. School officials suspended her for three days. Then José Angel and Luz Gutiérrez joined Lara and the students in planning a school board confrontation.

The work was done mainly by Mexican women because "the men were either afraid or simply did not feel it was their role to argue before a school board."[20] Through various means of persuasion, however, the protest organizers filled the December 8 board meeting with both women and men and were able to gain concessions. The outcry in the Anglo community, however, moved the board to abrogate the compromise made with the Mexican community, and WGP members decided to use the walkout tactic, by now a standard part of Chicano Movement strategy. Gutiérrez, Luz, Virginia Músquiz and other MAYO veterans joined with local leaders on the very night the board announced that it was reneging on its promises and "went from house to house recruiting the first one-hundred students to walk out the following day."[21]

The walkouts succeeded beyond the expectations of their originators: the third day, practically all the Chicano students walked out. To offset their effectiveness, the school board closed the school early for the holidays. During the Christmas break, the group, now called the Ciudadanos Unidos (CU—United Citizens) decided to continue the boycott into the following year and held rallies in Crystal City to maintain support for the effort. More than a thousand of the town's Mexican residents attended the first gathering and were heartened to hear that other Mexicans throughout Texas and the U.S. supported their undertaking.

On January 6, 1970, the walkout ended after the school board conceded to many of the student demands, which included democratizing extracurricular activities and adding Chicano content courses. Crystal City Mexicans felt empowered, but CU leaders knew that the Anglo power structure could easily rescind these concessions. Thus, the next move for Gutiérrez and the group was to gain political power. The walkout engagement is significant not so much because it initiated educational changes, which it did, but because from its base there emerged the most important third-party movement in Texas since the

According to Diane Palacios, it was not an easy decision for parents to support the walkouts: "A lot of the families that were at the walkouts sacrificed their jobs because they were employed by Anglos or worked at El Monte, but a lot of these people believed this so much, because of what it was doing to the students, that they sacrificed and were willing to take a chance."[19]

---

[19] On-camera interview with Diane Palacios.

[20] García, *United We Win*, p. 45.

[21] Ibid., p. 47.

People's Party of the nineteenth century—La Raza Unida Party (see Chapter Thirteen).

DIFFERENCES IN THE EXPRESSION OF *CHICANISMO*

As is evident above, the Chicano Movement in California and Colorado contrasted from the way it was expressed elsewhere, especially in Texas. These dissimilarities eventually led to clashes that contributed to the inability of the *movimiento* to coalesce beyond a certain stage (see Chapter Thirteen). To understand these variances, some tentative reasons will be offered here for consideration. In urban California, where the thrust of the *movimiento* took place, Chicanos had a longer road to traverse in order to achieve ethnic cohesion. In discussing the importance of Chicano art to the movement, the artist Amalia Mesa Baines points out that the medium was necessary

> To teach people the missing history and to reclaim cultural practices that particularly in California, Chicanos were distanced from. Unlike Chicanos in Texas or New Mexico or in enclaves that had a long ongoing tradition, California Chicanos were the furthest from the original family practices. . . and in northern California even more so. [22]

To be sure, in California a large part of the Mexican population advocated a folk-level *mexicanismo,* but it was brought in by migrants from Arizona, Texas and New Mexico and did not seem to survive in the social dynamics of California beyond the first generation as much as it did in other southwestern states. The poorest Mexicans were recently arrived immigrants, predominantly single men or families with very young offspring—a community that U.S.-born Chicano youth unconsciously saw as a separate ethnic group. Ironically, the *mexicanismo* of their parents or grandparents was not shared by the younger generation. In California more than in Texas, for example, much of the motivation for the early student movement participants was derived largely from intellectual perceptions of oppression rather a personal daily contact with severe discrimination and prejudice. This motivation was constructed from history, from reports on Mexican poverty in and outside California (e.g., the Grebler, Guzmán, Moore UCLA study)[23], from Vietnam casualty statistics, from political contact with the farmworker movement, from accounts of police brutality and from demeaning depictions of Mexicans in the media. What California Chicano students did experience directly was an identity crisis.

Yet, California Chicano activists, as shown in previous chapters, like members of all ethnic movements historically, required cultural assertion

In 1969 when the United Mexican American Students (UMAS) at UCLA needed funding to bring in Chicano speakers, Rosalío Muñoz remembers that "Moctezuma [Esparza] buttonholed me...and he says 'you're going to be in the movement.' He says, 'Look at yourself. . . *eres indio.* Look in the mirror. You're part of this whole thing.' So I got a bit more involved and felt a little bit more connected."[24] Also in taking a history course with Dr. Juan Gómez-Quiñones, Muñoz wrote a paper on agricultural workers in the 1930s that made him aware of the exploitation of Mexicans by California farmers. By the time UCLA students elected him president of the student body, Muñoz, whose teacher-father was active in Mexican Americanism, became part of the Chicano Movement. He subsequently became one of the organizers of the National Chicano Moratorium.

---

[22] Interview with Amalia Mesa Baines by Susan Racho, February 7, 1992, NLCC-GP.

[23] Leo Grebler, Joan W. Moore and Ralph Guzmán, *The Mexican American People: The Nation's Second Largest Minority* (New York: Free Press, 1970).

[24] Interview with Rosalío Muñoz.

and ethnic pride to propel them into taking the difficult steps to militancy and confrontational politics. Taking the seemingly successful African-American path to bolstering identity and pride, they focused on racial differences between themselves and Anglos, more than cultural differences, for identity development. But California Chicanos claimed extreme contrasts between themselves and Anglos, so the political stew needed cultural content. Not being conversant or interested in the folksy Mexicaness of older generations, myth-making ensued on a large scale. California was a hothouse for cultivating alternative lifestyles, an atmosphere that also stimulated identity experimentation.

As a consequence, Chicanos felt the identity crisis could be corrected by elaborating a self-image based on victimization, their racial characteristics, a pre-Columbian past and street-youth culture more than on the folk *mexicanismo* of their parents and grandparents. Ironically, the freedom and ability to function in mainstream culture, with its vast array of intellectual options, was an important foundation in California Chicano identity politics. The most important manifestation of this process was *El Plan Espiritual de Aztlán*, written at the Denver youth conference mainly by Californians. With its strong emphasis on race pride and provisions for an independent, separate spiritual plane for Chicanos, it became the constitution of the California *movimiento*.

Outside urban California, in communities where a youth culture which was an extension of previous *mexicano* generations was more intense, young Chicanos had grown up in an environment where not only were they unrewarded for being brown, but they were more categorically denigrated for being *very* Mexican, *very* poor, for having a Spanish first name, for speaking English with an accent, for wearing "Mexican" clothing, for taking *burritos* as school lunches and for living in dilapidated barrios, which contrasted radically with the ways Anglos lived. In Texas and Arizona, for example, school authorities consistently forbade Mexican youth to speak Spanish in schools. Basically, in these communities the division between Mexicans and Anglos was clear. In urban

California, the delineation was not that sharp while in Texas and Arizona an ethnic dichotomy served to create an acute resentment of a well-defined Gringo group. This was especially true in South Texas.

Mexican American students were also more politically and socially conservative outside of California, embedded as they were with the previous generation's values and outlook. And living under more repressive conditions, they had a greater fear of Anglo authority. In urban California, where the counterculture movement more successfully discredited the Establishment, Chicanos found it easier to eschew the middle-class values and dignified behavior which had been embraced by California Mexican American college students in the past (see Chapter Six).

In Texas, New Mexico and Arizona, then, the transition to militancy and confrontation was even more difficult to make; it did happen, nonetheless. But healthy doses of home-grown nationalism were necessary before this process could run its full course. Unlike in California, however, in these states there was less discussion of ideology among activists, and Chicano youth did not concentrate as much on dignifying an unrewarded *mestizo* race trait. They did romanticize their *mexicanismo*, a generational extension of their parents' culture and, to be sure, injected it with some California-generated myths. But Tejano Chicano nationalism, for example, ranked "Little Joe" y La Familia band in its pantheon of *movimiento* emblems ahead of Aztlán and *La raza de bronce*. In Tucson the emphasis was on local *tucsonense* culture while in New Mexico Tomás Atencio's efforts to romanticize village life resonated the most.

Moreover, resentment and dislike of Gringos was a given in states like Texas. In essence, as the rise of MAYO indicates in Texas, Chicanos had a head start in the arena of nationalism because of all the conditions discussed above. This provided them with the stamina to use confrontational and militant action. Finally, this dynamic helps explain why in the regions where repression had been the greatest—e.g., Texas—activists chose a more pragmatic approach; they were hungrier for material rather than cultural gains.

CONCLUSION

The two concepts of Chicano nationalism related above existed only in general contours and do not really fit neatly into a surgically divided geographic dichotomy. The only thesis pursued here is that one region had more of one portion of influence than the other. For example, Imperial Valley Mexican communities in California shared conditions akin to those in Arizona and Texas. It is also true that Chicano college students who became involved in Texas did not come from the poorest parts of their communities. But they still experienced the conditions of oppression more directly—the case of José Angel Gutiérrez is a perfect example.

We do know that low wages, poor educational attainments and inadequate housing were not as great in California as in other border states, especially Texas. The pathbreaking 1966 UCLA Mexican American Study Project demonstrated this. Mexicans, nonetheless, did not have parity with Anglos anywhere, not even in California. Moreover, just because almost castelike conditions in Texas and Arizona allowed Anglos greater latitude in repressing Mexicans that does not negate the fact that, in urban California, law-enforcement agencies and other institutions discriminated against Chicanos.

In the final analysis, the overall motivation of the *movimiento* was to give dignity and a positive identity to *los de abajo* (underdogs)—even if individual activists were not as directly affected as the *carnales* and *carnalas* (brothers and sisters in Chicano slang) they sought to help. Additionally, assimilation to Anglo society was equally rejected by all Chicano Movement participants, regardless of what source they used for their nationalism.

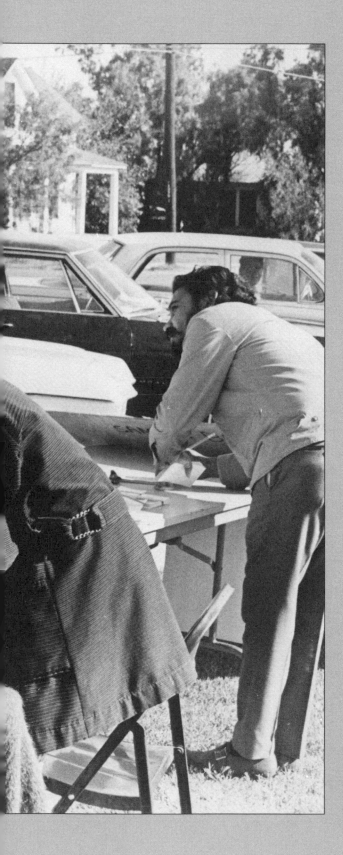

CHAPTER THIRTEEN

The Road to Political Empowerment

112. La Raza Unida Party registering voters in Crystal City. Photo by Oscar Castillo.

An enduring legacy left by the Mexican American generation was faith in the ballot box. But for a brief period in the beginning of the Chicano Movement, some leaders militantly rejected participation in politics as usual. One of these was Rodolfo "Corky" Gonzales, a one-time insider in Denver's Democratic Party machine. Without having an inkling that he would help forge the Chicano Movement, Gonzales resigned from the party in 1965 because, as he put it,

> I became disenchanted with the electoral system and disenchanted with the two political parties. And I recognized in my character that I could not compromise. Yes, I understood that politics is a game of compromise. I felt there were other people who could negotiate and do much better than I could. I felt more comfortable going home, even though financially I could have named my post or price.[1]

Instead, Gonzales went on in 1966 to found the Crusade for Justice (CFJ), which he and his supporters considered a civil rights organization without involvement in electoral politics. Another factor motivating Gonzales to quit was his dismissal as director of Denver's War on Poverty Program because he favored Mexicans over Blacks and whites.

A CHICANO QUIXOTIC QUEST?

Eventually, Gonzales became one of the founders of the unsuccessful Congreso de Aztlán, a vehicle which proposed a national Chicano political party to unite the Mexican American vote under one banner. This decision, according to the CFJ leader, did not betray his principle of "not working within the system" because it stayed within his philosophy of not collaborating in the two-party system. More than any other leader, Gonzales had been attempting to provide coordination and leadership to a potentially powerful but rudderless Chicano initiative. The idea for a Chicano party, as indicated in Chapter Ten, was

probably born at a pioneer youth conference called by Reies López Tijerina in 1967. After victorious campaigns in Texas in 1970, a spate of La Raza Unida Party (LRUP) groups appeared in a number of states, including Colorado. The party chapters, however, existed without national coordination. Many of them in reality were extensions of regional Chicano Movement drives with disparate agendas.

To rectify this lack of coordination, "Corky" Gonzales called for a national convention of the loose federation of LRUP entities for September of 1972. Invited were José Angel Gutiérrez and other members of the Texas LRUP who had run the successful South Texas elections and who were in the midst of a statewide campaign to elect a gubernatorial candidate. Gonzales also invited Reies López Tijerina, the New Mexico land-grant crusader, who had recently been released from prison. In bringing the LRUP factions together, Gonzales seized the reins of an idea that was more successfully being implemented in Texas.

By 1972 Gonzales was to become the main catalyst in promoting a national *movimiento*. Tijerina, his closest rival, had been removed from contention by his imprisonment and, upon his release, he had projected a zaniness and mysticism that worried even his most fanatic supporters. Union leader Cesár Chávez, the third renowned Chicano Movement leader, acquired that honor de facto—he never sought it nor did he show interest in the Chicano Movement per se. The MAYO activist and founder of the Texas LRUP, José Angel Gutiérrez, was at this point only an emerging notable. So Gonzales was for the time being alone in the field.

Gonzales's ambition to become the national leader of the *movimiento* had a long history. The hugely successful 1969 National Chicano Liberation Youth Conference sponsored by his CFJ was the first step in this process of consolidation and coordination. Then, by consistently engaging in other nationally prominent activities and by

---

[1] Interview with Rodolfo "Corky" Gonzales by Daniel Salazar, October 4, 1984, NLCC-GP.

113. Cover of *I Am Joaquín*, by Rodolfo "Corky" Gonzales.

disseminating his poem, *I Am Joaquín*, which became the *movimiento* anthem, Gonzales solidified his support. In August of 1969 the CFJ sponsored the Chicano Unity Conference. Its purpose was "to unite the various elements of the Chicano communities and their allies throughout the Southwest towards massive school walkouts on September 16, Mexican Independence Day."[2] The day would be known as "Chicano Liberation Day." In Denver the walkouts were highly successful, according to *El Gallo*, the official CFJ publication. The newspaper estimated that six to eight thousand students stayed out of class. It is unknown to what degree the call was heeded in

other areas, but in Hayward, California, more than one thousand students honored the boycott, according to the *Militant*, the Socialist Worker's Party newspaper.

Even if these agenda-propelled newspapers had exaggerated the turnouts, this action brought the CFJ more prominence among *movimiento* adherents. In November Gonzales traveled to Hayward, where his leadership was definitely acknowledged by area Chicano Movement pacesetters such as Armando Valdez, founder of the Mexican American Student Confederation (MASC) in the Bay Area, and Peter Camejo, a Socialist Worker's Party stalwart who later started a LRUP chapter in Northern California. At Hayward, Gonzales spoke at a Chicano symposium attended by some five hundred predominantly Northern California students. At the second National Chicano Liberation Youth Conference held in March of 1970, Gonzales now considered himself the unchallenged *movimiento* trailblazer for the formation of a national Chicano party; at the same time Texas's MAYO organization was establishing its own version of the LRUP.

It is possible that Gonzales decided to imitate the successful political party that was catapulting José Angel Gutiérrez and the other Texas "newcomers" to the *movimiento* limelight in order to forestall their meteoric ascendency. Nonetheless, within a short period of intense organizing, the CFJ built a formidable LRUP infrastructure. The Colorado strategy consisted of holding a number of conventions throughout the state in order to reach as many people as possible. The first convention was held at the University of Southern Colorado in Pueblo on May 16, 1970—only a month after the successful South Texas elections. It attracted eight hundred participants. At that meeting, the delegates nominated candidates under the LRUP banner to run for state offices. Albert Gurulé was selected as the entrant for the gubernatorial race in Colorado. Two weeks later a second meeting was

[2] Marín, *A Spokesman of the Mexican American Movement*, p. 14.

held in Denver, which designated even more nom-
inees for statewide and local posts. A third nominating convention was held in June to choose the
last of the LRUP hopefuls. The fourth and last par-
ley was held in July of 1970 to hammer out the
final platform; some one thousand participants
attended. For the most part, Gonzales's strategy at
these meetings consisted of little more than vague
promises of self-determination and cultural nationalism. But these resonated among a significant
portion of Colorado's Mexicans.

The LRUP, however, was not successful in
converting the enthusiasm exhibited in these
meetings into an electoral vote-getting machine.
Anticipating the August 29 Chicano Moratorium
in Los Angeles, speakers at the convention, many
of whom were candidates for office, delivered
speeches mainly on liberation or spoke out
against the war rather than addressing issues that
would attract rank-and-file voters to their cause.
For example, the candidate for state treasurer,
Juan Valdez, did not even address Colorado fiscal
issues. Instead he delivered a resounding con-
demnation of the war in Vietnam.

When the Colorado state attorney general,
Duke Dunbar, complained that some of the LRUP
candidates did not meet age requirements for
office, Gonzales countered by saying that his
group did not recognize Dunbar's authority to
make such a determination. This response in retrospect indicated that, rather than winning elections, political theater to raise consciousness was
foremost among the objectives of the Colorado
LRUP. The party's platform also reflected
Gonzales's incessant hammering on the need for
"Chicano liberation and self-determination" and
touched on issues that always punctuated
Gonzales's speeches: inadequate housing, police
brutality, land reform, redistribution of wealth,
opposition to the Vietnam War and noncoopera-
tion with the established state.[3]

But Gonzales did have solid objectives.

Foremost among them was to consolidate his
power within the Chicano Movement so that he
could plant the seeds of separatism. There is no
doubt that at this point he had no faith in the system's ability to solve problems. According to
Ignacio M. García,

> Gonzales. . . did not believe that Chicanos
> could work through. . . channels or would be
> allowed to systematically take control. The
> only alternative, then, was to develop La
> Raza's *conciencia* of its right to be free to a
> degree that would force a break. . . between
> Chicanos and the Anglo nation in which they
> lived.[4]

Come election day, the hard reality of electoral politics hit home: the Colorado LRUP lost its
electoral races by huge margins. The largest vote
count for the LRUP was only 5 percent in the
contest for the University of Colorado Board of
Regents. For other offices, party candidates
acquired totals ranging from only 1.8 to 3.5 percent of the vote. Considering the narrow message
provided by the LRUP campaign, these voters
were probably true believers in the Chicano
Movement. Despite this significant loss, Gonzales
announced the results as a victory and offered to
serve as a broker in the electoral process:

> We won the biggest number of votes that
> (has) been given to an independent party in
> the state of Colorado. . . . We've put on the
> line every social problem that the Mexicano
> has. . . . Both parties. . . came out with more
> Chicano candidates. . . . This resulted in two
> Chicanos being elected to the state House of
> Representatives.[5]

But while the LRUP did not attract a wide
range of Colorado Mexican voters, Gonzales was
determined to use electoral campaigns to muster
support for his vision of a national Chicano party.
However, Gonzales's arrest at the August 29
moratorium forced him to put that ambition on

[3] Marín, *A Spokesman of the Mexican American Movement*, p. 18.

[4] Ignacio M. García, *United We Win*, p. 102.

[5] Quoted in Marín, *A Spokesman of the Mexican American Movement*, pp. 22-23.

hold (see Chapter Eleven). At the third National Chicano Liberation Youth Conference in June of 1971, this concept began to take firmer shape. Gonzales invited José Angel Gutiérrez to give the keynote speech. Although the Texas LRUP stalwart was now beginning to rival Gonzales in national stature within the *movimiento*, the two seemed to agree on the need for a Chicano political entity that would never make compromises with traditional parties.

In the meantime, the LRUP concept had spread to other areas in such states as Arizona, California, New Mexico, Illinois, Wisconsin and Nebraska. In Tucson, Arizona, for example, Salomón "Sal" Baldenegro ran for city council in 1971 after a crusade to turn the Del Rio Golf Course into a "Chicano Park" began to get stale (see Chapter Twelve). Baldenegro states, "We asked ourselves 'Why is the city council not being responsive to us?. . . Because in this area [west Tucson], which is 90 percent Chicano, we never had a Chicano representative.' So we got together and decided someone had to run for city council and 'We'll run it as Raza Unida.'"[6] Baldenegro lost in his bid for a council seat, even in the "90-percent Chicano" west side barrios. Raúl Grijalva, one of the main LRUP organizers in Arizona, later became a successful politician only after shedding all aspects of LRUP affiliation and the *movimiento* rhetoric.

The greatest development of the LRUP outside of Texas and Colorado took place in California. The first LRUP group in that state appeared in Oakland in November 1970. It espoused the now standard LRUP line that "La Raza Unida will not support any candidate of the Democratic or Republican Party or any individual who supports these parties." California's LRUP preamble demonstrated its objectives of paralleling those of the Colorado organization, which was not necessarily to win elections but to raise political awareness among Chicanos. It stated that liberation could only come through action, not through mainstream politics. It also affirmed that "independent political action, of which electoral activity is but one aspect, means involving La Raza Unida Party at all levels of struggle, in action which will serve to involve and educate our people."[7]

Soon LRUP chapters existed throughout California, but unlike in Texas and Colorado, the idea spread informally rather than through a coordinated effort from a central clearinghouse. Members from these localized chapters met in regional conferences but made little progress in integrating the project statewide. At one of these gatherings at Oakland's Merritt College, José Angel Gutiérrez delivered a speech dismissing the emphasis on developing ideology as counterproductive. He felt that relying on an already existing familialism and Chicano brotherhood was all the ideology needed. For Gutiérrez, getting votes and influencing party politics was paramount, a point of view that became the hallmark of his pragmatic approach.

In 1971 the emerging California LRUP received a tremendous boost when Bert Corona, the veteran labor leader and MAPA organizer, lent his support. A long-time Mexican American era stalwart, Corona saw in the LRUP an opportunity to force the Democratic Party to account to California's Mexican community. An effective orator, Corona spoke on behalf of the LRUP at various locations in California, giving the movement a needed boost. In essence, Corona tried to sell Mexican American middle-class *políticos* on the LRUP concept, but his notion differed from that of "Corky" Gonzales and his followers in California. Corona saw the party as a vehicle for "maximum bargaining power," implying that it should eventually wrest concessions from one of the two parties.[8] In reality, the strategy was little different from what MAPA had done for years. Still, LRUP activists were

---

[6] Interview with Salomón Baldenegro.

[7] Both quotes in Muñoz, *Youth, Identity, Power*, pp. 107-109.

[8] García, *United We Win*, p. 100.

not about to look the proverbial gift horse in the mouth. Besides, Corona did not try to join the LRUP or meddle in its internal affairs.

In 1971 the California LRUP also entered into electoral engagement by fielding candidates. However, the attempt to achieve ballot status at the state level by filing petitions with the requisite number of signatures failed. This was one of many indications that the party was not sufficiently organized or experienced to meet such mundane requirements. Moreover, ideological orientations divided local chapters, hindering coalescing; even members within an individual chapter were often at odds on strategy and ideology. Strategically, LRUP chapters split between those who wanted to win campaigns, *al lo tejano,* and those who followed "Corky" Gonzales's example of using the party to raise consciousness levels.

The only election in which a LRUP candidate made an impressive showing was in Oakland's school board election in which a party candidate garnered thirty-three percent of the vote. The LRUP's showings throughout the rest of the state were dismal. As a consequence, California party members, consciously or unconsciously, followed the Colorado tack of losing and then turning the result into a victory; e.g., a loss, even when they wanted to succeed, could be explained away as an educational campaign.

But in Los Angeles party organizers saw an opportunity to win because of the city's large Mexican population. Raúl Ruiz, publisher of *La Raza* magazine and a college instructor who ran for the California Assembly, mounted the most formidable LRUP race. If Ruiz had not entered the contest, Richard Alatorre, a Mexican American Democrat favored to win, would have been cast only against Republican Bill Brophy. Ruiz only received seven percent of the vote, but that was enough to force a runoff election between Alatorre and Brophy, which the latter won. California LRUP organizers interpreted the results as a victory while Mexican American Democrats became bitter enemies of the upstarts who had spoiled their chances.

"CASI LLEGAMOS"—THE TEJANO BID

In Texas the LRUP, founded by MAYO's youthful organizers, forged a more pragmatic effort. The resounding success of the Crystal City High School walkouts in December 1969 brought José Angel Gutiérrez acclaim from Chicano Movement participants throughout the country. This allowed Gutiérrez a temporary shield from criticism as well as leeway in establishing national *movimiento* priorities. The MAYO activists "were being besieged with invitations to join the Democratic Party and change it from within," notes Ignacio García.[10] However, MAYO members leaned towards testing their ability, using the 1963 Crystal City

Looking back on why he endorsed the La Raza Unida Party, Bert Corona demonstrates that the Chicano Movement was not that far afield from the aspirations of his Mexican American generation. "I saw the Raza Unida Party as the beginning of the fullfillment of issues that were still on the agenda, that had been raised by Mexicano young people, young leaders back in the '30s, when the Mexican American Movement was formed. So I saw with the rise of this new generation in the '60s, a desire to build a political machine that would carry that burden of pushing reform, adopting of new changes, and bringing these issues forth to reality. I saw it as a great opportunity."[9]

[8] On-camera interview with Bert Corona by Ray Santiestaban, December 22, 1994, NLCC-GP.

[10] García, *United We Win*, p. 53.

victory as an example to gain real electoral power for Chicanos (see Chapter Twelve for a study of the 1963 takeover).

To appeal to the at-large Texas Mexican community, MAYO used shock tactics that garnered publicity but did not attract rank-and-file support. Wooing a general electorate differed drastically from political drama designed to draw attention to issues. A MAYO faction lead by Gutiérrez encouraged its members to shun "counterculture antics" that characterized much of the youthful *movimiento* behavior such as posturing as *vato locos* (crazy street dudes) espousing extremist rhetoric and cultural nationalism.

Gutiérrez espoused a militant cultural-nationalist approach, but one that resonated among Texas Chicanos. By now, the established Gutiérrez line was that the new party could appeal to moderate Texas Mexicans. In addition to rejecting counterculture antics, Gutiérrez distanced himself from Marxist rhetoric and solutions that could confuse the people. As Gutiérrez put it, "You don't come with your own agenda; we tried that. We tried coming in and telling people to fight against imperialism, colonialism and capitalism—that was like talking moon talk."[11]

To initiate the new electoral crusade, the Crystal City LRUP targeted the school board and the city council. On the school board, three out of five positions were to be selected in the April 1970 election. Gutiérrez decided to seek one of the seats, and the party chose Mike Pérez, a dance-hall owner, and Arturo González, a gas station attendant, to run for the other two. That same year the LRUP also fielded candidates for all of the open positions in Hidalgo, Zavala, Dimmit and La Salle Counties. Finding candidates to take the challenge proved difficult, however, because Mexicans understandably were afraid of repercussions from the Anglo power base if they ran under the LRUP banner.

The Crystal City Council had two positions open for the April election. Del Monte Company employee Ventura González and an auto parts store manager, Pablo Puente, were chosen to run by the LRUP. County officials disqualified Puente because he did not own property, but with the help of the Mexican American Legal Defense and Education Fund, the party reinstated his candidacy. LRUP opposition, which consisted mostly of the Winter Garden area's Anglos and some middle-class Mexican Americans, ran a slate of Mexican American candidates under the Citizens Association Serving All Americans (CASAA). In the meantime, the school board attempted to diffuse Mexican community resentment by reassigning the administrators who had most irked the Mexican American community during the school walkouts. The ploy was too little too late (see Chapter Twelve for walkouts in Crystal City).

José Angel Gutiérrez talks about how the 1963 Crystal City victory and the defeat that followed affected him: "I was one of the ones who received some patronage from that victory. . . . And I was the parks and recreation director, which meant I was in charge of the swimming pool. . . . I had the responsibility of having to throw out drunks. . . from the swimming pool and parks when they misbehaved. And it was very scary [some were Anglos]. And here I was, all of 18, and my government was crumbling [the newly elected council of Mexicans]. . . all being split asunder."[12]

[11] Ibid., p. 55.

[12] Interview with José Angel Gutiérrez by Jesús Treviño, January 27, 1992, NLCC-GP.

To discredit the LRUP campaign, CASAA pointed incessantly to José Angel Gutiérrez's record of militancy and hinted that, he was a Communist. It also charged that if elected, the humble background of the LRUP candidates augured poor performance and irresponsibility. On the day before the election, CASAA hired an airplane to drop thousands of leaflets with excerpts of a Gutiérrez speech criticizing the Catholic Church. The leaflet accused him of atheism. In turn, the LRUP concentrated on discrediting the Mexican American candidates as *vendidos* and boycotting businesses of uncooperative Mexicans.

On April 4 a record voter turnout gave the LRUP fifty-five percent of the vote, enough to seat Gutiérrez, González and Pérez on the school board. Three days later, slightly more than half of the voters elected the LRUP candidates to the city council. There were victories outside of Zavala County as well. Interspersed with their campaigning in Crystal City, Gutiérrez and other LRUP activists had spurred organizing in neighboring areas. In Cotulla, a town north of Crystal City, the party succeeded in placing its candidates on the school board. Also, Alfredo Zamora defeated Paul Cotulla, descendent of the town's founders, in the mayoral race. In addition, the mayor's office and two city council positions fell to LRUP-backed candidates in Carrizo Springs. "Chicanos were in a state of jubilation and euphoria. Gutiérrez. . . reacted by enthusiastically predicting that the LRUP would create 'Crystals' everywhere," writes the chronicler of MAYO, Armando Navarro.[13]

In the spring of 1970 the *movimiento* was at its apogee. The Denver Youth Conference the previous year had forged a national network of Chicano activists who easily communicated with each other. As Crystal City voters went to the polls, Rosalío Muñoz, from the National Chicano Moratorium Committee, was strengthening Chicano links across the nation as he organized

for the antiwar rally to be held in Los Angeles on August 29. The electoral achievements catapulted the LRUP, MAYO and Gutiérrez into a national prominence that made the attention they received after the walkouts pale by comparison and installed them solidly in the pantheon of Chicano Movement heroes. According to Ignacio M. García,

> The victory in Crystal City reverberated throughout Aztlán in communities similar in size, in urban centers, and in universities where Mexican Americans came together. The successful revolt symbolized what Chicanos everywhere could achieve with hard work and well-planned strategies. Within days of his election, Gutiérrez received several calls from Chicano activists nationwide. . . .Crystal City became a sort of political Mecca for Chicanos.[14]

But not all Mexicans in Texas supported such a brash assertion of Chicano power. Democratic Congressman Henry B. González, who had harshly attacked MAYO in previous years, saw the LRUP victory as ephemeral. It was based on "race pride," which he deemed a "slender and volatile glue upon which to build a political power base." LRUP's polarization of the white and Mexican communities could also backfire in the form of a backlash. Willie Velásquez, one of the original MAYO members who went on to found the Southwest Voter Registration Program as a Democrat, concluded that "ethnic movements and third parties were ill-fitted to survive in American politics." After resigning under pressure from MAYO, Velásquez "described himself as a Jeffersonian Democrat who believed in the system."[15]

After LRUP Chicanos came to power in Crystal City, significant changes took place. The school system hired more Mexican American teachers, the curriculum accommodated Mexican American studies, patronage was extended and free lunch programs were implemented. To finance the new system, the new administration

[13] Navarro, *Mexican American Youth Organization*, p. 223.

[14] García, *United We Win*, pp. 59-60.

[15] Ibid., pp. 60-61.

114. La Raza Unida Party campaign signs in Crystal City. Photo by Oscar Castillo.

sought out federal funding on a large scale and in the process made bargains that later led to charges of collaboration with the enemy. The local Anglo establishment, however, did not take all these changes lying down. Gutiérrez recalls,

> The Anglo community never gave up. They continued to fight. Their reaction was similar to what happened in the Black south when integration and the end of segregation occurred. White flight occurred out of the traditional institutions. . . . White Catholics opted for a different mass and even moved out, wouldn't go to church. . . . They [not just white Catholics] created their own private schools. . . transferred to neighboring school districts. . . many of them fired people [LRUP supporters] to see if that would scare us with economic sanctions. . . . They tried every machination in the book. It just made us stronger because we were enjoying the

power.[16]

The buoyant LRUP then set their sites on the November elections to compete for offices (sixteen in all) where Mexicans constituted a majority in communities throughout the Winter Garden area: in Dimmitt, La Salle and Zavala Counties. LRUP organizers knew that victories in these districts would establish the party as a permanent force in Texas. Massive organizing campaigns were launched. The opposition, however, also mustered a strategy to defeat the upstart Chicanos, believing that the Crystal City establishment had been caught off guard and that the majority of responsible Mexican Americans did not want the young radicals to represent them.

The main strategy used by the Anglo-run Democratic Party to head off the Chicano challenge was to mire it down in red tape. Since the

---

[16] Interview with José Angel Gutiérrez.

115. Muñiz banner at the La Raza Unida Party nominating convention. Photo by Oscar Castillo.

LRUP organizers had little experience in dealing with political bureaucracies, the strategy worked. One of the favorite tactics was having officials disqualify many of the nominating petitions, which denied LRUP candidates ballot status, supposedly because of "irregularities." In spite of spirited court challenges, election day arrived and the party entrants were not included on the ballots. The group had no choice but to attempt a write-in campaign. But a number of other obstacles were imposed, including illegal literacy campaigns and harassment at the polls. The result was a robust defeat. Of the fifteen seats that the LRUP vied for in the four-county region, it won only one. The euphoria of the April elections turned to bitter disappointment, but LRUP organizers rebounded, feeling determined to succeed. They were also becoming better acquainted with political realities.

After the April victories, Gutiérrez and the LRUP envisioned fielding candidates in state-level elections during 1972. This included nominating an aspirant for governor. The resounding November 1970 defeats, however, sobered up the LRUP leadership. While publicly maintaining enthusiasm for the effort, in private the leaders had misgivings about the efficacy of this approach; they began to believe that it was necessary to obtain local power first, region by region. José Angel Gutiérrez knew that the party lacked resources and, except for a few chapters in the Winter Garden area, most of the statewide groups were without political connections or constituencies.

When the LRUP faithful gathered in San Antonio in October of 1971 to assess their future, most members were convinced that a statewide campaign was possible. But the now more experienced Gutiérrez recommended the prudent approach, i.e., winning local contests before embarking on statewide campaigns. Mario Compeán, however, mustered support among the participants for the more ambitious option. Compeán agreed that organization beyond Crystal City and the few South Texas communities was fragile. But Compeán argued that a dramatic state-level campaign would serve as a catalyst to Chicanos who hungered for representation; it would also rally resources and volunteers faster than would regional offensives. It did not take much to sell this idea to a young *movimiento* constituency, whose rapidly growing enthusiasm did not leave much time for serious pondering of political realities. Compeán's position won out and Gutiérrez accepted the outcome in good spirits.

Now the search to find candidates for state posts was on. For the gubernatorial candidacy, LRUP leaders at first made overtures to prominent Mexican Americans who heretofore had not been associated with the party in order to attract mainstream support. They had no takers. When none of the party's insiders showed any interest in running for this highest of Texas posts, an informal procedure resulted in the selection of Ramsey Muñiz, a Waco lawyer who was peripherally involved with MAYO. It appears that the group chose him as a last resort after almost all other options had been exhausted.

To the luck and surprise of the LRUP insiders, the Muñiz choice turned out to be as good as if the LRUP had selected him through a public relations firm. Tall, well-built and good-looking, the former starter with the Baylor University football team projected an attractive and imposing figure. The well-dressed Muñiz would not alienate the more conservative Mexican voters in a Texas where all people, regardless of race, love their football. As his running partner, and as a concession to the women's caucus within the LRUP, Alma Canales, a MAYO activist from Edinburg and a leader in the Edcouch-Elsa high-school walkouts, was asked to run for lieutenant governor. Muñiz's faction was cool towards Canales because she projected a radical image that would chase away votes rather than attract them.

Canales, however, was supported by Compeán and other LRUP purists, who found compromise alien to their ideals. The eager Muñiz started campaigning almost immediately after he had announced as a candidate and went to every corner of Texas that held out a promise.

In June 1972 the slate was approved at the LRUP state convention, where Muñiz was presented to the at-large membership, many of whom had never met him but were suspicious of his lack of nationalistic fervor. At that meeting, however, the gubernatorial hopeful demonstrated a capability for winning over whatever audience he was speaking to. He used a militant tone that LRUP membership expected. At the same time, he looked polished and, alongside his attractive wife, Albina, he projected an image that mainstream politicians try to conjure.

The immediate challenge facing the LRUP, however, was to gather the necessary signatures to get on the ballot, a process which seemed to falter until Muñiz attracted a larger following of new volunteers. Still, the party did not meet the quota and party members had to falsify a great number of the signatures. After the primaries, Muñiz was pitted against rancher Dolph Briscoe, a conservative who had won the Democratic primary in a tight race against Frances "Sissy" Farenthold, a liberal. The Republicans nominated Henry Grover and were hopeful from the beginning that the LRUP would serve as a "spoiler" for Briscoe and the Democrats.

The LRUP welcomed the result of the Democratic primary because disenchanted liberal voters might be attracted. But Farenthold's camp was resentful, believing that the thousands of LRUP supporters might have opted for Farenthold over Briscoe if they had voted in the Democratic primary. LRUP organizers had asked supporters not to register as Democrats so that they could sign the LRUP nominating petitions. The Farenthold liberals, which included a significant group of Mexican Americans, never forgave the LRUP for this supposed betrayal. Sissy Farenthold remembers that she stood for issues that were dear to Texas Mexican Americans such as abolition of the Texas Rangers: "Mexican Americans, certainly in South Texas, had been my primary constituents." Nonetheless, she regrets,

> I was really left out to sort of twist in the wind. . . . So they didn't vote in the primary. . . those that saved their vote for Ramsey. . . . I am philosophical about it. I mean, the time has gone by, but I do have some ambivalence. . . . And maybe in the long run. . . they gained more by going their separate way. . . . Maybe there was a need for it. Certainly for those young leaders. . . . So I presume its part of the entire political process.[17]

During his campaign, Muñiz crisscrossed Texas accompanied by Albina, attempting to persuade Mexicans to change their Democratic voting ways and to woo disaffected white liberals and Black leaders. Indeed, the Reverend Ralph Abernathy, who inherited the helm of the Southern Christian Leadership Conference from Martin Luther King, endorsed Muñiz for governor. Most Texas liberals shied away from the LRUP, but as election day approached, some chose to support Muñiz over the conservative Dolph Briscoe, who had supported George Wallace at the Democratic Convention in Miami that summer.

THE LRUP GOES NATIONAL: DEFINING *CHICANISMO*

In the midst of the Texas and California LRUP campaigns, "Corky" Gonzales, as indicated above, called for the convention of a party which he felt he presided over nationally—with some justification. In many ways, he more than Gutiérrez had paved the way for its realization beyond the local level. In November 1971 he called a regional LRUP conference in Pueblo, which was attended mainly by Colorado followers of Gonzales's CFJ. There the national strategy was announced: Gonzales recommended that the LRUP should someday field a presidential candidate, hopefully himself. In June 1972 the CFJ convened another major LRUP meeting in Colorado, that attracted delegates from outside the state. Mario Compeán

represented the Texas party. He warned the conferees that the LRUP was not ready for a national plan. The delegates, nevertheless, overwhelmingly approved the Gonzales proposal.

If Gutiérrez questioned the viability of a statewide party, he definitely was at odds with a national-level organization. But he had traveled throughout the country, mainly to college campuses, encouraging students to form local chapters of the LRUP; he was therefore partially responsible for these aspirations. Besides, since he had wanted a leading role for himself in the Chicano Movement, he could ignore the Colorado LRUP initiative only at his own peril. Gutiérrez submitted to "Corky" Gonzales's wishes for a national party.

An assessment of the El Paso meeting reveals the procession of ideologies and general aspirations that had brewed for five years in the Chicano Movement cauldron. By then, *movimiento* activists had already acknowledged that in the course of the movement four leaders, representing different regions and political concepts, had emerged. These were César Chávez, Reies López Tijerina, "Corky" Gonzales and, the latest entry, José Angel Gutiérrez. The Gonzales faction wanted the convention to reflect that pantheon of "heroes," as historian Rodolfo Acuña terms them. Gonzales appointed himself as chairman and Gutiérrez as vice-chairman, and he provided an honorary position for Tijerina despite some *movimiento* activists considering him somewhat of a crackpot. Gonzales's beliefs did not allow him to invite César Chávez, whose leadership had been lionized at the National Democratic Party convention that summer. Those ties to the mainstream party were anathema to Gonzales and the Colorado LRUP.

In reality, Tijerina was dismissed by Gonzales and his group as a nonentity. In a recent interview, Ernesto Vigil noted that to them the aging land-grant warrior was

---

[17] On-camera interview with Cissy Farenthold by Rosa Hanson, September 7, 1995, NLCC-GP

116. Rodolfo "Corky" Gonzales developing coalitions. Photo by Oscar Castillo.

. . .pretty much away from what was going on in El Paso. He was just another personality on the side. We didn't see him representing any significant faction or tendency within the party. He was known as a leader of the land-grant struggle. We recognized that. We recognized his contribution.

As LRUP members arrived in El Paso's Liberty Hall Coliseum where the meeting was held, excitement and anticipation tinged the air as delegates milled around discussing the debate between the two competing philosophies represented by Gonzales and Gutiérrez. By then, the more pragmatic approach favored by Gutiérrez and his Texas followers was well known. Rumors were rife that he had asked George McGovern, the Democratic Party presidential candidate, to speak at the meeting.

In addition to their opposition to Chávez and Tijerina, Colorado LRUP leaders also opposed Gutiérrez. Fearful of his emerging strength, they were convinced that his pragmatic approach

would compromise the sanctity of independence and self-determination to which the group had committed itself consistently. As Ernesto Vigil remembers, the Coloradorans thought Gutiérrez was willing to cooperate with the Republican Party. Vigil maintains that,

> If you think that you are going to negotiate meaningful concessions, you have a chance of doing it with the incumbent far more than with the challenger. So I think José Angel Gutiérrez accepted that equation: that we have this power we're negotiating with the status quo and there are concessions we want. From [our] view it was inconceivable that you strike any kind of bargain with somebody like Richard Nixon.[18]

Gutiérrez concedes that, before the meeting, he entertained approaching the dominant parties to wrest concessions. As he put it in a recent interview, "People who run for office need to be asked, 'What are you going to do for me and

---

[18] On-camera interview with Ernesto Vigil.

what have you done lately?' as a prerequisite before getting my vote. Richard Nixon and George McGovern were no different. We asked them those questions then."[19]

The stage was set for a dramatic showdown. Gonzales carefully dressed in his standard all-Black "tough *vato*" uniform and gave the keynote address, which he punctuated with his simple but popular themes of Chicano nationalism, no compromise with the Establishment and self-determination. While he did not name Gutiérrez or the Texas LRUP, it was clear to whom he was referring when he alleged that any Chicanos willing to cooperate with the Establishment would be in cahoots with Republicans, the Mafia, Chicago's Mayor Richard Daley, George Wallace and George McGovern. The thunderous ovation after his speech convinced him that he stood alone as the primary leader not only of an emerging LRUP, but of the entire Chicano Movement. Never had so many U.S. Mexicans gathered in a political meeting of such magnitude. It did not bother Gonzales that his audience was overwhelmingly made up of students and other young people who had not yet legitimized themselves as representatives of the broad sector of Mexican Americans. He saw the assembly as a revolutionary vanguard that would eventually convert a cowed *raza* to his ultra-nationalistic message.

The more pragmatic Gutiérrez followed Gonzales to the podium, but the convention delegates were in no mood to hear his pragmatism. At this point back home, he was attempting to temper the militancy of Chicano politics that he and his MAYO cohorts had pioneered in Texas—not because it offended gringos, but because it alienated Texas Mexicans. Even his own following, that he and other MAYO pioneers had baptized into these tactics, prevented him from de-escalating the earlier strategy. In his speech

Gutiérrez carefully crafted his words so that it would not appear that he wanted to "negotiate with the enemy." Instead he spoke of unity, cautioning that they should not give the impression that Chicanos could not reach a consensus. He did aim a jab at the ideologically obsessed Colorado faction, saying that convention participants could not "afford the luxury of. . . bickering on minute rhetorical points. . . . We must display not who is more of a Chicano, but simply who doesn't need to debate what is a Chicano."[20] This rather noncommittal discourse also received a standing ovation.

Reies López Tijerina delivered the third major address in which he emphasized the pitfalls of debating ideological purity. Using the typical firebrand style that he had perfected as an evangelist, Tijerina reminded the delegates, in Spanish, that the Treaty of Guadalupe Hidalgo had given *la raza* in the U.S. rights that were betrayed and that, as far as Mexicans were concerned, the treaty symbolized the law of the land. Tijerina's admonishment was also well received. When he finished, Gonzales and Gutiérrez mounted the stage and, to an uproarious approval, the three linked upraised hands in a show of unity.

The meeting proceeded. The role of moderator fell to Gutiérrez, but since he had decided to run for chairman of the Congreso de Aztlán, the name picked for the planned national initiative, he asked Raúl Ruiz of Los Angeles to take on the task. Gutiérrez remembers,

> It was clear that Corky was making a big move to be the only person elected at the convention. . . . I decided to run against him. . . so then I turned to a fellow from California, Raúl Ruiz, to take charge of the convention, so that I could have time to run against Corky.[21]

Raúl Ruiz today laments that the party was

[19] On-camera interview with José Angel Gutiérrez by Hector Galán, December 12, 1994, NLCC-GP.

[20] Film clip of José Angel Gutiérrez addressing the El Paso Convention of La Raza Unida Party, NLCC-GP.

[21] On-camera interview with José Angel Gutiérrez

being divided by "personality types" rather than substantive issues: "There was a very strong competition and struggle with each other. We wanted it. . . to be solved."[22] As the two major players vied for votes, a platform was established. More than five hundred resolutions were considered. Some were predictable, such as supporting the UFW and the land-grant struggle in New Mexico. Curiously, as soon as a motion was read supporting the land-grant motion, a delegate immediately spoke against it because restoring land could benefit rich landowners and "Spaniards." Tijerina, who rarely used the word *Chicano* or invoked the concept of Aztlán, was considered to be Hispanophile by many Chicanos who leaned towards *indigenismo*.

Gonzales did introduce the no-compromise theme in his keynote speech, but as Ignacio M. García notes, "Ironically, the question of whether to support Nixon or McGovern in the presidential race did not become a major issue of discussion, even though group discussions had been going on during the conference on this topic." The only individuals who wanted to bring up the subject were Communist Party members, who pressed for an endorsement of McGovern for the sake of "stopping Nixon's reelection."[23]

Instead the method by which votes would be cast and counted, because this would determine the edge given to either Gonzales or Gutiérrez in the chairmanship bid, drew the most passionate debate. After much wrangling, the convention decided to count the vote of every delegate individually rather than by states. This procedure, opposed by Gonzales's supporters, probably gave Gutiérrez the advantage since more LRUP delegates from Texas were in attendance at the convention.

Raúl Ruiz recalls, "Of course José wanted the individual votes. . . because he could see that if it went that way, he would get the vote. 'Corky' wanted the block voting." Ernesto Vigil laments, "Going into the convention, we were operating against a stacked deck. . . so we weren't pleased. . . . We were more willing to. . . mix it up. We didn't go there to make friends."[24] But Ruiz concedes that not counting the vote of every individual smacked of an undemocratic procedure:

> How could we in our conference not count everybody's vote, regardless of whether it was against your interests. . . . As chair, I allowed the motion to go through. . . and in effect this. . . gave the chairmanship to José, which. . . made me the most unpopular guy in Colorado.[25]

Thus Gonzales lost; he gathered 170 votes to Gutiérrez's 256. When the vote was announced, Gonzales mounted the stage and gave Gutiérrez a conciliatory *abrazo*. Film footage of Gonzales's face as he ascends the stage betrays his discomfort and frustration; the same scene shows Gutiérrez elated. The disappointed Colorado delegation threatened to walk out, but Gonzales dissuaded them.

Gonzales then provided a moving message of unity and the importance of adhering to democratic ideals. He thanked all his supporters and reminded the "many young people" of their part in the "most historic event of the Chicano Movement. . . which cannot be prostituted by politics." He ended his farewell saying, "Whichever way the vote goes, our conscience, our direction, our principals will never waver and we will be part of La Raza Unida. Gracias!"

Gutiérrez's final words were also conciliatory. He applauded the skills of his opponents and their discipline and said he was proud to be in the same room with such formidable competition. He then asked that they put all differences aside and unite with him. But it was all for naught; the factionalism that became evident in the election

---

[22] On-camera interview with Raúl Ruiz by Robert Cozens, December 21, 1994, NLCC-GP.

[23] García, *United We Win*, p. 113.

[24] On-camera interview with Ernesto Vigil.

[25] Two quotes from Raúl Ruiz.

at the convention, that would have launched the only U.S. national party of Mexicans, destroyed that dream. Political scientist Carlos Muñoz concludes, "El Congreso de Aztlán, the national organizational structure that was established at the convention, failed to materialize. There was in fact no basis of unity on which to build a national organization."[26] In essence, no one who left the convention was committed to continue building the national organization; instead, they returned to their more provincial spaces of activism. Raúl Ruiz asserts, "We were a party that was not yet mature enough to be divided on issues. . . . You should have different positions, but come together in some acceptable consensus. . . . The party was divided before the conference and after. . . even more so."[27]

After Gonzales's defeat, Reies López Tijerina called for another meeting in Albuquerque for October 21-22, which he hoped would inject new life into the Chicano Movement and restore him to the helm of the *movimiento*. He called it the National Congress for Land and Cultural Reform. Seemingly it could also provide a platform for continuing the Congreso de Aztlán initiative which had come out of the El Paso conference. Tijerina invited "Corky" Gonzales, who refused to attend because the guest list included non-*movimiento* civil rights leaders and politicians. José Angel Gutiérrez did attend, taking time out from the busy Muñiz campaign. The meeting was marked by squabbling between the same factions that had divided the El Paso event, but it ultimately deteriorated into finger-pointing at Tijerina because he had invited moderate Mexican American bureaucrats to interact with militants. Tijerina walked out of his own meeting, as did most of the other participants, leaving it in disarray.

Another meeting of the Congreso took place almost a year later and it too turned into a fiasco because Gutiérrez, trying to keep his enemies away, did not invite LRUP activists from

California, New Mexico and Colorado. Many of these groups had been moving beyond cultural nationalism into the realm of Marxist internationalism, and Gutiérrez could not accept that. Slowly the little national infrastructure that had been established through the Congreso de Aztlán began to crumble and, by 1979, the few remaining members decided to hold their last meeting.

CALIFORNIA DREAMING

The El Paso conference was not the death knell of LRUP activism. As seen above, when Gonzales called the El Paso meeting, party members were in the midst of political campaigns, the most important ones taking place in Texas and California. When Raúl Ruiz and his Los Angeles LRUP cohorts went to El Paso, they left pending a campaign which they hoped would derail the election of another Mexican American Democrat, as had happened in the Alatorre defeat the previous year. Ruiz was challenging a Los Angeles incumbent in the state assembly: Alex García, whose record in the state legislature was less than stellar. The Republican candidate, Robert Aguirre, would have benefitted by a large LRUP turnout.

By California standards, Ruiz was a practical politician who wanted to win. He felt that the cultural vanguard notion hampered Gonzales from moving beyond narrow nationalism and connecting with a broader Mexican American base. His district was predominantly Mexican American, so the match would serve as a real test of the attraction the LRUP held for the *raza*. García obtained fifty-six percent of the vote to Ruiz's fifteen, however. After this resounding defeat, Ruiz was contrite, admitting that such failures could not be rationalized as a further step in "consciousness raising." Referring to the 1972 campaign, Ruiz wrote the following in his magazine *La Raza* in 1973:

> Now this does not mean that we are wrong in the establishment of a new political concept

[26] Muñoz, *Youth, Identity, Power*, p. 112.

[27] On-camera interview with Raúl Ruiz.

117. José Angel Gutiérrez. Photo by Oscar Castillo.

and structure. But it does mean that we have a difficult road ahead. We cannot expect to do away with a political party that has been using and confusing our people for. . . over half a century, with a few months of campaign activity. I think it presumptuous, and as a matter of fact, insulting that we should consider our people's beliefs so lightly.[28]

Still, as the words of this statement suggest, Ruiz held on to the notion that the LRUP served as a political vanguard and that, with education, Los Angeles Mexicans could turn to the party. Thus LRUP activists blamed their failures more on the false consciousness of Mexicans and did not consider that perhaps some of *la raza* were simply repelled by what appeared to be unqualified can-

didates and contentious campaign workers. Moreover, claiming victory because the LRUP had contributed to the victory of a conservative Republican over a liberal Mexican Democrat could not sustain LRUP growth or nurture political sophistication. Juan Gómez-Quiñones asserts that in the Alatorre campaign,

> The limits of the non-south Texas strategy of La Raza Unida became apparent; to abandon, for the time being, efforts to win seats and concentrate instead on the role of the "spoiler" was puerile, especially if the goal was ethnic representation.

LRUP members in California continued their advocacy, however, and in 1974 decided to run a

[28] Quoted in Muñoz, *Youth, Identity, Power*, p. 110.

Richard Santillán, now a university professor, has recalled his sentiments during the founding of the La Raza Unida Party: "So many of us who were barely getting our feet wet...at this time were becoming very angry and disillusioned at everything that represented the system.... That included people like Congressman Edward Roybal, Congressman Henry González and Julián Nava, who was on the school board at the time. I remember we took out a lot of anger and frustration against them because we largely blamed them for the condition of our community. We felt that they had not done enough and, in fact, they had sold out."[29]

candidate for governor, but they did not obtain the necessary signatures to be able to file. That same year, the Los Angeles LRUP under Ruiz had participated in a failed attempt to incorporate an unincorporated part of East Los Angeles that contained more than a hundred thousand people. According to Gómez-Quiñones, "LRUP demonstrated some of the most incompetent electoral efforts ever witnessed in Los Angeles. . . . A goal long sought by community activists was defeated."[30] The California LRUP never recovered, and this became its last major political act in the state.

Ironically, expediting the demise of the California LRUP was César Chávez's UFW. The party chastised the union for not pursuing a wider social agenda and for cooperating with the Democrats. Subsequently, Chávez sent his well-trained organizers to help defeat LRUP candidates in Los Angeles. When Dolores Huerta was asked to give reasons for the rift, she responded with a darker, albeit unsubstantiated, allegation that has plagued LRUP activists since the 1970s: "The Nixon campaign had given some money to some members of the La Raza Unida to attack the UFW. . . and when they started doing this in California, they discredited themselves. That was the main reason."[31]

SURVIVAL *A LO TEJANO*

In Texas the LRUP was making bigger waves. Gutiérrez and other LRUP members returned to the statewide campaign of Ramsey Muñiz for governor, and the El Paso conference quickly faded in importance. In many ways Gutiérrez, who was not ready for a national party, demonstrated a "dog in the manger" attitude. He could not really sustain the responsibilities of national leadership because they detracted from his Texas activities, but at the same time he did not want anyone else to have the mantle of national party chairman.

Muñiz had addressed the El Paso meeting but remained outside the deliberations made by the leadership. In reality, the Waco lawyer had never been an insider to LRUP politics, serving in 1972 mainly as a vote-getting attraction for the party. Besides, Muñiz was not conversant in classical Chicano Movement ideology. He was happiest when he could simply act as a traditional campaigner, once in a while emitting populist rhetoric, peppered with mildly spicy language. The Texas LRUP, through Muñiz, acquired numerous endorsements from old-line Mexican American Democrats, union leaders and other non-Chicano Movement activists. Without Muñiz in the front lines—even for the pragmatic Gutiérrez, who still guarded his reputation among Chicano purists—negotiating such matters would have proved difficult. Still, the

---

[29] On-camera interview with Richard Santillán by Robert Cozens, December 22, 1994, NLCC-GP.

[30] Last two quotes from Gómez-Quiñones, *Chicano Politics*, pp. 136 and 137.

[31] On-camera Interview with Dolores Huerta.

Texas LRUP made great strides in attracting a broad base of Texas Mexicans into the party. The LRUP continued to recruit Texas white liberals who did not support the conservative Dolph Briscoe, but since many believed that the Mexican party had siphoned away primary votes from Sissy Farenthold, they stayed away.

The Republican Party appreciated the LRUP, however, because it stood to remove a significant sector of the Mexican American vote from the ranks of the Democratic Party. Nixon's main campaign entity, the Committee to Re-elect the President (CREEP), made various efforts to support La Raza Unida. Some claim CREEP offered a bribe to Gutiérrez, which he declined. But Gutiérrez never quite gave up the strategy of wresting concessions. With Republican support, federal aid came into Zavala County and allowed Gutiérrez and the local LRUP to shore up county and municipal budgets and also allowed for extensive county and municipal patronage for supporters. Ironically much of the bargaining had taken place even before the El Paso conference, at the same time "Corky" Gonzales was condemning anything with the slightest hint of Establishment shade.

In the elections, Muñiz obtained six percent of the Texas vote, the vast majority of which had been cast by Mexican Americans. This surprisingly large margin denied Briscoe a majority over his Republican opponent. Other LRUP state office candidates such as Alma Canales, the lieutenant governor hopeful, obtained much smaller totals. The LRUP did better in some local elections such as Cotulla's, where it maintained or captured most of the municipal seats. Nonetheless, the party lost in Kingsville, where it had made a major effort to test its ability to capture power in a larger community.

In the final analysis, the Muñiz campaign was not much more successful than those in California. To be sure, the Texas LRUP campaign might have been more smoothly run than were the ones in Los Angeles, but the Texan party stood no chance of winning a statewide election; it only functioned as a potential "spoiler" that would benefit Republicans. After this failed campaign, the LRUP returned to Gutiérrez's first love: organizing in rural communities where Mexicans constituted the majority populations.

After three years of LRUP activity nationwide, its only significant wins were still those obtained in Crystal City and Cotulla, where the strategy had been to "polarize the town, discredit the *vendidos*, register voters and get them out on election day."[32] Indeed, in 1973, the party had garnered its biggest array of victories, all in South Texas and the Winter Garden area in such communities as Crystal City, Kyle, Hebronville, Edcouch-Elsa, Robstown, Beeville, Carrizo Springs and Marathon. The victories ranged from gaining one or two local seats to

Raúl Ruiz recalled his La Raza Unida days: "In political activity we were expert, we were committed. It wasn't just something that would just go away. We were already part of the struggle for years. This is why when Democrats like Richard Alatorre came to us to pull out and not run against them because, after all, they were Chicanos, we said NO! You should support us, we're the real candidates, we can effectively support our community much better than you because you have never been part of it. All you are is funded by the Democratic Party, and the only reason they are doing this is that they see a dynamic force rising from the community and all of a sudden they want to put a stop to it."[33]

---

[32] García, *United We Win*, p. 15.

[33] On-camera interview with Raúl Ruiz.

making complete sweeps. The triumphs, however, instead of bolstering Gutiérrez's one-region-at-a-time grand design, only emboldened the LRUP to increase its efforts to gain statewide strength.

Mario Compeán became chairman of the Texas LRUP in 1972; the statewide effort would now be under his watch. Ramsey Muñiz, still feeling victorious as a spoiler in the 1972 elections and heartened by the rural triumphs, decided early in 1974 to seek the governorship again. He made it clear from the start, however, that the campaign would reach out to all possible constituencies, not just the Texas Mexican population. He even explained that La Raza Unida meant "the people united," in order to steer away from appearing to use the race card. Muñiz wanted to win, and he would do what he could to achieve that goal. Compeán, on the other hand, rejected such an approach, insisting on continuing the nationalistic *movimiento* tact.

Compeán and Muñiz became bitter enemies, and at the 1974 state convention in Houston, their rivalry came to a head. After a particularly painful Houston confrontation between the two, Compeán decided not to run for reelection as chairman. Gutiérrez, who still wielded the greatest personal power in the LRUP although he only played a minor official role in the party by now, agreed. Muñiz chose Carlos Guerra, another MAYO pioneer and a onetime advocate of nationalistic rectitude, to chair his campaign. Unlike Compeán, Guerra was more willing to yield to what appeared to be the political realities of the time and concurred with Muñiz that a traditional campaign should be waged—this included wooing groups and individuals outside the party.

In a repeat performance of the 1972 election, Texas liberals again ran Sissy Farenthold, but she once again lost to Briscoe in the Democratic primary, and again the Democrats blamed the LRUP for drawing off Mexican American votes. White liberal support, as a result, was withheld from the LRUP to Muñiz's frustration, and in spite of repeating the ardent campaigning he had shown in 1972, the LRUP candidate received even fewer votes. He did not even duplicate the 1972 role of

spoiler because Briscoe, running against a weak Republican candidate, won handily. José Angel Gutiérrez, however, ran for Zavala County judge, the most powerful county post, and won.

After Muñiz's defeat, the LRUP convened a state meeting to discuss future plans. Gutiérrez, ever the power wielder, still advocated the regional approach but recognized that this would idle the many party chapters which had sprung up throughout the state and perhaps weaken the overall LRUP structure. So the option to try again for the governor's post was left open. Since party leaders deemed the 1974 Muñiz bid a failure, the former gubernatorial contender saw his influence wane within the party. Muñiz slipped into Robstown and started a law practice but fell in with bad company. In July 1976 he was arrested on federal charges of narcotics trafficking.

Although Muñiz did not play a major role in the LRUP, his arrest and later conviction was a serious setback for the party. Gutiérrez tried to insulate himself from the fallout by remaining the political boss of Zavala County. In Robstown Guadalupe Youngblood, the local LRUP leader, attempted to distance his efforts from the party by removing his local organization, the Familias Unidas (United Families), from party affiliation. In municipal elections during 1977 the Familias group launched a formidable campaign and a huge success was anticipated, but it suffered a disappointing loss.

In 1978 Mario Compeán collected the remnants of the party and launched himself as candidate for governor. He received less than two percent of the total votes cast. The Republican Bill Clements won against a liberal, John Hill, who had defeated Dolph Briscoe in the Democratic Party primary. Many former LRUP members had defected to his camp in the course of the year. Compeán's claims that his campaign was a spoiler for the Democrats rang hollow. However, asked recently if he thought that LRUP spoiled his chances of winning, Hill replied, "Who's to say? When you lose a close election, you can think of thirty-five reasons why you lost. But at least it certainly could have been the decisive factor."[34]

---

[34] On-camera interview with John Hill by Rose Hanson, September 7, 1995, NLCC-GP.

In the meantime, José Angel Gutiérrez, once unbeatable in South Texas, began to lose support among his followers, who formed a breakaway faction of the LRUP. Gutiérrez had evolved into a political boss and many of the young party members he had mentored began to question his increasing authoritarianism. In addition, the coalition that was forged within the local LRUP had been made up of various factions and it began to disintegrate. Gutiérrez was defeated in the same way that he came to power: through the ballot box. The political posts which he and erstwhile supporters had won fell into the hands of his Chicano opponents, often with the assistance of the Zavala County Anglos, anxious to see Gutiérrez get his come-uppance. In 1982 after a great amount of harassment by both Anglos and Mexican Americans, Gutiérrez quit Zavala County politics for good. Gutiérrez left the state, but eventually returned to Texas, obtained a law degree and set up a practice in Dallas.

In the rest of the country the LRUP also died a slow, painful death. On March 17, 1973, Denver police clashed with Crusade for Justice (CFJ) members after units arrived to break up a party at a CFJ-owned apartment complex. In the fracas, twenty-year-old Louis Martínez was killed after he had shot and wounded a policeman. Ernest Vigil, a CFJ leader, was shot in the back, and a bomb mysteriously destroyed part of the building. A debate ensued in Denver for months over who was at fault. The police were exonerated completely, but Crusaders insisted the police had provoked the incident. This outbreak, which led to the almost complete dissolution of the CFJ, was indirectly provoked by an incessant vigilance of Chicano Movement activities in Denver and throughout the rest of the country.

After 1978 Juan José Peña from New Mexico attempted to keep the fires burning at times almost alone, using his car as the LRUP headquarters. In Northern California many of the chapters reverted back to the Socialist Workers Party, which was what they were to begin with. In Los Angeles, Guillermo Flores and some of his associates transformed the LRUP Labor Committee into the August Twenty-ninth Movement (ATM), a short-lived Maoist-Marxist organization. Some activists even attempted to transfer the LRUP to untried territory: in the 1980s Daniel Ozuna, a Los Angeles party participant, brought the concept to Phoenix, where it serves to this day as a vehicle to instill in Chicano youth cultural pride through symbols such as *indigenismo*.

CONCLUSION

It became obvious that Mexican Americans could be persuaded to vote for the LRUP, but mainly if they were approached traditionally by the likes of a Ramsey Muñiz. The revolutionary vanguard approach espoused by Gonzales, it seems, had no long-term future in Mexican America and was doomed to remain insular. It is now a standard explanation that the LRUP left behind a political legacy that has allowed Chicanos greater participation in the two-party system. That assertion, while simply an interpretation, is probably correct.

In hindsight, the experience of the LRUP can provide contemporary political activists with a long list of what not to do. For example, whether or not militant and nationalistic tactics resulted in gains can be debated endlessly. There is no way of measuring what impact this strategy had on raising consciousness among Mexican Americans or whether it forced the Establishment to concede what it would have not otherwise done. It can also be said that the actions of LRUP were adventuristic or illegal and, as a consequence, "brought the man down on us." But that is only half the story. From the very first, the LRUP was seen as a threat to both Establishment Mexican Americans and Anglos, who consequently went out of their way to sabotage its effectiveness.

But the rise and fall of La Raza Unida Party is part of a larger question that will be addressed in the next chapter on the legacy of *el movimiento*. What does the Chicano Movement mean for us today and what does it portend for the future?

CHAPTER FOURTEEN

Legacy of the Chicano Movement

118. Students and staff in the Mexican American Studies Program at the University of Houston, along with the program director, Dr. Tatcho Mindrola, third from right in the back row.

The most often asked questions about the Chicano Movement are: "Did it succeed?" "Did it end?" "Was it betrayed?" Many a young Chicano, and not a few old ones, constantly stoke the ashes of the 1960s *movimiento* hoping to reignite the fire; some even become indignant at the suggestion that the movement has ended. Most present-day Mexican Americans, however, probably wonder what the excitement was all about. Assuming that the Chicano Movement began to die with the National La Raza Unida Party Conference in 1972, its legacy today is of such magnitude that it forms the most extensive watershed in Chicano history.

No Mexican American can escape its inheritance: not individuals who hated the *movimiento*, nor those who became too sophisticated for it, nor the ones who were indifferent to it. The *movimiento*'s legacy, in fact, affects a greater portion of the present-day U.S.-Mexican population than when it was at its apogee. Most present-day Chicano civil right leaders and politicians no longer insist on *El Plan Espiritual de Aztlán* as a guide to action, nor do they look to "Corky" Gonzales and José Angel Gutiérrez for leadership. But consciously or unconsciously, everyone follows more than one precept established during the movement.

Below is a discussion of the obvious and not-so-obvious concepts and institutions of this legacy. The *movimiento* endowment is manifest in identity, the arts, intellectual traditions, popular culture, civil rights activism, political behavior, gender identity and workplace defense. This does not mean that a completely new paradigm emerged from the *movimiento*. Certainly previous generations addressed all these issues; the Chicano Movement was the latest but most profound synthesis of them. It attempted to bring the largest number of *raza* ever into the fold of its political and social awareness and activism.

The base of the *movimiento* activists was

never very large. Consciously and unconsciously, the mainly student-led collective saw itself as a revolutionary vanguard which knew best what its people needed. In many ways, *movimiento* participants were not as directly affected by the ills they strove so hard to eradicate as were nonparticipants. Unlike workers whose motivation to join unions is fueled by self-interest, Chicano students and youth—except when confronting educational inadequacies or the possibility of being sent to Vietnam—joined causes for altruistic reasons. In large part, knowledge of social ills affecting their people sparked their initial commitment. But the sustaining fuel came from *Chicanismo*, a political identity that was usually instilled in college or institutions outside the barrio.

This sense of *Chicanismo* is the greatest monument left by the *movimiento*, even if at present it goes under different names. None of the Chicano Movement cultural or political pronouncements became part of an unchangeable dogma. Today only a small core of former Chicano Movement activists and their present-day followers adhere conservatively to the canon established in the 1960s. Among the Chicano Movement's less obvious but more enduring legacies is an obligation among a broad fraternity of Mexican Americans, especially those who participated in the *movimiento*, to identify with their working-class roots and to feel an obligation to their community. In the 1980s Francyn Molina conducted a study comparing former California activists who participated in the *movimiento* in the late 1960s and the early 1970s with a cohort group of non-participants. She concluded that the former activists maintained more liberal political views and a continuing sense of commitment to social causes.[1]

IDENTITY AND CIVIL RIGHTS STRUGGLE BEFORE THE *MOVIMIENTO*

To understand how the *movimiento* leadership successfully instilled in the U.S. Mexican

[1] Francyn Molina, "The Pychological and Political Development of Former Student Movement Activists: A View Fifteen Years Later" (Ph.D. Dissertation, Wright Institute, 1969).

community its democratic and populist impulses, past notions of identity must be reviewed. Mexican people left in the territories the U.S. acquired from Mexico in the nineteenth century had a "Lost-Land" identity. The term "lost" became more applicable after railroads, outside capital and entrepreneurs disrupted or eliminated the society forged by Hispanics and Anglos in the first few years of U.S. domination. Moreover, in the "Lost-Land" era, the link of Southwest Mexicans to central Mexico was weak. Even early immigrants crossing the border from northern Mexico found more intimacy with the Hispanic Southwest's culture and people than if they had gone in the opposite direction to the interior of their country. As a consequence, they too felt a sense of loss when Anglo-American hegemony subordinated and made barrios out of former Mexican towns. The loss of land, culture and political self-determination created the rationale for the civil rights struggle. No matter how hard Mexicans resisted these changes through individual or organized activity, their mobilization to stem these losses was unsuccessful.

The identity of this era, then, rested on an idealized and romanticized view of life before Anglos wrought modernization. But class differences abounded in the Mexican Southwest. Even after the Anglo takeover, some Hispanics amassed political and economic power within the total community as well as a degree of prestige and respect. To establish economic and political links, the Mexican elites mixed and married with newcomer Anglos. While the elites did not necessarily assimilate—it was more likely that Anglos would Hispanicize—they did collaborate with the more powerful Anglo newcomers. In the process they maintained their distance from the lower classes.

The arrival of large numbers of Mexican immigrants after 1900, who established *colonias* throughout the Southwest, created a *México Lindo* identity. These immigrants were segregated and subordinated, and, Anglos measured their value mainly in the labor market. Moreover, their barrios had little influence in shaping the image of the larger host communities. Survival and adaptation needs shaped political and defense strategies while their identity rested on an idealized and romanticized memory of the old country. While *México Lindo* consciousness emerged in old Hispanic communities such as San Antonio, it complemented a "Lost-Land" source of identity of that city. Conversely, in Los Angeles, immigration was of such magnitude that the "Lost-Land" ideal was inundated and hardly visible. In northern New Mexico, on the other hand, *hispano* villagers until recently maintained their "Lost-Land" identity intact. But even in the new societies wrought by immigration, class differences existed and were promoted by the purveyors of *México Lindo*, who were mainly middle- and upper-class exiled conservatives from the Mexican Revolution. They

In writing about a Christmas *posada* festival in nineteenth-century Los Angeles, journalist and author Arturo Bandini of the well-known *californio* clan reveals a typical attitude held by members of his class: "If you wish to know the rank, wealth or social standing of each individual, watch the actions of any proprietor of a booth; see how deferential his smile is to some, and with what humble but all-absorbing interest he listens to their conversation. But suddenly he straightens up, and stands on tip-toe, looks shocked and offended, but says loud enough to be heard by his visitors, 'Sh! sh!' What is the matter, you wonder. Why, he is only rebuking and silencing the two *pelados* (impecunious ones) for daring to talk in such presence."[2]

[2] Arturo Bandini, *Navidad* (San Francisco: California Historical Society, 1958), p. 17.

adhered to an elegant *mexicanismo* and looked with disdain at their uneducated poorer compatriots. No dignity and very little respect were attributed to their Spanish, their folk culture, their dress—these attitudes, of course, were class prejudices brought over from Mexico.

But when pitted against Anglo imperialism, *México Lindo* nationalism prompted immigrant leaders to come to the aid of compatriots whose civil rights were violated. Immigrant leaders also organized mutual aid societies that, while not unions in the strict sense of the word, were designed to help working Mexicans. In addition, the Mexican government through its consular system constantly revitalized *México Lindo* identity and served as a source of civil rights protection.

The rise of Mexican Americanism—a sense of permanency and a desire to live as the equals of other Americans within an Anglo-American system—usually occurred in the second or third generation. In urban Texas during the 1920s, the earliest large-scale manifestations of Mexican Americanism appeared when the state acquired the largest U.S.-born Mexican population in the country after 1910; from this base came a critical core that aspired to social mobility and equality. Geographically Mexican Americanization occurred in a staggered order that waited for U.S.-born Mexicans to come of age. By the 1940s there was no region in the U.S. where the process had not produced a large cohort group of individuals with the physiological and cultural characteristics of Mexicans, but for whom Mexico was a foreign country.

Mexican Americanization did not necessarily imply assimilation. Nonetheless, mainstream Anglo traditions infused the culture of educated and more affluent Mexican Americans, who profoundly desired social mobility and the degree of assimilation required to achieve their dreams. Mexican Americans with middle-class aspirations looked with disdain at their brothers and sisters who did not transcend the working-class Mexicaness that persisted beyond the first generation. Significantly, the Mexican American middle classes applied the word *Chicano* pejoratively to identify the lower classes. Despite their attitudes, Mexican American leaders launched an intensive

civil rights struggle to dislodge racist obstacles that prevented mobility, especially school segregation and job discrimination. In addition, all U.S.-born Mexicans, regardless of where they stood in the class hierarchy, resented mistreatment, especially in the form of police brutality or anti-Mexican violence. In the long run, these middle-class struggles benefited the children of the working classes, who also sought mobility.

More immediately, poorer Mexican Americans were more concerned with workplace conditions, which usually translated to a need for unions. Among the Mexican American middle class were individuals who made short-lived forays—through such organizations as the socialist Congress of Spanish-Speaking People of the 1930s and 1940s and the Asociación Nacional México-Americana (ANMA—Mexican American National Association) in the 1950s—to broaden the civil rights agenda to include working-class issues. Because of the pervasive antisocialist atmosphere in the U.S., these groups found it very difficult to survive.

In the process of Mexican Americanization, many Mexican Americans promoted themselves as white Americans of Mexican ancestry. For the mainly mestizo Mexican population, such an assertion was difficult to sustain, however. The claim constantly ran into racist, demeaning brick walls—a process witnessed by their children, many of whom became the promoters of a new Chicano identity.

CHICANOS ADDRESS THE IDENTITY CRISIS AND CIVIL RIGHTS

In the 1960s African Americans pioneered an assault on race denial by resurrecting a "Black Pride" movement which manifested itself through the promotion of self-esteem and the glamorizing of African history. The Black Pride movement saw the time spent by African Americans in the U.S. as demeaning and not a source of dignity. It did not take the emerging Chicano intelligentsia long to see parallels; often, however, the analogy was forced. Influenced by such writings as Franz Fannon's *Wretched of the Earth* and Elridge Cleaver's *Soul on Ice*, Chicano activists legitimately under-

119. Mexican American students in class at the University of Houston.

stood the contradiction of trying to be white or Anglo, especially in a society where racism prevented the fulfillment of such aspirations.

As a consequence, the Chicano Movement addressed the issue of identity and civil rights with a greater zeal than any other Mexican generation had in the U.S. The identity envisioned by *movimiento* leaders, and bolstered by *El Plan Espiritual de Aztlán,* had an impact everywhere the Chicano Movement was proclaimed. When dealing with the notion of denial, a catharsis emerged that put an emphasis on the acceptance of being brown or mestizo and not being ashamed of it. The 1920s work of the Mexican philosopher José Vasconselos, *La Raza Cósmica* (The Cosmic Race), with its message of a new hemispheric bronze people, resonated. The concept of Aztlán, the homeland of the Aztecs alleged to be the present-day Southwest, gave a heretofore unknown dignity to the mestizo-Indian aesthetic, which Chicanos had been conditioned to see in negative terms. Cultural trappings and myths formulated at the 1969 Denver youth conference and in the Chicano design for higher education, *El Plan de Santa Bárbara,* fueled the nationalism necessary to commit to social struggle.

CHICANO STUDIES

The most visible vestige of the *movimiento* is to be found in academia in the many university Chicano studies programs and departments that exist throughout the Southwest. The ability to bring about change at institutions of higher learning was a crowning achievement of the movement. The first Chicano Studies Department in the nation, founded in 1968 at California State College, Los Angeles, was established in response to protests by United Mexican American Students (UMAS). Ralph Guzmán, a professor of political science at the college, was named its first director. He soon ran into opposition from students who envisioned a department with independent courses while Guzmán wanted a traditional interdisciplinary academic program. After the meeting at the University of California, Santa Barbara which produced *El Plan de Santa Bárbara*, a spate of programs were pushed into existence through student militancy. The largest and the most intellectually dynamic was the UCLA Chicano Studies Center, founded primarily to conduct research.

Most of these centers and teaching programs—practically all of the California state colleges and universities instituted them—were traditional and did not adhere to the radical departures from academics-as-usual demanded by student activists. For example, *movimiento* students wanted programs that would actually teach liberation, impart cultural-nationalist inter-

120. Américo Paredes.

pretations and train activist cadres to organize in the community. The most well known department in the state system was directed by the activist-scholar, Rodolfo Acuña, at San Fernando Valley State College (now California State University, Northridge). Its fame was pegged more to Acuña's national recognition than to following the radical precepts demanded by students. Acuña published in 1972 the most read survey of Chicano history, *Occupied America*, containing the radical interpretation expected by Chicano students.

Chicanos established only a few formal programs outside California. The most important was at the University of Texas with renowned folklorist Américo Paredes as director. Its orientation was traditional, however, and did not provoke the intense debate over direction which characterized the California centers. At other institutions in the Southwest, a number of faculty with Chicano Movement orientation were hired by regular departments. Even if formal programs did not exist, Chicano studies courses and research within departments began to flourish throughout the country.

As indicated, there is no greater visible legacy than Chicano studies departments and programs at universities. Although many of these endeavors have been battlegrounds for feuds stemming from both ideological and personal politics, today every major southwestern universi-

ty houses a program whose purpose is the study of Chicanos. Some have been recently formed such as Arizona State University's, which was established in 1992, while others are more than twenty-five years old as is the program at California State University, Los Angeles. None has the orientation expected in *El Plan de Santa Bárbara*, albeit the spirit of commitment to the Mexican American community continues as an integral part of their mission.

Numerous journals of Chicano studies were established although most have not survived. In 1967 anthropologist Octavio Romano, a professor at the University of California, Berkeley, founded *El Grito: A Journal of Contemporary Mexican American Thought*. This independent publication served as a forum for a variety of themes, graphic arts and literature. Although its main purpose was polemically to attack previous Anglo-researched social-science studies of Mexican Americans, it was unable to offer alternative approaches consistently.

The journal *Aztlán*, founded and initially edited by Juan Gómez-Quiñones, had greater success as a respected academic periodical. Established at UCLA's Chicano Studies Center in 1970, its writers soon sought new paradigms with which to understand the Chicano experience. They dismissed cultural and race depictions that were proposed by Chicano nationalists as explanations for subordination. Their internal colony model viewed Mexicans in the U.S. as a colonized minority that existed in labor reserves, which were kept subordinated by an economic, social and racial web of control.

To internal colony proponents, cultural and race explanations by themselves would not create viable solutions. These were seen as a mere extension of the cure proposed by the Mexican American generation. For instance, Mexican Americans felt that individual self-improvement, in tandem with the elimination of racism, would vastly improve chances of getting a piece of the pie. Cultural nationalists wanted *Chicanismo* to be unequivocally accepted by white America and for it to energize *la raza* into collectively achieving economic integration and civil rights—this was still a piece of the pie. The internal colony

121. A scene from the Broadway production of Luis Valdez's *Zoot Suit*.

critique stated that race pride and cultural separatism served as Anglo Americans did for 1940's Mexican American activists—both versions were reformist and would result only in cosmetic changes. Internal colony proponents felt that the only solution for the predicament of Chicanos was revolutionary structural change.

This model won out for a time, and Chicano studies furthered that ideology. In 1973 the National Association of Chicano Social Scientists (NACSS) was formed by an emerging cadre of Chicano graduate students and entry-level professors. Later the group became the National Association for Chicano Studies (NACS) in order to accommodate a broader base of academic disciplines. Eventually, its main framework of analysis, the internal colony model, lost favor. Today, NACS reflects postmodernist trends, which radically

reconstruct European intellectual thought, including Marxism (from which the internal colony model acquired its analytic tools). Postmodernism has revived interest in the cultural position of the 1960s, especially among intellectuals in literature and the arts. NACS today, although it is undergoing a critical transition, is motivated primarily by a debate over gender in Chicano society.

THE CHICANO RENAISSANCE: ARTISTS AND CULTURAL NATIONALISM

The Promethean proportions of cultural nationalism produced within the California *movimiento* is related to that state's volume of Chicano artistic production. California artists initially served as the main purveyors of the Chicano Movement emblems of new identity. In 1971 literary critic Phillip D. Ortego accurately measured the pulse of the Chicano art movement of the time. He wrote,

> Perhaps the significance of the Chicano Renaissance lies in the identification of Chicanos with their Indian past. It matters not what etymologies are ascribed to the word "Chicano"; the distinction is not in whether the word is a denigration but in that it has been consciously and deliberately chosen over all other words to identify Mexican Americans who regard themselves as Moctezuma's children. They have thus cast off the sometimes meretricious identification with the Spanish templar tradition foisted on them by Anglo-American society because of its preference for things European.[3]

One of the most active promoters of the *movimiento* was guerrilla theater. Luis Valdez made the first attempt at this with El Teatro Campesino in order to provide political drama and motivation to the United Farm Workers Union under César Chávez. Numerous other similar efforts ensued. Wherever enough Chicanos gathered under the Chicano Movement rubric, *teatros* were established. The height of the *teatro* era was reached, with some one hundred twenty-five groups active, in 1976 when five festivals were held to attack the bicentennial celebration of the U.S. By then *teatros* had developed their own genres, themes and community bases from Southern California to the Midwest; even groups of Puerto Ricans and other Hispanics in New York and New Jersey were following this example.

Not too long after Ortego's "Chicano Renaissance" article was written, many Chicano artists transcended the *indigenista* phase and, as the Chicano Movement waned, cultural nationalism as an art form was severely criticized, especially by Chicano Marxists; they saw it as diversionary and escapist. After leaving Delano and the UFW, Valdez established a theater workshop in San Juan Bautista, California, where part of the daily excercises included praying to the Mesoamerican god Quetzacoatl as a reincarnation of Jesus Christ. Marxist intellectuals criticized his art because "its proposal for the resolution of material problems through spiritual means. . . was too close to the religious beliefs and superstitions that hampered La Raza's progress."[4] But surprisingly, this spiritual genre has survived to the present day. Protests to the 1992 observations of the 500-year anniversary of Columbus's arrival in America injected new life into the notion of Aztlán. But today Valdez and other participants in Chicano theater have gone to Hollywood, some achieving success as did Valdez in his films *La Bamba* and *The Cisco Kid*.

In Los Angeles and other California cities, a strong muralist movement emerged which employed strong Indian motifs, glorified interpretations of Chicano history and romantic allusions to mundane life in the barrios. Such artists as Eugenio Quesada of Phoenix, Peter Rodríguez of San Francisco, Melesio Casas from San Antonio and Ray Patlán of Chicago now pursue other art forms, but their original inspiration came from the social art movements of Mexican muralists such as Diego Rivera, José Clemente Orozco and David Alfaro Siquieros, who pioneered the rebirth of public art in Latin America. Highly influenced by the three Mexican greats, San Diego artists Salvador Torres, Victor Ochoa and David Avalos produced the most impressive mural project to date in Balboa Park, popularly known as "Chicano Park." Today murals are still being created by Chicanos and other community-based groups, but they do not have the same cultural orientation of the 1960s and 1970s. The young Phoenix muralist, David Murietta, for example, painted at least two giant murals of Charles Barkley, the Phoenix Suns basketball star, on barrio walls while other muralists, Los Cuatro from Los Angeles, now exhibit their giant neighborhood scenes in muse-

[3] Phillip D. Ortego, "The Chicano Renaissance," *Introduction to Chicano Studies,* Durán and Bernard, eds (New York: Macmillan Publishing Co., Inc., 1982), pp. 576-577.

[4] Nicolás Kanellos, "Theater," *The Hispanic American Almanac: A Reference Work on Hispanics in the United States,* ed. by Nicolás Kanellos (Detroit: Gale Research, Inc., 1993), p. 523.

Shattering the Myth:
Plays by Hispanic Women

122. The art of Yreina D. Cervántez featured on an Arte Público Book.

ums and galleries. The most innovative collective art group is ASCO, headed by Harry Gamboa. It produced living murals, guerrilla street happenings, avant garde photography and video documentation that is the essence of postmodernism.

Initially other Chicano graphic art appeared in *movimiento* tabloids of the 1960s, interspersed with the denouncements of racism, inadequate education and police brutality. The Chicano Press Association established a Southwest communication network of newspapers that interchanged items of all sorts, including art work. More recently, the plastic arts, whose origins are in the Chicano Movement, directly or indirectly have grown in respectability and institutional accep-

tance. Significant exhibitions such as the 1988 "Hispanic Art in the U.S.: Thirty Painters and Sculptor," and the more recent 1992 "Chicano Art of Resistance and Affirmation" were displayed in major museums throughout the country. Women artists such as Pattsi Valdez and Carmen Lomas Garza have achieved international renown, taking Chicano art to new heights of experimentation beyond the simple *movimiento* forms of the 1960s and 1970s.

Literature, primarily poetry, also appeared first as oral performances at movement events and in the CPA publications. The San Diego poet Alurista, the quintessential promoter of *Chicanismo* and *indigenismo* during the 1960s, was the most widely read of the Chicano writers. His 1960s and 1970s poetry idealized the pre-Columbian past and essentialized such mundane aspects of culture as the corn tortilla. As happened to Luis Valdez, Alurista's work was also faulted by Chicano Marxists and other critics for dwelling too much on cultural fantasies.

Eventually artists moved from publishing their works in the tabloids and onto the pages of Chicano Movement-inspired literary journals, most of which no longer exist. José Armas, an activist with Albuquerque youth, for example, founded *De Colores*; it ceased publishing in 1980. Others, to name but a few, included *Mango*, edited by Dorna Lee Cervantes in California; *La Palabra*, the only all-Spanish-language journal, started by Justo Alarcón at Arizona State University; and the *Bilingual Review*, the brainchild of Gary Keller in New York. The latter is still published at Arizona State University. The premier journal in the arts now goes under the name of *The Americas Review* and is published at the University of Houston. It began in 1973 as *Revista Chicano-Riqueña* in the unlikely place of Indiana University Northwest in Gary. The name reflected the ethnicity of its editors, Luis Dávila, a literature professor at Indiana University in Bloomington, a Texas Chicano, and Nuyorican Nicolás Kanellos, who then taught at the Gary campus. The original impulse for the journal, however, came from Chicano and Puerto Rican students at both campuses.

123. "Los Tejanos," a special issue of *Revista Chicano-Riqueña*, with the sculpture "Vaquero" by Luis Jiménez on

Like journals, a plethora of publishing companies emerged during and after the height of the *movimiento*. Octavio Romano, for example, shortly after launching *El Grito*, also founded Quinto Sol Publications, which published the first significant Chicano novels of the 1970s after running a competition for the best novel with a $1,000 *premio* (prize). In the 1970s José Armas ran Pajarito Press for a few years; in Ypsilanti, Michigan, Gary Keller established the Bilingual Review Press, now at Arizona State University, and Nicolás Kanellos now operates the largest Latino publishing house in the country, Arte Público Press, an outgrowth of *Revista Chicano-Riqueña*.

The legacy of Chicano literature is immense. Most writers in recent years have transcended the earlier *indigenismo* themes of Alurista, the strident polemics of the ex-convict turned poet, Ricardo Sánchez, and the romanticized street life of José Montoya. Now poets and novelists such as Gary Soto, Pat Mora, Graciela Limón and Victor Villaseñor express their *Chicanismo* through the mundane experiences of their lives with less idealism and anger. Still, contemporary writers dip back into the heart of the *movimiento* for inspiration. Long-time essayist, short story writer and poet Francisco Alarcón, for example, is the latest to resurrect the *indigenista* genre.

Some artists whose ascendancy came during the Chicano Movement understandably lament its passing. In 1992 pioneer Chicano artist and poet from Sacramento, José Montoya, lauded the mainstream Chicano "*artistas* [who] stayed on their stations, even after it was declared—'Hey!, there is no more race! You guys can stop running.'" But there is a recent resurrection according to the same artist, that "gives me a good sense that we are capable of bringing it around. . . of picking it up again."[5]

Little in his comments reveals notions of reviving the political aspects of the movement, however.

CHICANA FEMINISM: THE ARTS AND IDEOLOGY

It is Chicana writers today, however, who have taken the reins of the literary movement, many of them exploring feminist themes, styles and ideology. They focus on their subordination as women and lesbians of color. There seemed to be precious little during the height of the *movimiento* that augured a legacy of Chicana feminism, the women having been consigned to a support system for the male leadership. In 1969 an article entitled, "Genocide on the Chicano family," written by anonymous females in the Brown Beret magazine, *La Causa*, stated that, "Chicanas of the Brown Berets Organization are publicly protesting all conspired genocidal plans of the fascist government on behalf of 'La Raza Chicana' for the past 200 years." The piece denounced the Planned Parenthood efforts at birth control as fascist-inspired "genocidal programs." Birth control, it stated, was just a step to abortion and then sterilization. "La Raza's future depends on the health of all Chicanas in order for them to be able to continue bear[ing] healthy Chicanitos."[6]

By present standards such a view appears hopelessly backward and even submissive. Closer observation, however, demonstrates the

[5] Interview with José Montoya by Susan Racho, February 4, 1992, NLCC-GP.

[6] *La Causa*, March, 1969, clipping in the files of Edward Escobar.

124. Writers Ana Castillo, Evangelina Vigil-Piñón, Sandra Cisneros and Pat Mora after reading from their works at a NACS conference in Austin, Texas.

search for a Chicana feminist perspective. Chicanas started to demonstrate discontent with the *machista* attitudes shown by Chicano male leaders early in the movement. A founder of the Chicana Welfare Rights Organization, for example, Anna Nieto-Gómez, tried to put sterilization and the welfare rights of single mothers on the *movimiento* agenda in 1970 but was met with indifference by the male-dominated organizations. Nieto-Gómez's case demonstrates that the historical subordination of Mexican women and contemporary male chauvinism within the Chicano Movement contributed greatly to repressing Chicana activists. In November 1969 she wrote "Somos Chicanas de Aztlán," a poem replete with cultural nationalist allusions and challenges to the dominant attitude of *movimiento* males. She stated that the woman should no longer march behind her man or stay at home. Albeit some of the stanzas betray what Chicana feminists later would condemn as pandering to the male ego, she nonetheless provided a base for Chicana militancy:

> We are the soldaderas of our men
> We are the adelitas y las Juana Gallos de hoy. . .
>
> It shall be our love that shall nourish our men together
> Together, we shall plant the seed
> And the women shall bear the children of La Raza Nueva
> United we shall be La Familia Nueva[7]

"What is the Role of the Chicana in the Movement" was written by an anonymous woman from Long Beach in *La Raza*: "What role does the Chicana serve in the Movement? Just how important is she to the Movement that is dominated by men? The men in the movement only think of her when they need some typing done or when their stomachs growl, they ask her to run to the store, and buy food for them and cook it.

"Naturally, she is also needed for parties and to serve as hostesses for conferences. Few girls are invited to attend conferences and, if so, only to take the minutes of the conference or attend parties afterwards. Chicanas feel that it is the men who have the knowledge and the experience, they must train women in order to strengthen the Movement."

This last request is made so they can help children grow up with the right political orientation: "Help us to teach them to be revolutionary Chicanos for La Causa. Help us organize, train us and develop us."[8]

---

[7] *La Raza*, November 1969, clipping in the files of Edward Escobar.

[8] *La Raza*, November 1969.

Chicanas moved rapidly beyond that early feminism. With the demise of the *movimiento,* Chicana activists formulated a critique that was the harshest on the male participants of the *movimiento.* Marta Cotera, a La Raza Unida Party leader and cofounder of the Jacinto Treviño Alternative College, remembers,

> There were attempts to relegate women to a secondary position. These attempts were many times not successful. . . because women were constantly saying, 'Hey we gotta do this. We gotta be leaders or we gotta be *chingonas* (big shots), like the guys who are the *chingones.* . . . The attempts failed to relegate the women who were doing the work. . . . They were very much in evidence as. . . candidates, as organizers in leadership positions. Just simply because they were getting the work done.[9]

Indeed Chicanas in the LURP in 1972 formed a feminist caucus within the party, precisely to discuss those issues.

The Chicana intelligentsia, more than former activists, is responsible for developing a new intellectual evaluation by which the role of women in Mexican American and the greater Anglo society can be measured. At Indiana University in Bloomington, Norma Alarcón, as a graduate student in 1981, founded *Third Woman,* a literary journal designed to give voice to the emerging desire for liberation that Chicanas and Latinas felt had been denied them in the *movimiento.*

The feminist movement has spread swiftly and has invigorated the Chicano intellectual agenda. Historians like Vicky Ruiz and Antonia Castañeda, for example, do not see Mexican American women as just actors in a male-dominated society. Instead, they reconstruct the historical tapestry in which women interacted. In the forefront of the new radical critique by women of color are such essayists as Gloria Anzaldúa and Cherríe Moraga. Their works clearly delineate the different world inhabited by Chicanas, where borders exist for separating them from the white world and Chicano men.

A LEGACY OF WORDS AS SYMBOLS

Some of the lexicon used in the movement has survived to this day, albeit mainly in circles that have an unbroken tie to the movement: university students, artists, intellectuals, scholars, etc. The most apparent is the word *Chicano* itself. Outside of the academic environment, the term is met with indifference, and among Mexican immigrants it is scorned. But the struggle over its use no longer draws the same heat that it did when activists first proposed *Chicano* in the 1960s.

Much of the opposition to the expression in

125. Chicana poet and editor of a mid-1970s magazine, *Mango:* Lorna Dee Cervantes.

---

[9] On-camera interview with Marta Cotera.

126. Scholar Antonia
Castañeda.

the 1960s rested more on disapproval of "militants" than of the word itself although many Mexican Americans remembered how it was used to denote the lower classes. During the Los Angeles school walkouts in the spring of 1968, Lincoln High School teacher Carmen Terrazas, an opponent of the strike, wrote a letter to the *Los Angeles Times* condemning the word *Chicano* as demeaning to Mexican Americans. Soon after, there appeared in *La Raza* a "La Adelita Letter to La Malinche." La Adelita was the name for female camp followers and soldiers during the Mexican Revolution, and La Malinche was the consort of Hernán Cortés, who legend has it betrayed her people. "As for the term Chicano," wrote La Adelita, "I suggest Terrazas do some research into its origin. We have always referred to ourselves as Chicanos. . . . We gave it to ourselves, the Anglo did not. . . . Terrazas insists on referring to herself as an American of Mexican descent. . . she suffers from an inferiority complex for which I pity her."[10]

During this era, both sides constructed elaborate etymologies of *Chicano*. To those who wished for the word to represent the movement, *Chicano* derived from the ancient Nahuatl word *mexicano* with the "x" being pronounced as a "shh" sound. Among the many versions that detractors used to disqualify the term was that it came from *chicas patas,* an extremely pejorative reference used to denote new arrivals from Mexico.

In Phoenix, Chicanos por la Causa (CPLC) was founded in 1969 as an organization of militant advocates for change. It evolved into a community development organization that dispenses services but does not engage in the more radical activity that characterized it in earlier years. During the 1980s, known as the "Decade of the Hispanic," the group's name presented difficulties for some board members. But despite pressure to change it, the staff never succumbed but maintained the militant sounding moniker given it by the activists of another era.

---

[10] *La Raza*, March 28, 1969, clipping from the files of Edward Escobar.

In the 1980s the word *Hispanic* came into use as a self-identifier. Soon Chicanos formulated a fanciful conspiracy theory that asserted the term was coined either by the Nixon, the Carter or the Reagan administration, and was foisted on Mexican Americans as a nondescript word which stripped them of their particular ethnic identity. According to this critique, the term put Chicanos in an ethnic category with other Latinos to which they did not belong and diluted their power as the largest Latino population group. With the resurgence of utopian *indigenismo* in the last few years, Mexican Americans who use the word *Hispanic* are accused of pathologically denying their Mexican-Indian background.

These attempts to manipulate the use of self-identifiers by a cultural vanguard is definitely part of the *movimiento* legacy and demonstrates just how durable these politics can be. Ironically, even as Mexican Americans employed the word *Hispanic*, they exhibited a profound degree of ethnic pride that did not exist before the Chicano Movement.

The word and concept of Aztlán have also survived, albeit confined to the same circle that uses *Chicano*. The journal *Aztlán* has provided the word, if not the concept, endurance beyond the *movimiento* era. Ironically in the 1970s intellectuals who were criticizing the cultural nationalism which gave birth to the concept of Aztlán were writing in *Aztlán*. But just as post-modernist trends among Chicanos have helped revive *indigenismo*, accompanying this same course is an increased use of the word *Aztlán*. The poet Alurista, in recalling the assaults on his art in the late 1960s when he was a student at San Diego State College, said that Chicano infiltrators from the Socialist Workers Party (SWP) had denounced him for inventing Aztlán because "it was a form of mystification and a way of confusing people." But he defended himself from these "close-minded," dogmatic ideologies, he claims, by telling them, "You guys don't understand metaphors. . . sym-bols. . . what collective consciousness is all about." In spite of all the ridicule he endured, Alurista gloats, "The fact of the matter is that Aztlán has prevailed and has become *the* unifying symbol I intended it to be."[11]

CULTURAL NATIONALISM VS. *MOVIMIENTO* MARXISM

From the outset the Chicano Movement declared itself to be a radical grassroots crusade, different from its Mexican American predecessors. It appropriated the farm-worker movement of César Chávez as part of its initiative. During its height, most Marxist or socialist philosophies were rejected, but some activists adhered to a circumstantial and vague socialism tinged with a Third-World orientation. In reality, few activists studied or applied a rigorous Marxist analysis to their formulations. As a consequence, in the arena of civil rights and political empowerment, the Chicano Movement left a legacy not too far astray from what Mexican Americanism strove for.

Before 1972 the Socialist Worker's Party had attempted to infiltrate the *movimiento*, but its participation was so intrusive and problematic that eventually most groups denied it participation in the Chicano Movement. Extremist nationalistic leaders, who dominated the *movimiento*, often said that they rejected a structured Marxist method because its European orientation was not valid for the Chicano experience. An underlying reason for such rejections, however, was that, in spite of increasing militancy and separatist rhetoric, the Chicano thrust was not that far removed from the reformist goals of the Mexican American generation: in essence, to remove the racist obstacles to mobility. Few activists knew about the Congress of Spanish-Speaking People or AMMA, and if they had, it is doubtful they would have emulated their orientation. The devotion and physical efforts exerted by *movimiento* participants in assisting farm-worker unions were on a

---

[11] Interview with Alurista.

part-time basis and temporary. By 1972, as was evident at the La Raza Unida Party Conference in El Paso, César Chávez was looked upon with disdain by many activists.

Some structured Marxism did influence the movement, however. After the failure of LRUP, which announced the beginning of the end for the *movimiento,* many participants began to question the ability of cultural-nationalist prescriptions and race-identity politics to provide solutions to the problems of Chicanos. At that point, many former activists turned to traditional politics within the system. Some *movimiento* participants who did not abandon radical activism, nevertheless, looked to more defined Marxist structural explanations and sought praxis through this approach. The *Centro de Acción Social Autónoma— Hermandad General de Trabajadores* (CASA— HGT Center for Autonomous Social Action-General Brotherhood of Workers) launched the most extensive Marxist effort to push the Chicano Movement away from reformist goals. Bert Corona, the perennial activist with roots in Mexican American-era radical politics, and Magdalena Mora, along with former members of *Católicos por la Raza* (Catholics for the Race) and the UFW, began CASA-HGT in 1968 to help undocumented immigrants obtain legal status. In the mid-1970s the group was reorganized, Corona lost his preeminence and its members began openly espousing a Marxist-Leninist ideology. CASA had the largest participation of Chicanas in leadership positions of any Chicano organization. Its newspaper, *Sin Fronteras* (Without Borders), for example, was edited by Kathy Ochoa. According to Juan Gómez-Quiñones,

> CASA achieved a significant record of success. They pushed forward ideological and organizational development by providing militant leadership in a wide set of activities nationally and in Los Angeles. . . . The newspaper *Sin Fronteras* was clearly the best militant print organ of the movement.[12]

Plagued by internal leadership conflicts similar to ones experienced by other leftist organizations of previous decades, CASA activities came to an end. Its appeal did not go beyond a tightly disciplined circle of organizers. But in its short life, the group brought to the forefront the previously ignored issue of immigrant workers, especially the undocumented.

The attention paid to the issue of undocumented workers by Mexican Americans allowed José Angel Gutiérrez in 1977 to make his final bid to remain a major player in Mexican American politics. By then, LRUP was in its death throes. Gutiérrez, after being denied a large federal grant because of a Democratic party-led vendetta, was losing his grip on power in Zavala County. He then organized the First National Chicano/Latino Immigration Conference in San Antonio. Its aim was to oppose an effort initiated by President Jimmy Carter's administration to stem illegal immigration. Unlike typical Chicano Movement meetings, this one attracted every major Mexican American organization in the country. Besides LRUP members, representatives from CASA-HGT, the GI Forum, LULAC, Mexican American Legal Defense and Education Fund (MALDEF) and even from the hard-to-insult SWP attended. The odd mix unfortunately led to extreme sectarian squabbling, and the conference adjourned without reaching an accord. The immigrant-worker issue continues today as a major legacy left for today's civil rights activists by the Chicano Movement. It is an issue that can be traced in large degree to CASA-HGT activism within the Chicano Movement.

Other socialist groups also made inroads into the movement. The Socialist Workers Party, in spite of conflict with the *movimiento* mainstream, continued to attract significant numbers of Chicanos as did the Communist Labor Party. The August 29th Movement, an organization identified with Maoism but made up of Chicanos, also attempted to instill radical consciousness among

---

[12] Gómez-Quiñones, *Chicano Politics,* p. 151.

Mexican Americans, primarily in California. All in all, none of the Marxist groups drew the same degree of attention among the general Mexican American population as did the mainstream *movimiento* nationalism.

Since *movimiento* participants were not involved in labor organizing efforts to any large degree, with the exception of the VFW, there is little of that left today that can be directly traceable to the movement. To be sure, many former activists such as Joe Razo, the former publisher of *La Raza*, are now active in labor issues that affect Latino immigrants, a concern that has been prompted by the dramatic rise in immigration during recent years. But those efforts do not apply Chicano Movement symbolism and they bear little resemblance to the CASA outlook.

THE CHICANO MOVEMENT SPIN TO TRADITIONAL POLITICS

The founding of the Mexican American Legal Defense and Education Fund (MALDEF) and the Southwest Voter Registration and Education Project (SVREP) are among important projects which were funded by the Southwest Council of La Raza (SWCLR), a creation of the Ford Foundation's attempts to bring about social change—both were initially headquartered in San Antonio in the late 1960s. Although both were outgrowths of *movimiento* activity, they strove to bring about change through the system. Lawyers Pete Tijerina and Gregory Luna secured the funding for MALDEF in 1968, which over the years and until the present day has pursued numerous cases affecting Mexican Americans collectively, such as those dealing with educational neglect, bilingual education, affirmative action and the rights of undocumented workers. Its first director was lawyer Pete Tijerina. Mario Obledo, who in the 1980s went on to become LULAC's most strident president, was the first general consul of MALDEF. In 1969, before Obledo's involvement in MALDEF, he had collaborated with Willie Velásquez in the Raza conferences which led to the formation of MAYO. After that, however, he drifted away from LRUP activism.

In 1973 the MALDEF board hired Vilma Martínez, a native of San Antonio, who oversaw the organization's rise to prominence. Although Martínez pursued cases through assertive persistence, typical of the *movimiento* style, she did not cultivate a direct tie to the Chicano Movement. Both Martínez and Obledo, however, sympathized with LRUP. One of the most publicized MALDEF achievements was the 1982 *Plyer v. Doe* case; the organization successfully argued before the U.S. Supreme Court to force the Houston Independent School District to educate the children of undocumented workers.

Tommy Espinoza, director of Chicanos por la Causa in Phoenix, asserts that "the only way you could get elected was to go through a business group that would hand-pick their candidates and then you might run. But then you were working for their interests and not that of the Mexican community."[13]

Similarly Texas state legislator, Pete Torres Jr. recalls, "The climate in San Antonio in the early sixties was not so unique from other southwestern cities. We had a business establishment that had been running the city for some fifteen years. They ran the candidates citywide. Since elections were 'at-large,' the local Mexicanos and local labor and liberal leadership...we were all cut out from participation in city hall."[14]

[13] Interview with Tommy Espinoza by Jesús Treviño, n.d, NLCC-GP.

[14] Interview with Pete Torres Jr. by Jesús Treviño, January 30, 1992, NLCC-GP.

Despite the failure of LRUP as a political strategy, electoral involvement provided the *movimiento* valuable lessons which were put to effective use later. Prior to the movement, Mexican American leaders understood that mass registration of their people could pave the road to empowerment in electoral politics. But during the *movimiento*, Chicanos through the LRUP focused attention on such obstacles as gerrymandering, which prevented solid Mexican voting districts from existing, and the at-large election system, which diluted the voting power of solidly Mexican sections at both the state and municipal levels. This procedure allowed Anglo elites to control who would get elected.

127. Willie Velásquez, founding director of the Southwest Voter Registration and Education Project.

MALDEF, from its inception, strove to end such discrimination in the electoral process. In 1972 it attacked the at-large system in the *White v. Register* case, in which its lawyers demonstrated that the at-large process had disenfranchised Mexican Americans politically. MALDEF won the case at the state level and then before the Supreme Court when the state of Texas appealed the decision. Now a candidate running for office had to represent a specific district and only registered voters from that district were allowed to vote in his or her election. In 1975, San Antonio converted to single member districts, making possible the election of more Mexican Americans to the city council and eventually the election of Henry Cisneros as mayor.

At the time that MALDEF was winning its landmark decision of *White v. Register*, Willie Velásquez was pursuing his dream by building an organization that would focus on registering Chicanos to vote: the SVREP. Velásquez, along with José Angel Gutiérrez and Mario Compeán, was one of the founders of MAYO. But in 1969 he parted with the group because he did not agree with the concept of LRUP. He felt that Chicanos should work through the existing structure, in this case the Democratic Party. This perspective created a chasm between his ideals and those of Chicano Movement leaders (see Chapters Twelve and Thirteen). Nonetheless, the Ford Foundation-funded SVREP, like MALDEF, tapped into the Chicano consciousness which *movimiento* activists had instilled among Mexican Americans.

The SVREP directed its resources to registering Mexican American voters and, in cooperation with MALDEF, to engaging in litigation to assure that the electoral system complied with the 1965 Voting Rights

Andy Hernández, ex-director of the Southwest Voter Registration and Education Project, recalls Velásquez's unrelenting vision: "Willie said, 'We got to build a voter organization effort within our community like no other Chicano has ever seen before. Andy, we're going to build a registration drive that is going to last ten years! We're going to register all those Mexicans to vote and by the time we're finished, we're going to elect all of our people to political power, and every goddamn gringo political caucus is going to respect us!' I thought to myself, here is this guy up here in this tiny office, sitting in a folding chair with a folding table for a desk, and he is telling me we're going to build an organization that is going to have gringos shaking in their boots. Yeah, sure!"[15]

[15] Interview with Andy Hernández by Jesús Treviño, January 30, 1992, NLCC-GP.

Act. Velásquez modeled the organization after a similar effort made by Black civil rights leaders in Atlanta. The SVREP sought to obtain funds by applying for nonprofit status with the Internal Revenue Service in 1970, but the effort was stymied by bureaucratic stonewalling. It was years before Velásquez's vision was able to get off the ground. SVREP organizers suspected that the Republican-controlled administration was using the IRS to forestall its formation. With Nixon out of office in 1974, however, the organization finally received its nonprofit status and immediately set out to register Mexican Americans.

The combined efforts made by MALDEF and SVREP are responsible for the considerable gains Mexicans have made through the ballot box in recent years. The first opportunity to put this two-pronged assault to a test came in 1975 in Denver, where redistricting MALDEF and massive registration SRVEP drives resulted in the election of Stan Sandos and Sal Carpio to the city council. Sal Carpio had been a member of Colorado's La Raza Unida Party. More recently, the election of Ed Pastor in 1992 as Arizona's first Mexican American congressman is also the result of redistricting and registration drives.

The dream of the Mexican American generation was achieved by a strategy it had espoused to begin with, but the drama created by LRUP accelerated the process. The confluence of the efforts of both generations succeeded in achieving an age-old objective. Velásquez remained the director of the SVREP until his untimely death in 1988.

GRASSROOTS EMPOWERMENT EFFORTS

Perhaps the most visible legacy of the *movimiento* is related to the formation of economic and community empowerment organizations. In part, this effort exists because of the consciousness raised by militant Chicanos who pressured mainstream Mexican American leaders in the 1960s to reassess old prescriptions for solving long-standing social problems. Initially the main vehicle for this effort was the Ford Foundation-funded Southwest Council of La Raza (SWCLR), which empowered local community-action

groups in San Antonio, Oakland, Phoenix and Los Angeles. Started by such Mexican American era stalwarts as the scholar-union organizer Ernesto Galarza and United Mine Workers Union executive Maclovio Barraza, the SWCLR established two headquarters, one in Phoenix and the other in San Francisco. San Antonio's Mexican American Unity Council (MAUC), which provided an organizational base for the Mexican American Youth Organization (MAYO), was one of the organizations funded by the SWCLR (see Chapter Twelve).

In Phoenix, Maclovio Barraza assisted *movimiento* activists in founding Chicanos por la Causa (CPLC) in 1969, also with funding from the SWCLR. The organization began with militant fervor by organizing school walkouts and an attempted school board takeover. Eventually, CPLC became an efficiently run community development program, which continues today as one of the largest in the nation. It administers drug rehabilitation and senior citizens centers and acts as a liaison with Chicano small businesses and the federal government.

But the most well endowed community initiative, which still exists, emerged in Los Angeles. After the walkouts had politicized Mexicans in the city, the United Auto Workers (UAW) union and some other labor groups financed the formation of The East Los Angeles Community Union (TELACU). It first provided economic development inside the barrios and assisted self-help groups in obtaining funding. This experiment originated in a UAW policy inspired by its long-time president, Walter Reuther, to help stem the deterioration of the inner cities. The two UAW officials chosen to administer TELACU, Esteban Torres and Glen O'Loane, were at first met with suspicion by traditional organizations and even new ones such as the Brown Berets. But when it became clear that TELACU controlled many of the resources necessary to deal with East Los Angeles problems, the two union men were accommodated into the fold.

With funding from outside the unions, TELACU extended its activities to include crime-prevention and drug-abuse counseling and, at one point, it even attempted to take over an ailing mattress factory. Eventually millions of dollars were dispersed through the organization, and Torres became a political king maker. Some of the more idealistic radicals never accommodated to what they called "poverty pimping," but more often funds from the group bought it widespread allegiance and it came to dominate East Los Angeles social activism.

Over the years TELACU became involved in political issues, including the 1974 attempt to incorporate East Los Angeles. The organization received large-scale funding from the federal Office of Economic Opportunity (OEO), which allowed it to expand its vast empire even further—in 1985 TELACU's assets were valued at eighty million dollars.

Ultimately the Chicano Movement accelerated the struggle to end discrimination in hiring, a movement pioneered in the 1940s by Mexican American advocates such as George I. Sánchez, and which was continued into the 1960s by such groups as PASO, LULAC and the GI Forum. Indeed the militancy shown by Mexican Americans when they walked out of an Equal Employment Opportunity Commission in Albuquerque in 1966 to draw attention to discrimination served as a model for future *movimiento* activists (see Chapter Ten). There is no doubt that affirmative action compliance for Mexican Americans would have been slower if not for the intensity of demands made during the Chicano Movement.

The efforts of the Mexican American Community Service Organization (CSO) were replicated with the founding of San Antonio's Communities Organized for Public Services (COPS) in 1974 and the United Neighborhood Organization (UNO) in Los Angeles in the late 1970s. Both organizations, which use the Saul Alinsky Industrial Area Foundations (IAF) methods on which César Chávez relied, are funded by the Catholic Church. The basic methodology is to identify the problems that most antagonize a community and then organize its inhabitants

around these issues. Confrontational tactics are used, but without ideological underpinnings other than self-interest. The organizers of both groups are all Chicanos, but they are not allowed to use nationalism as a motivation. In San Antonio, for example, COPS was successful in conducting a political campaign and electing candidates based on the propensity of flash floods to devastate west side neighborhoods.

But even these organizations, which seem to avoid cultural identity and Marxist politics, are connected to the *movimiento*. Many of their activists were politicized during the Chicano Movement, including Ernie Cortés, the main impetus behind both COPS and UNO. He began his political career as a member of MAYO. Significantly, most of the presidents of COPS chapters have been women.

CONCLUSION

If the persistence of the Chicano Movement is measured only by vestiges which are directly tied to the movement, then the *movimiento* is dead. A much broader perspective has to be taken, however, one that traces the civil rights of U.S. Mexicans beyond the narrow period of the *movimiento*. It would be sad to think that the Chicano struggle for success hinges on whether we can resurrect the Brown Berets. The Crusade for Justice still exists in Denver, espousing a dogma that the real Aztlán of the Aztecs is the Southwest. If "Corky" Gonzales were to make a call for a national meeting, it is doubtful it would have the impact of the 1969 youth conference— even if as many people attended. Almost every university in the Southwest has a Movimiento Estudiantil Chicano de Aztlán (MECHA) organization. While many chapters simply sponsor social events and cultural celebrations, others are more politically active. Even so, the attention-getting platform which existed for Chicano student organizations in the 1960s is no longer there. So what is left?

[16] Author interview with Alfredo Gutiérrez, November 12, 1995.

A successful politician-businessman in Arizona who was also a pioneer in the *movimiento* told this author that, "the majority of activists were just having a good time," including himself. "All the gains we made in civil rights and political representation would have been gotten without all the shouting," he asserted. "Look at what Willie Velásquez did."[16]

That opinion, coming from one of the former shouters, could be valid, and perhaps someday we can have a social science method of measuring such a conclusion. Until then, there will be room for many other assessments, such as those offered in this chapter.

Let us conclude this book on a positive note. Joe Razo, the founder of Los Angeles's *La Raza* newspaper who was arrested during the 1968 walkouts, concedes that the *movimiento* lapsed into extremes of nationalism and socialism, and activists religiously believed "our own propaganda." He includes his own publication in this. But those were just learning stages, according to Razo, and far from seeing the *movimiento* as

dead, he thinks that "we are still building, this movement is still in its infancy. There are a lot of fights [left]. . . and for some of us who love to get into struggles, that's the beauty of it."[17]

It took about five years before the activists spent their passion or the political environment changed to where they lost their platform. Many Mexican Americans with a modicum of power within the "system," who were made uncomfortable during this era because of militancy and demands to account to *movimiento* goals, welcomed its demise. This does not mean that they did not benefit or that they remained unaffected by the Chicano Movement.

Rosalío Muñoz, organizer of the 1970 National Chicano Moratorium, thinks back on the impact of the movement and concludes that "it helped crystallize for people making a commitment, just like in my own life, a commitment from there to go on. Let's start setting up the basis to win what the program was in those days. And I think our generation then. . . did that, and it has begun coming into fruition now."[18]

[17] Interview with Joe Razo,.

[18] Interview with Rosalío Muñoz.

BIBLIOGRAPHY

ARCHIVAL AND MANUSCRIPT COLLECTIONS

American Legion Repatriation Files, East Chicago, Indiana Historical Society.

Archivo General de la Nación, Mexico City, Presidentes.

Archivo Histórico de la Secretaría de Relaciones Exteriores (AHSRE), Consular Records.

Arizona Historical Society Archives, Tucson, Arizona.

Carey McWilliams Papers, Special Collections, University of California, Los Angeles, Research Library.

Chicano Collection, Arizona State University Library.

Colleción Porfirio Díaz, Hemeroteca, Universidad Iberoamericana, Mexico City.

Federal Writers Project, Bancroft Library, University of California, Berkeley.

Espy, M. Watt, and John Ortiz Smykla. Executions in the United States, 1608-1687: The Espy File (Ann Arbor: Interuniversity Consortium for Political and Social Research, 1990), Machine Readable Data File 8541.

Manuel Gamio Papers, Bancroft Library, University of California, Berkeley.

National Latino Communications Center and Galán Productions, Interview Collection, Los Angeles and Austin.

NEWSPAPERS AND MAGAZINES

Arizona Republic (Phoenix)
Calumet News (East Chicago, Indiana)
Católicos por la Raza (Los Angeles)
La Causa (Los Angeles)
Chicago Daily Tribune
The Chicano Student (Los Angeles)
El Cosmopolita (Kansas City)
El Defensor (Edinburg, Texas)
Forward (Los Angeles)
El Imparcial de Texas (San Antonio)
El Nacional (Chicago)
Latino Americano (Phoenix)
The Los Angeles Star
The Mexican Voice (Los Angeles)
New York Times
La Opinión (Los Angeles)
La Prensa (Los Angeles)
La Prensa (San Antonio)
La Raza (Los Angeles)
El Tucsonense (Tucson)
Weekly Arizona (Tucson)

INTERVIEWS

Interview transcripts. Provided by National Latino Communications Center, Los Angeles and Galán Productions, Austin:

Rodolfo Acuña, March 6, 1992.
Alurista by Enrique Berumen, March 2, 1995.
Salomón Baldenegro by Jesús Treviño, February 25, 1992.
Carlos Cadena by Jesús Treviño, n.d.
Larry Calloway by Jesús Treviño, July 23, 1992.
David Cargo by Claire Jones, February 3, 1994.
César Chávez by Luis Torres, April 20, 1992.
Jerry Cohen by Myléne Moreno, January 20, 1994.
Marta Cotera by Jesús Treviño, January 29, 1992.
Paula Crisóstomo by Jesús Treviño, February 15, 1993.
Tommy Espinoza by Jesus Treviño, n.d.
Joe Fernández by Jesús Treviño, July 27, 1992.
Rodolfo "Corky" Gonzales by Daniel Salazar, October 4, 1984.
José Angel Gutiérrez by Jesús Treviño, January 27, 1992.
Andy Hernández by Jesús Treviño, January 30, 1992.
Dolores Huerta by Luis Torres, March 19, 1992.
Severita Lara by Jesús Treviño, January 31, 1992.
Amalia Mesa Baines by Susan Racho, February 7, 1992.
Carlos Montes by Enrique Berumen, February 6, 1994.
José Montoya by Susan Racho, February 4, 1992.
Carlos Muñoz by Susan Racho, February 6, 1992.
Carlos Muñoz by Jesús Treviño, October 7, 1995.
Rosalío Muñoz by Jesús Treviño, December 30, 1993.
Gil Padilla by Myléne Moreno, January 14, 1994.
Joe Razo, March 4, 1992.
David Sánchez by Enrique Berumen, January 22, 1994.
David Sánchez by Jesús Treviño, July 22, 1992.
Alfonso Sánchez by Jesús Treviño, July 24, 1992.
Reies López Tijerina by Luis Torres, December 29, 1989.
Pete Torres Jr. by Jesús Treviño, January 30, 1992.

On-camera interviews, National Latino Communications Center, Los Angeles, and Galán Productions:

Joe Aguerrebere by Susan Racho, January 18, 1995.
Bert Corona by Ray Santiesteban, December 22, 1994.
Marta Cotera by Robert Cozens, January 18, 1995.
Charles Cotrell by Ray Santiesteban, October 14, 1994.
Sissy Farenthold by Rose Hansen, September 7, 1995.
Jessica Govea by Sylvia Morales, December 5, 1994.
Carlos Guerra by Robert Cozens, October 15, 1994.
José Angel Gutiérrez by Hector Gálan, December 12, 1994.
John Hill by Rose Hansen, September 7, 1995.
Dolores Huerta by Sylvia Morales, January 13, 1995.
Eliseo Medina by Sylvia Morales, November 18, 1995.
Carlos Montes by Susan Racho, December 1, 1994.

Diane Palacios by Robert Cozens, October 15, 1994.
Raúl Ruiz by Robert Cozens, December 21, 1994.
Richard Santillán by Robert Cozens, December 22, 1994.
Lionel Steinberg by Sylvia Morales, December 7, 1994.
Sabine Ulibarrí by Myléne Moreno, April 18, 1995.
Ernesto Vigil by Myléne Moreno, February 14, 1995.

Interviews conducted by author:
José Anguiano, East Chicago, September 14, 1974.
José Cruz Cervantes, Houston, March 21, 1976.
Mercedes García de Rosales, Tucson, October 15, 1991.
Alfredo Gutiérrez, November 12, 1995.
Ana Navarro de Garza, Schererville, Indiana, 1975.
Eleazar Risco, September 21, 1995.
Refugio Rosales de Dalton, Tucson, October 15, 1991.
Armando Valdez, September 17, 1995.
Jovita Yáñez, Houston, March 29, 1976.

PUBLISHED PRIMARY SOURCES

Bandini, Arturo. *Navidad*. San Francisco: California Historical Society, 1958.

Crónicas diabólicas de "Jorge Ulica"/Julio G. Arce, edited and introduced by Juan Rodríguez. San Diego: Maize Press, 1982.

García, Andrew. *Tough Trip through Paradise*, edited by Bennet H. Stein. Boston: Houghton Mifflin, 1967.

La migración y protección del mexicano en el extranjero. México, DF: Imprenta de la Secretaría de Relaciones Exteriores, 1928.

"Report of Frank Buckley of the Bureau of Prohibition, Treasury Department, Submitting Detailed Information Relative to a Survey of Prohibition Enforcement in the State of Texas." In *United States, 71st Congress, 3d Session, Enforcement of the Prohibition Laws; Official Records of the National Commission on Law Observance and Enforcement*, Vol. 4, 923-970. Washington, DC: United States Government Printing Office, 1931.

Ruiz de Burton, María Amparo. *The Squatter and the Don*, edited and introduced by Rosaura Sánchez and Beatrice Pita. Houston: Arte Público Press, 1992.

Vallejo, Guadalupe. "Ranch and Mission Days in Alta California." *The Century Magazine* 41 (1881): 183-192.

Venegas, Daniel. *Las aventuras de Don Chipote, o cuando los pericos mamen*, edited and introduced by Nicolás Kanellos. Mexico City: Secretaría de Educación Pública, 1984.

Weeks, O. Douglas. "The League of United Latin American Citizens: A Texas Mexican Civic Organization." *The Southwestern Social Science Quarterly* 10 (December 1929): 257-278.

BOOKS

Acuña, Rodolfo. *Occupied America: A History of Chicanos*, 3rd ed. NY: Harper and Row, 1988.

Alvarez, Jr., Roberto R. *La Familia: Migration and Adaptation in Baja and Alta California, 1800-1975*. Berkeley: University of California Press, 1987.

Balderrama, Francisco E. *In Defense of La Raza: The Los Angeles Mexican Consulate and the Mexican Community, 1929-1936*. Tucson: University of Arizona Press, 1982.

Balderrama, Francisco E. and Raymond Rodríguez. *Decade of Betrayal: Mexican Repatriation in the 1930s.* Albuquerque: University of New Mexico Press, 1995.

Broyles-González, Yolanda. *El Teatro Campesino: Theater in the Chicano Movement.* Austin: University of Texas Press, 1994.

Camarillo, Albert. *Chicanos in a Changing Society: From Mexican Pueblos to American Barrios in Santa Barbara and Southern California, 1848-1930.* Cambridge: Harvard University Press, 1979.

Campa, Arthur. *Hispanic Culture in the Southwest.* Norman: University of Oklahoma Press, 1979.

Cardoso, Lawrence. *Mexican Emigration to the United States, 1897-1931.* Tucson: University of Arizona Press, 1980.

Chávez, John R. *The Lost Land: The Chicano Image of the Southwest.* Albuquerque: University of New Mexico Press, 1984.

Coerver, Don M. A. and Linda B. Hall. *Texas and the Mexican Revolution: Study in State and National Border Policy, 1910-1920.* San Antonio: Trinity University Press, 1984.

Degler, Carl N. *Neither Black nor White: Slavery and Race Relations in Brazil and the United States.* New York: Macmillan Publishing Co., 1971.

De León, Arnoldo. *Not Room Enough: Mexicans, Anglos and Socioeconomic Change in Texas, 1850-1900.* Albuquerque: University of New Mexico Press, 1993.

_____ *Ethnicity in the Sunbelt: A History of Mexican Americans in Houston.* Houston: University of Houston, Mexican American Studies Monograph Series No. 7, 1989.

_____ *Mexican Americans in Texas: A Brief History.* Arlington Heights, Ill: Harlan Davidson, 1993, 38.

_____ *The Tejano Community, 1836-1900.* Albuquerque: University of New Mexico Press, 1982.

_____ *They Called Them Greasers: Anglo Attitudes toward Mexicans in Texas, 1821-1900.* Austin: University of Texas Press, 1983.

Gamio, Manuel. *The Life Story of the Mexican Immigrant: Autobiographical Documents Collected by Manuel Gamio.* New York: Dover Publications, 1970.

_____ *Mexican Immigration to the United States: A Study of Human Immigration and Adjustment.* New York: Dover Publications, Inc., 1971.

García, Ignacio M. *United We Win: The Rise and Fall of La Raza Unida Party.* Tucson: MASRC, University of Arizona, 1989.

García, Mario T. *Desert Immigrants: The Mexicans of El Paso, 1880-1920.* New Haven: Yale University Press, 1981.

_____ *Mexican American Leadership: Ideology and Identity, 1930-1960.* New Haven: Yale University Press, 1990.

Gledhill, John. *Casi Nada; A Study of Agrarian Reform in the Homeland of Cardenismo.* Albany, NY: The University at Albany, SUNY, Institute for Mesoamerican Society, 1989.

Gómez-Quiñones, Juan. *Chicano Politics: Reality and Promise, 1940-1990.* Albuquerque: University of New Mexico Press, 1990.

_____ *Mexican Students Por La Raza: The Chicano Student Movement in Southern California, 1967-1977.* Santa Barbara, CA: Editorial La Causa, 1978.

González, José Amaro. *Mutual Aid for Survival: The Case of the Mexican American.* Malabar, FL: Robert E. Krieger Publishing Company, 1983.

González, Luis. *San José de Gracia: A Mexican Town in Transition.* Austin: University of Texas Press, 1972.

Grebler, Leo, Joan W. Moore and Ralph Guzmán. *The Mexican American People: The Nation's Second Largest Minority.* NY: Free Press, 1970.

Griswold del Castillo, Richard. *The Treaty of Guadalupe Hidalgo: A Legacy of Conflict.* Norman: University of Oklahoma Press, 1990.

_____ *The Los Angeles Barrios, 1850-1890: A Social History.* Berkeley: University of California Press, 1980.

Gutiérrez, David G. *Walls and Mirrors: Mexican Americans, Mexican Immigrants and the Politics of Ethnicity.* Berkeley: University of California Press, 1995.

Hart, John M. *Revolutionary Mexico: The Coming and Process of the Mexican Revolution.* Berkeley: University of California Press, 1987.

Heyman, Josiah McC. *Life and Labor on the Border: Working People of Northern Mexico, 1886-1986.* Tucson: University of Arizona Press, 1991.

Hoz, Santiago de la. *El Cuaderno Libertario,* Los Angeles, 1904; *El Labrador,* December 30, 1904.

Isuaro, Durán and H. Russell Bernard, eds. *Introduction to Chicano Studies.* NY: Macmillan Publishing Co., 1982.

Justice, Glenn. *Revolution on the Rio Grande: Mexican Raids and Army Pursuits, 1916-1919.* El Paso: Texas Western Press, 1992.

Kanellos, Nicolás. *A History of Hispanic Theatre in the United States: Origins to 1940.* Austin: University of Texas Press, 1990.

Knight, Alan. *The Mexican Revolution,* Vol. 1. London: Cambridge University Press, 1986.

Luckingham, Bradford. *Phoenix: The History of a Southwestern Metropolis.* Tucson: University of Arizona Press, 1989.

Marín, Christine. *A Spokesman of the Mexican American Movement: Rodolfo "Corky" Gonzales and the Fight for Chicano Liberation, 1966-1972.* San Francisco: R and E Research Associates, 1977.

Marín, Marguerite V. *Social Protest in an Urban Barrio: A Study of the Chicano Movement, 1966-1974.* Lanham MA: University Press of America, 1991.

Márquez, Benjamin. *LULAC: The Evolution of a Mexican American Political Organization.* Austin: University of Texas Press, 1993.

Martínez, John. *Mexican Emigration to the United States, 1910-1930.* San Francisco: Arno Press, 1971.

Martínez, Oscar J. *Troublesome Border.* Tucson: University of Arizona Press, 1988.

_____ *Fragments of the Mexican Revolution: Personal Accounts From the Border.* Albuquerque: University of New Mexico Press, 1983.

McWilliams, Carey. *North From Mexico: The Spanish Speaking People of the United States.* Westport, CT: Greenwood press, 1968.

Mirandé, Alfredo. *Gringo Justice.* Notre Dame: University of Notre Dame, 1987.

Montejano, David. *Anglos and Mexicans in the Making of Texas, 1836-1896.* Austin: University of Texas Press, 1987.

Muñoz, Carlos, *Youth, Identity, Power: The Chicano Movement.* London: Verso, 1989.

Nabokov, Peter. *Tijerina and the Courthouse Raid.* Albuquerque: University of New Mexico, 1969.

Navarro, Armando. *Mexican American Youth Organization: Avant-Garde of the Chicano Movement in*

Texas. Austin: University of Texas Press, 1995.

Officer, James. *Hispanic Arizona; 1836-1856.* Tucson: University of Arizona Press, 1989.

Pitt, Leonard. *The Decline of Los Californios: A Social History of Spanish-Speaking Californians, 1846-1890.* Berkeley: University of California Press, 1971.

Raat, W. Dirk, *Revoltosos: Mexico's Rebels in the United States.* College Station: Texas A&M University Press, 1981.

Reisler, Mark. *By the Sweat of Their Brow: Mexican Immigrant Labor in the United States: 1900-1940.* Westport, CT: Greenwood Press, 1976.

Richmond, Douglas W. *Venustiano Carranza's Nationalist Struggle, 1893-1920.* Lincoln: University of Nebraska, 1983.

Romo, Ricardo. *East Los Angeles: History of a Barrio.* Austin: University of Texas Press, 1983.

Rosenbaum, Robert J. *Mexicano Resistance in the Southwest: "The Sacred Right of Self-Preservation."* Austin: University of Texas Press, 1981.

Rozwenc, Edwin C. and Thomas Bender. *The Making of American Society.* NY: Alfred A. Knopf, 1978.

Ruiz, Vickie L. *Cannery Women, Cannery Lives: Unionization and the California Food Processing Industry, 1930-1950.* Albuquerque: University of New Mexico Press, 1987.

Sánchez, George J. *Becoming Mexican American: Culture and Identity in Chicano Los Angeles, 1900-1945.* NY: Oxford University Press, 1993.

Sandos, James A. *Rebellion in the Borderlands: Anarchism and the Plan of San Diego, 1904-1923.* Norman: University of Oklahoma Press, 1992.

San Miguel, Guadalupe. *"Let All of Them Take Heed": Mexican Americans and the Campaign for Educational Equality in Texas, 1910-1981.* Austin: University of Texas Press, 1987.

Santibáñez, Enrique. *Ensayo acerca de la inmigración mexicana en los Estados Unidos.* San Antonio: The Clegg Co., 1930.

Sheridan, Thomas E. *Los Tucsonenses: The Mexican Community in Tucson, 1854-1941.* Tucson: University of Arizona Press, 1986.

Shockley, John Staples. *Revolt in a Texas Town.* South Bend, IN: Notre Dame University, 1974.

Skerry, Peter. *Mexican Americans: The Ambivilant Minority.* NY: The Free Press, 1993.

Taylor, Paul S. *An American Mexican Frontier: Nueces County Texas.* Chapel Hill: University of North Carolina, 1934

_____ *Mexican Labor in the United States: Chicago and the Calumet Region.* Berkeley: University of California Press, 1931.

Turner, Frederick C. *The Dynamic of Mexican Nationalism.* Chapel Hill: University of North Carolina Press, 1968.

Valdés, Dennis Nodín. *Al Norte: Agricultural Workers in the Great Lakes Region, 1917-1970.* Austin: University of Texas Press, 1991.

Vargas, Zaragoza. *Proletarians of the North: A History of Mexican Industrial Workers in Detroit and the Midwest, 1917-1933.* Berkeley: University of California Press, 1993.

Venegas, Daniel. *Las aventuras de Don Chipote, o cuando los pericos mamen,* edited and introduced by Nicolás Kanellos. Mexico City: Secretaría de Educación Pública, 1984.

Weber, David J. *Foreigners in Their Native Land: Historical Roots of the Mexican Americans.*

Albuquerque: University of New Mexico Press, 1973.

Zamora, Emilio. *The World of the Mexican Worker in Texas.* College Station: Texas A&M University Press, 1993.

ARTICLES AND CHAPTERS IN BOOKS:

Aguilar, John L. "Expressive Ethnicity and Ethnic Identity in Mexico and Mexican America." In *Mexican American Identity*, edited by Marta E. Bernal and Phylis I. Martinelli, 55-67. Encino, CA: Floricanto Press, 1993.

Betten, Neil and Raymond Mohl. "From Discrimination to Repatriation: Mexican Life in Gary, Indiana, during the Great Depression." *Pacific Historical Review* 42 (August 1973): 270-388.

Cardoso, Lawrence. "Labor Emigration to the Southwest,1911-1920: Mexican Attitudes and Policy." *Southwestern Historical Quarterly* 84 (April 1987): 400-416.

Chávez, César. "The Organizer's Tale." In *Introduction to Chicano Studies*, edited by Livie Isuaro Durán and H. Russell Bernard, 338-345. NY: Macmillan Publishing Co., Inc., 1982.

Christian, Carole. "Joining the American Mainstream: Texas's Mexican Americans during World War I." *Southwestern Historical Quarterly* 92 (April 1989): 559-595.

Escobar, Edward J. "The Dialectics of Repression: The Los Angeles Police Department and the Chicano Movement, 1968-1971." *The Journal of American History* 79 (March 1993): 1483-1514.

García, Mario T. "La Frontera: The Border as Symbol and Reality in Mexican American Thought." *Mexican Studies/Estudios Mexicanos* 1 (Summer 1985): 195-225.

García, Richard A. "The Chicano Movement and the Mexican American Community, 1972-1978: An Interpretive Essay." *Socialist Review* 40-41 (July-October 1978): 117-136.

_____ "The Mexican American Mind: A Product of the 1930s." In *History, Culture and Society: Chicano Studies in the 1980s*, edited by Mario T. García, et. al., 67-92. Ypsilanti, MI: Bilingual Review Press, 1983.

Gómez-Quiñones, Juan. "Piedras contra la luna: México en Aztlán y Aztlán en Mexico: Chicano-Mexican Relations and the Mexican Consulates, 1900-1920." In *Contemporary Mexico: Papers of the IV International Congress of Mexican History*, 494-527. Mexico City: El Colegio de México and UCLA Latin American Studies Center, 1975.

_____ "Plan de San Diego Reviewed." *Aztlán* 1 (Spring 1970): 124-132.

González, Henry B. "The Hate Issue." In *Introduction to Chicano Studies*, edited by Livie Isauro Durán and H. Russell Bernard, 561-567. NY: Macmillam Publishing Co. Inc., 1982.

Harris III, Charles H. and Louis Sadler. "The 1911 Reyes Conspiracy: The Texas Side." In *Border Revolution* edited by Harris and Sadler, 27-52. Las Cruces, NM: Center For Latin American Studies/Joint Border Research Institute, New Mexico State University, 1988.

_____ "The Plan de San Diego and the Mexican-United States War Crisis of 1916: A Reexamination." In *Border Revolution,* edited by Harris and Sadler, 71-100. Las Cruces, NM: Center For Latin American Studies/Joint Border Research Institute, New Mexico State University, 1988.

Kanellos, Nicolás. "Theater." In *The Hispanic Almanac: A Reference Work on Hispanics in the United States*, edited by Nicolás Kanellos, 505-542. Detroit: Gale Research, Inc., 1993.

Krenek, Thomas. "The Letter from Chapultepec." *The Houston Review* 3 (Summer 1981): 268-271.

Marín, Christine. "Go Home, Chicanos: A Study of the Brown Berets in California and Arizona." In *An*

Awakened Minority: The Mexican Americans, edited by Manuel Servín, 226-247. Beverly Hills: Glencoe Press, 1974.

McBride, James D. "The Liga Protectora Latina: A Mexican American Benevolent Society in Arizona." *Journal of the West* 14 (October 1975): 82-90.

Mellinger, Phil. "The Men Have Organizers: Labor Conflict and Unionization in the Mexican Mining Towns of Arizona, 1900-1915." *Western Historical Quarterly* 23 (August 1992): 323-348.

Menchaca, Marta. *Mexican Outsiders: A Community History of Marginalization and Discrimination in California.* Austin: University of Texas Press, 1995.

Ortego, Phillip D. "The Chicano Renaissance." In *Introduction to Chicano Studies,* edited by Livie Isuaro Durán and H. Russell Bernard, 568-584. NY: Macmillan Publishing Co., Inc., 1982.

Padilla, Genaro. "The Recovery of Nineteenth-Century Autobiography." *American Quarterly* 40 (September 1988): 286-306.

Rosales, Francisco A. "Mexicans, Interethnic Violence, and Crime in the Chicago Area During the 1920s and 1930s: The Struggle to Achieve Ethnic Consciousness," *Perspectives in Mexican American Studies* 2 (1989): 59-98.

_____ "The Regional Origins of Mexicano Immigrants to Chicago During the 1920s." *Aztlán* 7 (Summer 1976): 187-201.

_____ "The Mexican Immigrant Experience in Chicago, Houston, and Tucson: Comparisons and Contrasts." In *Houston: A Twentieth Century Urban Frontier,* edited by Rosales and Barry J. Kaplan, 58-77, 192-194. Port Washington, NY: Associated Faculty Press, 1983.

_____ "Shifting Self-perceptions and Ethnic Consciousness among Mexicans in Houston, 1908-1946," *Aztlán* 16, (1985): 96.

_____ "Mexicans in Houston: The Struggle to Survive, 1908-1975." *Houston Review* 3 (Summer 1981): 224-248.

Rosales, Francisco A. and Daniel T. Simon. "Mexican Immigration to the Urban Midwest; East Chicago, Indiana, 1919-1945." *Indiana Magazine of History* 77 (December 1981): 333-357.

Santillán, Richard. "Rosita the Riveter: Midwest Mexican American Women during World War II, 1941-1945," *Perspectives in Mexican American Studies,* 2(1989): 115-146.

Sepúlveda, Ciro. "Research Note: Una Colonia de Obreros: East Chicago, Indiana." *Aztlán* 7 (Summer 1976): 237-336.

Shankman, Arnold. "The Image of Mexico and the Mexican American Black Press, 1890-1935." *Journal of Ethnic Studies* 3 (Summer 1975): 43-56.

Simon, Daniel T. "Mexican Repatriation in East Chicago, Indiana." *Journal of Mexican American History* 2 (Summer 1974): 11-23.

Smith, Michael M. "Mexicans in Kansas City: The First Generation, 1900-1920." *Perspectives in Mexican American Studies* 2 (1989): 29-58.

Treviño, Roberto. "Prensa y Patria: The Spanish Language Press and the Biculturalization of the Tejano Middle Class, 1920-1940." *The Western Historical Quarterly* 22 (November 1991): 451-472.

Weber, David J. "The Spanish Legacy in North America and the Historical Imagination." *Western Historical Quarterly* 23 (February 1992): 5-24.

UNPUBLISHED SOURCES:

Dimas, Pete. "Perspectives on the Career and Life of Rubén Salazar." M.A. thesis, Arizona State University, 1980.

Escobar, Edward J. "Race and Law Enforcement: Relations Between Chicanos and the Los Angeles Police Department, 1900-1945." Unpublished manuscript in author's files.

Harlan, Anita. "The Battles of 'Ambos Nogales.'" Typescript, Arizona Historical Society Archives.

Knowlton, Clark S. "Reies L. Tijerina and the Alianza Federal de Mercedes: Seekers After Justice." Unpublished manuscript in author's files.

Laird, Judith Fincher. "Argentine, Kansas: The Evolution of a Mexican American Community, 1905-1940." PhD dissertation, University of Kansas, 1975.

Macías Jr., Leonardo. "Mexican Immigration and Repatriation." M.A. thesis, Arizona State University, 1992.

Molina, Francyn. "The Psychological and Political Development of Former Student Movement Activists: A View Fifteen Years Later." PhD dissertation, Wright Institute, 1969.

Rocha, Rudolfo. "The Influence of the Mexican Revolution on the Mexico-Texas Border, 1910-1916." PhD dissertation, Texas Tech University, 1981.

Rosales, Francisco A. "The Lynching of Antonio Rodríguez: An Historical Reassessment." Unpublished manuscript in author's files.

Rosen, Gerald. "Political Ideology in the Chicano Movement: A Study of the Political Ideology of Activists in the Chicano Movement." PhD dissertation, University of California, Los Angeles, 1972.

Ruiz, Manuel. "Latin American Juvenile Delinquency in Los Angeles: Bomb or Bubble." Typescript in Carey McWilliams Papers, Special Collections, University of California, Los Angeles Research Library.

Solliday, Scott W. "The Journey to Rio Salado: Hispanic Migrations to Tempe, Arizona." Master's thesis: Arizona State University, 1993.

CHRONOLOGY

■ **1836** - The Republic of Texas gains its independence from Mexico. After being defeated at the battle of San Jacinto by General Sam Houston, General Antonio López de Santa Anna signs a document giving Texans their independence.

■ **1845** - Texas is officially annexed to the United States.

■ **1846** - The United States invades Mexico under the banner of Manifest Destiny.

■ **1848** - The Treaty of Guadalupe Hidalgo officially ends the Mexican War. Under the treaty, half the land area of Mexico—including Texas, California, most of Arizona and New Mexico, and parts of Colorado, Utah and Nevada—is ceded to the United States.

■ **1848** - The gold rush lures a flood of Anglo settlers into California, which becomes a state in 1850.

■ **1849** - The Foreign Miner's Tax affirmed the rights of Anglos to exclude Mexicans and other non-Anglos from the public domain mines of California.

■ **1853** - General Santa Anna returns to power as president and, through the Gadsden Treaty, sells to the United States the region from Yuma, Arizona, along the Gila River to the Mesilla Valley, New Mexico.

■ **1857** - Anglo freighters attack and kill Mexican cartmen in the San Antonio environs in order to run them out of business.

■ **1859** - The Cortina War begins when Mexican landowner Juan Nepumenco Cortina shoots an Anglo lawman in a street in Brownsville, precipitating border warfare between Anglos and Mexicans for the next few years.

■ **1880s** - Mexican immigration to the United States is stimulated by the advent of the railroad.

■ **1890s** - Land usurpation in New Mexico leads to the formation of the "Gorras Blancas," night riders that attempt to forestall the development and modernization that threaten the Hispano way of life.

■ **1894** - The Alianza Hispano Americana is founded in Tucson, Arizona, and quickly spreads throughout the Southwest.

■ **1907-1908** - A recession creates conditions for the first major repatriation program of destitute Mexicans in the United States.

■ **1910** - The Mexican Revolution begins, with hundreds of thousands of people fleeing north from Mexico and settling in the Southwest.

■ **1917** - An immigration act is passed by Congress making literacy a condition for entry. During World War I, "temporary" Mexican farm workers, railroad laborers, and miners are given a waiver to the immigration law so they can enter the United States to work.

■ **1921** - A recession provokes extreme anti-Mexican feelings. *comisiones honoríficas mexicanas* are founded by the Mexican consular service in the United States to assist in repatriation and defense.

■ **1925** - The Border Patrol is created by Congress.

■ **1929** - The League of United Latin American Citizens (LULAC) is founded in Texas by frustrated Mexican Americans who find avenues for opportunity in the United States blocked.

■ **1931-1932** - During the worst years of the Great Depression, thousands of Mexicans are repatriated only to find themselves destitute in Mexico.

■ **1933** - Mexican farm workers strike in the Central Valley, California, cotton industry, supported by several groups of independent Mexican union organizers and radicals.

■ **1938** - Young Mexican and Mexican American pecan shellers strike in San Antonio.

■ **1943** - Prompted by the labor shortage of World War II, the U.S. government makes an agreement with the Mexican government to supply temporary workers, known as "braceros," for American agricultural work.

■ **1943** - The so-called "Zoot Suit" riots take place in Southern California.

■ **1947** - The American G.I. Forum is organized by Mexican American veterans in response to a Three Rivers, Texas, funeral home's refusual to bury a Mexican American soldier killed in the Pacific during WWII.

■ **1950s** - Immigration from Mexico doubles from 5.9 percent to 11.9 percent, and in the 1960s rises to 13.3 percent of the total number of immigrants to the United States.

■ **1950** - In spite of the resurgence of Mexican immigration, Mexican Americans cannot help but become Americanized when more and more are educated in Anglo school systems, live in integrated suburbs and are subjected to Anglo-American mass media, especially television.

■ **1954** - In the landmark case of *Hernández v. Texas*, the nation's highest court acknowledges that Hispanic Americans are not being treated as "whites." The Supreme Court recognizes Hispanics as a separate class of people suffering profound discrimination.

■ **1954 -1958** - Operation Wetback deports 3.8 million persons of Mexican descent. Only a small fraction of that amount are allowed deportation hearings.

■ **1962** - The United Farm Workers Organizing Committee in California, begun as an independent organization, is led by César Chávez.

■ **1963** - In Crystal City, the Political Association of Spanish-speaking Organizations (PASO) and local Teamsters (mostly Mexican Americans) unite to take over the city council for two years.

■ **October 8, 1963** - La Alianza Federal de los Mercedes (The Federal Alliance of Land Grants) is incorporated by Reis López Tijerina.

■ **1965** - Rodolfo "Corky" Gonzales is appointed director of Denver's War on Poverty Program.

■ **September 16, 1965** - The National Farm Workers Association (César Chávez and Dolores Huerta) meet in a Delano church hall and vote to join the Agricultural Workers Organizing Committee strike.

■ **Late November-December 1965** - Chávez's National Farm Workers Association begins the grape boycott, targeting Schenley Industries and DiGiorgio Corp.

■ **1966** - Rodolfo Acuña starts teaching the first Mexican American history class in Los Angeles.

■ **March 28, 1966** - At an EEOC meeting in Albuquerque, only one commissioner shows up and fifty Chicano leaders, including "Corky" Gonzales, walk out, protesting the lack of Mexican American staff and efforts.

■ **March 17- April 11, 1966** - César Chávez and the National Farm Workers Association march from Delano to Sacramento, taking 25 days and arriving on Easter Sunday, April 11.

■ **April 29, 1966** - "Corky" Gonzales is fired from the Neighborhood Youth Corps directorship, promising that "this day a new crusade for justice is born." He subsequently founds the Crusade for Justice in Denver.

■ **June 1966** - The farm-worker solidarity march from the Rio Grande to Austin takes place. Here, many future leaders participate, including José Angel Gutiérrez.

■ **July 2-4, 1966** - The first Alianza public protest takes place: a three-day march from Albuquerque to Santa Fe to make demands to the governor.

■ **August 22, 1966** - The AFL-CIO executive council admits the United Farm Workers Organizing Committee, merged from NFWA and AWOC into the AFL-CIO.

■ **October 15, 1966** - Tijerina and 350 members of La Alianza occupy Kit Carson National Forest Camp Echo Amphitheater on behalf of the "Pueblo de San Joaquín de Chama." Within a week state police, Rangers and sheriff's deputies move in. La Alianza "arrests" two rangers and, on October 2, tries them for trespassing.

■ **1966** - The UFW wins a contract at DiGiorgio Corp.

■ **1967** - The Mexican American Youth Organization (MAYO) is formed on college campuses in Texas.

■ **1967** - The Mexican American Legal Defense and Education Fund (MALDEF) is incorporated in San Antonio.

■ **March 13, 1967** - 250 students representing seven Los Angeles colleges and universities meet to form United Mexican American Students (UMAS).

■ **June 5, 1967** - Tijerina conducts an armed raid in Tierra Amarilla on the Rio Arriba County Courthouse to make a citizen's arrest of D.A. Alfonso Sánchez.

■ **August, 1967** - The UFW wins contracts with Gallo, Almaden, Franzia, Paul Mason, Golberg, the Novitiate of Los Gatos and Perelli-Minetti.

■ **August 19, 1967** - The Alianza Federal de Las Mercedes changed its name to Alianza Federal de Pueblos Libres.

■ **October 21-22, 1967** - The Alianza Federal de Pueblos Libres national convention is held in Albuquerque, organized by Tijerina. Here the idea for La Raza Unida is discussed.

■ **December, 1967** - David Sánchez dissolves Young Citizens for Community Action to form the Brown Berets self-defense group in L.A. The Berets begin a series of pickets in front of sheriffs' offices and police stations.

■ **December 27, 1967** - More than a hundred Chicanos demonstrate at the East L.A. sheriff's substation against police brutality.

■ **1968** - Betita Martínez founds *El Grito del Norte* newspaper in Albuquerque, New Mexico.

■ **February 15, 1968** - César Chávez begins a 25-day fast at Forty Acres near Delano. He states he is fasting in penitence for farm workers' moral problems and talk of violence.

■ **March 3, 1968** - More than 1000 students peacefully walk out of Abraham Lincoln High School in L.A. Lincoln High teacher Sal Castro joins them. By afternoon, 100 more students walk out of four other schools: Garfield, Wilson, Belmont and Roosevelt.

■ **March 10-11, 1968** - César Chávez breaks his fast at a mass in a Delano public park

with 4000 supporters, including Robert Kennedy at his side.

■ **April 9, 1968** - 700 Chicano students walk out of Lanier High School in San Antonio. Soon, 600 more walk out from Edgewood High School.

■ **April 16, 1968** - Denver Chicanos begin a boycott of Coors for discriminatory hiring.

■ **May 27, 1968** - A grand jury indicts the L.A. 13 for conspiracy to disrupt the peace in organizing the school walkouts.

■ **June 1968** - East Los Angeles native José Sánchez, 19, is the first Chicano to resist the military draft publicly.

■ **September 10-24, 1968** - Students and parents picket Lincoln High School and the LAUSD Board of Education, demanding Sal Castro's reinstatement.

■ **September 26-October 2, 1968** - Chicanos sit in at the LAUSD Board of Education: 35 parents, students and Brown Berets protest Sal Castro's suspension.

■ **October 3, 1968** - LAUSD board votes to return Sal Castro to the classroom.

■ **November 4, 1968** - The United Mexican American Students (UMAS) and the Black Student Union (BSU) unite, and Rosalío Muñoz is elected UCLA student body president.

■ **March 27-31, 1969** - The First National Chicano Youth Liberation Conference is sponsored by the Crusade for Justice.

■ **April 1969** - A three-day conference is organized at Santa Barbara by the Chicano Coordinating Council of Higher Education to create a plan for curricular changes and provide service to Chicano students. Student organizations statewide change their name to El Movimiento Estudiantil Chicano de Aztlán, MECHA.

■ **September 16, 1969** - The first "Chicano Liberation Day" is organized by "Corky" Gonzales.

■ **November, 1969** - Rosalío Muñoz refuses to be drafted at the induction center in downtown Los Angeles.

■ **December 20, 1969 -** Católicos por la Raza clashes with police as it demands church programs for Chicanos in front of St. Basil's Cathedral in L.A.

■ **February 28, 1970 -** The Second National Chicano Moratorium Committee demonstration takes place in L.A. with 6,000 people assembled.

■ **April, 1970 -** La Raza Unida Party wins four of seven seats on the Crystal City school board.

■ **May 16, 1970 -** The first Colorado La Raza Unida meeting takes place at Southern Colorado State College. "Corky" Gonzales is elected state chair.

■ **July 20, 1970 -** The National Chicano Moratorium Committee marches in Houston, drawing 5000 people to its rally.

■ **August 29, 1970 -** The third Moratorium protest in Laguna Park, with 10,000-30,000 people attending, takes place. A liquor store theft provides police with the excuse to break up the peaceful gathering. Some protesters respond by throwing things back. At the Silver Dollar Bar, Rubén Salazar is shot in the head with a tear-gas missile.

■ **October 2, 1970 -** More than 600 Chicano students walk out of an East Chicago, Indiana, school after the vice principal says, "Mexicans are lazy and ignorant."

■ **October 14, 1970 -** Los Angeles County District Attorney Evelle J. Younger announces he will not prosecute Deputy Thomas Wilson for Salazar's death.

■ **November 22, 1970 -** The Oakland-Berkeley chapter of La Raza Unida Party has its first meeting.

■ **1971 -** The FBI Counter Intelligence Program infiltrates and provokes Chicano organizations.

■ **May, 1971 -** The Houston Chicana Conference attracts more than 600 Chicanas from 23 states.

■ **May 5, 1971 -** La Marcha de la Reconquista, a march from Calexico to Sacramento, begins

with Rosalío Muñoz, David Sánchez and the Brown Berets.

■ **February 9, 1972 -** Ramsey Muñiz announces his bid for Texas governor under the La Raza Unida Party banner at a press conference in San Antonio.

■ **February 12, 1972 -** The United Farm Workers Organizing Committee (UFWOC) charters the United Farm Workers (UFW), AFL-CIO.

■ **August 14, 1972 -** The UFW files suit in Phoenix to bar enforcement of the new Arizona Agricultural Relations Act, which will prohibit harvest-time picketing.

■ **August 28-September 26, 1972 -** The Brown Berets invade Catalina Island and take a campsite.

■ **September 1-4, 1972 -** La Raza Unida Party holds its national convention in El Paso. Some 3000 Chicanos attend. Gutiérrez beats Gonzales for the national chair in a decisive campaign that leads to the division of LRUP into two camps.

■ **November 3, 1972 -** Muñoz garners 6.28 percent of the Texas gubernatorial vote, nearly undermining Democrat Dolph Brisco's victory.

■ **January 23, 1973 -** A shootout with police takes place at a Crusade for Justice apartment building, Escuela Tlatelolco, next door to its headquarters.

■ **1974 -** The Southwest Voter Registration Education Project is established. Willie Velásquez, a former member of MAYO and La Raza Unida, becomes its director.

■ **November, 1974 -** Raúl Castro becomes the first Chicano governor of Arizona.

■ **1975 -** The Voting Rights Act of 1965 is extended to Hispanic Americans.

CREDITS FOR ILLUSTRATIONS

llustrations in each of the chapters appear thanks to the courtesy of the following sources and photographers:

CHAPTER ONE

1. California State Library. 2. Library of Congress. 3. California Historical Society. 4. Library of Congress. 5. California Historical Society. 6. Library of Congress. 7. Los Angeles County Museum of Natural History. 8. Museo Histórico "Casa Mata," Matamoros, Tamps., Mexico. 9. Western History Colection, University of Oklahoma. 10. Archives Division, Texas State Library. 11. Sever Center for Western History, Natural History Museum of Los Angeles County. 12. Recovering the U.S. Hispanic Literary Heritage, University of Houston. 13.Library of Congress. 14. Huntington Library, San Merino, California.

CHAPTER TWO

15. Biblioteca Nacional, Mexico. 16. Library of Congress. 17. *Los Angeles Times*. 18.Recovering the U.S. Hispanic Literary Heritage Project, University of Houston. 19.Recovering the U.S. Hispanic Literary Heritage Project, University of Houston. 20.Recovering the U.S. Hispanic Literary Heritage Project, University of Houston. 21.Recovering the U.S. Hispanic Literary Heritage Project, University of Houston.

CHAPTER THREE

22. Arizona Historical Society Library. 23. Library of Congress. 24. Library of Congress. 25. The *Houston Chronicle*.

CHAPTER FOUR

26. Arizona Historical Society Library. 27. Sever Center for Western History Research, Natural History Museum of Los Angeles County. 28. Houston Metropolitan Research Center, Houston Public Library. 29. Castillo Family Collection, Houston Metropolitan Research Center, Houston Public Library. 30. Recovering the U.S. Hispanic Literary Heritage Project, University of Houston. 31. Arizona Historical Society Library. 32. Recovering the U.S. Hispanic Literary Heritage Project, University of Houston. 33. Recovering the U.S. Hispanic Literary Heritage Project, University of Houston. 34. Arizona Historical Society Library. 35. Recovering the U.S. Hispanic Literary Heritage Project, University of Houston. 36. Arizona Historical Society Library. 37. Houston Metropolitan Research Center, Houston Public Library.

CHAPTER FIVE

38. Henberger Collection, Harry Ransom Center, University of Texas at Austin. 39. Library of Congress. 40. Recovering the U.S. Hispanic Literary Heritage Project, University of Houston. 41. Harry Ransom Center, University of Texas at Austin. 42. Recovering the U.S. Hispanic Literary Heritage Project, University of Houston. 43. Bancroft Library, University of California. 44. Secretaría de Relaciones Exteriores, Mexico City. 45. Library of Congress.

CHAPTER SIX

46. Houston Metropolitan Research Center, Houston Public Library. 47. Houston Metropolitan Research Center, Houston Public Library. 48. The Institute of Texan Cultures, *The San Antonio Light* Collection. 49. Houston Metropolitan Research Center, Houston Public Library. 50. Arizona Historical Society Library. 51. F. Arturo Rosales. 52. Houston Metropolitan Research Center, Houston Public Library. 53. F. Artuo Rosales. 54. Jensen Elliot Collection, Austin History Center. 55. Houston Metropolitan Research Center, Houston Public Library. 56. Houston Metropolitan Research Center, Houston Public Library. 57. Mireles Papers, Texas A&M University-Corpus Christi. 58. *Los Angeles Times.* 59. Library of Congress. 60. Benson Latin American Library, University of Texas. 61. Benson Latin American Library, University of Texas. 62. Edward Roybal Congressional Office.

CHAPTER SEVEN

63. Héctor P. García Papers, Texas A & M University-Corpus Christi. 64. Library of Congress. 65. Library of Congress. 66. Library of Congress. 67. Secretaría de Relaciones Exteriores, Mexico City. 68. Library of Congress. 69. Houston Metropolitan Research Center, Houston Public Library. 70. Houston Metropolitan Research Center, Houston Public Library.

CHAPTER EIGHT

71. Archives of Labor and Urban Affairs, Wayne State University. 72. Archives of Labor and Urban Affairs, Wayne State University. 73. Archives of Labor and Urban Affairs, Wayne State University. 74. Archives of Labor and Urban Affairs, Wayne State University. 75. Oscar Castillo. 76. Oscar Castillo. 77.Archives of Labor and Urban Affairs, Wayne State University. 78. George Rodríguez. 79. Oscar Castillo. 80. Archives of Labor and Urban Affairs, Wayne State University. 81. Archives of Labor and Urban Affairs, Wayne State University. 82. Archives of Labor and Urban Affairs, Wayne State University. 83. Oscar Castillo. 84. Nicolás Kanellos.

CHAPTER NINE

85. Oscar Castillo. 86. Recovering the U.S. Hispanic Literary Heritage, University of Houston. 87. Museum of New Mexico (Neg. No. 22468). 88. Oscar Castillo. 89. Lyndon Baines Johnson Library, The University of Texas at Austin.

CHAPTER TEN

90. Oscar Castillo. 91. Arte Público Press. 92. Arte Público Press. 93. Western History Department, Denver Public Library. 94. Western History Department, Denver Public Library. 95. Arte Público Press. 96. Oscar Castillo. 97. Oscar Castillo. 98. Recovering the U.S. Hispanic Literary Heritage

CHAPTER ELEVEN

101. George Rodríguez. 102. Oscar Castillo. 103. George Rodríguez. 104. Oscar Castillo. 105. *Los Angeles Times* Photograph Collection, University Research Library, UCLA. 106. Oscar Castillo.

CHAPTER TWELVE

107. Oscar Castillo. 108. Arturo Rosales. 109. Recovering the U.S. Hispanic Literary Heritage Project, University of Houston. 110. Oscar Castillo. 111. Oscar Castillo.

CHAPTER THIRTEEN

112. Oscar Castillo. 113. Arte Público Press. 114. Oscar Castillo. 115. Oscar Castillo. 116. Oscar Castillo. 117. Oscar Castillo.

CHAPTER FOURTEEN

118. Mexican American Studies Program, University of Houston. 119. Mexican American Studies Porgram, University of Houston. 120. Arte Público Press. 121. Arte Público Press. 122. Arte Público Press. 123. Arte Público Press. 124. Nicolás Kanellos. 125. Arte Público Press. 126. Recovering the U.S. Hispanic Literary Heritage Project, University of Houston. 127. Library of Congress.

INDEX